D1477412

THIS IS THE COAST GUARD

Coast Guard Rescue Trio Underway. HH-3F helicopter refueling from the 210-foot U.S.C.G. Cutter *Venturous* while the 378-foot U.S.C.G. Cutter *Mellon* keeps pace alongside, off San Diego. (Photo by William G. Bradshaw, Oakland, California. *Courtesy:* United States Coast Guard.)

THIS IS THE COAST GUARD

By

H. R. Kaplan

and

Lcdr. James F. Hunt, USCG

I

THE UNITED STATES COAST GUARD
An Interpretive History

II

MISSIONS AND FACILITIES

III

COAST GUARD PROFILES

1972   Cambridge, Maryland

CORNELL MARITIME PRESS, INC.

ISBN 0-87033-160-4

Library of Congress Catalog Card Number: 74-153146

Contents

Frontispiece
Acknowledgments   vii
Foreword   ix

I

THE UNITED STATES COAST GUARD
AN INTERPRETIVE HISTORY

The Roots   1
Against Piracy and Slavery   9
Alexander Fraser Takes Command   13
Civil War   19
Of Reconstruction and Continued Growth   27
1898: The United States Flexes Its Muscles   33
World War I   43
The Rum Fleet   49
Prelude to World War II   59
At War Again   65
A Changing Service for a Changing World   73
In Vietnam Waters   81
The Past Is Prologue   89

II

MISSIONS AND FACILITIES

Aids to Navigation   97
  Boston Light Station, A National Historical Landmark   103
  Lightships
    Nantucket   106
  Offshore Towers
    Chesapeake Light Station   110
  Loran Stations
  Kure Island   112
  Loran—A Layman's Explanation   115
  Cape Flattery Light Station   117
  Buoy Tenders—*Bittersweet*   121
Boating Safety   127
Icebreaking   131
  Polar Icebreakers—*Northwind*   137
  Great Lakes Icebreaker—*Mackinaw*   143
  International Ice Patrol   145
Law Enforcement   147
  Reliance, 210-foot class   151
  Merchant Marine Inspection Offices—MIO New York   156
Military Readiness   161
  Taney, 327-foot class   163
Ocean Stations   165
  Chincoteague, 311-foot class   169

Oceanography   171
Port Safety and Security   177
Reserve Training   183
Search and Rescue (SAR)   187
   Hamilton, 378-foot class   195
   Pontchartrain, 255-foot class   199
Raritan, 110-foot Harbor Tug   205
Command at Sea   207
   Cape Knox, 95-foot class   207
   Point Warde, 82-foot Patrol Boat   208
   Self-Bailing, Self-Righting Motor Lifeboat, *44303* 210
Automated Merchant Vessel Report System (AMVER)   215
Coast Guard Aviation   217
Aircraft   225
   The HH-3F Helicopter   225
The U.S. Coast Guard Academy   227
Eagle, The Extraordinary Classroom   233
Kukui, One of a Kind   235
Supply Depots   237
   USCG Supply Depot, New Orleans   237
Miscellaneous Training and Support Facilities   239

III

COAST GUARD PROFILES

Alexander Hamilton, *Founding Father*   245
Louis McLane, *Builder of a Service*   249
The Legacy of John Canfield Spencer   253
Joshua James, *Greatest Lifesaver of Them All*   255
Mike Healy, *Black Hero of the North*   259
David H. Jarvis, *Leader of the Overland Expedition*   265
Admiral Russell R. Waesche, *Wartime Leader*   269
The Burning Sea (Story of John Allen Midgett)   275
Death on an Icecap (Story of John A. Pritchard)   279
The Gift of Douglas Munro   283
Grand Haven, Michigan, Coast Guard City, U.S.A.   287

Bibliography   291
Index   295

Acknowledgments

This book could not have been written without the generous assistance of many persons. We are especially indebted to Rear Admiral Russell R. Waesche for his contribution of materials on his father, the late Admiral Waesche, wartime Commandant of the Coast Guard; Mr. Gerard Richardson for his beautiful sketches of the first cutters; Mr. Paul Johnson, Librarian and Curator, Coast Guard Academy; Miss Elizabeth A. Segedi, Photo-Editor of Coast Guard Headquarters at Washington, D.C.; Miss Anna T. Jarvis of New York City for providing hitherto unpublished photographs and information on her father, Captain David H. Jarvis, leader of the famed Overland Expedition of 1897-1898 to relieve whalers stranded at Point Barrow, Alaska; Chief Warrant Officer Joseph Greco, Jr., of the Public Information Division, Coast Guard Headquarters; Captain Robert I. Price; Commander William J. Bickford; Commander John W. Duenzl and Peggy; Commander Joseph F. Smith; Rear Admiral Oscar C. Rohnke (Ret.) and Gladys; Commander Robert E. Williams (Ret.); Rear Admiral Louis B. Olson (Ret.); Captain Donald C. Davis; Captain Joseph C. Fox, Jr.; Captain Walter C. Ochman; Captain Charles L. Blaha; Captain William S. Schweb; Commander Alva L. Carbonette (Ret.); Commander Berry L. Meaux; and Commander Hal F. Olson.

Our thanks also go to Rear Admiral John D. McCubbin; Rear Admiral William F. Rea III; Rear Admiral Austin C. Wagner; Captain John P. Latimer (Ret.); Captain James H. Durfee; Captain Fred T. Merritt; Captain Harold D. Muth; Captain William L. Aitkenhead; Captain William F. Tighe, Jr.; Captain Robertson P. Dinsmore; Captain Archibald B. How; Captain Donald J. McCann; Captain Robert A. Duin; Captain Clarence R. Hallberg; Commander Clarence C. Hobdy, Jr.; Commander David M. Kaetzel; Commander Gilbert P. Sherburne; Commander William E. Lehr, Jr.; Commander Walter D. Fox; Commander Thomas H. Rutledge; Commander Clyde T. Lusk, Jr.; Commander James A. Wilson; Commander Charles A. Biondo, USCGR; Commander Daniel L. Charter; Commander Robert J. Ketchel; Commander William F. Roland; Commander Dalton J. Beasley; Lcdr. Albert D. Super; Lcdr. James D. Webb; Lcdr. Ronald M. Polant; Lcdr. Lawrence Graham; Lcdr. Harry E. Obedin; Lcdr. Anthony B. Ford; Lcdr. Wade M. Moncrief, Jr.; Lcdr. Clifford E. Banner; Lcdr. Gilbert Shaw. Lcdr. Maurice Dumas, USCGR; Lt. Walter N. Smith; Lt. Gabriel G. Gustafson, USCGR; Lt. William G. Bradford III; Lt. (jg) John M. Robinson, USCGR; Lt. Rob R. Hathaway; Lt. (jg) Theodore J. Flynn, USCGR; Lt. (jg) Frank Couper, USCGR; Lt. (jg) Howard E. Copeland, USCGR; Lt. (jg) Samuel H. Pope, USCGR; Lt. (jg) Graham J. Chynoweth, USCGR; Boatswain's Mate, First Class, R. P. Milligan; Chief Boatswain Luis M. Lopez; Chief Boatswain Bernard A. Kincaid; Chief Warrant Officer J. E. Sparks; Chief Warrant Officer C. Keith, Jr.; Ensign Ronald A. Fritzche, USCGR; B. C. Roberts, Superintendent, Cape Hatteras National Seashore; and Vincent Mrazek, Chief Ranger, Cape Hatteras National Seashore.

Foreword

Originally, it was our intention to prepare a book portraying the operating units and facilities by which the Coast Guard carries out its diverse missions. But as we proceeded further into the work, we could see that this approach would not do full justice to a service with a rich and colorful history going back to the very roots of the Republic. To separate the Coast Guard from its history would be like separating the heart from the body. Moreover, in the Coast Guard, more than in most other government agencies, functions evolved out of historical necessity. To be fully understood, we believed that each mission should be seen in its historical perspective. We think that the history will serve this purpose.

Although we have tried to present as broad a range of functions and activities as possible, we are very much aware that some of you will note the absence of an activity with which you have been associated. If so, do not regard this as a value judgment, but rather as a condition imposed upon us by the exigencies of research and the availability of materials. In the event of future revisions, we hope that many of these omissions can be corrected.

It should be understood that during the time between preparation and publication of this book there is the possibility that changes in procedures and facilities have occurred.

In selecting subjects for the "Coast Guard Profile" section, we realized that many other persons equally deserving of the honor could have been chosen. But once again, certain practical limitations dictated our choice. Perhaps our readers can supply us with the names of other persons who should be included in any future editions.

But above all, we want you to enjoy your literary excursion into what is probably the most fascinating and certainly the most versatile Service in the world. Happy reading.

THE AUTHORS

I

THE UNITED STATES COAST GUARD
An Interpretive History

The Roots

On the thirtieth of April, 1789, on the balcony of the Federal Building on Wall Street, New York City, George Washington raised his right hand to take the oath as the first President of the United States. In his brown broadcloth suit with buttons of spread eagles, white silk stockings, silver shoe buckles and dress sword, he was the very image of authority. After administering the oath, Chancellor Robert Livingston, Chief Justice of New York,

Already, two principal currents of thoughts were emerging which would shape the young Republic's political future. There were the Federalists, including Washington and one of his chief aides, the young Alexander Hamilton, soon to be the first Secretary of the Treasury, who believed in the necessity for a strong, centralized government. In opposition to this was the group headed by Thomas Jefferson, who, remembering the British

George Washington taking oath of office. Photo: National Archives

stepped to the railing of the balcony and cried out: "Long live George Washington, President of the United States." The thousands massed in the street responded with thunderous cheers. Washington bowed gravely several times, and then walked slowly into the Senate Chamber. Thirteen years after the colonies had declared their independence from Great Britain, a new nation was ready to take its place in the world.

Yet the nation Washington was to govern was far from united. It was torn by factional rivalry.

experience, was very suspicious of any deeply entrenched central authority. Out of this debate was to grow a system of government carefully balancing these two principles.

In the summer of 1790, one year after Washington entered upon the presidency, a new crisis confronted the country. The federal treasury was nearly empty. Unless additional revenues could be raised, the country faced the prospect of bankruptcy and a breakdown of federal authority.

Primary cause for the financial stringency was

1

smuggling, a practice begun originally as a means of circumventing unjust British duties. It had developed into such a profitable business that it was being continued after the Revolution had been won. It was diverting desperately needed tax dollars from the national treasury. Somehow, this practice had to be stopped and the money rechanneled to national purposes. Continuance of smuggling was due in part to the failure on the part of the average American to understand the federal concept. In a time of slow and limited communications, his thinking tended to be restricted to local issues. The federal entity was too shadowy a thing to be taken seriously.

But the brilliant, 32-year-old Alexander Hamilton, first Secretary of the Treasury, was fully aware of the dimensions of the crisis. As he saw it, the crisis was not only financial but administrative. A federal government without funds could not assert its prerogatives, and an impotent government spelled the end of nationhood. The country would deteriorate into a loosely bound group of states, each squabbling for advantage. Such a country could not present a very strong position to the world. For months Hamilton grappled with the problem. His proposed solution—the establishment of a Treasury Fleet charged with the enforcement of all customs laws. He had already experimented with such a fleet on the Schuylkill River, flowing past Philadelphia.

After some debate, the Congress agreed with the Secretary. On August 4, 1790, it authorized the construction of "ten boats for a collection of revenue." The new fleet, known variously as the Revenue Marine and Revenue Cutter Service was a reality. From that modest beginning was to develop a service whose responsibilities increased steadily over the years until it became not only the foremost U.S. agency for maritime safety in all its aspects but also one of its armed forces, asserting American sovereignty on the oceans of the world. As the years passed, it was to take an increasingly prominent place in oceanic sciences, research and development, and many other fields not conceived of in Hamilton's day.

Since the Revolutionary Navy had been disbanded in 1790, Hamilton realized that the new fleet would have to serve for a time as the nation's naval arm. Therefore he urged that its officers be commissioned, holding the same rank as those held formerly in the Navy. Hamilton reasoned that suoh rank "would attach them to their duty by a nicer sense of honor." Much of Hamilton's correspondence during this period stresses the attribute of personal honor. It was the mark of the 18th century "gentleman" and was one of the many views held in common by Hamilton and his leader, George Washington, who also lived by the same high code. The relationship between these two men was one of the most extraordinary in history. To the young Hamilton, Washington was the exemplar of statesmanlike conduct. The older man had an almost paternal feeling for his bright young subordinate.

Hamilton's revenue fleet represented part of a bold economic plan to reestablish federal credit and to shore up its sagging financial structure and prestige. Another part of the plan called for repayment of the $70,000,000 debt incurred during the Revolution by the states, and the defrayment of government expenses from revenue. The Revenue Act of 1789 had made provision for levying a tariff for revenue.

Hamilton also sought to insure the industrial independence of the nation by advocating protectionist measures. As part of the British Empire, the colonies had served mainly as sources of raw materials for the mother country. This had to be reversed if the country were to acquire the industrial independence necessary to its survival. This farsighted man also saw that the American merchant marine, severely depleted in the war with England, had to be rebuilt and that a Lighthouse Service would have to be created to protect the fleet against the dangers of rocks and shoals. This foreshadowed the development of federal responsibility for the safety of merchant shipping, one of the Coast Guard's primary functions.

The cost of the fleet was extraordinarily low even by the prices of those far-off times. Each of the cutters was to cost approximately $1,000. Hamilton estimated the cost of the fleet as follows:

10 Captains at 40 dollars a month	$4,800
10 Lieutenants at 25 dollars a month	3,000
60 Seamen at 8 dollars a month	5,000
Provisions	3,000
Wear and tear	2,000

Yet even this modest estimate was pared down by a parsimonious Congress. It also disregarded Hamilton's advice on naval commissions for officers and ordered instead a master, a first, second, and third mate, four mariners, and two boys for each cutter. Masters were to receive a salary of $30 a month and the subsistence allowance of a Captain of the United States Army. The frugality which characterized the first Treasury Fleet has become traditional with the modern Coast Guard which sets great store on stretching tax dollars as far as they will go. It was not a very lavish start, but as least it was a start.

In 1791, the first cutter of the revenue fleet, *Massachusetts*, slid down the runways at Newburyport, Massachusetts. Her construction had been closely supervised by Captain John Foster Williams. By the time the cutter was completed, she cost more than twice the sum originally authorized. But Williams was a man who knew what he wanted, and it was traditional to comply with a master's construction needs.

As if to underscore the military character of the new Service, the *Massachusetts* and her sister cutters were soon involved in defending American merchant ships against predatory French privateers. By an irony of history, the United States had become embroiled in an undeclared war at sea with France, its former ally in the recent War of Independence. By the late 1790's, French vessels had already seized more than 340 United States ships. The ten small revenue cutters now had to assume the defense of the United States coastline as well as carry on their usual duties

First Revenue Cutter *Massachusetts;* 50 feet, 70 tons. Completed 1791, Newburyport, Mass. First of "ten boats" built when Congress authorized construction.

Williams, however, was not the first to receive his commission as master. At the top of the masters' list was Hopley Yeaton, of New Hampshire. His commission was the first to be issued by President Washington to any officer afloat. Eventually, under a provision of the Act of 1799, military ranks of "Captain" and "Lieutenant" were authorized for cutter officers in place of "Master" and "Mate." The military character of the young Service was clearly established at that time. It has remained so ever since.

against smugglers. In the meantime, the regular Navy was being constructed. Until such time as the vessels were ready to put to sea, the revenue cutters would have to serve as a war fleet.

While the quasi-war with the French was underway, the Congress ordained in 1799 that "Revenue Cutters shall, whenever the President of the United States shall so direct, cooperate with the Navy of the United States." On August 4, 1949, Congress put it more strongly: "The Coast Guard as established January 28, 1915, shall be a military service and a branch of the armed forces of the United States at all times. The Coast Guard shall be a service in the Treasury Department, except when operating as a Service in the Navy." This still obtains today, although the Coast Guard now is a component of the Department of Transportation to which it was transferred in April, 1967. But both by statute as well as by historical experience, it is one of the Armed Forces of the United States.

In 1799, Stoddert ordered four fleets of 20 ships to sea against the French raiders. Eight cutters were a part of this force. Of 20 French ships captured by the combined fleets, 16 were taken by revenue cutters. The 187-ton cutter, *Eagle*, set a record by capturing five French ships, recapturing seven American vessels, and assisting in the capture of ten others.

The performance of the doughty little cutters

The U.S. Revenue Cutter *Pickering*, one of the first ten cutters built to form the earliest seagoing Service of the United States, presently known as the U.S. Coast Guard. (Photographed from a sketch by an unknown artist.)

Anticipating the 1799 Act of Congress, President John Adams had put the cutters under the command of Benjamin Stoddert, first Secretary of the Navy, in 1798. Their duties included patrolling between Nantucket and Cape Henry, and escorting the new frigate, *Constitution*, on her maiden cruise. They also performed the first convoy duty, guarding American merchantmen against the French privateers.

opened the Navy's eyes to the fighting qualities of the small fleet. They were excellent combat allies, and the Coast Guard has ever since played an assigned role in emergency and wartime naval operations. The foundation for that enduring partnership was laid in that distant time.

One of the most remarkable records in the hostilities with the French was made by the revenue cutter, *Pickering*. A sister ship of the

Eagle, she fought a notable engagement with the privateer, *L'Egypte Conquise*, on October 18, 1799. In preparation for the encounter, the French ship had been specially fitted out and doubly manned to capture the *Pickering*. Against the former's 14 nine, and 4 six-pounders and crew of 250, the cutter had only 14 four-pounders and a crew of 70. For nine hours the vessels fired broadside after broadside at one another. And then, incredibly, the larger ship hauled down the tricolor and surrendered. American hardihood and seamanship had gained a notable victory which would go down in the annals of the country. Later, in 1800, the *Pickering* was to meet a tragic end when she was lost with all hands in a storm.

It was also about this time that the revenue cutters began to fly what are known today as the Coast Guard ensign and pennant. In authorizing these banners in 1799, Congress declared: "Whenever any ship or vessel, liable to seizure or examination shall not bring to, on being required to do so, or on being chased by any cutter or boat, which has displayed the pennant and ensign prescribed for vessels of the Revenue Service, the master of such cutter or boat may fire at, or into, such vessel, after such pennant and ensign has been hosited and a gun fired by such cutter as a signal . . . " The right of search and seizure remains an important part of the Coast Guard's functions.

But time was moving swiftly on, and the old century was nearly over. The cutters which had served so well in those exciting years since 1791 were showing signs of wear. Also, while they were fast, they were too small and too lightly armed for the needs of the dawning 19th century. But they had given the country a breathing spell and had also won respect for American seamanship and national sovereignty. On February 3, 1801, a treaty with France ended the Coast Guard's first partnership with the Navy. But it was not to be for long. The United States was still far too weak to be taken seriously by the mighty powers of Europe, particularly England. The English were still not reconciled to the existence of the upstart nation on the North American continent. To many Englishmen, it seemed that the Yankees needed to be taught a lesson.

England, engaged in a long-drawn-out war with Napoleon, sought to cripple French trade by seizing American ships and by impressing U.S. seamen into the British Navy. This outrageous practice fanned enormous resentment in this country. President Thomas Jefferson, fearing to engage so formidable an enemy as the British fleet,

requested that an Embargo Act be passed, forbidding all international trade to and from American ports, effective December 22, 1807.

As might have been foreseen, the effect of the act was economic depression. The new nation depended desperately upon its merchant shipping for survival. Sooner or later, it would have to meet the challenge head on. The Jeffersonian approach was doomed to failure.

The Revenue Cutter *Pickering* capturing a French prize. She was one of the best fighting ships of her time, ton for ton.

Like the expert politician that he was, Jefferson did a quick about-face. He requested that Congress authorize the building of additional revenue cutters, the original vessels being generally unseaworthy after long use. In 1809, Congress gave its assent to the construction of 12 cutters. War with Britain was inevitable.

When the United States declared war on Great Britain on June 19, 1812, the Treasury had 16 cutters, each with six to ten light guns and carrying 15 to 30 first-rate sailors. It was an audacious undertaking by a small, weak country against an

Defending the *Eagle* in the War of 1812.

Another hand-to-hand encounter was less successful. On June 12, 1813, under cover of darkness, three barges from the British man-of-war *Narcissus* tried to take the 75-ton cutter, *Surveyor*, by surprise in the York River of Virginia. Though outnumbered 50 to 15, the cutter crew wounded seven and killed three of the enemy before yielding. British Captain John Crerie was so impressed by the "determined way in which her deck was disputed, inch by inch," in hand-to-hand fighting, that he returned to Captain William Travis of the cutter "the sword you had so nobly used."

It remained for the revenue cutter, *Eagle*, to bring the Revenue Marine its greatest fame in the war. A British sloop had been raiding shipping off Long Island. On October 10, 1814, word was received that the American ship, *Susan*, out of New Haven, Conn., had been captured by the British vessel. The cutter, *Eagle*, with 40 volunteers added to its crew, set out in search of the sloop. After an

The U.S. Revenue Cutter *James C. Madison*, 1813. In July 1812, the *Madison* captured the 300-ton British Brig *Shamrock* armed with 6 guns and 16 men, and took her prize to Savannah. On Nov. 24, 1812, the *Madison* was captured by the British near Savannah. Captain Brooks and his officers were taken prisoners to New York by the Cartel Brig *Diamond*. (From a watercolor by C.J.A. Wilson.)

empire whose seapower was many times greater than that of the United States. As it turned out, the War of 1812 was fought by nine cutters. The war was less than a week old when the revenue cutter *Jefferson* captured the British vessel, *Patriot*, the first prize to fall into American hands. Altogether, the cutters took 14 enemy ships. The *Madison* brought in the 300-ton brig *Shamrock*, and shortly after, the schooner *Wade*, carrying $20,000 in gold and silver. The *Vigilant* took the British privateer, *Dart*, in a running battle between Newport, Rhode Island, and Block Island. The British vessel had captured a score of New England ships. In the final phase of the fight, the cutter ran alongside the *Dart* and boarded her, killing *Dart's* first officer and overwhelming her crew.

English brig and Revenue Cutter (early U.S. Coast Guard cutter) at right in the War of 1812. (From a painting by an unknown artist.)

U.S. Coast Guard Combat Artist Hunter Wood gives his watercolor conception of the engagement between the U.S. Coast Guard brig *Nancy* and the French brig *Mehitabel* in the War of 1812.

all-night search, they found the sloop. Beside the sloop was H.M. brig, *Dispatch*, with 18 thirty-two-pounders to oppose the *Eagle's* six four-pounders. No breeze stirred as the *Eagle* drifted towards the shore. The British warship drifted toward the *Eagle*, preparing for the kill.

Finally, the *Eagle's* crew ran her aground on an island and then dragged her cannon to the top of a bluff where they had the drop on the enemy. When ammunition ran low, five of the crew returned to the *Eagle* for more, but only three of them made it all the way. Aboard the ship, they replaced the ensign that had been shot away. The British fired a full broadside at them, and the Americans salvaged the small shot that riddled the hull. Back on the bluff, they made cartridges of bits of cloth and pages from the cutter's log and fired the shot back at the British. So accurate was their fire, that the enemy was unable to land to take the bluff and had to withdraw. It was only a short respite, for early the next morning, as the wounded cutter limped to port, the British warship found and captured her. But the *Eagle's* exploit had captured the imagination of the American people. The performance of the entire Revenue Cutter Service had been so outstanding that it kindled a new pride in the ability of United States sailors and in the Revenue Service particularly.

Against Piracy and Slavery

During the interlude between the undeclared war with the French and the War of 1812, the revenue fleet had not been idle. America's growing trade was making new demands on the Revenue Marine and would make even greater demands in the years to come. Eventually, protecting the

different character was looming on the horizon. This would not be a war against the forces of a foreign power but against something even more malignant—piracy and slavery. In 1815, the cutters were ordered into service to suppress these prac-

Left: Suppressing Gulf Pirates. During the period from 1800 to 1825, the Gulf Coast was the happy hunting grounds for scores of pirates, among them the notorious Jean Laffitte. The cutters *Louisiana* and *Alabama* became famous for their fights against the freebooters, both on the sea and at their shore bases, many of which they burned. *Right:* Attacking a Seminole Indian Stronghold. In 1836 a party of United States troops sent to subdue the warlike Seminole Indians was ambushed and massacred, beginning the Seminole War. The Revenue Cutters were sent to Florida to cooperate with the Army and Navy in putting an end to the fighting. The cutters finally cleaned up—after two and a half years of chasing elusive savages through the swamps.

the years to come. Eventually, protecting the safety of merchant shipping would become one of its principal peacetime missions.

The brilliant showing made by the Revenue Marine against the British Navy had won renown for the United States. But the Service had little time to rest upon its laurels. A war of a very

tices. The cutter, *Active*, captured a number of privateers in Chesapeake Bay between 1816 and 1819. The *Dallas* seized others in 1819 off Savannah, Georgia.

During the early years of the 19th century, pirates infested the waters off the eastern seaboard, operating boldly and with apparent impunity. The

9

matter was made worse by letters of marque sold by France to any sea captain who believed he could make a profit out of buccaneering. From his base near New Orleans, the swaggering Jean Laffitte built a pirate empire. He and his brother Alexander had become so rich and successful that they lived in the manner of grandees, with citizens of New Orleans courting their favor. The Florida Keys were another favorite haunt of these freebooters who were fast becoming the scourge of the Atlantic seacoast. The United States depended too much on foreign trade to permit these rascals to check its flow.

In its need, the country turned once again to the vessels best suited to hunt down and destroy the pirates. The government had no faster or better equipped vessels for this purpose than the Revenue Marine cutters. Two new cutters, the *Alabama* and the *Louisiana*, were built in 1819 to help take on the pirate fleet. Each was 57 feet long, 17 feet in beam and had a shallow, six-foot depth of hold. Both sailed south to drive the pirates from the seas. They and other cutters sailed into the very heart of the pirate empire in the Gulf and off Florida, and succeeded in smashing the entire vicious trade.

By the second decade of the 19th century, the free and easy trade of piracy had lost much of its attraction. A punitive squadron headed by Commodore David Porter was dispatched by the government to scour the Atlantic for pirates. The British in the West Indies were also beginning to crack down on the pirate gangs. Any buccaneer caught would be certain to find himself dangling from a British gibbet. By 1840, piracy was practically finished in American waters, and it was the Revenue Marine which was primarily responsible for its unlamented demise.

In the 1830's there were already indications that the issue of secession would haunt the country. The year was 1832, and the State of South Carolina had "nullified" the tariff on imports entering through her ports. This was open defiance to the federal government and threatened, if unchecked, to destroy the unity of the nation. Five cutters were sent to Charleston to enforce the collection of customs. In supporting this move, President Andrew Jackson declared: "If a single drop of blood shall be shed in opposition to the laws of the United States, I will hang the first man I can lay my hands on upon the first tree I can reach." This was very blunt language and the message was clear indeed. Vessels arriving with sugar from Havana anchored under the guns of the cutters and their cargoes were impounded in Fort

Moultrie until the import duties were paid. It took the skill of Henry Clay to end the crisis with the tariff compromise of 1833. But it was a portent of more troubled times to come.

Trouble with the Seminole Indians of Florida, long festering, burst into the open in 1836. Southern planters were complaining that runaway slaves were being given refuge by the Seminoles. Some had even intermarried with the Indian population. Since 1819, when Florida became part of the United States, the Seminoles had been pushed steadily out of their lands. Under mounting pressure, the Seminole chief, Osceola, precipitated the Second Seminole War by killing Florida's governor, General Wiley Thompson, and four of his men at Fort King. On the same day, other Seminoles ambushed an Army column under Brevet Major Francis Dade, killing him and 107 of his 110 men. This was to be a fight to the finish.

Eight cutters were ordered to the scene. The cutter, *Washington*, arrived just in time to land men and guns to save beleaguered Fort Brook. This was the first amphibious landing by combined forces in U.S. history, anticipating by more than a century similar operations accomplished by the Coast Guard during the Second World War.

So effective were the cutters in protecting settlers and in frustrating Indian attacks, that in 1836, Congress raised service pay to $100 a month for captains, $65-$80 for lieutenants, $16 for seamen, and $6-$10 for cabin boys. In appreciation, Florida offered land as homesteads for any cuttermen desiring them.

One of the most important developments in the history of the Revenue Marine took place in the early 1830's when the Secretary of the Treasury ordered the first winter cruise to aid seafarers and ships in distress. Cutters were charged in 1836 "to aid persons at sea, in distress, who may be taken aboard" and in 1843 to preserve property found aboard wrecks and to secure the cargoes for the owners. This was an event of the first magnitude for the Service, clearly establishing the humanitarian character which it bears to this day. Thus, far back in its history, the Coast Guard already had a dual peacetime and military function. This concept was to be greatly expanded and elaborated in the years to come, but the foundation for it had been laid in those early years of its history.

In the 1840's a new era dawned for the Revenue Marine under the able direction of Secretary of the Treasury John C. Spencer. Spencer set out to reorganize the Service along more efficient and modern lines. For the first time since its founding, the Revenue Marine was established as a bureau in the Department of the Treasury. It had accounting, engineering, personnel, operations, intelligence and legal branches, and a captain was selected to head the bureau.

Spencer made a brilliant choice in selecting Alexander V. Fraser, a veteran captain of the Revenue Marine, to head the streamlined organization. Fraser proceeded to overhaul the Service and to redress many of the injustices which had crept into its administration. One of his primary objectives was to build a high esprit in officers and enlisted men. Military customs and etiquette were to be strictly observed, and promotions were based on merit rather than political influence. Fraser also tried to cut the bureau away from the heavy hand of the regional Customs Collectors.

Alexander Fraser Takes Command

In a time of widespread corruption and heated factionalism, Fraser maintained not only his integrity, but strove in every way to create a Service with a distinctive tradition and high morale. He was a ray of light in the otherwise dark history of the Revenue Service during the 1840's.

Fraser was a New Yorker who as a youngster had attended the Mathematical, Nautical, and Commercial School in New York City. Even at that early age he showed promise. In writing a recommendation for Fraser in 1826, an instructor, M. Nash, certified that he had acquired a "very accurate and complete knowledge of Navigation and Nautical Astronomy as well as a distinguished reputation as a practitioner, especially in finding Longitude by Lunar Observations and the use of a Chronometer."

Fraser's first practical experience at sea came in the East India trade. A few years after leaving school, he served as a mate and later as master of a merchantman. He learned at first hand how to deal with hurricanes, the Horse Latitudes, and Zulu pirates. Those who came through this experience successfully were tough, confident skippers who took no nonsense from anyone. They had proved their seagoing mettle.

In 1832, Fraser applied to President Andrew Jackson for a commission in the Revenue Marine. He was appointed a second lieutenant, reporting for duty on the cutter, *Alert*, commanded by Captain W. A. Howard. The *Alert* and several other cutters were on duty in Charleston, South Carolina, upholding the supremacy of the federal government with respect to enforcement of a protective sugar tariff. For a time, South Carolina threatened to "nullify" the tariff, but eventually backed down under the president's determined stand.

But Fraser was now on his way up the ladder of promotion. He secured letters from Captain Howard, who wanted him on his ship, and from private firms such as C. Price & Morgan, and Hollingshead, Platt & Company of Philadelphia, Pa. Despite Fraser's proven merit, it remained necessary for him to obtain the backing of powerful sponsors to advance in rank. There was no merit system at the time. In 1835 Fraser was still attempting to obtain a first lieutenancy by transmitting lengthy letters of commendation signed by leading members of the powerful Democratic Clubs of the city and county of New York. It was to no avail, and Fraser decided to accept an excellent commercial offer. He received a two-year furlough from the Service which he spent as master of the *Himmaleh* on a voyage to Japan, China, and the Malayan Archipelago.

When Fraser returned to New York in March, 1838, he immediately wrote the following letter to Secretary of the Treasury Woodbury:

"Sir:

I have to report my arrival at this port after a long and tedious passage from China. I am informed of my promotion and hope I may deserve it. The *Alert* being without a First Lieutenant, and being certain that Captain Bicker would wish me with him, I would request that should it meet with the views of the Department I might be appointed to that vessel . . .

Your Obt Servt
Alex V. Fraser
U.S. Rev. Cutter Service"

This time, Fraser had better fortune and his request was granted. He boarded the *Alert* in time to start the newly instituted winter cruising.

These were colorful times in the American merchant marine. For about a quarter of a century, from 1830 to 1855, the U.S. clipper fleet was giving foreign competition a hard run for its money. The U.S. mercantile fleet was burgeoning, and by the middle 1850's the fast, beautiful clipper ships were familiar sights in all the harbors of the world. The premium was on speed. The faster the ship, the greater the profit she could make for her owners. These sailing ships were so successful that they may well have delayed the United States' entrance into steam propulsion. As a result of this delay, England took the lead in steamship construction to compete with the successful sailing ships of the United States.

Considering the primitive navigational equipment of the time, the sailing fleet took

Top: U.S. Coast Guard Cutter crossing the bar at the mouth of the Tabasco River, Mexico, June 14, 1847. From a lithograph by Sarany and Major, engraved and drawn by Lt. H. Walke, USN. (Courtesy of the Library of Congress) *Bottom:* USRC *Walter Forward*, 1841-1865. Photograph of an oil painting more than 100 years old, done by an unknown artist shortly after the Mexican War of 1845-47. The original painting was presented to the U.S. Coast Guard in 1958 by Dr. York Nones Pitkin of Cleveland, Ohio, descendant of Captain Henry B. Nones, USRCS, who commanded the *Forward* throughout her career in the U.S. Revenue Cutter Service and who won distinction with the *Forward* in the Mexican War.

14

enormous risks, especially in a wintry crossing of the North Atlantic. During this period, about 90 American ships were wrecked each year. Many of these tragedies took place on the coasts of Long Island, Cape Cod, and New Jersey. These mishaps gave added impetus to the search and rescue activities of the Revenue Service. In the highly embellished language of the time, a civilian chief of the Revenue Marine Bureau wrote:

"Those aware of the privations and perils incident to ordinary coasting in the winter season, will not regard the discharge of these duties as pastime, nor suppose these triumphs over storm and wave are achieved without hazard. Conquests that 'wrest from the greedy sea its prey' are rarely easily won, and often demand a heroism as great as ever was displayed on a field of battle." Nevertheless, the ornate language did not belie the facts.

For Alex Fraser, his three years on the *Alert* were to provide him with valuable experience for his future work. Captain Bicker was growing old. Increasingly, Fraser was called upon to carry out the winter cruising duty. His record was so impressive that, when he sought promotion to captain, New York's marine insurance underwriters gave him their unqualified endorsement. His promotion came in 1842, when he was named captain of the newly constructed cutter, *Ewing*.

The Service had been running into heavy weather. There was much discontent on the part of Congress with the manner of funding the cutter fleet which was supported not by appropriations but by the Secretary of the Treasury out of the public revenue. Out of this period of controversy came a new determination on the part of Treasury Secretary John C. Spencer to establish a strongly centralized Revenue Marine Bureau under the Department and headquartered in Washington, D.C. His choice to head the new Bureau was Captain Alexander V. Fraser.

For the hard-pressed Revenue Cutter Service, the appointment of Fraser to head up the Bureau was a momentous development. At last the organization had a centralized, unified command under the direction of an able and experienced officer. Fraser had the further advantage of enjoying the full confidence and support of Secretary Spencer. In the short time that the two men worked together they were to make Service history.

Fraser wasted no time in taking over. Within a short time after assuming his new position, he ordered Second Lieutenant George Hayes to Washington as his assistant. On January 9, 1844, he submitted the Service's first annual report, summarizing the situation as Fraser saw it and recommending changes to be made.

From the very beginning of his tenure, the first Captain-Commandant of the Revenue Service strongly advocated the construction of iron steamers. This was not a new idea first advanced by Fraser. As a matter of fact, the House of Representatives in 1840 had instructed its Committee on Naval Affairs to look into the desirability of using armed steamers in the Revenue Service. A new construction policy had been initiated in 1842, but no new cutters had been launched when Fraser came to Washington. Among the advantages of iron steamers, Fraser noted the costliness of repairs and replacements caused by dry rot in wooden vessels; the rapid destruction of wooden ships in southern waters by borers and rot; as well as the superior ability of steam-propelled iron ships to give chase to smugglers running the twisting inside coastal passages. He was so persuasive that in January, he was able to report that steam cutter construction was already six months underway.

But it wasn't all smooth sailing. From his survey of power engineering, Fraser concluded that the only reliable means of propulsion was the side-wheel. In this he was overruled by other authorities who had opted for underwater propulsion. In the 1840's this was a very new naval engineering concept and the planners had very little experience to guide them. The results were disastrous and delayed the use of steam in cutters for a decade. The experiment had been very costly, nearly bankrupting the Service. It was a classic example of an overoptimistic attempt to utilize the force of steam whose potential and characteristics were still largely unknown. Also unknown to the engineers of the 1840's was the relation of power and form to speed and ship resistance. Sailing ships on the other hand had evolved gradually over the centuries and their builders were more artists than engineers. However, the building of iron ships was another matter, requiring strict adherence to mathematical formulae.

When the United States declared war on Mexico in May, 1846, the Revenue Service promptly became a part of the Navy. In its fleet were a number of the poorly designed steam cutters of the early 1840's. The cutters *Bibb*, *McLane*, *Dallas*, and *Spencer* were equipped with hopelessly inefficient, submerged, horizontal paddle wheels. The former cutter, on her voyage to Mexico, began to leak so badly that she had to be beached. The *Polk* leaked on launching and never went into service. Because of defects, the *Spencer* was used as a lightship at Hampton Roads, Virginia. The *McLane* had her machinery removed and was converted into a lightship in 1848. The *Woodbury* and *Van Buren*, while not steamers, were not considered worth repairing. The *Legare* was taken out of service because of a dangerous boiler and transferred to the Coast Survey. The *Walker*, also transferred to the Survey, was run down and foundered off Barnegat, New Jersey. Modern naval

Service, transforming it into an efficient and well-disciplined military organization. So far as was possible they tried to eliminate the pernicious practice of obtaining advancement through politicial intrigue with regional Customs Officers.

With an eye to the future, the canny Fraser effected a closer liaison with the long-established Lighthouse Service. About a century later, the Services were to be officially united.

Not all of the reforms went down easily. The abolition of flogging as "healthful" punishment drew a tart comment from none other than

This meticulously detailed oil painting of the famous Revenue Cutter *McCulloch* was done by the American painter, John Bard, in the 1850's. For many years the painting was improperly stored in a suburb of Washington, D.C., accounting for its cracked surface. Bard was a member of the Hudson River School of painting whose works are now regarded as collectors' items.

engineers consider it a miracle that all of the ill-fated vessels didn't explode in view of their use of sea water in square-shaped boilers. It was an inglorious chapter for the Service, and Fraser had to face some harsh criticism although he had in fact argued against the type of construction employed in the cutters.

Despite the steam fiasco, Fraser retained his post as Chief of the Revenue Marine Bureau for several years. Even after Spencer left the Treasury, he managed to muster enough political backing to permit him to follow the course he had charted.

The Spencer-Fraser combination left a permanent impact on the Service. By the force of their personalities and their skillful leadership, the two men completely overhauled the Revenue

Captain Winslow Porter. Said the autocratic Porter:

"The regulations of the Service are a miserable compilation framed by a set of fawning pimps in Washington such as Fraser, Howard, and others, to tickle the ears of John C. Spencer." But in spite of Porter's tough talk, the reforms remained.

In 1848, Fraser's term as Captain-Commandant of the Revenue Marine Bureau came to an end. At that time, the revenue laws were extended to include the Oregon and California Territories and a new customs district was established to administer this function. To this district, the revenue cutter, *Lawrence* built in 1848, was assigned. Realizing that he would be transferred out of Washington, Fraser requested and was given command of the new cutter. His voyage in the *Lawrence* around the

Cape Horn to San Francisco and his work during the frenetic days of the Gold Rush were to become an epic of naval history.

Seldom has a voyage been so beset with problems as was Fraser's on the *Lawrence*. Three of his lieutenants were political appointees with no sea experience. The ship's surgeon, a Dr. Overstreet, was professionally competent but so gullible that he was easily taken advantage of by crewmen feigning illness. The boatswain, an old whaling ship sailor, attempted to employ whaling methods in handling the cutter. At last, in Valparaiso, he tendered his resignation and was put ashore drunk and disorderly.

In the more than two months of sailing for Rio de Janeiro, the *Lawrence* was buffeted by squalls, heavy thunder, lightning and heavy rains. When the cutter finally reached Brazil, Fraser found that she was so badly in need of repairs that it would not be possible to continue the voyage for some time. To make matters worse, the Brazilians completely ignored Fraser's demands for haste and performed at their more leisurely Latin pace. For two long months Fraser chafed at the delay. Then in March, he embarked on the perilous trip around the Horn at the worst time of the year.

Yet such was Fraser's control that he ran the *Lawrence* as if it were a training ship. The inexperienced members of the crew had a chance to learn navigation by the best method of all—that of performing shipboard duties under the guidance of a master navigator. The men were assigned professional reading which they were expected to master along with their practical experience. By the time the *Lawrence* arrived in San Francisco months later, the young officers had acquired considerable knowledge of their profession and could regard themselves as saltwater sailors.

Fraser remained on the west coast until 1852 when he was transferred to the Atlantic. His term of duty spanned the fantastic time of the Gold Rush when men by the thousands came to California lured by the prospect of sudden wealth. The best testimony as to the effectiveness of Fraser's administration is to be found in a letter written to him by the Collector of Customs at San Francisco in November, 1850:

"... Few men have had more difficult or responsible duties to perform ... When it is to be remembered that you have been in a harbour where from five to six hundred vessels were riding at anchor, in the midst of great excitement, with crews insubordinate and lawless, without the aid of civil tribunals or civil process, and when day and night you have been called upon to render assistance and to aid masters, of vessels in suppressing mutiny and violence, surely it becomes me to bear willing testimony to the necessity of your presence and your promptness in the discharge of your onerous duties. To me your services have been invaluable ... May you have a safe and prosperous cruise...

> J. Collier
> Collector"

Captain Henry Benjamin Nones, U.S. Revenue Cutter Service (1804-1868). Early uniform of a captain of the Coast Guard. Mexican War period and Civil War.

Other cutters followed *Lawrence* to patrol the waters of America's westernmost territories, but Fraser had been the trail blazer and he had established a standard of service which was to be a model for others.

On Fraser's return to the east coast in 1852, a pleasant surprise awaited him. Steam cutters were once again being considered for use in the Revenue Service. The result was the construction of the *Harriet Lane*, named after President Buchanan's niece who presided over the White House during his administration. This time, the engineering was more sophisticated and the misfortunes of an earlier day did not recur.

Yet at this point in his career so filled with achievement, Fraser met his nemesis. He had ardently supported the building of a steamer for New York, a project opposed by an Assistant Secretary of the Treasury. Arbitrarily, his commission was revoked in 1856—a sorry repayment for a lifetime of dedication to the Service. It was not until the outbreak of the Civil War in 1860 that Fraser applied for reinstatement in the Revenue Service. Eventually, through President Lincoln's full support, he received a new commission on July 1, 1863. But by this time, it was no longer possible for Fraser to accept the appointment. Nevertheless, he had won out in his advocacy of steam, and the *Harriet Lane* was the result.

From the time Fraser left Washington in 1848 until the start of the Civil War, the Revenue Service deteriorated steadily. The many innovations and improvements made by Spencer and Fraser were administrative rather than statutory and as such could be easily undone. Little by little, the bad practices of an earlier day—the political corruption, favoritism—crept back into the Service. It was a low point not only for the Service but also for the nation it served. On the horizon were dark clouds ready to erupt momentarily into that most dreaded of all conflicts, civil war.

Civil War

The causes of the Civil War are so tangled that they cannot be explained by any simplistic theory. Long before the first shot was fired on Fort Sumter, tensions had been building up between North and South. The country still remembered South Carolina's futile attempt to nullify a federal tariff a generation ago. The incident continued to rankle in southern hearts. Strangely enough, it was a southerner, President Andrew Jackson, who had met the issue head on. In the face of "Old Hickory's" iron determination, South Carolina had backed down. But the debate between supporters of a strong Federal Union and the advocates of a States' Rights philosophy of government was by no means over.

Also at issue were two fundamentally different ways of life—the slave-based agricultural economy of the South versus the growing industrialization of the North. Politicians were finding it increasingly difficult to straddle the issue of slavery. The Supreme Court's Dred Scott decision did nothing to soothe the country's heated passions.

Even those who were not abolitionists recognized that slavery was grossly immoral. It was a cancer on the body politic, deforming and distorting the image of freedom which the United States sought to present to the world. In 1859, tough old John Brown had made his desperate attack on a federal arsenal at Harper's Ferry, West Virginia. It was a part of his crusade against slavery and the officer to put it down was a young West Point graduate, Robert E. Lee. Brown was hanged, but only after a trial during which he made a speech that had the thunder of Old Testament prophecy. Men, as Freud has pointed out, are much more moral than they realize. Sooner or later they know there has to be a reckoning.

Rational men on both sides sought as best they could to avoid the awful prospect of fratricidal war. In 1830, and again in 1850, the "great compromiser" Henry Clay had managed to stave off conflict. But more and more these efforts had the look of appeasement and pleased no one.

On March 4, 1861, President Abraham Lincoln in his inaugural message made it sternly clear that "the power confided to me will be used to hold, occupy, and possess the property and places belonging to the Government . . ."

To the South, the president's words constituted a direct challenge, amounting nearly to a declaration of war. For them, federal sovereignty no longer existed. The Confederacy's Stars and Bars were already flying over lighthouses, lightships, arsenals, customs houses, dockyards, many forts and over some revenue cutters. As the dreaded moment of decision approached, brave and honest men on both sides had to make one of the most difficult choices of their lives. Among these were many officers and men of the Revenue Cutter Service.

A dramatic case of conflicting loyalties involved Captain James J. Morrison, commanding officer of the revenue cutter *Lewis Cass*, at Mobile, Alabama. A southerner, Captain Morrison had served his country well in the Seminole and Mexican wars. Now with the approach of war, he found himself, like his great countryman, General Robert E. Lee, unable to take up arms against his native state, his relatives, his children, and his home. He chose to put his services at the disposal of the Confederacy. On January 30, 1861, he turned his ship over to the State of Alabama. On the other hand, Third Lieutenant Charles F. Shoemaker, later Commandant of the Revenue Cutter Service, chose to remain loyal to the federal government. With his fellow officers and the entire crew of the *Lewis Cass*, he made his way through the full length of the hostile South. On reaching Northern territory, Shoemaker reported aboard the *Crawford* in July, 1861, just in time to serve as part of Flag Officer S. H. Stringham's naval force in Hampton Roads, Virginia.

Another southerner who elected to stand with the Confederacy was Captain John G. Brushwood, commander of the cutter *McClelland*, stationed at New Orleans, Louisiana. Treasury Secretary John A. Dix, suspecting possible surrender of the cutter by its captain, sent a courier with orders that Brushwood proceed immediately for New York. When the captain refused, Dix wired: "Tell Lieutenant Caldwell to arrest Captain Brushwood, assume command of the cutter, and obey the order. If Captain Brushwood, after arrest, undertakes to interfere with the command of the cutter, tell Lieutenant Caldwell to consider him as a mutineer, and treat him accordingly. If anyone

19

attempts to haul down the American flag, shoot him on the spot."

With the bombardment of Fort Sumter by the Confederacy on April 12, 1861, the storm which had been threatening so long finally broke. The die was cast. Henceforth, the long debate would be settled not in the halls of Congress but on the battlefield. On hand to watch the spectacle was the revenue cutter *Harriet Lane*, lying off the bar at the entrance to Charleston Harbor. She had been sent there by Lincoln's Navy Secretary, Gideon Welles, to join a relief squadron.

The *Harriet Lane* had one of the most unusual histories in the annals of the Revenue Service. She had been built only a few years before the war, and was the Service's first successful steam cutter. A side-wheeler, built at the then high cost of $140,000, she had already served as part of a flotilla sent to enforce a trade agreement between the United States and Paraguay. It had been classical "gunboat diplomacy" but it had one redeeming virtue: it worked.

Later in the war, the *Harriet Lane* would take part in the first Union victory: the capture of Fort

Harriet Lane, United States Revenue Service Cutter.

But the effort came too late. *Harriet Lane* and others in the relief squadron watched helplessly as Confederate artillerymen poured more than 3,000 rounds into the fort and finally bludgeoned its commander, Major Anderson, into surrender on April 14. During the action, the cutter, *Harriet Lane* hailed the steamer, *Nashville*, but the latter refused to show her colors. The cutter's commander, Captain Faunce, then ordered a shot thrown across her bow which "had the desired effect." Thus, the *Harriet Lane* is credited with firing the first shot from any naval unit in the long and terrible war to preserve the Union.

Clark and Fort Hatteras, serving as bases for blockade runners in the Hatteras Inlet, North Carolina area. Assigned to the Navy, she served as the flagship for Admiral David Porter. But *Harriet Lane* was not destined to serve out her time in the Union fleet. She was captured by Confederates at Galveston in a bloody, rough-and-tumble boarding with guns and cutlasses. After that she went to sea under the Stars and Bars, General Magruder of the Confederacy deeming her services "absolutely necessary for use as a government gunboat." Years later, operating as a freighter, she ended her days off Pernambuco, Brazil.

Soon after the shelling of Fort Sumter, Lincoln issued a call for 75,000 volunteers to check the Confederacy on land. But it was quickly apparent that troops alone would not be able to meet the emergency. The Union would have to establish a blockade from Chesapeake Bay to the Rio Grande. This curtain of ships was aimed at keeping cotton from going out of the Confederacy and to prevent arms, ammunition, clothing, salt, medicines and every other necessity from coming in. It was to be a tightening stranglehold on the southern war economy.

For the Revenue Cutter Service, the outbreak of war meant a substantial expansion of the scope and importance of its operations. Invoking the Act of March 2, 1799, President Lincoln ordered many of the cutters into combat in cooperation with the Navy. Cutters assigned to naval forces helped to achieve federal objectives at sea. These were economic isolation of the South by blockade and by seizure of confederate shipping, provision of security for Union shipping, and supplying of naval support for Union military ventures.

As the tempo of war accelerated, Secretary of the Treasury Salmon P. Chase, issued a Circular Letter which reviewed the President's Proclamation closing the ports of Virginia, North Carolina, South Carolina, Georgia, Florida, Alabama, Louisiana, Mississippi, and Texas—the whole of the Confederacy. "You will bear in mind," his order directed, "that all persons or parties in armed insurrection against the Union, however such persons or parties may be organized or manned, are engaged in levying war against the United States . . ."

"Use your utmost vigilance," the Secretary urged the Customs Collectors and Revenue Captains, "to prevent the prohibited shipments and to detect and bring to punishment all who are in any way engaged in furnishing supplies to such insurgents . . ."

The war had been in progress for only a short time, but already five former revenue cutters flew the Confederate flag. Another vessel, *William J. Duane*, dismantled and undergoing repairs, was lost to the federal government when Union forces hastily withdrew from the Norfolk Navy Yard.

At the beginning of the war, Secretary Chase's fleet totaled 28 cutters. Four were based on the Pacific Coast, six on the Great Lakes, and the remaining 18 operated from Atlantic ports in the North. Five of the cutters on the Great Lakes were ordered to the Atlantic Coast, and the Treasury Department hunted desperately for additional ships.

So great was the need that the federal government put into service nearly anything resembling a cutter. The veteran steamer, *Bibb*, still in the Coast Survey after having been transferred from the Revenue Service in 1847, was recalled to duty. Other Survey vessels released for duty with the Revenue Service included *Crawford, Corwin, Vixen, Howell Cobb, Commodore Perry, Arage,*

Harriet Lane firing first shot in Civil War.

and others. The federal government also bought vessels usable as cutters, and accepted yachts offered by private citizens.

One of the most unusual vessels acquired by the government from private owners was the *Naugatuck*, sometimes referred to in the records as *Ironsides* or *E. A. Stevens*, after her former owner and designer, of Hoboken, New Jersey. He had designed the ship to demonstrate some of the revolutionary theories involved in the construction of his famous "Stevens Battery." The latter was an ironclad which had been under construction by the Navy for 20 years and which was never launched. A contemporary of the famed *Monitor* and *Virginia*, *Naugatuck* was one of the first ironclads to go into action. She was semi-submersible; she could take aboard sufficient water ballast in fifteen minutes to sink her almost three feet, and she could pump it all overboard again in eight minutes.

The strange looking *Naugatuck* proved her mettle when she tested the iron sides of *Virginia* in company with the *Monitor*. She shared in the bombardment of Sewall's Point, opening up the

of a duel with the battery attempting to cripple and sink the vessels, and the sharpshooters picking off the men at the guns.

During the action, *Naugatuck's* Parrott gun poured round after round of 100-pound shells into the Confederate works. Suddenly, the overheated weapon burst with a tremendous explosion and its part in the fighting was over.

The expedition started dropping downstream, with *Naugatuck* following, raining shell and canister from her starboard guns. But the Confederate shore defenses were too strong to be overcome by naval attack. Troops would be

Model of the U.S. Revenue Cutter *Fessenden* (1865-1908), built by the Smithsonian Institution for its naval exhibit in 1963. Photo: Smithsonian Institution

James River to Union forces. Again, together with the *Monitor*, she led an expedition up the river to reduce the enemy's work along the way, spike their guns, blow up their magazines, and get to Richmond and shell the city into surrender.

Eight miles below Richmond, at Drury's Bluff, the *Naugatuck* found the channel blocked by two barricades. One of them was built of spikes driven into the river bed, and the other formed by steamboats and sailing vessels loaded with stones until their keels rested on the bottom. A heavy Confederate battery planted on the bluff, supported with rifle pits manned by sharpshooters, looked down on the river. When the flotilla appeared, it boomed into action. That was the start

needed to dislodge the foe. The first Union attack on Richmond had been unsuccessful.

Gradually, the Treasury expanded its cutter fleet by a modest building program. Six steamers were built late in 1863; *Ashuelot, Kankakee, Kewanee, Mahoning, Pawtuxet*, and *Wayanda*. Several of these cutters escorted a "cotton fleet" from Savannah to New York early in 1865, thus helping to reopen the American source of supply for Northern factories.

The sea war, however, was not entirely a Northern affair. The South was aware that trade was vital to the Northern economy. On the other hand, England was dependent on American western wheat. Between 1860 and 1862, England increased her wheat imports from 17½ million bushels to 62 million. This trade helped to bring in urgently needed gold revenues and tended to assure English neutrality.

By the close of 1862, the federal government had built up a strong naval force, including several blockading squadrons. They served in the north and south Atlantic, in the Gulf of Mexico, and on several strategic rivers. The "North Atlantic Blockading Squadron" by itself, commanded by Admiral S. P. Lee, totaled nearly 90 ships. The ring of steel had been forged; it was beginning to exert its deadly pressure.

Blockade duty was not glamorous, but consisted of hard, unrelenting vigil to prevent all commerce with the embattled South. Mostly it was a routine affair, but it involved considerable effort to intercept English attempts at running the blockade. Although England was nominally neutral, popular sympathy was largely with the South. In November, 1862, the U.S. Consul at Glasgow, Scotland, wrote: "Glasgow is now the great resort of Southern emissaries for the purchase and outfitting, and also for the building of iron steamers, either to run our blockade as merchant vessels or to ravage the seas as ships of war." During the same month a similar letter was received from the American Consul at Liverpool, England.

Despite federal efforts, Southern raiders caused heavy damage to Northern shipping. Early in the war, they accounted for 110,000 tons of Yankee commerce and forced another 750,000 tons into foreign registry. To counter this threat, the federal government had to put into service every revenue cutter and Navy ship that could be spared to protect lanes of commerce. Yet even in this grim time, the cutters assigned to blockade duty managed to assist an average of 115 distressed vessels annually between 1861 and 1865. Protection of federal revenues assumed even greater importance in wartime.

As the war progressed, it became evident that strangulation of Southern commerce by blockade and other measures offered a powerful weapon for victory. Ultimately, revenue cutters were assisting on blockade duty along the Atlantic seaboard, in the Chesapeake, and in the Potomac region and provided very valuable help to the Naval Patrol Force.

To help stem the strong Confederate tide early in the war, the federal government had purchased a number of private vessels for use in blockade duty. Among them was the *Lady Le Merchant*, built on

the Clyde in Scotland in 1853. She had an English oak frame, teak planking, and copper fastenings and seemed like a bargain at $25,000. Secretary Chase authorized her purchase, and she entered the Revenue Cutter Service as *Miami*. She was to figure in one of the dramatic episodes of the war. On a cloudy night of May, 1862, her cabin was the setting for a council of war attended by General Egbert Viele, Commander of Union Forces in Virginia, Secretary of War Edwin M. Stanton, Secretary of the Treasury Salmon P. Chase, and

1st Lt. Alvan A. Fengar, U.S. Revenue Marine, after receiving appointment in that rank, Oct. 9, 1861.

President Lincoln. For some time the Union army had been bogged down before the city of Norfolk, although militarily, there seemed to be no obstacle to assault and victory. On that historic night, the *Miami* ran close in to the beach, and Lincoln was put ashore to walk on Confederate soil. Investigation showed that assault on Norfolk was not only feasible but easy. The President and Stanton ordered an attack the following day and Norfolk fell to the Union forces. The conference on the *Miami* had produced a victory when it was most needed to restore flagging Northern morale.

From James Gordon Bennett, Jr., son of the famed editor of the *New York Herald*, the federal government purchased the yacht *Henrietta*. Secretary Chase accepted the vessel and commissioned the 20-year-old Bennett as a First Lieutenant to serve aboard the yacht.

The story of the revenue cutter *Caleb Cushing* is an extraordinary one, with many of the elements of a suspense thriller. It began in June, 1863, when Lieutenant Charles W. Read, commanding the

Captain Amasa L. Hyde commanded the Cutter *Tiger* on patrols between Baltimore and New York from November 2, 1861, to February 28, 1862. He then commanded the Cutter *Jeremiah S. Black* off the New England coast.

Confederate raider, *Clarence*, appeared off the Virginia Capes, burned three vessels, captured two others, then set fire to his own ship after transferring her armament and stores to the *Tacony*, a third capture.

News of the exploit shook up the Union high command. President Lincoln quickly sent a dispatch to Secretary Chase to cooperate with the Navy in cracking down on the "rebel depredations on American commerce and transportation and in capturing rebels engaged therein."

Instead of backing down for a while, Lieutenant Read, a bold and resourceful officer, decided on a bold gamble. He sailed up the coast of Maine and picked Portland, station of *Caleb Cushing*, as the place for a raid ashore. Realizing that Union vessels were on the alert for *Tacony*, he switched to another ship, *Archer*, which he disguised as a fishing vessel. He succeeded in getting safely past the forts guarding Portland Harbor where the crew strolled casually ashore in small groups. They were to meet in the town and destroy two gunboats under construction and set fire to the city's wharves.

But things don't always work out according to plan. The fire would not take hold, and Read was almost ready to give up the plan when he learned that Captain Clarke, commander of *Caleb Cushing*, had died of a heart attack a few hours earlier. Immediately a new plan formed in Read's mind. At about one o'clock in the morning, after the moon had set, small boats made stealthily for the *Caleb Cushing*. Before the crew of the cutter could recover from their surprise, they were overpowered and the vessel was in rebel hands. At first Read tried to sail her. But there was not enough wind and she had to be towed from the harbor by two boats.

A dramatic sea chase developed, Jehediah Jewett, Portland Collector of Customs, quickly organized a flotilla of three steamers—the tug *Casco*, the side-wheeler *Forest City*, and *Chesapeake*. About ten miles offshore, the pursuers caught up with the *Caleb Cushing*, and eventually, *Archer*, along with its commander, Lieutenant Read, were taken prisoner. However, during his two weeks of cruising, the Confederate raider had run up an impressive score. It included 19 sailing vessels burned and bonded. Read had obviously intended to destroy *Archer* and sail on in the *Caleb Cushing*.

Other revenue cutters made fine records for themselves in the war. *Forward* lent substantial support to Union General Butler at Annapolis, Maryland. *Nemeha* cooperated with the Union Army and Navy on the Atlantic coast and received General Sherman on board at the end of his famous "march to the sea." *Forward*, *Brown*, *Agassiz*, and *Antietam* served with distinction in North Carolina waters, while *Jackson*, *Tiger*, *Hercules*, and *Phillip Allen* gave a good account of themselves in Chesapeake Bay.

All the while that the revenue cutters were helping to prosecute the war, they were also carrying out some of their regular duties. Assistance to Union vessels in distress now meant direct assistance to the federal war effort. Cruising in protection of shipping now meant cruising against Southern privateers as well as against natural dangers. The cutters were an important part of the Union naval effort.

Less sensational than the work of the revenue cutters but vitally important was the contribution of the Lighthouse Establishment. This old government agency had been a part of the Revenue Cutter Service until it was detached in the 1840's and set up as a seperate administrative unit under the general supervision of the Secretary of the Treasury.

Records of the Civil War period show that the destruction of lighthouses and other navigation aids was heavy. The enemy destroyed 164 lights and nearly all of the lightships south of Chesapeake Bay were captured. Some lightships were sunk by the Confederates to obstruct entrances to harbors. But the spirit of the Service remained undaunted. In a statement freighted with some political overtones, Secretary of the Treasury Chase said: "In disregard of repeated warnings of impending danger in December last, the Secretary of the Treasury in office at the time, neglected to take the necessary measures to secure the vessels and other movable property connected with the lighthouse establishments. This property, therefore, became the easy prey of insurrectionary violence. Acts of rapine and plunder followed each other in quick succession as the rebellion spread, until the lights of commerce were extinguished along the whole coast—except at Key West and some neighboring points protected by the power of the Union—from the capes of the Chesapeake round to the western limits of Texas. In other parts of the country, the lighthouse system has been extended and improved, until it is surpassed in aids and benefits to navigation and commerce by that of no other country. Under the direction of the Secretary also, as the rebellion has been suppressed in district after district, the lights have been rekindled. Already, from the coasts of the Chesapeake, from the banks of Hatteras, from the islands of Port Royal entrance, and from Chandeleur Island in the Gulf, they shine once more as the safeguards and symbols of fraternal commerce and peaceful civilization. May we not hope that the time is not far off when every extinguished light shall be in like manner restored amid the rejoicings of a reunited people?"

They were moving words, but the hope they expressed was not to be realized for several long years of war. But as the Union Armies gained control in one area after another, rekindling of the lights went on. They relit the guiding lights which had been extinguished by war.

As the war progressed, it became clear that the era of the sailing ship was over. The need was for steam rather than sail. Also, by this time, naval technology had proceeded to a point at which the earlier difficulties with steam had been overcome.

It was during the war that the Revenue Cutter Service came to the attention of the American public more forcefully than ever before. The Service was accorded a new respect for its fighting abilities and its humane functions. It was a Service adapted both for peace and war. A marine editor, in 1864, indicated an awareness of this when he wrote.:

"Keeping always under steam and *ever ready*, in the event of extraordinary need, to render valuable service, the cutters can be made to form a *coast guard* whose value it is impossible at the present time to estimate." This prescient editor foresaw the future of the Service, "Semper Paratus," "Always Ready," and its future appellation, U.S. Coast Guard.

Of Reconstruction and Continued Growth

In 1865, the terrible Civil War finally came to an end, but the country had paid a dreadful price in blood and treasure. Never again would it return to the simpler America of an earlier time. The farm, which had hitherto been the central point of its economic and cultural life, was being supplanted by rapid industrialization and a swing toward urbanization. This trend was to continue indefinitely. The late sixties and the decades to come were times of growing awareness of the richness of the United States' natural resources and of the enormous profits to be made by their exploitation. The country's goods were beginning to move in significantly greater quantities to foreign markets. Factories were starting to pour their goods into the market, and in general, it seemed as though the nation was determined to put the holocaust of the war behind it and to roll up its sleeves and get to work.

There was no question that the production of war material by northern factories had given American industry a strong impetus to develop methods of mass production. Under the pressures of war, manufacturers had been forced to compress economic development which would normally have taken a decade into a few brief years.

It was during the late sixties, also, that the name of the Service changed from Revenue Marine to the Revenue Cutter Service. The name would not become official for another few years, but references to the Service in legislation and other written documents eventually established the latter title as the organization's commonly accepted name.

As is usually the case between wars, the Revenue Cutter Service, and the federal establishment generally, came under the harsh scrutiny of Congress. But the greatly increased tempo of foreign and coastal shipping saved the Service from excessive mutilation in the name of economy.

Ships were being built of iron now and they carried larger cargoes and more passengers, requiring greater protection. This meant that lighthouses and other aids to navigation were more urgently needed than ever and had to be maintained in a state of efficiency. If the protection of the Revenue Cutter Service were diminished or withdrawn, hordes of smugglers were

ready to move in and reap their illicit profits. So, for the time being, the Service was spared the dismantling which usually occurs in peacetime.

Nevertheless, the new Secretary of the Treasury, George S. Boutwell, was determined to prune the costs of running the Service. His subordinate, the civilian Chief of the Revenue Cutter Service, Sumner I. Kimball, decided that, the cost of iron

Sumner I. Kimball, first civilian chief of the Revenue-Marine Bureau. Kimball also headed the Lifesaving Service.
Photo: National Archives

ships being too high, the new, badly needed cutters would be made of wood. The total of petty officers and enlisted men was substantially cut and the pay reduced. Kimball also carried out a vigorous housecleaning of incompetent and extravagant officers, and saw to it that discipline was tightened. A special object of his censure was the use of cutters as personal yachts by local Customs officials as a perquisite of office. Once again, following on the footsteps of Captain Fraser, Kimball put into effect a merit system to determine promotions. He also made one other great contribution to the quality of the Service by establishing, in 1877, a "School of Instruction" to train young officers on an old schooner, named *Dobbin.* From this move developed today's U.S. Coast Guard Academy, which trains the bulk of the Coast Guard's career officers.

Captain Douglas Ottinger built and equipped the first Lifeboat Stations on the New Jersey shore.

The attempts to build an effective Lifesaving Service, interrupted by the war, were continued by Kimball in the 1870's. He succeeded in convincing Congress of the need for appropriating funds for the establishment of such a Service. Officers of the Revenue Cutter Service were placed in charge of this project. Thus, the familiar lifesaving stations, which were to dot the coastline of the United States, had their genesis under the direction of this remarkable man. The stations were to be manned by full-time, professional crews, known as surfmen. These brave and dedicated men were to leave a heritage of valor and humane concern never surpassed in marine history. The close union between the Revenue Service and the Lifesaving Service was probably the most important partnership in marine safety ever undertaken in this country. It was to pay enormous dividends in

the saving of human life and property in the years to come.

But while the money allotted to the Service was relatively small, the number of duties assigned to it in the decades following the Civil War was large. In these crucial years of U.S. development, when American energy and industry were making giant strides in resource development, the Service acquired one responsibility which was to leave its stamp permanently upon the Pacific Northwest. This was in connection with the development of the huge Alaskan Territory, purchased in 1867 by President Andrew Johnson's Secretary of State, William H. Seward, from the Imperial Russian government for the amazingly low price of $7,200,000. It was easily one of the best real estate bargains ever made by the nation. Yet at the time, Seward was assailed in the press and elsewhere for buying what was thought to be a frozen, worthless wasteland. Even persons who should have known better, referred to the new territory as "Walrussia," "Seward's Folly," and "Seward's Ice Box." Time has shown how wrong they were.

With the purchase of Alaska went the need for exploration of this sprawling land and an inventory of its resources. Clearly, this was work for the Cutter Service.

In July, 1867, the revenue cutter, *Lincoln,* hauled anchor at San Francisco, bound for Sitka and the first U.S. exploration of the waters and resources of Alaska. Out of that first voyage developed the Alaskan Patrol and a partnership in the building of Alaska from a rude and brawling territory into the nation's 49th state. This partnership continues, although nowadays, many of the functions of the Patrol have been taken over by the state. But in the early days of a century ago, the cutters and their captains were virtually the only representatives of law and order in an otherwise lawless land. The cutters often served as floating courts where justice was dispensed, sometimes roughly, but fairly. They were the spearhead of progress in an area whose civilization was essentially nomadic, and at least several centuries behind the modern era. For the Navy Department, the cutters gathered military intelligence. For the Post Office Department they carried the mail. And for the Interior Department they carried teachers to their posts and checked up on sanitation, guarded timber and game.

The cutters of the Alaskan Patrol (formerly the Bering Sea Patrol) made surveys of the coast and regional industries for the Department of Commerce, and they brought dentists and doctors to

Top: The U.S. Revenue Cutter *Lincoln* at anchor at Victoria, B.C., November 1870. *Bottom: Manzanita,* 152-foot vessel, old sail and steamer, built 1878-79.

Lifeboat from U.S. Lifesaving Station, Cape Henry, Va., investigating grounded schooner, c. 1890's. Photo: Smithsonian Institution

remote native villages which had never known such care before. They were strongpoints of civilization in the northern wilderness, pioneers in the fullest sense of the word.

The historic voyage of the *Lincoln* also was the first oceanographic study of northern waters ever carried out by the U.S. government in this area and represented the start of a flourishing program in the marine sciences carried on in the Coast Guard over the past century. It laid the foundation for such work and its significance in shaping the character of the modern Coast Guard cannot be overestimated.

Out of this colorful period, two names emerged

which will be forever remembered in Coast Guard history: the cutter *Bear*, and Captain Michael A. Healy, her most famous commander and one who was to command her for a longer time. By the time the Coast Guard acquired the *Bear* she had already acquired fame as one of the toughest vessels in the far north. Her builders, the firm of Alexander Stephen and Son of Dundee, Scotland, had a reputation for building the best vessels in operation in the sealing trade. That was to be the *Bear's* mission, and when launched in 1874, she gave promise of being an outstanding sealer. Time quickly confirmed this judgment. Before she entered the service of the cutter fleet, she had served not only as a sealer, but had taken part in the rescue of Lieutenant Adolphus Washington Greely, of the U.S. Army Signal Corps, and other members of the Lady Franklin Bay Expedition of 1882.

The expedition was one of a long series of attempts by the nations of the world to penetrate the secrets of the polar regions. There was a growing awareness on the part of the world's scientific community that these desolate regions held some of the world's most valuable secrets. For the most part, efforts to learn these secrets had ended in disaster, the most notable one being the failure of the 1845 expedition by Sir John Franklin. This was undoubtedly very much in the mind of Greely when he set out on his mission in 1882.

But somehow, despite the carefully prepared plan, disaster overtook the Greely venture. Two years after the expedition had set out, Greely and his men were trapped in the vast and icy prison of the Arctic. Spurred by a rising tide of public indignation at the indifference displayed by Congress to the expedition's fate, the Secretary of the Navy made up his mind to act. For some time he had been negotiating for the purchase of a rescue fleet. One of the vessels was the *Bear*, which had won renown for her northern exploits.

On March 17, 1884, the *Bear* and three other ice ships began their rescue attempt. At this time, the *Bear* had become a ship in the U.S. Navy. It turned out to be a harrowing voyage, as voyages in northern seas often are. But like the tough ship she was, she weathered all the difficulties that beset her. Months later, the rescue flotilla found the first evidence of Greely's presence at Cary Island in the middle of Baffin Bay. From then on, the story mounted steadily to the climax when on June 21,

1884, a search party discovered the emaciated, broken survivors of the Greely expedition. Only seven had survived out of the original twenty-five. Greely was among them. The men had been so weakened by starvation and disease that they no longer had the strength to bury their dead, but laid them, instead, in shallow trenches scooped out of the ice. They had been reduced to eating the dirty oil-stained covering of Greely's sleeping bag, as well as moss. The pitiful survivors of the expedition were brought back to the United States to a hero's welcome.

On her return from the successful rescue of Greely, the *Bear* was declared unfit for further service in the Navy, and she was decommissioned for sale out of the Service. It seemed like an ironic twist to a great story. But, fortunately, that wasn't the story's end. The Revenue Cutter Service had been looking for a sturdy ship for northern cruising. In the *Bear*, they knew a good ship when they saw one. By Act of Congress, March 3, 1885, with the concurrence of the Navy, she was transferred to the Treasury Department. Her domain was to be in the icy waters of Alaska and the Arctic Ocean.

This was the ship that was turned over in February, 1886 to Captain Healy, who had by this time achieved a formidable reputation in the northwest as an Arctic skipper. Ship and commander were well suited to each other, although at first Healy was not at all enthusiastic about the *Bear*. A few cruises in her, however, soon changed his mind. This vessel had endurance and staying power such as were seldom found in any ship.

Healy and the *Bear* were to make history on the Bering Sea Patrol and in their vigilant guarding of the resources entrusted to them, notably, the valuable Pacific fur seals, with rookeries in the fog-shrouded Pribilof Islands. In a part of the world formerly ruled by savage exploitation of the natives, Healy introduced a measure of justice and compassion. Healy was joined in this noble work by Dr. Sheldon Jackson, General Agent for Education in Alaska. Both of the men were deeply concerned about dwindling supplies of food for the Eskimos. Their numbers had been so decimated by lack of food that there was a good possibility that in a relatively short time they would be wiped out. Healy's remarkable story will be recounted at greater length elsewhere in this book.

Top. Cutter *Hudson* rescuing the disabled Navy torpedo boat *Winslow* from under enemy shore batteries and impending destruction at Cardenas, Cuba, May 11, 1898, during the Spanish-American War. (From a painting by an unknown artist.) *Bottom:* Built in 1882 by the Pusey and Jones Co., of Wilmington, Del., the 148-foot Coast Guard cutter *Forward* was the second of three vessels named after a former Secretary of Treasury, Walter Forward. She carried out patrol duties in the Gulf of Mexico, the Caribbean, and along the south Atlantic coast of the U.S. During the War with Spain, in 1898, she patrolled the Straits of Florida.

1898: The United States Flexes Its Muscles

By the close of the 19th century, the wounds made by the Civil War had begun to heal. The country was anxious to get on with its business. The industrial revolution, which had begun in the United States in the middle of the century, was well advanced. From a largely agricultural nation the United States was turning increasingly into an industrial one. The dream of spanning the North American continent had been achieved. In the nearly three centuries between the founding of the colony at Jamestown, Virginia, and the inauguration of President McKinley in 1897, a mighty nation had come into being and was only now beginning to feel its strength.

Behind much American thought and action lay the mystical concept of "manifest destiny" which according to orators and editorialists decreed that the United States assume its world role as the dominant power of the Western Hemisphere. This idea had already been formalized by President Monroe in the doctrine bearing his name.

The Monroe Doctrine rested on the proposition that the basic interest of the American people should be concentrated on their continental opportunities. The hemisphere was also to be kept independent and protected against further colonization and conquest of foreign powers. Conversely, the U.S. was to stay aloof from the Pandora's Box of European politics. But by 1890, the doctrine had begun to weaken. The restless energies of the people demanded new theaters of action. The Revenue Cutter Service was to be a part of this surge to power.

United States politicians, including Theodore Roosevelt, were intoxicated by the prospect of their country's becoming a "world power." The time had come, they felt, for the United States to take its place on the world stage.

Actively helping to build the new image of America was the United States naval strategist, Alfred Thayer Mahan. Through books, articles and other publications, he urged that United States welfare, and indeed its very existence, demanded the building of a large naval establishment. Dominance of the seas was essential to the development of United States commerce throughout the world. The Navy would assert the United States presence everywhere and put the world on notice of the new giant among nations.

The Mahan doctrine of sea power was heady wine for Theodore Roosevelt, a young and rising politician, and for other public men of the time anxious to tread the path of empire. Associated with them was the Massachusetts Senator, Henry Cabot Lodge, son of a wealthy Boston merchant active in the China trade. Together, these men fanned the flames of nationalism. They were eager to join the nations of Europe in the game of empire building.

Only about 90 miles from Key West, Florida, lay the Island of Cuba, one of the last New World possessions of Spain. The mighty empire established centuries ago by the brave but ruthless conquistadors had faded. Generations of ruinous wars and maladministration had reduced that once-feared nation to a shell of its former greatness. There had been several abortive attempts at revolution against Spanish rule in Cuba, but they had come to nothing. In 1851, Captain T. C. Rudolph, commander of the cutter, *Taney*, had received orders to proceed from New York to Savannah without delay. This mission was to prevent an invasion attempt by a General Narcisco Lopez from leaving the Florida coast for Cuba. That attempt ended in failure and the death of Lopez by garroting.

Over the next forty years, the announced neutrality of the United States was severely strained by U.S. adventurers and gunrunners who saw a chance for money and excitement in the idea of a Free Cuba. On February 24, 1895, the last of a long series of Cuban rebellions broke out, creating the atmosphere for the confrontation with Spain three years later.

Waves of Cuban exiles had poured into the United States so that by 1895, about 40,000 were in this country. Their revolutionary councils kept a flood of dollars pouring into the coffers of the rebel leader, Jose Marti, regarded as the George Washington of Cuba. This turmoil kept the revenue cutters constantly busy. Between 1895 and 1898, the cutters *Boutwell, Colfax, Forward, Hamilton, McLane, Morrill, Windsor,* and *Windom* cruised more than 75.000 miles along the Florida coast, through the Gulf of Mexico, and the Caribbean to discourage and prevent Cuban invasions. They captured seven vessels and 115 Cubans and Cuban sympathizers, broke up two expeditions, and blockaded thirteen other vessels illegally loaded in the U.S. with arms, ammunition and provisions.

The newspapers, notably those of William Randolph Hearst in New York, and of Joseph Pulitzer in St. Louis, carried moving stories of the cruelty and oppression of the Cubans by the Spaniards. Something had to be done quickly by the United States, they urged, to relieve the suffering of the Cuban people. The stories were written in the colorful journalistic style of the period and were deliberately calculated to stir the ever-present sympathy for the underdog in the U.S. character. Here was a perfect opportunity for the United States to play the part of liberator and avenger of wrong. It would also help to divert the attention of the American people from the worsening economic situation at home.

Then came the explosion on the U.S. battleship, *Maine*, stationed in Manila Bay, in 1898 to "safeguard American interests." This took place on February 15 of that year. By the time the battleship had settled to the bottom of Havana Harbor, the United States was virtually ready for war with Spain. It had been a terrible disaster in which two officers and 258 members of the crew had lost their lives. Spanish officials were accused of the act. However, they denied it, and to this day the origin of the explosion has never been found.

President McKinley, essentially a peaceful man, sought to settle the matter by diplomatic means. For his efforts he was described by Roosevelt as having "the backbone of a chocolate eclair." Negotiations went forward for a couple of months when, suddenly reversing his course, McKinley sent a message to Congress calling for a resolution authorizing him to expel the Spanish forces from Cuba. In response to the message, both Houses of Congress adopted a resolution demanding Spain's withdrawal from Cuba. The President backed this up by proclaiming a blockade of Cuba's northern coast. The war was on.

It was scarcely an equal contest, and there was never any real doubt as to the outcome. Spain was long past her prime as a world power, and the Spanish forces were no match for the young enthusiastic forces arrayed against them. In the United States a near holiday atmosphere prevailed. The young war hawk, Theodore Roosevelt, was delighted at the prospect of foreign adventure. The years of peace since the Civil War had made the country soft, he said. The nation "needed a war" to regain its virility and to find new living room for Americans who were running out of land on the continent. More than three decades later, views

strikingly similar to these were to be expressed by the German leadership of the middle 1930's as justifying a course of conquest. Even in 1897, the views expressed by Roosevelt and others were not new but had been held by many other would-be world conquerors in the past.

"Remember the *Maine!*" became the battle cry. The formal declaration of war came on April 25, 1898, when the government stated that it considered itself at war with Spain since April 21.

At the outbreak of hostilities, the revenue cutter, *McCulloch*, was underway to San Francisco via the Mediterranean and the Suez Canal. At Singapore she was ordered to join Admiral Dewey's forces in the Philippines. A few days later, the cutter joined the U.S. squadron in Man-o'-War Anchorage, Hong Kong, where she was repainted a "war" color—leaden gray.

On April 24 the squadron shifted anchorage to Mirs Bay, China, where all vessels prepared for action. On April 27, at Dewey's signal, the squadron stood out to sea on its fateful mission. At a speed of eight knots they headed for Manila Bay and their rendezvous with destiny. Aware of the danger bearing down on him, the Spanish Governor General of the Philippines issued the following proclamation to the crews of the Spanish warships:

"The North American people, constituted of all the social excrescences, have. . .provoked war with their perfidious machinations, with their acts of treachery, with their outrages against the Law of Nations.

"A squadron manned by foreigners, possessing neither instruction nor discipline, is preparing to come to this archipelago, with the ruffianly intention of robbing us of all that means life, honor and liberty.

"The aggressors shall not profane the tombs of your fathers; they shall not gratify their lustful passions at the cost of your wives' and daughters' honor."

The insolent proclamation, when read to the crews of the U.S. squadron, provided the final incentive to action. As one observer described it: "The cheers which followed the reading could be heard from ship to ship throughout the squadron."

On the afternoon of April 30, the squadron arrived off Subic Bay. No enemy warship appeared to challenge them. Quietly, the American naval force moved closer to the enemy strongpoint on El Fraile Rock. At a quarter past twelve, just as the *McCulloch* was passing the Rock, soot in the cutter's stack caught fire, sending up a pillar of flame. Minutes thereafter, a shot rang out from the battery at El Fraile, followed quickly by a second one. The *Boston*, just in front of the *McCulloch*

At 5:30 a.m., as dawn broke over Manila Bay, Dewey maneuvered into position to fire his

Cutter *McCulloch*, 1897-1917. The Cutter *McCulloch* is seen here in original sail rigging lying at anchor in a port. In April 1898 the new Revenue Cutter *McCulloch*, with orders to cooperate with the Navy, arrived at Hong Kong, China, and reported for duty with Commodore Dewey, USN, Asiatic Station. Sailing with Dewey's squadron on its historical mission to Manila Bay, she guarded the supply ships *Nanshan* and *Safiro* during the trip and the ensuing battle with the Spaniards, and subsequently acted as Dewey's dispatch vessel. Aboard the *McCulloch* was a crew of about 8 officers and 95 men, and six guns.

answered with a 6-inch gun. The cutter then fired three projectiles of her own. The enemy had been fully alerted and a major engagement was only hours away.

opening salvo. The *McCulloch* had been assigned the duty of guarding the storeships, *Nanshan* and *Zafiro*. After herding her two charges into a safe position, she took up her own post "close in rear of our line of battle." Enemy shells fell all around the cutter. As the mist cleared on the morning of May 1, 1898, the Americans discovered the Spanish fleet. It lay alongshore, about six miles off, moored between Cavite Arsenal and Sangley Point.

Promptly, Dewey's flagship, *Olympia*, changed direction, bearing directly towards the enemy, disdaining its shore batteries. For forty minutes Dewey did not reply to the furious enemy shelling. Then, lowering his field glasses, he leaned over the bridge-rail and calmly told the captain of the *Olympia*, "You may fire when you are ready, Gridley." Those words have since become enshrined in American tradition. Between the early morning and half-past twelve, including time out for breakfast, the U.S. squadron had destroyed the whole of Spanish Admiral Montojo's fleet without the loss of a ship or a sailor! It was undoubtedly one of the greatest naval victories in history. The United States had flexed its naval muscles with devastating results. In doing so it had put this country into the center of the world scene, and the haughty powers of Europe could no longer look with condescension upon the young nation. This was a power to be feared and respected. Isolationism of the past was over and done with. There could be no returning to the America of an earlier day. The victory at Manila Bay changed the entire course of American history.

Four days later, the *McCulloch* started for Hong Kong and its cable facilities to send the dramatic message to the American people: "The Spanish fleet destroyed." Great triumphal celebrations broke out throughout the country.

Along the Atlantic and Gulf coasts, the Army mined important harbors against possible entry by the Spanish fleet. The cutters *Dexter*, *Dallas*, *Guthrie*, *Penrose*, *Winona*, *Smith*, and *Galveston* patrolled the mine fields, guarding against sabotage, and piloting traffic to safety. The cutter *McLane* spent the war on the 130-mile cable line between Sanibel Island and the Naval Base at Key West, Florida.

Although the victory at Manila Bay was by all odds the high point of the war, a gallant episode took place some time earlier off Cardenas Bay, Cuba. Late in April, 1898, U.S. Admiral Sampson had established a blockade of Havana and the Cuban northern coast. After Admiral Cervera took his Spanish fleet to cover in Santiago, the blockade was extended to keep that port "bottled up." The *San Francisco Examiner* of April 24, 1898 reported: "The *Morrill*, *Hudson*, and *Hamilton*, formerly revenue cutters and recently armed for service in the Mosquito Fleet, passed through Hampton Roads today and, after asking formal permission of the Commodore, proceeded to Key West. From that point they will join the Cuban blockading fleet."

The *Hudson* was a 96-foot tug, carrying a shield on her pilothouse and two six-pounders on her deck. On joining the fleet the small ship was assigned to blockade the entrances to Matanzas and Cardenas Bays and ordered to issue arms and ammunition to rebel Cuban groups whenever possible. She soon found that three lightly-armed Spanish gunboats were in Cardenas harbor. These vessels hindered the *Hudson's* contacts with rebel bands. The *Hudson's* skipper, First Lieutenant Frank H. Newcomb, tried vainly to lure the Spanish ships into a fight. But the Spaniards refused to take the bait. Newcomb then conceived of a plan to bring the battle to them. Through hazardous patrol action, he discovered that a clear, narrow channel, running close by several islands led to the Cardenas waterfront. It was a very dangerous route since the harbor was filled with mines and debris. But it would have to do.

A few days later, the Navy sent its gunboats *Machias* and *Wilmington*, and the torpedo boat, *Winslow*, to join *Hudson* in a raid on the bay. They arrived off the entrance on May 11. But the *Machias* took too deep a draft to clear the narrow channel. Therefore, she remained outside to shell the mango swamps and to discourage snipers. The other ships undertook the run through the hazardous channel. Once inside, the *Wilmington* steamed down the center of the bay, while the *Winslow* and *Hudson* covered the south and north shores. The adventure had begun.

On shore, there was no suspicion that anything was amiss. A few merchant ships laying at anchor off Cardenas were sighted. It was only after the raiders arrived directly in front of the town that they sighted the hunted gunboats moored alongside some sugar wharves. *Winslow* immediately moved towards them to blast them at close range. But before the Americans could open fire, Spanish shore batteries began zeroing in on the *Winslow*. Within a few minutes a furious fire-fight was on. *Hudson* closed towards *Winslow* at full speed, the two vessels steaming back and forth near the waterfront, probing with their guns for enemy emplacements. *Wilmington* remained farther out in the bay, supporting their attack with four-inch broadsides.

Since the Spanish gunners used smokeless powder, they would be located only by intermittent flashes. Smoke from black powder used by the Americans hampered their shelling, but they kept up a rapid fire, shooting at every flash on shore. The *Hudson* in 20 minutes hurled 135 shells at the enemy. All through the action, Savage, the black steward, stripped and sweating, passed up ammunition in a steady stream, as he roared out "There'll Be a Hot Time in the Old Town Tonight!"

The Spaniards were not especially proficient marksmen, but they held certain advantages over their foe. They were able to blanket the raiders in a hail of fire which poured down on the small ships from five different directions. The shelling churned the water around the cutter into a white froth.

Then the *Winslow's* luck failed her. Two shells tore into her, wrecking her steering engine and a boiler. Helpless, she rode before a rising breeze onto the shoals, reaching to shore and into point-blank range of the Spanish guns, and possible doom. Once she hit the beach she would be raked by remorseless enemy fire.

Lieutenant Newcomb and his crew decided that they were not going to let the *Winslow* perish unaided. The tug moved shoreward into shallow water to take the *Winslow* in tow and save her from destruction.

Because the *Hudson* was deeper-hulled than the torpedo boat, she soon found herself nearly aground. For about 20 minutes, under murderous Spanish fire, she backed and filled and ploughed her way along. Lieutenant Bernadou, the *Winslow's* commander, was wounded. But Lieutenants Scott and Mead kept up a steady return fire.

In moments that seemed to stretch into infinity, the *Hudson* gradually pulled within heaving-line distance of the other ship. Lieutenant Scott stood by the tugboat's rail, ready to throw a line to Ensign Worth Bagley on the *Winslow's* deck. Suddenly, Bagley and three other crewmembers of the *Winslow* were cut down by a shell which exploded in their midst. Other men caught Scott's line and made it fast as the *Hudson* began her mission of rescue. As she slowly pulled the torpedo boat to safety, the *Wilmington's* shells finally silenced the Spanish guns. The *Winslow* had been saved from the very jaws of destruction. It was one of the most heroic episodes of the war.

Although the engagement was not a major one, the heroism of the *Hudson's* crew did not go unnoticed. President McKinley in a letter to the Congress urged: "I recommend that in recognition of the signal act of heroism of First Lieutenant Frank H. Newcomb, United States Revenue Cutter Service, above set forth, the thanks of Congress be extended to him and to his officers and men of the *Hudson;* and that a gold medal of honor be presented to Lieutenant Newcomb, a silver medal of honor to each of his officers, and a bronze medal of honor to each member of his crew who served with him at Cardenas."

Captain Francis S. Van Boskerck, Jr., shown here in the white dress uniform of 1st Lieut. in the U.S. Revenue Cutter Service after his appointment in that rank in 1902. He was composer of the lyrics to the U.S. Coast Guard marching song, "Semper Paratus."

The *McCulloch's* victory message touched off a wave of celebrations throughout the United States. National confidence soared to new highs. And even in the ancient capitals of Europe there was the feeling that the fulcrum of power was shifting from the Old World to the New. Americans were more convinced than ever of a special destiny in world affairs. Their country had moved into a position of world leadership. As they were to find out in the decades to come, the price of that leadership

Top: The U.S. Revenue Cutter *Grant* (1871-1906) was the first vessel of the United States to make practical use of radio. Regular use of wireless telegraphy by the Revenue Cutter Service, predecessor of the modern U.S. Coast Guard, was inaugurated by the *Grant* on November 1, 1903. *Bottom:* Built in 1897, the 205-ft. U.S. Coast Guard Cutter *Manning* served at Santiago during the Spanish-American War—1898, and was stationed at Gibraltar as a convoy escort ship during World War I. She performed many Bering Sea Patrol cruises and rescues of ships in distress during her career. She was decommissioned at Norfolk, Va., on May 22, 1930, and sold on December 6, 1930 for the sum of $2,200.00.

would be grievously high. But that was still a long way off and could not dampen their elation.

Just before the coming of the 20th century, a new phenomenon appeared which was to span oceans and forever change the nature of world communications. This was the wireless, developed by Guglielmo Marconi, the brilliant son of an Italian father and an Irish mother. With the wireless telegraph, he ushered in the start of an

Republic, on January 23, 1909. Immediately after her ramming, her wireless operator, Jack Binns, began tapping out the SOS of that time, CQD. The signal was picked up by other vessels in the vicinity. Meanwhile, the other vessel, the steamship *Florida* of the Lloyd Italiano Line, incoming and heavily loaded with immigrants, was taking passengers off the *Republic*. Although *Florida* had a hole in her bow, she was in no immediate danger.

U.S. Lighthouse Service Tender *Hyacinth* underway in Lake Michigan where she tended aids to navigation. Home port, Milwaukee; built around 1902.

electronics revolution in communications whose end is not yet in sight. From this beginning was to grow a host of electronic devices, considered indispensable in peace and war. Wireless laid the foundation for a new aids-to-navigation system, including radar, Long Range Aid to Navigation (Loran), and all of the other techniques of war, navigation and rescue employed by the Coast Guard today.

The incident which first brought wireless to national attention was the ramming and subsequent sinking of the White Star liner,

The *Republic* was settling steadily deeper in the water. Six passengers had been killed. Help was desperately needed. Then Binn's batteries weakened, and his messages could no longer be transmitted.

But he had been instrumental in bringing other ships to the assistance of the stricken *Republic*. Among these were the Coast Guard cutter, *Gresham*, out of Provincetown, Mass., the cutter *Seneca*, and the British vessel, *Furnessia*. The *Gresham*, the *Seneca*, and a tug kept their searchlights on the *Republic* as passengers and crew were speedily removed. Finally, the *Gresham's* wireless proclaimed triumphantly, "All hands saved." Marconi's miraculous invention had worked its first magic. Overnight, radio operators became the nation's new heroes. A new humanitarianism in the age-old battle of men against the sea was now possible. With this new electronic means, all kinds of help could be made available to stricken ships and their passengers. The Coast Guard's hand of mercy could be outstretched much farther as the result of the wireless and the other electronic marvels which would follow it.

The short interval of peace between 1900 and World War I was an uneasy period for the Treasury fleet. A commission appointed by President Taft to search for ways of reorganizing government for greater efficiency critically examined the Service and found that many of its duties, acquired in bygone periods, were now obsolete. They, accordingly recommended that the Service be abolished and its duties taken over by the Navy. Usually, these bureaucratic storms blew themselves out in time, but on this occasion, the recommendations of the committee were approved by the President, who requested that they be put in the form of legislative changes. Congress, however, disagreed with the President, holding that the duties carried out by the cutters were of a highly specialized character and to assign them to the Navy would burden it unduly and detract from its primary function of military effectiveness. The Service had survived one of its severest crises.

However, the debate begun by the Taft Commission had raised some important questions. One of these was: Why not consolidate the Revenue Cutter Service with the Lifesaving Service? Both agencies were primarily concerned with the safety of life at sea, and a union would enhance the effectiveness of the entire function. The outcome of the discussion was the enactment on January 20, 1915 of a bill, combining the Revenue Cutter Service and Lifesaving Service, into a new agency to be known as the United States Coast Guard. The modern era of the Service had begun. It was the greatest single development in the history of a service which had been struggling for a century and a quarter for parity with the other military services. Under the new organization this would no longer be in doubt. The small revenue fleet envisaged so long ago by Hamilton had at last come into its own.

Only a few years before the birth of the modern Coast Guard, the world was stunned by one of the worst disasters in marine history. It was the sinking of the British luxury liner, *Titanic*, after colliding with an iceberg off Newfoundland on her maiden voyage. The tragedy took place on April 14, 1912, after she had left Southampton, England four days before. Her passenger list read like a "Who's Who" of American society, including some of the most prominent personalities of the time. She had been built at the then enormous cost of $7,500,000 and had been widely billed as "unsinkable." The *Titanic's* passengers and crew totaled about 2,224, but of these 1,513 lost their lives. No other sea tragedy has been so celebrated in music, poetry, and drama. Even today, more than half a century since that dreadful night, the name *Titanic* instantly recalls disaster at sea.

So shocked was the maritime world by the loss of the *Titanic* that about two years later, a conference of the leading maritime nations was convened in London, England, to consider ways of preventing similar tragedies. The result was the inauguration in 1914 of the International Ice Patrol. The cost of the Patrol was to be defrayed in fixed proportions by the nations benefited. Since the Coast Guard had already begun operating a patrol over the heavily traveled North Atlantic shipping lanes in 1913, operation of the International Ice Patrol was added to its already numerous responsibilities for the safety of life at sea. Except for the years of World War I and II, the Patrol has operated continuously and with conspicuous success. In all the time that the Coast Guard has performed this duty, no ship has been lost through collision with an iceberg.

Originally conceived as a surface patrol by Coast Guard cutters, the Patrol has evolved over the years into aerial reconnaissance of the approximately 33,000 square miles of North Atlantic under its surveillance. This is roughly the size of the state of South Carolina. During the ice season, from February through August, the area is heavily blanketed by fog and an average of 400 bergs drift southward towards the busiest shipping lanes in the world. In view of the vastness of the area, the generally poor visibility, and the great number of bergs calved off the Greenland glaciers, it is quite possible that occasionally a berg may find its way into the shipping lanes unobserved. But the advanced scientific detection techniques used by the Coast Guard makes this unlikely.

As the years have gone by, the Patrol has become increasingly a part of the Coast Guard's specialization in the oceanography of far northern waters. Its oceanographic ship, *Evergreen*, in its post season cruises has contributed much valuable data on this phase of marine science. Data made available by the Patrol, the Ocean Station Vessels, the Alaskan Patrol and other marine science units of the Coast Guard are of great value to the world's scientific community in the never ending quest to learn the secrets of one of man's oldest but least discovered frontiers—the ocean. Today's Coast Guard is one of the leading marine science agencies in the federal government. This too is a beneficial offshoot of the tragedy of the *Titanic*. The assumption of the Ice Patrol reflected the flexibility and responsiveness of the Coast Guard to emergencies. "Semper Paratus," "Always Ready," was an appropriate motto for the Service.

Commodore Ellsworth P. Bertholf, USCG Commandant, 1911-1919. (In command when U.S. Revenue Cutter Service merged with Life Saving Service to become U.S. Coast Guard—1915.)

Top: The Revenue Cutter *Snohomish* in Port Angeles, Washington harbor in April 1909. *Bottom:* Cutters *Onondaga* (l.) and *Algonquin* at Newport News shipyard, September 17, 1907. Photo: The Mariners Museum, Newport News, Va.

World War I

By the end of the first decade of the 20th century, the glow of Admiral Dewey's magnificent victory at Manila Bay had begun to fade. The country was absorbed in internal matters such as developing its resources and with the growing economic power of huge business combines known as "trusts," the days of laissez-faire economy were drawing to a close. A policy of protectionism necessary when the nation was struggling to build its industries, had created economic Frankensteins. "Muckraking" journalists, such as Lincoln Steffens and others, were alerting the people to the dangers of monopoly. Theodore Roosevelt, with the shrewd instinct of a good politician, recognized a popular issue when he saw one. He proclaimed himself a crusader against the "soulless corporations" and their greed. The "trust-busting" campaign was very effective and gave him a national image.

Now in 1912, under the administration of President Woodrow Wilson, the intellectual former president of Princeton University, the country was determined to put its economic affairs in order. The "plutocrats" and their lobbyists had to be controlled before their enormous economic power corrupted the political system.

Former President William Howard Taft, a perceptive observer, had noted: "For thirty years, we had an enormous material expansion in this country, in which we all forgot ourselves in the enthusiasm of expanding our material resources and in making ourselves the richest nation on earth. We did this through the use of the principle of organization and combination, and the development of our national resources. In the encouragement of the investment of capital, we nearly transferred complete political power to those who controlled corporate wealth and we were in danger of a plutocracy."

So preoccupied were Americans with their domestic problems that they paid little attention to the assassination of the Archduke Francis Ferdinand of the Austro-Hungarian Empire on June 28, 1914, in the provincial town of Sarajevo. After all, the Balkan countries had always been turbulent, and another political killing was one more violent incident in a long history of violence. What the American public did not realize was

that for 30 years Europe had been a hotbed of diplomatic intrigue. The continent was crisscrossed with alliances, ententes, and secret pacts, setting one group of powers against another. A crisis had been building up between these competing sovereignties. A long, civilized era of peace was nearing its end. A "golden age" of European civilization was receding into history.

Seminole at Newport News shipyard July 17, 1908. Photo: The Mariners Museum, Newport News, Va.

The killing of the Archduke set in motion one of history's greatest holocausts. With the inevitability of Greek tragedy, events unfolded, one after the other. Austria seized upon the murder of the Archduke as a pretext for invading Serbia. Russia, honoring its defense pact with Serbia, declared war on the decaying Austro-Hungarian Empire. This gave Kaiser Wilhelm, last of the Hohenzollerns, the cue he had eagerly awaited. The Kaiser, who loved military pomp and gorgeous uniforms (all cleverly concealing his withered left arm), now had an opportunity to deploy his splendidly trained and equipped armies. He declared that Germany regarded itself at war with Russia.

Then France and England entered the war against the central powers, including Germany, the Austrian Empire and Turkey. It was only a question of time before all Europe would be a battleground. But in 1914, the prospect of American involvement seemed remote. This was a European affair. Let those nations work out their problems as best they could.

At the start of the war, President Wilson had declared the neutrality of the United States. Public opinion, however, was not entirely neutral. Many citizens of German descent, notably in the Midwest, favored Germany. Others favored the Allied cause.

The United States maintained its shaky neutrality until April 1, 1917. In the 1916 presidential campaign, Wilson had used the fatuous slogan: "Too proud to fight." But the situation was becoming intolerable as the Germans mounted their unrestricted submarine warfare. The breaking point came in April 1917, after German raiders had sunk four American ships in one week. Obviously shaken, the President sent a special message to Congress:

"It is a fearful thing to lead this great peaceful people into the most terrible and destructive of all wars . . . but the right is more precious than peace." After nearly 20 years of peace, the nation was again at war. But this time the holiday spirit of 1898 did not prevail. Arrayed against the United States was not the feeble naval power of Spain but the mightiest military powers of Europe. It would be one of the cruelest wars in U.S. history. In spite of all its efforts to remain neutral, the country had been drawn into the holocaust. It was learning the cost of being a "world power."

Although the duration of U.S. involvement in the first World War was brief, it was very eventful. For the Coast Guard, participation began on April 6, 1917 when it received the laconic message: "Plan 1, Acknowledge." This meant that the United States was at war and that the Coast Guard's 15 cruising cutters, 200 officers and 5,000 men were to go into action with the Navy. Mostly, the naval action revolved about undersea warfare. The Coast Guard was in the thick of it, convoying cargo ships and transports.

Outstanding among the antisubmarine units of the Atlantic Fleet was Squadron F, Division 6. It was made up of Coast Guard cutters *Ossippee, Seneca, Yamacraw, Algonquin, Manning,* and the *Tampa.*

On April 28, 1918, the *Seneca* was escorting ships towards Gibraltar when at 2:45 a.m. the convoy ran into a pack of three German U-boats. The British sloop *Cowslip* was nearly cut in two by a torpedo. Ordinarily, the *Seneca* would have been justified in sailing on to look after the safety of other ships. But she stopped three times to put off lifeboats and to pick up 81 survivors.

Tampa on convoy duty during World War I. Under the command of Commander Charles Satterlee, she set a splendid record in her work, protecting 18 convoys without losing a ship. She was sunk with all hands in Bristol Channel, September 28, 1918.

During another *Seneca* convoy mission, the British collier *Wellington* was torpedoed. She was abandoned but remained afloat. Her crew refused to go on board again, though 19 of them later changed their minds when 20 of the *Seneca's* crew manned her and got up steam for Brest, France. That night a gale came up, and at 4 a.m. the *Wellington* went down. At dawn, the British destroyer *Warrington* picked up seven seamen and one Coast Guardsman in a lone lifeboat. Floating on makeshift rafts were another seven British seamen and eight Coast Guardsmen. Eleven of the *Seneca's* crew, including two Navy petty officers, and five of the collier's crew were lost.

The incident made a deep impression on the British. Said the British Admiralty: "Seldom in the annals of the sea has there been exhibited such cool courage, and such unfailing diligence in the face of almost insurmountable difficulties." If these words have a Churchillian ring, it is because they were written by Sir Winston himself who at the time was First Lord of the Admiralty.

Not long afterward, the cutter *Tampa*, bound for England after having brought a convoy safely into Gibraltar, vanished into the sea with a loud explosion. Some wreckage and two unidentifiable bodies were the only traces ever found of the ship and of the 111 Coast Guardsmen and four Navy men aboard her. There were indications that she had been hit by a torpedo.

On the other side of the Atlantic, a tower lookout at the Coast Guard's Chicamacomico, North Carolina, station saw the British tanker *Mirlo* torpedoed seven miles off shore. The station's motor surfboat made three trips through fiercely burning gasoline and heavy seas in gathering darkness to save 36 British seamen. For his heroism, the keeper of the station, John Allen Midgett, member of a famous Coast Guard family, was awarded the Victory Medal and a Congressional Lifesaving Medal. The British expressed their gratitude by having a special medal struck off for Midgett and each of his crew. The British Board of Trade gave Midgett a silver loving cup.

The Coast Guard suffered greater losses in proportion to its strength than any other of the U.S. Armed Services in World War I.

The awful destruction of war was forcibly brought home to the American people by a terrible explosion at a major shipping terminal at Black Tom's Island, New Jersey. This small strip of land, just across the Hudson River from New York in the heart of the metropolitan area was a central storage point for explosives destined for the war fronts. On July 31, 1916, windows in office buildings, apartments and homes were suddenly shattered by the force of the explosion at Black Tom's Island. Showers of glass filled the streets in the surrounding communities. However, since the blast took place at 2:00 a.m., no one was seriously injured. But property damage was estimated at about $22 million. The incident also pointed up

the need for more careful guarding of port and waterfront areas against the dangers of sabotage and fire. No one has ever found the immediate cause of the explosion, although sabotage was quite widely suspected.

Quick to arrive on scene was the Coast Guard cutter *Hudson* the same vessel which had so gallantly braved enemy fire to pull the crippled *Winslow* out of the range of Spanish guns in 1898. She still bore the honorable scars of that engagement. Her captain, Alex Foss, brought her alongside a lighter loaded with ammunition and turned streams of water into the vessel while shells rained on his deck. There were indications that the disaster could have been caused by a fire on a barge laden with high explosives. But this could not be confirmed.

The effect of the Black Tom's explosion was to speed Congressional enactment of the Espionage Act of 1917. It authorized the President to delegate the Coast Guard the protection of ports and waterfront areas. Security in each harbor was to be controlled by a Captain of the Port. Thus, out of the Black Tom's disaster was born one of the Coast Guard's major duties, Port Security. Although the Espionage Act was to last only for the duration of the war, Port Security continues to be one of the Coast Guard's functions.

One of the most important developments to come out of World War I was the emergence of Coast Guard aviation. This, together with spectacular advances in communications, gave the Service a scope of activity never before possible. With the advent of aviation on a major scale, the Coast Guard began to assume its present shape.

Aircraft gave the Service what it had dreamed of for generations—a flying lifeboat. But the full realization of that dream was still some time off.

From the start, the Coast Guard had had a hand in aviation. When the Wright brothers made their epochal first flight at Kitty Hawk, North Carolina, three members of the nearby Kill Devil Hill Lifeboat Station were on hand to help them. When a strong gust of wind flipped the flimsy plane over after the flight, all three grabbed it and helped secure it.

Two of the most earnest advocates of aircraft for search and rescue were Coast Guard Lieutenants Elmer F. Stone and Norman B. Hall. Their advocacy was so persuasive that by the summer of 1916 they were flying missions in a plane borrowed from a company that built them, the Glenn Curtiss organization. That led the Coast Guard to send Stone and five other officers to the

This is the NC-4 model of plane which Lieut. Elmer F. Stone of the U.S. Coast Guard piloted on its historical flight from the United States to Europe in May 1919. The NC-4 was the only one of three (the others were NC-1 and NC-3) that successfully completed the journey, and the first airplane to fly the Atlantic. Lt. Stone was the only non-Navy man in the Squadron that was to test the long-range capabilities of an aircraft in ocean crossing. The journey began on May 8 from Rockaway, N.Y., and with only brief stops for refueling at Newfoundland and at the Azores, flew on to touch down on May 27, and then continued to Plymouth, England, where it landed on May 31. Photo: National Archives

Navy Aviation School at Pensacola, Florida. Hall was sent to the Curtiss Company to study aviation and engineering. In that same year, Congress authorized the Coast Guard to establish ten air bases along the seacoasts and the Great Lakes. But money did not accompany the authority. When World War I came, the Coast Guard pilots used their skills flying for the Navy.

ers were strung out along their route in the event of a forced landing at sea. That was good planning, because a destroyer rescued the five-man crew of the NC-3 after it had drifted at sea for two days.

The world followed the route of the surviving NC-4 avidly. Banner headlines in the newspapers announced that the plane had flown the 1,200 miles to the Azores in fifteen hours and five

The 190-foot U.S. Coast Guard Cutter *Seneca* (1908-1936).

The enthusiasm for aviation carried over into peacetime. In his newfound mastery of space, man aspired to nothing less than the spanning of the Atlantic Ocean. To most, it seemed a rash adventure. But others, including Stone, thought it quite feasible.

The Atlantic Air Sweepstakes began on May 16, 1919, when three seaplanes took off for the Azores. They were the NC-1 (Navy-Curtiss), 3, and 4. They were big aircraft with a 126-foot wing-spread and four engines. They carried wireless capable of transmitting over 350 miles and were able to communicate with one another through the brand-new wireless telephone. Twenty-one destroy-

minutes. The successful pilots were Lieutenant A. C. Reade of the Navy, and First Lieutenant Elmer Stone of the Coast Guard. Some time later, the plane landed at Plymouth, England, where it received a triumphant welcome. The rash young men had made their dream come true.

Despite these early triumphs, it was not until 1925 that Coast Guard aviation received appropriations from Congress. The reason was that the Prohibition Amendment, forbidding the importation and sale of alcoholic beverages, had ushered in a new era of smuggling which was to lead to the Coast Guard's "Rum War" of the next decade.

Top: A Coast Guard "First." The only photograph of man's first flight taken by J.T. Daniels, then a member of Kill Devil Life Saving Station, one of the witnesses (December 17, 1903). The plane, piloted by Orville Wright, has just taken off from the monorail. Wilbur Wright, running at the side, had held the wing to balance the machine until it left the rail. Kitty Hawk, east coast of North Carolina. *Bottom:* U.S. Coast Guard's First Aviation Group. (L. to r.): C. T. Thrun, J.F. Powers, George Ott, C. Griffin, John Wicks, Robert Donohue, C.E. Sugden, E.A. Coffin, S.V. Parker, P. B. Eaton, E.F. Stone, Ora Young, W.R. Malew, J. Meyers, J. Medusky, R.F. Gillis, W.S. Anderson and L.M. Melka. Of the 18 pictured, nine remained in the U.S. Coast Guard, three became Rear Admirals, one a Vice Admiral, while another won the Congressional Medal for a historical contribution to aviation. Stone received the Congressional Medal May 23, 1930 for extraordinary achievement in making the first successful trans-Atlantic flight.

The Rum Fleet

Passage of the National Prohibition Act in 1919, popularly known as the "Volstead Act" after its sponsor, Congressman Andrew J. Volstead of Minnesota, injected the Coast Guard into one of the most tumultuous periods of American history. The fourteen years of the "noble experiment" spawned an era of widespread disrespect for law and well-organized syndicates of hoodlums who waxed rich catering to the great national thirst.

Racketeers became national heroes and the corruptive influence of organized crime was felt at all levels of government. It produced social consequences of enormous importance.

Psychologically, the 18th Amendment could not have come at a worse time. The country wanted to relax from the tensions of a major war. The Puritan Ethic, so strong in an earlier America, was weakening. Men who had been to war came back

Eighty-five-foot Harbor Cutter; built in San Francisco. Later stationed in Seattle, she outdid other vessels catching rumrunners.

The Coast Guard, as the nation's seagoing law enforcement agency, was in the forefront of the effort to prevent the smuggling of liquor from the sea. The unpopularity of Prohibition increased the difficulty of its task. There was little glory and much frustration in its war against the rumrunners.

In the perspective of history, we can see that Prohibition was nothing less than an effort to legislate morality and therefore doomed to failure.

with different values. Old values were losing their appeal. A new morality was coming into being, directly in conflict with the sterner code of the past. Defiance of the Prohibition law became a mark of sophistication, as did the frequenting of "speakeasies" or illicit bars which did a smashing business. In a few years, respect for authority, so much a part of American character gave way to a new permissiveness. The country was never again

Top: The U.S. Coast Guard Destroyer *Terry* (CG-19), an early 20th century 742-ton, three-stack oil burner, pickets the French rumrunning schooner *Mistinguette* on the North Atlantic coast, outside of the 12-mile limit. Smugglers with foreign registry could not be seized on the high seas and usually lay outside of territorial limits until contact was made by fast speedboats which smuggled the contraband into port. The trailing method proved most effective against such smugglers. *Bottom:* The rumrunner *Linwood* is set afire by her crew after being pursued by a Coast Guard patrol boat, May 1923.

Top: An early 20th century four-stack oil burner, the Destroyer *Downes* (CG-4) (ex-Navy number DD 45) was one of the original 20 destroyers transferred from the U.S. Navy to the U.S. Coast Guard under Act of Congress dated April 21, 1924, for use in an all-out battle to suppress smuggling. *Bottom:* A group of U.S. Coast Guard 75-ft. patrol boats in "V" formation take off from an Atlantic coast base in the 1920's to hunt down smugglers.

to return to its more innocent past. Prohibition as well as the normal questioning of values following a great war were shattering the old society. The consequences of this development were incalculable. They are, in fact, still being felt.

By 1924, the situation had deteriorated so badly that President Calvin Coolidge, in his inaugural address, made what constituted an official declaration of war on the liquor syndicates. In this, he was responding to an urgent demand from Rear

Top: Seventy-five-foot patrol boats from Base 7 picketing two rum-laden schooners, Gloucester, Mass. *Bottom:* Contraband cargo from the seized motorboat K-10193, captured by the 75-ft. Coast Guard patrol boat CG-128 on December 30, 1929, in New York Harbor.

Admiral F. C. Billard, Coast Guard Commandant, who had asked for $28,500,000 to build a fleet capable of handling the seagoing part of the "rum war." Billard estimated that an appropriation of this size was required to build 20 new cutters, about 200 cabin cruisers and 91 smaller motorboats. It would also permit him to operate them with about 3,535 additional officers and enlisted men.

Considering the magnitude of the task, Billard's request was reasonable. "Rummie" fleets were swarming around the coasts of the United States and in the Great Lakes. The Coast Guard's small fleet was completely outmatched by the smugglers' superior numbers. The liquor traffic flourished most lucratively off the Atlantic coast. Just beyond the three-mile limit lay the fleets of rumrunners. They operated with amazing audacity. At sundown, the lights of their ships blinked cheerfully to their associates on shore, telling them that another profitable cargo of liquor was ready for unloading. The risk was not very great and the penalties, even if caught, were not too severe. With reasonably good luck, an enterprising rumrunner could in a few good seasons make enough money to go on a long vacation or enter a more respectable business. Operating on regular schedules, fast, powerful small boats would pull alongside the rum boats and take on board cases of Scotch and other popular liquors, and dart for shore. There, trucks would be ready to reload the liquor and move it inland. Rummies often boasted that their liquor was "right off the boat." Those who could not afford to pay the steep prices demanded for good whiskey sometimes resorted to crude, homemade products often causing death, poisoning or blindness.

Congress pared Billard's request to $13,000,000 and made such an appropriation in April, 1924. Steps were also taken to recondition 20 Navy destroyers and transfer them to the Coast Guard. Although this was below the amount requested by the Coast Guard, it would definitely put more teeth into its law enforcement machinery.

The news was heralded to the world by the *New York Times* which announced that the Coast Guard was "... declaring open warfare on rumrunners and dope smugglers."

Dope, however, at that time, was by far the lesser part of the Coast Guard's problem. Admiral Billard, himself, took a more conservative view. "It is indeed a large problem for a service as small as ours to undertake," he stated. "We have been given this job to do, and the way in which we do it is going to have tremendous influence on the future welfare and prestige of the Coast Guard. I have taken the position here in Washington that the Coast Guard has never fallen down in any task assigned to it, and that we will stop rumrunning on our coasts if given the funds for which we asked. For the honor and prestige of the Service, we must not fail and we will not fail."

This ringing announcement was also a highly perceptive one. The Admiral was shrewd enough to realize that this was an opportunity for his Service to shed its obscurity and attain national stature. In this he was quite correct.

Less than three months after Billard's announcement, Coast Guard seizures of liquor and rumrunning craft had exceeded $10,000,000, or nearly the total amount appropriated for the Service. The Coast Guard was giving good value for the money received, but a long and frustrating struggle still lay before it.

One immediate result of the Coast Guard's attack on the rummies was that "rum row" no longer hovered off the coast. But the traffic was still considerable and the lure of quick, high profits attracted ships of many nations. But now, the tactics of the rumrunners had grown more sophisticated. Instead of taking up a line offshore, they constantly changed their positions, making their location more difficult.

But the sweetness of success was mixed with the bitterness of frustration. The most effective tactic of the cutters was to stand by and keep the rumrunners under close watch. Any of the rum boats foolhardy enough to make a dash for the coast usually wound up in Coast Guard custody. The picketing also discouraged local dealers from coming alongside and taking on a load. The increased hazard of bringing in liquor also had the effect of raising prices. In Atlantic City, New Jersey, for example, the price increase was about one to two dollars a case. But business was booming and the demand for liquor so great that it easily absorbed the increase.

Rumrunners not only had a good deal of popular support but even some judges and law enforcement officials were inclined to deal leniently with them. Unquestionably, there also was some bribery of local officials who conveniently looked the other way. Newspapers sometimes made a slapstick comedy out of a deadly serious enforcement effort.

To the Coast Guard, the rum war was anything but funny. The grimness of the situation was illustrated in the Florida Straits in 1927. Reports had been received that rumrunners were buying liquor in Bimini in the Bahamas with counterfeit money. Chief Boatswain's Mate, Sydney Sanderlin, skipper of Patrol Boat No. 249, and his seven-man crew were sent to check the matter out. They carried as a passenger, Secret Service Operator Robert K. Webster. His mission was to find the plates and presses and smash the counterfeiting ring with the help of British authorities.

Schooner *Silvatrice* with 2,000 cases of alcohol aboard seized off Cape Cod Canal, December 16, 1922, being towed to Boston by the U.S. Coast Guard Cutter *Acushnet*.

Several miles out of Fort Lauderdale, Florida, the patrol boat sighted a motorboat speeding towards the Florida coast. Sanderlin's long experience told him it was a rumrunner. He stopped the boat with warning shots over her bow. On boarding her he found that she was carrying 160 cases of liquor.

Two men were in the smuggler's boat: Alderman and Weech. Sanderlin told the men that he was taking them into custody. However, he first had to obtain permission from Fort Lauderdale since he had been authorized only to carry Webster to Bimini. While this was going on, Coast Guardsmen began unloading the liquor.

While Sanderlin was sitting at the radio, sending his message to Fort Lauderdale, Alderman saw several pistols on a table in the pilothouse. Grabbing one, he pointed it at Sanderlin's back and killed him.

The shot alarmed Machinist's Mate Victor Lamby who started to go below to get a gun and bring the rumrunners under control. But Alderman had the reflexes of a cat. Wheeling and firing simultaneously, he dropped Lamby down the companionway, fatally wounded.

The killer ordered the remaining Coast Guardsmen to reload liquor on his boat. Then he stated that he planned to kill them all and burn the patrol boat. To carry out this vicious plan, he sent Weech below to smash the gas lines and start a fire. Somehow, Weech's match would not ignite. The strain was beginning to tell on Alderman, and, nervously, he told Weech to warm up the engine of their boat for a quick takeoff so that they would be well out of the way when the Coast Guard craft blew up. But in talking to Weech, he made the mistake of turning his head. In that instant, the Coast Guardsmen rushed him. Alderman's pistol discharged, and a bullet ripped through Webster's heart. Two more shots rang out, sending another Coast Guardsman overboard with a wounded shoulder and a blinded eye.

Now the tide turned. Using an ice pick and a deck scraper, the remaining crewmen of No. 249 stabbed Alderman and knocked him unconscious to the deck. Weech was knocked on the head and taken prisoner as he came up the companionway. Subsequently, Weech testified for the state against Alderman. Alderman was convicted of three murders and hanged at the Coast Guard Base at Fort Lauderdale.

Sometimes the pursuit of the rum smugglers raised questions of international law, as in the case of the Canadian rumrunner, *I'm Alone*. This bizarre case involved the pursuit of the Canadian vessel in international waters on two successive days. The Coast Guard claimed it had been in "hot pursuit." But the court disagreed, noting that the pursuit had not been continuous but by two different cutters on two different occasions. Eventually the matter was settled by arbitration.

By the 1930's the gaudy Prohibition era had nearly run its course. Repeal of the 18th Amendment in 1933 put an end to the law enforcement nightmare. But on balance, the Coast Guard had come out very well in the rum war. The nation gained a new respect for a service whose operations generally tended to be overlooked.

The war against the "rummies" resulted not only in the expansion of the Coast Guard's air fleet, but also in the acquisition of new and faster cutters to cope with the rising tide of lawlessness.

At the end of the Prohibition Era, the Service had a good deal more muscle than it had had before.

Faced with urgent need to end liquor smuggling, Congress had been obliged to loosen its purse strings and make money available for aircraft. Experience had shown that no other type of vehicle could provide the same surveillance capability as aircraft. This trend was given new impetus in 1934 when Secretary of the Treasury Henry Morgenthau made the Coast Guard responsible not only for coastal surveillance but also for keeping an eye on inland international borders. Formerly, this function had been carried out by the civilian U.S. Border Patrol. By placing all flying functions of the Treasury within the Coast Guard, Secretary Morgenthau gave the Service a major air arm. Suddenly it acquired 15 Customs Service planes and six from the Navy, along with bases at Buffalo, San Antonio, and San Diego. The struggle for recognition of the Coast Guard's aviation function was over.

Since those distant 1930's, Coast Guard flyers have logged many air miles and have pioneered in many phases of aviation, notably the helicopter. The Service was quick to see the value of the "whirlybird" for sea rescues as well as disaster relief operations. More recently, they have served as reconnaissance vehicles for all new Coast Guard cutters. The Coast Guard's icebreakers in the far north all carry specially trained helicopter crews.

The Coast Guard's HH-3F model helicopter, currently in use, is one of the most sophisticated aircraft to be found in any air fleet. Carrying an airborne navigational computer, this vehicle is the first to be equipped with so advanced an avionic system for peacetime uses. The result has been to

One of two Chance Vought UO-4 float seaplanes commissioned by the Coast Guard in 1926. They did valuable work in apprehending rumrunners during the prohibition era.

USCG Cutter *Faunce*, patrol boat.

extend greatly the scope and effectiveness of aircraft. It has helped to make the odds a little more favorable for persons or vessels waiting for assistance in an angry sea. As such, it constitutes a safety dividend for the entire maritime community.

The end of the "Rum War" did not mean that happy days had returned for the Coast Guard or the nation. During the tragicomedy of Prohibition,

corners hawking apples and other trifles. The textbook virtues which generations of Americans had been taught to revere—diligence, thrift, and sobriety—seemed meaningless. Old people saw their carefully hoarded savings disappear in bank failures. Young people found that the doors of opportunity were closed to them. Jobs, even menial ones, were eagerly sought after by educated men who would ordinarily have disdained them.

Contraband runner *Mary Langdon* flanked by the U.S. Coast Guard Cutter *Redwing* (l.) and 75-ft. patrol boat
CG-237 after her seizure on June 10, 1925.

another enemy had struck—the great Depression of the 1930's. It had begun with the stock market crash of 1929 and had been growing steadily worse. The booming optimism of the late 1920's was turning to despair as people watched their carefully laid plans for the future vanish.

The country's huge industrial plant, once the envy of the world, slowed down to a crawl. Grey-faced men who had formerly held responsible positions in business found themselves on street

There were bread lines and soup lines and people living in tar paper shacks on the outskirts of cities.

The lady who held "the lamp beside the golden door" in New York harbor, slammed it shut, cutting the once heavy flow of immigrants to a trickle. At a time when the storm clouds were darkening in Europe, the country ceased to be a sanctuary for the oppressed. What had become of the American Dream of an unlimited future?

In the ensuing disenchantment, Americans

searched within themselves for answers to calamity. They questioned and examined the values and institutions hitherto regarded as sacrosanct. The idea of material progress as the key to happiness or the good life was under special scrutiny. Yet, the common misfortune bred a certain compassion not known in happier times. It was a traumatic time which would leave its mark upon the nation for generations.

The Coast Guard was not immune to the corrosive effects of the Depression. It had never known the luxury of a large budget. Now, faced with the need for greater economies, it had to take such painful steps as the downgrading of chief petty officers to seamen and the termination of enlistment contracts. Some Coast Guardsmen were sent to Civilian Conservation Corps camps set up by the Roosevelt administration to provide work for the unemployed. Morale in the Service suffered.

The Great Depression was not the only shadow over the country. In Europe, aggressive nationalism was on the rise. This was especially true in Germany, Italy and Spain. Sooner or later, it boded no good for the Free World. The militaristic character of the regimes of those countries foreshadowed eventual conflict. The smell of war was once more in the air.

The American people, more sophisticated than they had been in 1914, realized that it would be difficult, if not impossible, to keep out of another European war. The decade of the 1930's was ending on a somber note.

Just before it ended, however, the Coast Guard acquired one of the most historic federal agencies, the U.S. Lighthouse Service. In July, 1939, the agency was transferred from the Department of Commerce to the Coast Guard.

Historically, the Lighthouse Service was older than the Coast Guard, having been established in August, 1789. Alexander Hamilton was directed by Congress to set up and maintain lighthouses, beacons, buoys, and public piers at "any bay, inlet, harbor or port of the United States, rendering the navigation thereof easy and safe." Throughout their histories, the two agencies had maintained a close association, varied occasionally by administrative changes. With the official transfer, however, the Coast Guard assumed the primary responsibility for the maintenance and operation of the federal aids to navigation program, a major and difficult assignment.

The Lighthouse Service had a luster of its own, its records being filled with the achievements of its men. One exploit in particular involved the repulse of an attack of hostile Seminole Indians during the war with the latter in the 1830's. The heroic lighthouse keeper was John W. Thompson of the Cape Florida Light, a few miles from what is now Miami. On the afternoon of July 23, 1836, Thompson saw a band of Indians moving stealthily towards the lighthouse. Calling to his Negro assistant, he barred the door of the lighthouse and retreated to the tower just in time to frustrate the Indians who were pounding on his door. For 24 hours, Thompson and his brave assistant kept up a stream of fire at the marauding Indians, resorting at last to blowing up the stairs of the lighthouse to prevent its capture. Thompson's assistant was killed, and the keeper's clothes were nearly burned off him but somehow he managed to resist. He was at last rescued from his predicament by the arrival of a force of cutters.

Transfer of the Lighthouse Service into the Coast Guard was followed by a flurry of intensive research aimed at developing a worldwide system of electronic aids. The most noteworthy development to emerge from this activity was the Service's Loran (Long Range Aid to Navigation) system which enables transoceanic ships and planes to pinpoint their positions to distances of several hundred miles. First to use such a system were the British, shortly after the outbreak of war in Europe. However, the Coast Guard pioneered in developing several increasingly refined classes of this sophisticated navigation aid. Today, the Coast Guard's Loran network is global, extending from Greenland to southeast Asia and from the Arctic to the Antarctic. Altogether, the Service operates more than 48,000 aids. Research is constantly going forward to find new and more effective ways of performing this important function at lower cost to the U.S. taxpayer.

In September, 1939, the calamity which all reasonable men had hoped to avoid, became a reality. The German armies, poised to strike a lightning blow at Poland, ruthlessly smashed across the Polish borders. World War II was on. In ferocity and destruction, it would surpass anything that mankind had ever known. As the United States watched developments abroad, it also prepared to strengthen its defenses at home.

Top: U.S. Coast Guard Cutter *Shawnee* (WAT-54). *Bottom:* U.S. Coast Guard Cutter *Northland* in Greenland.

Prelude to World War II

The war which was supposed to "make the world safe for democracy" had done nothing of the sort. It had merely sown the seeds of a greater war. In Russia, it had brought a Communist dictatorship into being. As the dreary 1930's drew to a close, the United States, in addition to an economic crisis at home, faced a rising tide of Fascism in Italy and Germany. The term "Fascism" was derived from the Latin word "fasces" or "bundles" from the bundle of sticks surmounted by an axe borne before Roman magistrates as a symbol of authority. It was an apt symbol, emphasizing the collective strength of the state, as compared to the relative weakness of the individual.

Founder of the first fascist, or Corporate State, was Benito Mussolini, journalist and social revolutionary. In 1922, at the head of a small band of black-shirted followers, he had made his famous "march on Rome" to confront the Italian government. A show of force by the government could easily have smashed the movement. But the government was weak and indecisive and played into Mussolini's hands.

Through a Machiavellian use of threats of force, guile and political assassination, Mussolini rose to the top of Italian leadership. He was a dynamic, effective orator and a competent journalist.

The ideology of Fascism was elitist and profoundly anti-democratic. It repudiated democratic government as weak and exalted the virtues of total obedience to and faith in its leaders. Its credo was summed up in the slogan: "Believe, obey, fight." Military prowess was the principal yardstick against which a nation's greatness could be measured. Only in war could a nation achieve its true greatness. The Fascist ideology had, in fact, some of the "superman" overtones of Nietzsche's thought, and it is not surprising that it took root in Germany a few years later.

It remained for the evil genius, Adolf Hitler, World War I corporal in the Austrian Army and failed artist, to become the exponent of the German brand of Fascism. Hitler, who discovered he had a genius for politics and demagoguery, preached a doctrine similar to Mussolini's except that it placed greater emphasis on German nationalism. In his hoarse, rasping voice, he exploited the resentment of the German people of the harsh terms imposed on them by the Versailles Treaty, ending World War I. To this he added a virulent anti-Semitism, holding the Jews to blame for Germany's economic plight after the war. His followers called themselves National Socialists, shortened to "Nazi." They wore brown instead of black shirts and by the middle of 1930's numbered in the hundreds of thousands. Germany's wrongs could be redressed only on the field of battle. At this point, many persons were inclined to dismiss "the little man with the mustache" as a slightly ridiculous figure. They were very much mistaken.

Then came the tragic Spanish Civil War in 1936 when the rebel forces of Colonel Francisco Franco, with the help of the Germans and Italians, overthrew the Spanish Republic and set up a Fascist dictatorship. The democracies provided scarcely any aid to Spain in her hour of travail. There were Brigades which fought as volunteers with the loyalist forces, but they were poorly armed. Ironically, the only major assistance came from the Soviet Union which was concerned not so much with maintaining Spain's constitutional government as with strengthening Russia's own position on the Iberian Peninsula.

Flushed with their Spanish success, the German and Italian dictators forced the western democracies to make one concession after another.

Confronting the ranting Hitler was the ineffectual Neville Chamberlain, English Prime Minister and the very prototype of the Edwardian gentleman, with his wing collar, rolled umbrella and diffident, understated manner. Nothing, it seemed, could stop the advance of the dictators. In September, 1939, when the German armies smashed the Polish frontiers and began their systematic destruction of that unhappy country, it was clear to everyone that no promises made by Hitler or his partner Mussolini to refrain from further aggression were worth the paper they were written on. Ready or not, the democracies would have to fight after all.

As early as 1937, President Franklin D. Roosevelt foresaw the war threat posed by developments in Europe. In a Chicago speech, he had said: "Let no one imagine that America will escape, that it may expect mercy, that this Western

Hemisphere will not be attacked." He then went on to urge concerted efforts by the free nations to restrain the enemies of freedom.

Roosevelt was also worried about the ruthless Japanese expansion in the Pacific. For some years they had been embarked on their "Greater East Asia Co-Prosperity" program, a euphemism for eventual Japanese hegemony in Asia. As a nation with important interests in the Pacific, the United States could not look on complacently while Japan continued its aggression. But at the moment, Europe was the main point of crisis.

This was to be a war to the death between the forces of totalitarianism and the free world. Both France and England were ill prepared for such a war. Without massive assistance from the United States, they could fall to the Axis powers, as the union of Italy and Germany was called. Later Japan was added to the confederation.

President Roosevelt called upon Congress to modify the strict neutrality laws to permit the sale of munitions and other war material to France and England. This he did in the cause of national security, pointing out that the domination of Europe by the Axis would leave the U.S. isolated and prey to the further designs of the dictators. Through intelligence reports received daily, Roosevelt knew also that eventually Japan would join in the war, creating a two-ocean conflict for the United States. Congress approved the President's request, although a number of legislators did so with many reservations. Nevertheless, the United States, for the present, was in the position of a "benevolent neutral" towards its hard-pressed allies. Most Americans sympathized with the Allied cause, but were very reluctant to become embroiled in another war.

In 1940, the Coast Guard began its Port Security operations under the revived Espionage Act of 1917 and the newly enacted Dangerous Cargo Act. This was part of a general program to minimize the danger of sabotage in port and waterfront areas. The function has been maintained until the present. The Coast Guard's Organized Reserve Port Security Training Program (ORTUPS), prepared reservists to go into action to protect vital harbor areas within 24 hours after a declaration of national emergency.

By 1941, the German Armies had occupied Norway and Denmark, and had crushed Holland, Belgium and France. Britain now stood virtually alone against the Nazi blitz. In 1940, the city of London had undergone punishing attacks by the Luftwaffe and much of the city had been destroyed. But under the leadership of the great Sir Winston Churchill, the British had found their fighting spirit and defied the might of the Nazi war machine.

The U.S. Coast Guard was the first of the Armed Forces to enter the arena of war. In 1941, the cutter *Comanche*, carrying the first U.S.Consul to Greenland, arrived in May at Ivigtut, site of the world's largest deposit of cryolite, a mineral essential to the production of aluminum used in aircraft construction. The move had been arranged by the United States with the Danish government in exile.

In these anxious moments, a new danger threatened the burgeoning U.S. effort. On May 22, 1941, a message was flashed to the British Admiralty that the powerful German battleships, *Bismarck* and *Prinz Eugen*, had, under cover of fog, slipped out of Bergen Fjord where they had been under British surveillance, into the sea-lanes. They now menaced the convoy routes. In the path of the battleships were two cutters, *Northland* and *Modoc*, which were later joined by the smaller cutter, *General Greene*. They were searching for survivors of a convoy en route to England which had suffered heavy losses at the hands of a German submarine "wolfpack." In the foul weather and confusion of battle, the *Modoc* was very nearly hit by the *Bismarck*. The German battleship managed to sink the British warship, *Hood*, but suffered serious battle casualties. Later, the *Bismarck* was sunk with only 100 of her 2,100 men surviving.

From now on, however, the guarding of the convoy routes was going to be on a much more extensive scale. In the summer of 1941, the Coast Guard organized its Greenland Patrol. It included the cutters, *Modoc*, *Comanche*, *Raritan*, and *Bowdoin*. Their area of surveillance covered south Greenland waters. Off northeast Greenland cruised *Northland*, *North Star*, and the indestructible old *Bear*. The Patrol was commanded by Commander Edward H. "Iceberg" Smith, a pioneer in oceanography.

Commander Smith's orders were "to do a little of everything." It was a major assignment, including keeping convoy routes open, as well as air routes for planes; breaking ice; finding leads in the ice for Greenland convoys of merchant ships and escorting them; rescuing survivors of submarine attacks; building and maintaining aids to navigation; reporting weather and ice conditions; and providing air and surface patrols. Besides all this, Commander Smith was ordered to find and destroy enemy weather and radio stations in

Greenland; continue the hydrographic survey; maintain communications between U.S. and Greenland government posts; carry supplies to Eskimos and small Danish settlements; escort cryolite ships; and perform rescue missions. All these duties were carried out faithfully by the Patrol.

fishermen, but of electronic specialists. A scientist and a female nurse were also on board. Under further questioning, the men admitted that they had been dispatched to erect a radio shack 500 miles to the north.

Not long after, a small boat from the *Northland* made a night landing a mile from the shack.

The Coast Guard knocks out Nazis' weather station in remote Greenland. The Coast Guardsman atop the shanty is Alphonse Szumiel, chief gunner's mate, of Buffalo, N.Y.

To keep an eye on any suspicious developments along Greenland's bleak coastal areas, Commander Smith organized a sled patrol manned by Danes and Eskimos, using dog teams. They soon turned up information leading to the first American naval capture of World War II. A group of men had landed in a deserted fjord from a fishing trawler, the *Buskoe.* The trawler had sailed away, but Smith's suspicions had been aroused. He took the vessel into port for questioning. Further investigation revealed that it was crammed with radio equipment and that its crew consisted not of

Lieutenant Leroy McCluskey, USCG, in charge of the party, and twelve Coast Guardsmen, smashed in the door and surprised three German radio operators, lying on their bunks. Found in the shack were plans for other secret radio transmitter shacks in Greenland. This took place on September 12, 1941, only about three months before the Japanese attack on Pearl Harbor and the formal U.S. entry into the war.

Shortly thereafter, the cutters *Duane* and *Northland*, carried out surveys of Greenland's west and east coasts to determine the feasibility of setting up airfields and seaplane bases and weather and radio stations. In April, 1941, a Danish-U.S. agreement was announced, declaring that Greenland's defense against German invasion was essential to the security of the Western Hemisphere.

After this, events crowded one upon the other. On April 10, 1941, the President transferred ten Coast Guard cutters to England, stating that he found the defense of the United Kingdom vital to the defense of the United States. The cutters were of the 250-foot Lake class, consisting of the *Cayuga, Itasca, Saranac, Sebago, Shoshone, Champlain, Mendota, Chelan, Pontchartrain,* and *Tahoe.* In Long Island Sound, Coast Guardsmen trained British crews to operate the cutters.

In the rising tempo of the war, the Coast Guard had seized 39 German, Italian and French ships in United States ports. They were taken into "protective custody" when it was discovered that Italian crews were sabotaging their vessels' machinery.

As the United States developed into "the arsenal of democracy," the sea-lanes leading to Greenland and Iceland became steadily more important. To assist the convoys and transoceanic aircraft, the Coast Guard established light stations and radio beacons. But it was hard duty, and soon Commander Smith augmented his fleet with ten trawlers selected from the New England fishing fleet. These small vessels were commanded by yachtsmen and other personnel making up the

Saranac, 250-foot Lake class.

As part of the campaign against Nazi submarines and to prevent the establishment of new bases, the United States occupied Greenland, and also Iceland. United States Navy ships began to escort huge convoys of U.S. merchantmen to Iceland. In the course of this operation, the Germans torpedoed two American destroyers, the *Kearny* and the *Reuben James.*

Since November, 1940, Rear Admiral Russell R. Waesche, the dynamic Commandant of the Coast Guard had been strengthening his Service. By November, 1941, when the president ordered the Service into the Navy, its strength had risen from 17,000 to 30,000. At war's peak, the Coast Guard would number more than 17500.

Coast Guard Reserve created in 1939. Many of these men were unaccustomed to the rough water and foul weather of the Greenland area, but they did an effective job, nevertheless.

Inevitably, the Coast Guard suffered losses during its operation of the Greenland Patrol. One of the most serious of these occurred on January 29, 1942 off the coast of Iceland when the 327-foot Coast Guard cutter, *Alexander Hamilton,* was towing a disabled Navy supply ship to a rendezvous with a Navy tug. Soon after casting the tow loose, an explosion in the engine room shook the cutter, killing all on duty there. No submarine was sighted. In a heavy sea, the *Hamilton's* crew took to the lifeboats after the cutter developed a steep list. It looked for a while as if the cutter could be saved, but the attempt was given up when she turned bottom up. There was no alternative but to destroy her with gunfire. She was one of the newest and finest ships in the Coast Guard fleet. The tragedy cost 26 Coast Guardsmen their lives.

Tragedy also overtook another cutter, *Escanaba*, which had formerly been berthed in Grand Haven, Michigan. On June 13, 1943, the *Escanaba* along with the *Mojave, Tampa, Raritan, Algonquin,* and *Storis* was escorting a convoy on its way from Greenland to Newfoundland. Suddenly, men on the *Storis* saw a nuge cloud of flame and smoke blot of the *Escanaba.* She went down so rapidly that no signals could be sent. Only two enlisted men out of a crew of 105 survived.

Just a short time before, the *Escanaba* had spent eight hours in submarine-infested waters, rescuing survivors from a torpedoed transport, *Dorchester.* Both the *Escanaba* and the *Comanche* had searched for the submarine to no avail. Then they had set about pulling survivors out of the water, which was only two degrees above freezing. No one could live long in such cold. Only two of the *Dorchester's* fourteen lifeboats had been launched. Working through the bitterly cold night, the cutters saved 299 men. When dawn at last broke, the rescuers could see hundreds of dead men, tossing on the rough sea in their life jackets. It was a scene conveying the full horror of war.

The *Dorchester* was also renowned as the ship on which one of the most heroic episodes of the war took place. As the doomed ship settled quickly in the sea, its four Army chaplains gave their life jackets to soldiers and calmly waited for death. They were Father John P. Washington, Rabbi Alexander D. Goode, Reverend George L. Fox, and Reverend Clark V. Poling. How sad that such nobility should be evoked only in the terrible crucible of war!

Before the Greenland Patrol was over it had taken its share of Coast Guardsmen. The *Natsek*, a sturdy 115-foot trawler out of Boston, was lost without leaving a trace. Another converted trawler, *Nanok*, suffered a similar fate in December, 1942, during a storm.

It was during the operation of the Patrol that the heroic Lieutenant John K. Pritchard and his equally gallant Radioman Benjamin A. Bottoms, lost their lives in a brave attempt to rescue the crew of a Flying Fortress lost for two weeks on the Greenland Ice Cap. Under the most hazardous conditions, they made the difficult landing on the ice cap to rescue a part of the crew. Then against the advice of the captain of the cutter, *Northland*,

to which Pritchard was attached, he went back to rescue the remainder. This time he didn't make it, and the world had lost two very brave men.

For all practical purposes, the Patrol was part of the unofficial war with the Axis powers which existed before the formal declaration. Yet even during that period, there had been sufficient indication of the enormous toll which would be exacted by this greatest of all conflicts.

During the period preceding the entry of the United States into World War II, the Coast Guard instituted its Ocean Station Vessel Program. The year was 1940 when two Coast Guard cutters were assigned to observation stations between Bermuda and the Azores. They provided weather data and other information for transoceanic planes and

USCG *Natsek*, June 25, 1942.

ships. Until then, this information had been supplied by merchant ships. But this had been discontinued after the start of war in Europe forced ships of belligerents into radio silence.

At war's end there were 11 Coast Guard ocean stations in the Atlantic, serving as plane guards and radio beacons, as well as watching the weather. The number of cutters on this patrol was cut back after the war. At present, the Coast Guard operates four ocean stations in the North Atlantic and two in the Pacific. They patrol a 210-mile square of ocean (44,100 square miles). It is a rough, monotonous but vital task. Besides relaying meteorological and other data to ships and planes, the cutters also carry out extended oceanographic studies and are an important source of oceanic information.

America's official neutrality was ended on the "day of infamy," December 7, 1941, by a swarm of Japanese bombers, streaking in from an aircraft carrier off Hawaii to bomb Pearl Harbor, the United States' most important naval base in the Pacific. The nation was at war again.

Top: Coast Guardsmen on the deck of the U.S. Coast Guard Cutter *Spencer* watch the explosion of a depth charge which blasted a Nazi U-Boat's hope of breaking into the center of a large convoy. *Center:* Coast Guardsmen from the Cutter *Spencer* picking up survivors from the Nazi U-Boat just before it made its final dive. Meanwhile, the convoy steamed on. *Bottom:* The deadly fire of the Cutter *Spencer* ended the career of this Nazi submarine. The German crewman standing by the stanchion disappeared just after this picture was taken.

At War Again

The Japanese attack on Pearl Harbor was the spark that ignited the Nation's immense energies. On December 8, 1941, the United States officially declared war on Japan. It was joined by Great Britain. Three days later, Germany proclaimed war on the United States and agreed with Japan, their Axis colleague, not to make a separate peace. This, however, so far as Germany was concerned, was little more than a formality. An undeclared state of war had existed between the U.S. and Germany since October 27, 1941. At that time, President Roosevelt had informed the country that Germany had started war on the United States. Said the President: "Hitler has attacked shipping in areas close to the Americas . . . Many American-owned ships have been sunk on the high seas. One American destroyer was attacked on September 4. Another destroyer was attacked and hit on October 17. Eleven brave and loyal men of our Navy were killed by the Nazis. We have wished to avoid shooting. But shooting has started . . . America has been attacked." The most terrible war in the history of the world was now fully under way.

As had the German Kaiser a generation before, the Nazis underestimated the might of an aroused America. Once Americans were convinced of their cause and determined on a course of action, they could build a military machine capable of sweeping all before them. It was a fatal miscalculation for Hitler and his minions.

The Coast Guard organization which took its place with the Navy in World War II had come a long way in more than two decades since the first world conflict. Both its air and surface fleets had become considerable, due in part to the needs of the "Rum War." Ready to take their places in the line were seven 327-foot "Secretary" class cutters, considered among the most advanced ships in the U.S. naval service, with a speed of 15 to 18 knots and a cruising range of more than 8,000 miles. They carried 200 officers and men and were equipped with a small seaplane for scouting and observation. They were in effect, early aircraft carriers. To meet wartime needs, their fire-power was stepped up to three five-inch guns, three 3-inch/50 antiaircraft guns, several 50-calibre and 20-millimeter machine guns, depth-charge racks, and Y and K guns for projecting depth charges.

Next in size were the 250-foot cutters of the Lake class, carrying 150 officers and enlisted men. Ten of these had been built between 1928 and 1932. They bore the names of American lakes: *Champlain*, *Cayuga*, *Chelan*, *Itasca*, *Mendota*, *Pontchartrain*, *Sebago*, *Saranac*, *Shoshone*, and *Tahoe*.

Altogether, 267 cutters were in the Coast Guard fleet, as well as 199 picket boats 34 to 65 feet long, 39 lightships, numerous auxiliary craft for repair work, freight carrying, maritime training, cable-laying, and icebreaking. Aircraft, operating out of eight stations, in addition to a patrol detachment at Cape May, New Jersey, totaled 55. Alexander Hamilton would have been gratified to see the healthy growth of his brain-child.

Nevertheless, for the time being, the Axis powers had the advantage. It had taken a relatively long time for the American people to recognize the dangers facing them, and military rearmament could not be achieved overnight. It would be at least a year to eighteen months before the weight of U.S. power could be brought to bear on the aggressors. In the meantime, a large share of the defense of the United States fell to the Coast Guard fleet.

The cutters performed valiantly, but were not able to provide adequate defense for the country's immense coastline. Alert submarine commanders were quick to take advantage of American weakness. They made daring attacks on tankers off Cape Hatteras and found the unarmed freighters sitting ducks. Shaping up was the crucial Battle of the Atlantic which was in the long run to decide the outcome of the war. It was the United States' announced intention of providing a "bridge of ships" spanning the wide Atlantic with enormous convoys carrying troops and supplies to all the fighting fronts of Europe. If the Germans could frustrate this strategy, their plan for world dominion would be well advanced. No one knew this better than Admiral Russell R. Waesche, the Coast Guard Commandant. He was determined that, whatever sacrifice it cost, the Coast Guard would throw every ounce of its reserves, both human and materiel, to assist in furthering this vast enterprise for freedom.

But in those dark days of January, 1942, Americans were stunned to learn of one sea disaster after another. Thirteen ships were sunk by

German submarines in the last half of that month. Their boldness increased to the point where they became openly contemptuous of U.S. defenses, sometimes making attacks in daylight in the full sight of viewers, as was the case of the destroyer, *Jacob Jones*, sunk off Virginia Beach, south of Chesapeake Bay.

Lt. Maurice D. Jester, Commanding Officer of the 165-foot Cutter *Icarus*.

The Coast Guard, however, did have one advantage, contributing to its military readiness. As the agency primarily responsible for enforcing U.S. neutrality at sea, it had already undergone considerable preparation prior to the nation's formal entry into the war. As Admiral Waesche put it: " . . . the Coast Guard as the law enforcement arm of the Federal Government upon the high seas and navigable waters of the United States, immediately swung into action to enforce the neutrality laws . . . and was in a position to render a greater service than ever before in a time of national emergency."

That was one of the few bright spots in the generally dismal picture of U.S. military preparedness in 1942. The country's entire military and industrial potential was being harnessed to war requirements but the changeover was of such magnitude that it could not be accomplished quickly.

Meanwhile, German submarines were having things very much their own way. Particularly bad news came from the Gulf Sea frontier, including the Florida coast, Gulf of Mexico and part of the Bahamas and Cuba. The only naval forces available to defend this large stretch of coastline were a group of three Coast Guard cutters at Key West, Florida, a converted yacht, 19 unarmed Coast Guard aircraft, and 14 Army planes carrying .30 calibre machine guns. The Germans showed their contempt for these meager defenses by striking in this area late in February, 1942. They sent four ships to the bottom in four days. As ship losses increased, the Coast Guard moved to strengthen its defenses with additional cutters and aircraft. But the wounds inflicted had been severe. Forty-one vessels were picked off by German submarines in the month of May alone.

One of the torpedoed vessels included the Coast Guard cutter, *Acacia*, while it was en route to Antigua, British West Indies, on March 15, 1942. The wooden superstructure of the *Acacia* was set afire by submarine shelling, turning her into a burning trap. As the flames mounted, a submarine sailed up close and completed the cutter's destruction. The *Acacia's* crew in three lifeboats had their first look at the frightening face of war. It was a humiliating time for the country and an impatience began to build up for reprisal. Finally, in the third month of the war, two German submarines were sunk by Navy planes. In April, 1942, the U.S. destroyer, *Roper*, sank the U-85 near Hatteras. But, on the whole, it had been a disappointing showing. In four months of war, only four enemy submarines had been dispatched while German shipyards were turning out new subs at a rate of about one a day.

The really good news came on May 9, and it was the Coast Guard cutter, *Icarus*, patrolling off Cape Lookout which was responsible for it. The cutter had picked up a peculiar sound contact off its port bow. As the sound grew louder, a torpedo was seen to explode about 600 feet off the port quarter. No periscope was showing, but the cutter continued to stalk the enemy vessel until it could hear the sub's propeller sounds very clearly. Then contact was lost at 180 yards. At this time, Lieutenant Maurice D. Jester quickly calculated the sub's position and dropped five depth charges.

After the noise and turbulence of the explosion had subsided, the *Icarus* again could hear the submarine moving in a westerly direction. Depth charges were dropped again, flushing the U-boat to the surface. German gunners burst out of the conning tower and made for the deck gun. But before they could get there, the waiting gunners on the *Icarus* flung them back with heavy fire. An order was given to ram the U-boat. Seven of the *Icarus'* shells had homed in on the submarine, crippling her. The German sailors threw themselves overboard. The result: a dead submarine and a large oil slick and wreckage, as well as 33 survivors. It turned out that the submarine was the new 500-ton U-352, making its maiden raid.

The elation produced by these early successes soon turned to despair when the U-boat toll of merchant ships rose to more than three a day. The country and the Free World could not sustain this rate of loss for long. 1943 saw the peak of the Battle of the Atlantic. The Germans had developed refined underwater warfare techniques and were now operating in murderous "wolf packs," lying in wait for the convoys.

Far from the embattled armies on the European battlefronts, the fate of free peoples everywhere was being decided in the vast stretches of the Atlantic. The United States showed a little ingenuity of its own by developing a high-frequency direction finder. The cutters, *Campbell* and *Spencer*, 327-footers of the "Secretary" class, were equipped with them. During this crucial period of the war at sea all of the Coast Guard's cutters of this type were employed on convoy duty.

The new direction finder was able to locate with great precision the position of a submarine. The task of the cutters was made simpler by the frequent radio communication maintained between

Vice Admiral James A. Hirshfield, Assistant Commandant, USCG (Ret.).

Sub-sinking Skipper of the Cutter *Campbell*, Commander James A. Hirshfield, USCG.

the submarines and the German Admiralty. This typically German penchant for tight, centralized control of fighting units proved to be a vulnerability which the cutters could exploit.

It was in the wind-lashed North Atlantic in February, 1943, that the new equipment proved its worth. Both the *Campbell* and the *Spencer* were helping to guard a huge, 63 ship convoy on a westbound course. The first inkling of danger came when the cutters picked up a babble of German. It indicated that a wolf pack lurked close by. The *Campbell* and *Spencer* charted a course for the undersea craft, but at first were unsuccessful in locating them. Then the *Campbell* responded to a call for assistance from a ship which had straggled out of the convoy. In the interval, *Spencer* and *Dianthus* made their way to an area where three enemy submarines were being bombed by aircraft. As the U-boats undertook evasive action, *Spencer* spotted another sub. She bore directly on it, blazing away with her guns and dropping depth charges. Although it could not be ascertained at

The captain of the U-606 was a tenacious commander, and he doggedly tracked the convoy. That night, the sky was lurid with the glow of distress rockets. In the course of the action, the Polish vessel, *Burza*, detected a distant sound and headed towards it. Upon reaching the area of contact, she released depth charges. In an effort to avoid damage from the charges, the submarine went down to a depth of 780 feet where the pressure ruptured her hull. When she emerged, she was alongside the *Campbell*.

Immediately, the *Campbell* gave pursuit. The submarine appeared to have vanished when suddenly she reappeared. Commander (later Vice Admiral) Hirshfield ordered that the *Campbell* proceed on collision course at a top speed of 18 knots. As she came on, her guns kept up a fusillade of gunfire, killing the German commander and part of his crew. The force of the collision cut gaping holes in the *Campbell's* bridge and her engine room, but the sub was finished. Twelve of her crew were rescued. Hirshfield, who was slightly wounded by splinters from the gun shield of the

U.S. Coast Guard 83-foot patrol boats at Long Beach, Calif. 11th Coast Guard District.

the time whether the submarine had been hit, she never was seen again.

But there were still four submarines in the vicinity of the convoy. On the following morning, they managed to sink two freighters. *Campbell* immediately gave pursuit, but was not able to locate the subs.

Campbell, was awarded the Navy Cross.

There were still many days ahead, but slowly, the full force of America's enormous war machine was being turned on the enemy. The Axis powers were gradually losing the advantages of surprise and the initiative was passing to the Allies. Although other American ships would be lost to

Top: Nazi gunners knocked out this Coast Guard LCI during the initial invasion of the French coast on D-Day. *Bottom:* This striking panorama of the French invasion beach was made by a Coast Guard combat photographer from a hillside cut with trenches (foreground) of the ousted Nazi defenders.

underwater marauders, the scale was so reduced that it no longer presented the threat of disaster.

American invaders clamber from a U.S. Coast Guard LCI (L) into a landing barge for the last lap of the English Channel crossing which will bring them into the fight to liberate France.

Members of the Coast Guard shore patrol; trained to repel attempts of enemy spies and saboteurs on our shores.

In the Pacific, the U.S. was well on its way to eliminating Japanese strongpoints in that immense theater of war. The enemy was being forced back,

island by island, and the Coast Guard had a major part to play in the campaign. As in the Atlantic,

In a highly technological age, man and dog made an effective beach patrol team as they maintained their vigil against possible enemy agents during World War II.

Coast Guardsmen manned a wide variety of vessels, including those of the Army and Navy. They saw action in every theater of operation, from Normandy, North Africa, Sicily and Anzio to Guadalcanal and other Japanese bastions in the Pacific. Coast Guardsmen manned the landing craft, bringing assault troops to the beaches, their special training in the handling of small craft making them especially valuable for such duty. They also served on many of the huge assault transports, carrying barges and troops within striking distance of the beaches.

In the D-Day landings in Normandy in June, 1944, a flotilla of fifty 83-foot cutters distinguished itself by serving as a rescue fleet under the fire of German guns. The flotilla had been selected for that duty by the Commander-in-Chief himself, President Roosevelt, who as a former Secretary of the Navy and a yachtsman, was well aware of the Coast Guard's expertise in the operation of small boats in restricted waters. More than 1,400 men were plucked from the chill waters of the English

Channel and enabled to rejoin their units to fight once again. It was one of the epics of courage of the war. That wooden "matchbox fleet" will be long remembered.

The war in the European and Pacific theaters did not diminish the need for security at home. On the contrary, it imposed additional duties on the Coast Guard to protect the home front from saboteurs and other enemies. We have already noted the formation of a fleet of volunteer small craft to make up the Coast Guard Reserve. These men, many of whom served without pay, maintained a

should be employed. But it had the overriding virtue of working.

The most spectacular incident involving beach patrol duty came in June, 1942. It had been a quiet night with nothing to indicate that anything out of the ordinary would happen, when Seaman Second Class John C. Cullen prepared to patrol his beat from the Coast Guard Station at Amagansett, Long Island. About 300 yards down the beach, he saw four men at the water's edge. Something about their manner made Cullen suspicious. He questioned them about their business and was told

Eighty-three-foot cutter in action.

Legion of Merit winner, Coast Guardsman John C. Cullen, Boatswain's Mate first class.

constant vigil off our coasts. Their picket boats performed valuable service. In 1942, the present-day Coast Guard Reserve was organized and the earlier organization became the Coast Guard Auxiliary, a body of volunteer small boatmen who have distinguished themselves in advancing the cause of recreational boating.

An interesting outgrowth of the war was the creation of the Coast Guard's Beach Patrol, utilizing that ancient but very effective combination of men, horses and dogs. It seemed a paradox that, in a war placing such stress on sophisticated armaments, so primitive a technique

that they were Southampton fishermen who had run aground in the fog. Cullen invited them to come to the station to wait for morning.

The leader of the group who had been amiable until then, suddenly turned ugly. When he saw that the Coast Guardsman was not impressed he changed his tactics. Holding out a roll of bills to Cullen, he said: "Why don't you forget the whole thing?"

Cullen decided to play along until he could relay the information to the authorities. He returned to the station and gave the alarm. Later, his testimony was largely responsible for bringing a death sentence to the four men who were revealed to be Nazi saboteurs, landed by a U-boat, and with funds to carry out their plans. Cullen's report put the FBI on their track. All four men died in the electric chair.

In that same climactic 1942, President Roosevelt signed legislation authorizing a Coast Guard Women's Auxiliary of commissioned and enlisted personnel to relieve Coast Guardsmen for sea duty. Its first head was Lieutenant Commander Dorothy C. Stratton, formerly Dean of Women at Purdue University. The organization was known as the Spars, a combination of the first letters of the words in the Latin and English versions of the Service motto: Semper Paratus; Always Ready.

In 1942 while the war was still in progress, the Bureau of Marine Inspection and Navigation of the Department of Commerce became a part of the Coast Guard and the Service's modern identity was virtually complete. There was no question now that the Coast Guard was the foremost federal agency for marine safety in all its aspects.

When the guns of World War II fell silent in 1945, the Coast Guard had carved one more niche for itself in history. The little revenue fleet had become a far-ranging, diversified Service, with the most modern and extensive capabilities in the arts of war and peace, and possessing a versatility unequalled by any other service in the world.

A Changing Service for a Changing World

With the surrender of the Japanese in August 1945, the Second World War came to an end. It had been a prodigious effort in which the country had unleashed the full power of its military and industrial capability. In that time the Coast Guard had reached a peak strength of more than 175,000—by far the greatest in its history. Under the spur of wartime necessity it had developed a host of new techniques and devices to carry out its functions. Many of these advances were in the field of electronics, an area in which the Coast Guard was to score some outstanding successes in the years ahead. Its work in the maritime safety sector has been substantially broadened by the addition of disaster-prevention programs to its already well-recognized function of rescue at sea.

The Coast Guard's successful performance of its varied tasks during the war constituted one more outstanding response to emergency. And as had happened so often in the past, its responsibilities had grown accordingly. Such had been the case since the earliest days of the Republic.

By 1945 the Coast Guard had assumed the essential elements characterizing the present Service. Classically it could be defined as an Armed Force of the United States and the chief federal agency for maritime safety and law enforcement. That, of course, is a highly compressed definition of its function and indicates a compartmentalization of function which does not in fact exist. The war had illustrated that there was no neat separation of "peacetime" and "wartime" duty in the Coast Guard. Some of its most important aspects, such as concern for safety of life at sea, had expanded during the war. During the dark days of the Battle of the Atlantic, it had rescued more than 4,200 seamen from torpedoed vessels and from other emergencies. At no time during the war crisis did the Coast Guard suspend its marine safety efforts.

As the country neared the decade of the 1950's, electronics loomed ever larger in service operations. The high-speed electronic computer and its revolutionizing effect on government and industry was only a few years away. But some of the wizardry of electronics had already gone into

In 1966, the Service celebrated a half century of aviation. Most numerous of its aircraft in the 1966 fleet were HU-16E'S, known to many as the Grumman Albatross.

73

Top: This 45-foot inland buoy boat was developed for Coast Guard use during the early 1960's. *Bottom:* The decade 1960-1970 saw the Coast Guard's old wooden-hulled 83-foot patrol boats replaced by modern, air conditioned 82-footers such as *Point Highland* pictured here. *Point Highland* is based in Crisfield, Md.

the development of the Service's famed Long Range Aid to Navigation (Loran) system. At the war's close, Loran establishments dotted the world, turning out to be just as useful to peacetime navigation as they had been during the war. This same expertise extended to the designing of other advanced navigation aids and a more centralized means of operating them.

made upon the Coast Guard were more extensive and complicated than ever before.

As things settled down, the Coast Guard gradually returned to its normal day-to-day activity, centering mainly about marine safety. It was because of the largely transportation-oriented nature of the Service that it would, some years later, in April, 1967, leave its traditional home in

The self-bailing, self-righting 44-foot motor surfboat and the HH-52A amphibious helicopter were among the many additions to the Coast Guard's sea and air fleets during the mid-1960's.

In those busy wartime years, the Coast Guard had been moving ahead in the use of aircraft, especially the utilization of helicopters for search and rescue, adding a new dimension to its work. Its naval architects and engineers had been designing and assisting in the building of new and advanced classes of cutters. Clearly, the Coast Guard, along with the rest of the Nation, recognized that it stood on the threshold of a new era.

But while the Coast Guard's duties continued to expand, its personnel did not. The ending of the war produced clamorous demands for instant demobilization from Congress and other segments of American society. Millions of men and women had to be funnelled back into the civilian mainstream, and this at a time when the demands

the Treasury Department where it had been since 1790, for a new place in the Transportation Department. There it would function as one of the components of America's first Department devoted to the needs of this vital field.

The key phrase to the Coast Guard's development in the post-war years is "transportation-oriented." By the middle 1950's, about 20 percent of its officers were involved in a comprehensive program to make the U.S. merchant marine the world's safest. That is still the case. It entails a comprehensive Commercial Vessel Safety Program extending from a vessel's blueprint on the drawing board throughout its operating life until the final scrapping. Not only does the Coast Guard inspect American ships to make certain they conform to safety standards but it is also concerned with the qualifications of their officers and crews. It serves as the official U.S. representative on international bodies dealing with world maritime safety standards, the most important of these being the Intergovernmental Maritime Consultative Organization (IMCO), an agency of the United Nations. IMCO is responsible, among other things, for formulating the international safety code for the maritime world.

The technological revolution in the United States was especially noteworthy in the Coast Guard's far-flung navigational aids network, useful both in peace and war. In addition to the highly sophisticated Loran system with its advanced position-finding capability, there were many thousands of other devices, ranging from relatively simple river buoys to highly sophisticated devices capable of providing significant oceanic data as well as providing navigational assistance.

To help establish a greater uniformity in navigation aids, the Coast Guard has worked with the Federal Aviation Administration of the Department of Transportation, and with the Department of Defense to set up a National Navigation Plan. The Plan aims at the development and operation of a federal system and represents the first time that the problem has been approached on a national basis. It represents a major advance in marine safety.

As the years sped by after the war, the Coast Guard found itself hard at work modernizing its approach to the ancient problem of rescue at sea. When the high-speed electronic computer began to appear on the scene in the mid-1950's, Coast Guard electronic engineers were quick to see its possible application to search and rescue. A result of their efforts was the Automated Merchant Vessel Reporting System (AMVER) which made its debut at New York City in 1958. Basically, AMVER is a computerized search and rescue network, employing the latest electronic techniques for this humane objective. Heart of the system is a computer network linking the AMVER Communications Center in New York with Coast Guard Headquarters in Washington. Emergency calls come in daily from distressed vessels in the major oceans of the world. Through the use of ship and shore radio relays and a high-speed electronic computer memory bank and retrieval system, the Coast Guard is able to keep track of thousands of ships, so that, within minutes after a call for assistance is monitored, it can furnish the precise locations of ships with medical facilities closest to

the endangered vessel or person. The AMVER system is voluntary and international, depending on the cooperation of foreign flag ships or radio stations around the world. It is a truly international undertaking on behalf of the safety of life at sea. The response has been so encouraging that it represents one of the few unifying factors in a world given over increasingly to national rivalries.

The Coast Guard's ability to respond to new national developments was well illustrated in the field of recreational boating, one of the country's most popular outdoor activities. Once regarded primarily as a rich man's sport, boating now numbers more than 8 million enthusiasts, reflecting the growing affluence of the American economy. With additional thousands of citizens taking to the water each year, the Coast Guard has developed a program for maintaining high safety standards for recreational boatmen. It is a responsibility shared by the Coast Guard with the states and it is paying dividends in reducing accidents and loss of life. One of the Coast Guard's major instrumentalities for fostering safe boating practices is the Coast Guard Auxiliary, a voluntary organization of boatmen, with flotillas throughout the United States. Working without salary, these public-spirited citizens devote much of their free time to patrolling regattas and other outdoor marine events, to conducting boating safety courses, and to performing courtesy motorboat examinations. They also take part in search and rescue and have helped to save many lives.

In response to the deepening crisis with Cuba since the Castro takeover in 1959, the Coast Guard in 1961 was assigned the function of trouble shooter and humanitarian agency to tackle the many problems posed by the constant flow of refugees across the Straits of Florida to Key West and freedom. Those 90 miles of water between Cuba and the United States became the Western Hemisphere's equivalent of the Berlin Wall. The situation became especially acute in 1965 when, due to a change in Cuba's emigration policy, hordes of refugees fled their unhappy homeland. Out of this crisis was born the Cuban Patrol, consisting of cutters and aircraft, flying constant surveillance over the Straits to keep an eye on the situation there and to assist stranded voyagers in their flight to freedom. So eager were these people to escape that they put to sea in every imaginable kind of craft, including even flimsy rafts. Often, they would run out of fuel midway in their journey and would drift in the burning heat in their exposed boats until they were spotted either

Top: Edisto and other Navy icebreakers were taken over by the Coast Guard in the mid-60's. *Bottom:* The Coast Guard assisted thousands of desperate Cuban refugees during the Cuban exodus which began in 1961.

by a Coast Guard cutter or aircraft. At such time, they would be taken aboard the cutter and given food and rest. When they had been refreshed their boat would be fueled to complete the trip to the United States.

Gradually, patterns evolved in the refugees' efforts to reach the United States. Coast Guard surveillance planes learned to fly over certain islands to look for Cubans waiting for assistance. The Coast Guard Base at Key West had to be expanded and improved to serve the heavy migration of Cubans.

The Patrol, however, also served another function, and this was to enforce U.S. neutrality by preventing the transportation of men and arms from the United States by Cuban exiles seeking to build resistance points in their oppressed country. During this period, the Cuban missile confrontation occurred when the Soviets introduced these lethal weapons into the island nation. In their proximity to the United States mainland—just 90 miles away—they presented an intolerable threat to national security. New tensions gripped the world as the superpowers squared off against one another. Fortunately, the crisis was resolved by a Russian backdown.

The result of the missile crisis was to stimulate an even greater exodus from Cuba. This required a broadening of the Patrol to include larger Coast Guard cutters, including the *Diligence* and the *Androscoggin*, as well as intensified air surveillance of the Straits. Again the Coast Guard did its job well. With the return of calmer conditions to the Caribbean, surveillance activities have been reduced but not discontinued.

In 1965, an agreement was arrived at between the Navy and Treasury Departments to transfer all of the former's icebreakers to the U.S. Coast Guard. That literally made the Coast Guard "king of the ice." The agreement was an outgrowth of the increasingly tense international situation, necessitating the deployment of Navy fleet units to a growing number of crisis areas. The transfer would free significant numbers of Navy vessels for combat duty, should that become necessary.

Historically, the move was a logical extension of the Coast Guard's traditional function of icebreaking in the harbors and waterways of the U.S. Its work in this sector went back to the early days of the Service when cutters on rescue missions often had to punch their way through ice to reach endangered ships. Over the years, this responsibility was broadened to include icebreaking on the Alaskan Patrol, the Great Lakes, and the Northeastern Atlantic coast.

Under the expanded function, Coast Guard icebreakers will take part in a variety of peacetime operations in polar regions. The Coast Guard will also assign icebreakers to Navy operational control for seasonal deployment to the Arctic and Antarctic in support of the national interest. To the extent practicable, the Coast Guard will participate in polar scientific programs sponsored by the Navy, Coast Guard, National Science Foundation, and other federal or private agencies having approved scientific missions requiring icebreaker services.

During Operation Deep Freeze, 1967, the Coast Guard for the first time in its long association with U.S. Naval Support Forces For Antarctic Sciences, operated four icebreakers.

In late August, 1969, the Coast Guard began a new chapter in the long history of the Arctic exploration when its icebreaker, *Northwind*, accompanied the supertanker icebreaker, *Manhattan*, on the first leg of her epic voyage across the top of North America to Prudhoe Bay, Alaska, and its newly discovered oil fields. Her mission was to determine the feasibility of a transcontinental, deeper-water, all-season tanker route to northern Alaska via the famed Northwest Passage. The 1,005-foot *Manhattan* was the largest and best-equipped vessel ever to attempt such a crossing, but she was not the first to do so. In the summer of 1957, the Coast Guard cutters, *Storis*, *Bramble*, and *Spar*, successfully negotiated the passage in the first polar circumnavigation of the North American continent. In July, 1969, the *Northwind* had transited from Point Barrow, Alaska to Greenland earlier in the season than had ever been done before. These were much smaller ships, drawing far less water than the mammoth *Manhattan*. The icebreaker, *Staten Island* escorted the supertanker on her return voyage. The entire venture was part of a great push to open up for commercial use the oil and mineral wealth of the great northwest.

The decades following the second World Conflict saw a great reawakening of mankind's interest in the totality of his environment. A major beneficiary of this scientific renaissance was the field of oceanic science. The Coast Guard had been one of the first federal agencies to be concerned with oceanography. Its work in this area dated from 1867 when the Revenue Cutter, *Lincoln*, departed San Francisco on the first government effort to explore the waters of Alaska, a territory which the United States had only recently acquired from the Imperial Russian Government. Its work in the ocean sciences has been going on ever since. By the 1960's, it was one of the principal contributors to the scientific investigation of Arctic waters. Making information available to this field of study were the Alaskan Patrol, the Coast Guard-operated International Ice Patrol, the Ocean Station Program, and other studies conducted in collaboration with private or other governmental agencies. With the signing of legislation by President John F. Kennedy, the Coast Guard acquired official status as a federal oceanographic agency authorized to conduct its own studies.

Closely linked to the revived interest in oceanographic science was a shocked awareness that many of earth's most common environmental features, including the oceans, could no longer be taken for granted but were in grave danger due to unwise or excessive exploitation. Tankers growing ever larger in size posed new dangers of massive oil spills with their consequent killing of seabirds and marine creatures. The science of ecology, hitherto regarded as the preserve of academicians, became an absorbing public interest. Alarmed by the disastrous potential of irreversible poisoning of the oceanic environment, new studies were undertaken in the late 1960's to study means of combatting this danger. The Coast Guard, with its special association with the marine environment, was given a key role in the undertaking. Its marine scientists and engineers became deeply involved in finding solutions to the menace of pollution of the oceans by oil or other adulterants. Today this ecological concern extends across the entire spectrum of our lives, and bids to become a problem of critical proportions. At stake is nothing less than the survival of mankind. For the first time in the nation's history, a concerted attack on the problem is being made with the support of all segments of the American community. It is the great problem remaining before us.

It was in the 1960's that man saw himself for the first time not merely as an exploiter of earth resources but as a conservator. The United States in particular became aware that the elements of life itself, earth, air and water, could no longer be taken for granted. Human resources were, after all, limited.

The role of conservator of marine resources was not a new one for the Coast Guard. It had long been charged with the enforcement of many conservation treaties entered into by the United States and foreign governments to preserve certain species of marine life. Outstanding among these arrangements was the convention to prohibit unrestricted hunting of the North Pacific fur seal, a species

nearly rendered extinct by hunters in the closing years of the 19th century.

In the 1960's the country moved into an era of unprecedented prosperity. American living standards were easily the highest in the world. This should have created an atmosphere of euphoria, but it did not. Somehow, it seemed to many that the "American Century," to which Dewey's great victory at Manila Bay had been a prelude, was not living up to its promise. There had been a major

Admiral E.J. Roland, the Coast Guard's dynamic postwar Commandant, held office from 1962-1966, supervising a period of great change and growth for the service.

Depression, two World Wars, as well as a more limited but vicious conflict in Korea, all in the space of half a century. These crises had sapped much of the nation's energy. Perhaps it was war weariness or the disenchantment which inevitably comes with world power. The pragmatic, materialistic philosophy that had served so well in frontier days appeared to have little application to the modern era. As the country entered into the second half of the century, it was learning the heavy cost of world leadership.

The malaise was heightened by disturbing events in the former French colony of Indo-China, long a battleground of many races and nations. The withdrawal of the French after their defeat at Dien Bien Phu had created a power vacuum into which native Communist forces, abetted by China and the Soviet Union, threatened to flow. Ho Chi Minh, leader of the Communist Party in North Vietnam had already begun to infiltrate the south. His aim was clear: to set up a Communist dictatorship for all of Vietnam. The people of what is now the Republic of Vietnam did not want such a dictatorship, but that was what was in store for them unless help arrived soon. Only one nation had the capability to resist Communist aggression: the United States. It was part of the American tradition to assist any nation struggling for independence.

By 1965, substantial U.S. forces were in the menaced Republic. It was in that year that the Coast Guard, at the request of the U.S. Navy, began to deploy its forces to take part in the sea war in southeast Asia. The story of that involvement represents so unusual a chapter in the history of the Service that it deserves to be taken up by itself.

In Vietnam Waters

The struggle to prevent the destruction of the Republic of Vietnam by Communist invaders escalated sharply in 1965. This resulted in the intensification of both the land and sea phases of the conflict. One of the Republic's most vulnerable points was its long and sparsely defended coastline. In consequence, the northern attackers were able to maintain a large and steady flow of men and materials by sea routes.

The U.S. Navy, recalling the Coast Guard's long experience in dealing with seaborne infiltration, called on the Coast Guard to assist in its coastal surveillance of the South Vietnamese coast. The Coast Guard's response was to dispatch Squadron One, consisting of twenty-six 82-foot cutters. The tiny cutters were shipped to the Philippines on board large merchant vessels, but travelled the remaining distance to Vietnam under their own power. They were to form the nucleus of the U.S. Navy's Operation Market Time. The Operation was aimed at defeating North Vietnam's attempts to utilize coastal routes for the resupply and reinforcement of Viet Cong fighting units in the South. The operation derived its name from the thousands of commercial junks plying Vietnamese coastal waters daily, bringing cargoes of vegetables and other products to native markets. Not all of the cargoes were innocent. Sometimes they consisted of Viet Cong detachments headed for the battle zones.

U.S. Coast Guard 82-foot patrol craft *Point Garnet* (WPB-82310) and *Point Grey* (WPB-82324) are bedded down in cradles on board the *SS Steel Admiral* ready for departure for South Vietnam duty. The permanent home port of both craft is Norfolk, Va.

81

United States' efforts to bar infiltration by sea started in February, 1965, when a large cache of arms was found in Vung Ro Bay by members of the U.S. and Vietnamese Navies. A 130-foot junk had been sighted by a helicopter on a medical mission out of Qui Nhon. Aircraft called to the scene sank the vessel in shallow water. Later, it was discovered that she was carrying enough equipment to outfit an entire Viet Cong battalion. Further investigations revealed additional caches of weapons, ammunitions and explosives. Papers found on the vessel showed that it was of North Vietnamese registry and engaged in infiltration. To the Navy this indicated an urgent need to strengthen its coastal surveillance, and the incident signalled the beginning of an accelerated sea war against the Communist invader.

Squadron One was deployed along the Vietnamese coast in three divisions—11, 12, and 13. Division 11 operated out of An Thoi on the island of Phu Quoc in the Gulf of Thailand. Division 12 was based at Da Nang near the demilitarized sector

On patrol near Duong-Dong, South Vietnam, the 82-foot U.S. Coast Guard Cutter *Point Comfort* (WPB-82317) inspects a junk.

of Vietnam just south of the 17th parallel. Division 13's cutters operated along Vietnam's central coast and were based at Cat Lo, about 40 miles south of Saigon. Headquarters for the Squadron were at Saigon.

The following year, a decision was made to increase the effectiveness and scope of the coastal surveillance by detailing another Squadron of oceangoing Coast Guard cutters. Known as Squadron Three, it consisted of five cutters with headquarters at Subic Bay, Republic of the Philippines. The deployment of Squadron Three to the Vietnam theater of operation represented a tribute to the effectiveness of the coastal surveillance work of Squadron One and was also a substantial shot in the arm for the hard-working 82-foot cutters. Each of Squadron Three's cutters carried a complement of 159 officers and enlisted men, for a total of about 795. This added to the approximately 500 Coast Guard personnel of Squadron One plus special detachments assigned to missions such as aids to navigation, merchant marine inspection, and explosives loading brought the total Coast Guard participation to around 1,500. This was a considerable undertaking for a small service whose entire military complement numbered around 35,000 officers and enlisted men.

Both of the Coast Guard Squadrons, together with Navy units and naval craft of the Republic of Vietnam made up the Coastal Surveillance Forces. They threw a ring of steel around the Republic's coastline.

Work on patrol was a grinding, monotonous, seven-day-a-week affair, punctuated occasionally by fierce fire fights with an elusive and usually unseen foe. In miserable sub-tropical temperatures, the cutters kept constantly on the alert for suspicious looking native craft. Once one was sighted, the cutter headed for it. In a businesslike but courteous manner, the inspector (usually a Vietnamese petty officer) checked out the junk's registry and the crew's credentials. In many cases the occupants of the junks were well-known to the inspectors and the tone was generally good natured. Food, packages, medicine, cigarettes and other highly-prized items were distributed.

Sometimes, however, a less holiday atmosphere prevailed. This was true when in May, 1966, the cutter, *Point Grey*, spotted two bonfires burning on the beach. They could have been signals for possible infiltrators. The cutter waited alertly in the darkness, waiting for the enemy to make his move. Then a radar contact with a metal-hulled

vessel brought the *Point Grey* into action. She challenged the vessel, forcing it aground. Instantly, the cutter was raked by intense fire from the beach. The cutter returned the fire with its machine guns and mortar. Soon other Market Time

A crewman on board the 82-foot patrol Cutter *Point Garnet* of Division 11, U.S. Coast Guard Squadron One, loads a 61 mm mortar during a firing demonstration in the Gulf of Thailand.

units arrived. The grounded enemy ship was hit by fire from the *Point Grey* and from the air. The assault was so heavy that the 125-foot enemy vessel was ripped apart by an internal explosion. Afterwards, salvage crews removed 15 tons of weapons and ammunition from her charred and shattered hull. About 80 tons of war materiel were destroyed by explosions.

The foregoing incident is typical of many other shoot-outs on coastal patrols. Sometimes a fanatically resisting enemy has resorted to such desperation measures as destroying his own vessels rather than surrender. In the five years of operation in Vietnam waters, the crews of the Coast Guard cutters became veterans. They learned to live with the possibility of sudden death.

They learned that the cardinal rule in Vietnam was never to let down one's defenses. To do so

Top: The 82-foot U.S. Coast Guard Cutter *Point League* stands off watching the burning 100-foot steel Viet Cong trawler that the cutter forced aground near the village of Ba Dong, South Vietnam, during several hours of gun battle to keep the enemy from entering Co Chien River on June 20, 1966. Fire began with an explosion on board the trawler at 6:15 a.m., and was extinguished at 2:00 p.m. by Coast Guard and Vietnamese crews. Salvage crews removed an estimated 250 tons of arms and supplies which the trawler attempted to infiltrate to Viet Cong ground forces. *Bottom:* While assigned to U.S. Coast Guard Squadron Three at South Vietnam, the 255-foot Cutter *Owasco* (WHEC-39) is seen unrepping with the USS *Guadalupe* (AO-32) after refueling from the Navy tanker during Market Time patrol.

Top: This unique "piggy-back" gun mount combines a .50 calibre machine gun and an 81 mm mortar. The mount was developed by the Coast Guard specifically for use in Vietnam. *Bottom: Point Slocum* on Vietnam patrol.

could mean quick death. They also found out that the enemy had many faces. He could be a waiter by day and a Viet Cong warrior by night. Frail-looking men and women, and occasionally children, could prove to be spies or terrorists. It was a war unique in the Coast Guard's and the Nation's experience.

But coastal surveillance was only one part of the Coast Guard's work. Several of its personnel were detailed to improve port security, especially in the port of Saigon which is highly vulnerable to infiltration and sabotage. The accelerated tempo of shipping to Vietnam had created major headaches for Vietnamese port officials, for their procedures were keyed to the more leisurely pace of French colonial days. Coast Guard experts helped to teach port workmen the basics of safe handling and loading of explosives and other dangerous cargoes. Other service personnel, helping to set up a modern aids to navigation system suited to the needs of today's shipping, installed lighted and unlighted buoys, and ranges and day beacons. Also a Loran (Long Range Aid to Navigation) network was constructed for U.S. and allied forces in Southeast Asia.

To handle disciplinary problems stemming from the growing numbers of merchant seamen in the port cities of the Republic of Vietnam, the Coast Guard created the post of Shipping Advisor to the U.S. Navy's Military Sea Transportation Service. It is a rigorous job, demanding almost continual travel from one trouble spot to another.

In February, 1969 the Coast Guard began "Vietnamizing" its operations in Southeast Asia. Through an innovative and highly successful plan designed to teach South Vietnamese Navy personnel how to operate the Coast Guard's 82-foot cutters, all 26 of these miniature men-of-war had been turned over to the Republic by mid-August, 1970. A similar training plan resulted in the turn-over of the cutters *Bering Strait* and *Yakutat* on January 1, 1971, and in turn-over of the cutters *Castle Rock* and *Cook Inlet* in December, 1971. These 311-foot vessels are now the capital ships of South Vietnam's budding Navy.

With the turn-over of *Castle Rock* and *Cook Inlet*, the Coast Guard ended its participation in Operation Market Time. After nearly six years and 5.5 million miles of combat patrol duty, the

Hazards of the Vietnam conflict included the ever-present danger of being trapped by the outgoing tide. For more than 24 hours in late 1968, the Cutter *Point Partridge*, pictured here, was a sitting duck for the enemy. Fortunately, she was refloated by the next tide and escaped without further incident.

Service could point to an impressive box score, including the completion of 5,975 successful gunfire support missions credited with: the killing or wounding in action of 1,721 enemy personnel; the destruction of 2,642 enemy junks, trawlers, and sampans; and damage or destruction of 9,687 enemy strongpoints. In contrast, the Coast Guard lost none of its own cutters, although seven heroic personnel lost their lives in action. Another 59 personnel were wounded in action.

During the same period, Coast Guard Explosives Loading Detachments supervised the safe loading of more than 5,000,000 tons of potentially destructive cargoes vital to the war effort. The token advisory forces which the Coast Guard presently retains in Vietnam continually add to the legacy of this stirring historical era for the Service.

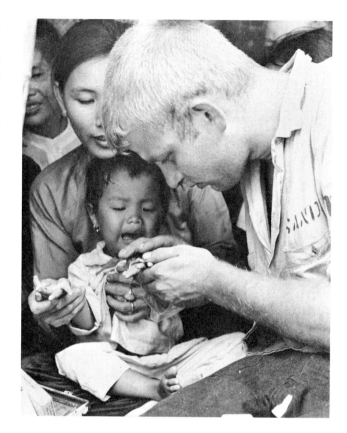

Right: Medical Corpsman rendering medical aid to a tiny Vietnam refugee.

Department of Transportation and Coast Guard Headquarters. This handsome edifice, the Nassif Building, is located at 400 Seventh Street SW, Washington, D.C. It was first occupied in spring 1970.

The Past Is Prologue

On April 1, 1967, the Coast Guard ended its 177-year association with the Treasury Department to enter the newly created Department of Transportation. It had seen the nation grow from a fledgling republic hugging the Atlantic seaboard to the mightiest power of the Free World. Its duties had proliferated to such an extent that the scope of its activities extended far beyond the continental limits of the United States. Despite its relatively small numbers, it had played a major part in the saga of American growth.

The creation of the new department was far more than a federal "houskeeping" operation, but represented a new direction in the federal government's approach to the problems of transportation. The urgency of these problems could no longer tolerate the fragmented approach of the past. Agencies charged with safety responsibilities for the various modes of transportation would now be housed in a single department where each component would contribute its expertise to the solution of problems and to the formulation of national policy. The Coast Guard represented the marine component of the department.

For the Coast Guard, the transfer had important implications. Not only had the Service changed its organizational base of operations, but it had entered a new frame of organizational reference which would shape its future development.

This gigantic rubber-coated bladder is a principal element of the Service's ADAPTS system.
Photo: UNIROYAL, Inc.

The Service moving into the new department was in no way diminished by the transfer. The legislation authorizing the move expressly stated that the Coast Guard's functions were to remain intact. That meant it would continue to be the nation's chief agency for marine safety and maritime law enforcement as well as one of the Armed Forces of the United States. The law also confirmed the Coast Guard's burgeoning program in marine science and research and technology.

As a matter of fact, two new functions were immediately added to the Coast Guard's duties. They were administration of the Great Lakes Pilotage Staff, and responsibility for safe clearances of bridges over navigable waters. The latter function previously had been under jurisdiction of the Army Corps of Engineers.

The Service which entered the Department of Transportation had changed substantially from the one of twenty years earlier. Its orientation was becoming increasingly scientific and technological. It had made striking advances in marine research, especially in the phenomena of far northern waters. Long before it was apparent to others, the Coast Guard had realized that knowledge of the oceans was more than a peripheral matter and essential to man's continued survival. Now in the latter years of the 20th century it was part of mankind's great adventure to probe the secrets of the deep and to preserve the quality of our environment from the pollutants constantly entering it.

The marine aspects of ecology, especially as they bear upon the problem of marine pollution, promised to be one of the most crucial sectors in the broadening effort to prevent environmental deterioration. The Coast Guard's work in this area continued to gain momentum, and in 1970 it allocated nearly 4.5 million dollars of its budget for Research and Development towards the control and reduction of marine pollution. Another four million dollars was requested for this purpose in the President's budget for fiscal 1971.

Currently, the Service is vigorously evaluating anti-pollution systems and techniques. They include application of infra-red, ultra-violet and micro-wave devices for the surveillance and detection of pollution. An Air Deliverable Anti-Pollution Transfer System (ADAPTS) tested in 1970, yielded promising results in combating pollution resulting from grounded tankers. Highly sensitive methods of detecting pollution are very important to prevent the discharge of ships' ballasts under cover of darkness. In addition to this

danger, it is estimated that about 7,500 accidental oil spills occur each year in U.S. waters alone. Each spill poisons the sea for months and even years. Contracts were awarded in 1970 for the development of prototype systems capable of containing and recovering oil on the high seas.

1970 also witnessed two coordinated major studies of pollution caused by oil spillage and by other dangerous substances. Legislative measures were also considered and recommendations forwarded to the President. The first of the studies dealt with pesticides, explosives, heavy metals and other materials. It was based on data obtained from 50 state and federal agencies and from industries manufacturing and transporting hazardous substances. Consideration was also given to information provided by conservation groups.

In the area of marine conservation, the Coast Guard continued to collaborate with the Interior Department in the enforcement of conservation treaties entered into between the United States and foreign governments. Mostly, the treaties deal with various species of marine life and seek to restrain excessive harvesting practices. This is a sector in which the Coast Guard has been active since the turn of the century.

The passage of Water Quality Improvement Act of 1970 gave the Coast Guard added responsibilities in an area of law enforcement in which it has been active for more than 70 years.

The battle against environmental deterioration has been joined, and the Coast Guard will prosecute its part of it with all of the energy at its command.

The Coast Guard's program to replace its aging fleet with vessels of the most modern design is continuing at a good pace. In September, 1971, its twelfth high endurance cutter, *Midgett*, was launched at Avondale Shipyards, New Orleans, Louisiana. Powered by 36,000 horsepower gas turbines, she has a cruising speed of 20 knots, a maximum speed of 29 knots and a cruising range of 14,000 miles. Nine of her sister ships have made proud records for themselves in active service, and wear battle ribbons for duty in Vietnam. On November 21, 1970, two of these fine cutters, *Rush* and *Sherman*, combined with the *USS Endurance* to sink a North Vietnamese trawler attempting to smuggle enemy arms into South Vietnam.

Since 1965, Coast Guard pilots flying "Jolly Green Giant" helicopters have helped to save the lives of numerous U.S. Air Force crews downed by the enemy in the Vietnam war. Nearly all these rescues took place in the jungle nowhere near the water.

The Coast Guard's air arm in 1970 continued to develop. Contracts were let for six more of the effective HH-3F "Pelican" helicopters to strengthen the existing fleet of 22. Another six of these aircraft were ordered in 1971. Deliveries for the 12 aircraft will start in calendar year 1972.

Traditionally interested in all means of improving navigation, the Coast Guard in 1971 made new progress towards the goal of reliable automation, compatible with reduced costs. Work went forward to develop a Loran "C" receiver which may eventually be available to pleasure boat operators for less than $2,000. Loran "C" is a refined low-frequency system originally conceived for Department of Defense use. It transmits at only 100 kilohertz and relies on the matching of carefully controlled frequencies. Its greatly expanded range nearly doubles the efficiency of the original Loran.

The navigation aids network operated currently by the Coast Guard consists of more than 50,000 devices, ranging all the way from simple daymarks to sophisticated Loran stations costing millions of dollars. The most promising aid to emerge in recent years is a navigational buoy designed to replace the lightships with their 16-man crews. These large navigational buoys (LNB's) represent a new generation of nautical signposts. They are disc-shaped, constructed of steel, 40 feet in diameter and 7-1/2 feet deep. The hull supports a 38-foot tower housing a 7,500 candlepower light, a fog signal and a radio beacon antenna which points the way electronically. It requires no crew and can perform effectively in a 13-foot sea churned up by a 60-knot wind in a temperature down to a frigid one degree Fahrenheit. Its cost is a modest $250,000 or about one-twelfth that of a lightship and it presents few maintenance problems.

The first of the LNB's made its debut at Sandy Hook, off the New Jersey coast. This versatile aid is used as a lighthouse where the bottom terrain is unsuitable for the construction of a building. The rapid advance of automation has reduced the number of manned lighthouses from about 400 at the turn of the century to less than 100 today. The lonely lighthouse keeper is fast fading into history.

The National Oceanographic Atmospheric Administration (NOAA), created in 1970 as an agency of the Department of Commerce, took over some functions formerly performed by the Coast Guard

Concern for the ecological impact of oil spills in the Arctic motivates the Coast Guard's studies in this remote part of the world. The growing oil needs of a heavily industrialized society highlight the importance of these testing procedures.

Top: Opening of the Arkansas River Waterway in 1971 has brought Coast Guard cutters to the states of Arkansas and Oklahoma for the first time. Pictured here is the small river tender *Patoka* stationed in Sallisaw, Oklahoma. *Bottom:* Coast Guard's new Air Cushion Vehicles (ACV's) *Hover 01* and *Hover 02*, demonstrate their high speed in a race with 82-foot *Point Chico* (MPB-82339) during evaluation tests off the coast of San Francisco.

and the two agencies will work closely together in the future. Much of the Service's basic research and developmental work has been made available to NOAA. The Coast Guard will also make available ships to support the work of the new agency.

A portent of what the future holds in store for navigation aids is the experimental Harbor Advisory Radar System (HAR) which is now being operated experimentally in San Francisco. HAR promises to reduce the incidence of collisions in congested operating areas. Electronic computers are a principal component of the HAR system. They are helping not only to improve traffic control but will also eventually make possible the automatic detection and simultaneous tracking of 500 targets by radar.

In the Coast Guard's never-ending war with the perils of the sea, search and rescue has always had a high priority. In a typical year, it saves more than 2,000 lives and assists in preserving property valued at about 3 billion dollars, or nearly six times its annual budget. 1971 was no exception in this regard. The Service responded to about 50,000 calls for assistance. Other statistics show that the Commercial Vessel Safety Program annually prevents 1,100 fatalities and 14,000 injuries while preserving about $150,000,000 in property. Outstanding progress also has been logged in recreational boating which is growing at a rate of more than 5,000 boats a week. Despite this increase, boating accidents have shown no increase, underscoring the effectiveness of the Coast Guard's program.

Under study are new prototype Search and Rescue (SAR) boats, 36 and 42 feet long. These craft were tested intensively during 1971. Faster than their predecessors, the new boats have aluminum hulls, and require less maintenance. Ultimately, it is anticipated that they will replace the Coast Guard's entire aging small-boat SAR fleet. The program will continue over a seven-year period.

SAR radar is also being dramatically improved and two experimental sets of radar are now being built specifically for Coast Guard uses. Initial tests will be conducted aboard a Coast Guard HC-130B aircraft. It is expected that the new equipment will be able to detect with pinpoint accuracy a 16-foot fibre-glass boat in five-foot waves at a distance of ten miles, even in moderate rain, fog or darkness. If the equipment performs with the accuracy expected, it will be one of the greatest breakthroughs ever attained in the difficult art of search and rescue, reducing aircraft search time by half. It is an exciting possibility with immense importance to the future of marine safety.

In a world reminiscent of science fantasy, the Coast Guard has pioneered in developing SAR vehicles. Satisfactory tests of an Air Cushioned Vehicle capable of 80 miles an hour were carried out in San Francisco Bay in 1970. The vehicle is powered by a jet engine. Efforts are now centering on the development of a motor surf boat(MRBX) for use in highly strenuous situations, such as those in the Columbia River bar in Oregon where a rapidly shallowing bottom generates violent waves.

All of the foregoing illustrates the ferment of activity and dynamism actuating today's Coast Guard. Many more brilliant accomplishments could be cited but what we have seen is enough to reveal the trend of its development and its promise for the future.

Yet in our preoccupation with facilities, it is imperative that we do not overlook the most important of all the Coast Guard's resources—its brave and dedicated men. Without them, no facilities, however ingenious, could accomplish their purpose. In early spring, 1972, Coast Guard personnel numbered approximately 5,600 civilians and 38,000 military men and women. They are the heart, the one indispensable resource of the Service. The world has changed greatly since the Coast Guard's first ten small cutters took to the ocean, but the quality of the personnel making up the Service is as high, perhaps higher, than ever. This augurs well for the future of the Service and the nation.

II
MISSIONS AND FACILITIES

Top: Hospital Point Light, Massachusetts. This structure dates back to the late 19th century. *Bottom:* A civilian worker at a Coast Guard Depot poses beside the largest and smallest buoys used by the Service in 1955.

Aids to Navigation

The Coast Guard's oldest mission, in terms of a federally provided public service, is that of aids to navigation. During the 180-plus years in which the U.S. has operated navigational aids for the benefit of its mariners, vast technological changes have taken place but the basic mission requirement has remained virtually unchanged. That mission, as stated in the ninth act ever passed by the U.S. Congress, included "the necessary support, maintenance and repairs of all lighthouses, beacons, buoys, and public piers at the entrance of, or within any bay, inlet, harbor, or port of the United States, for rendering the navigation thereof easy and safe . . .". Passed on August 7, 1789, the act gave the Secretary of the Treasury authority over existing navigational aids and anticipated the construction of new aids where necessary. The act also provided for federal expropriation of 12 lighthouses, seven unlighted buoys, and a few miscellaneous fog signals formerly operated by the colonial governments.

During the first few years of American independence, operating this small but growing system of navigational aids was an item of foremost national priority. This is clearly evidenced by the substantial number of historical documents relating to the system and bearing the signatures of such luminaries as George Washington, Alexander Hamilton, and Thomas Jefferson.

The first lighthouse built by the federal government was completed in 1792 at Cape Henry,

Left: A first order Fresnel lens developed for lighthouse illumination by the French physicist Augustin Fresnel in 1822, utilizing the refractive properties of glass to produce light beams. It represented one of the most important advances in aids to navigation. Photo: The National Archives. *Right:* Buoy tending in inland waters.

Top: Repairing electric lighted buoy, Gedney's Channel, N.Y., 1892. *Bottom:* The Lighthouse Tender *Crocus* which operated out of Detroit in the Great Lakes and U.S. Lighthouse Service is shown here tending old-time buoy.

Virginia. This project, however, had been originated by the Virginia colonial authorities. Montauk Point Light in New York was the first lighthouse for which Congress made a specific appropriation of funds. As is the case with many of these durable old structures, the Montauk tower, built in 1797, is still in service.

contemporaries. The venerable Fifth Auditor seems to have been both capable and conscientious but lighthouse administration was nothing short of deplorable. The country was simply growing too fast for the government to keep up with it. Aids were built to meet immediate and pressing local needs, without regard to any general system or

Left: Wolf Trap Light in Chesapeake Bay. *Right:* The Staten Island, N.Y., Rear Range is an example of Victorian architecture in lighthouse construction.

During the first thirty years which elapsed after lighthouses came under federal control, their numbers increased from 12 to 55. Supervision of the lights alternated between the Secretary of the Treasury and his Commissioner of Revenue, a policy which changed as periodic reorganizations occurred within the Treasury Department. In 1820, an act of Congress became effective which made the Fifth Auditor of the Treasury "General Superintendant of Lights." For nearly 33 years, Stephen Pleasanton, as Fifth Auditor, supervised all lighthouse affairs.

No matter how severely bureaucratic inefficiency may be criticized today, general government administration has improved dramatically since the days of Pleasanton and his

plan. Although lighthouse keepers' jobs were neither sinecures nor especially lucrative, they were dispensed through political patronage, and were apparently in great demand. Many well qualified, dedicated men served as keepers during this period but tenure was entirely subject to political vicissitudes.

For many years the supply, and even the inspection of the lighthouses was performed mainly by contract. Under this system the contractors virtually administered the lighthouse organization, exercising wide discretion in performing their contracts. In 1835 a contractor changed Mobile Point Light from a fixed to a revolving light without previous instructions. Sub-letting of contracts was commonly practiced, so that in many instances those actually engaged in the lighthouse work were not directly responsible to the government.

Buoys were a major source of complaint. Without any uniform system of shape, color, or placement, they were often more confusing than helpful. Nevertheless, like "Topsy," the unwieldy

A major step forward occurred in 1843 when a qualified civil engineer was detailed to inspect the seventy-odd lighthouses along the New England coast. This was the first instance in which an engineer had been employed in an important capacity on behalf of the service. His report indicated the desirability for changes in both the

Left: Cape Hatteras Light on North Carolina's outer banks. *Right:* The Coast Guard's most modern lighthouse is this 163-foot structure in Charleston, South Carolina. It consists of a concrete foundation supporting a steel frame surrounded by porcelainized aluminum panels. It is the only lighthouse in the U.S. equipped with an elevator.

system "just grew." By 1840 there were 234 lighthouses compared to scarcely more than 50 when Pleasanton took charge. More than 900 lesser aids were in service. Lightships, which had been introduced in this country in 1820 now numbered 30. 1840 also marked the year when the Lighthouse Establishment acquired its first seagoing tender, the former revenue cutter *Rush.*

The expansion had brought no improvement in efficiency and criticism began to pour into Washington. Among the most influential critics were the publishers of *Blunt's Coast Pilot,* who wrote the Secretary of the Treasury that "the whole lighthouse system needs revision, a strict superintendence, and an entirely different plan of operation."

Service's illuminating apparatus and its administration. Two years later, Treasury Secretary Walker succeeded in having two officers of the Navy sent to Europe to procure any information which might be useful in improving the lighthouse system of the U.S. The report developed from this investigation pointed out quite clearly that the U.S. system was far inferior to those of most European countries. A number of constructive proposals were included in the report, but Congress failed to react.

In 1850, the situation improved markedly with the passage of a law establishing a systematic marking system for buoys. From that date forth, pilots of inbound vessels could, with assurance, pass even-numbered red buoys on the starboard hand and odd-numbered black buoys on the port.

Other special situations were covered by the establishment of appropriate standardized markings.

The most significant administrative changes of the era came with the creation of the first Lighthouse Board in 1851. Composed of two senior officers of the Navy, two of the Army Corps of Engineers, two civilian scientists, and a junior Navy officer who served as Secretary, the Board immediately brought sweeping improvements to the Service. Many well remembered figures in history graced the Board during its 59 years of existence, including Admiral George B. Dewey, Admiral W. B. Shubrick, future Civil War Generals Meade and Beauregard, and the distinguished Smithsonian Institution scientist, Joseph Henry.

A technological revolution was underway. The famous prismatic lenses originated by the French physicist, Augustin Fresnel, were installed throughout the lighthouse system by 1859. Barrel-stave and solid wooden buoys, which had hardly changed since colonial days, soon gave way to durable metal structures with the new standardized markings. Bell buoys appeared in 1855, followed by whistle buoys in 1876. A marvel of the age—the steam fog signal—was introduced in 1857. Geographical expansion also began to accelerate. The first Pacific lighthouse was completed on Alcatraz Island California in 1854. Responsibility for maintaining and operating navigation aids was extended to the Mississippi, Ohio, and Missouri Rivers in 1874.

Technological changes in illuminating agents were somewhat slower in coming. Burning agents such as whale oil and rapeseed oil were inexpensive, reliable, and generally quite adequate. Kerosene, when introduced around 1877, proved so very cheap and efficient that it continued as a lighthouse illuminant long after electricity appeared on the scene. Indeed, a 1926 report on the Lighthouse Service discusses the replacement of cotton mantles by silk ones in a section highlighting major recent improvements. The Lighthouse Board never hesitated to experiment, although it was completely pragmatic in its approach. In 1888, the Board attempted the lighting of a buoy by electricity. Three years later the project was abandoned as impractical; the electric cable kept breaking. In 1910 the first lighted buoys employing acetylene proved to be an overwhelming success.

When the Lighthouse Board was abolished on June 17, 1910 it could take credit for having lifted the U.S. Lighthouse Service from a formless, inefficient source of bureaucratic embarrassment to an organization generally considered to be the finest of its kind in the world. Previously, in 1903, the Service had been transferred from the Treasury Department to the Department of Commerce and Labor.

Undoubtedly, there were some who must have been apprehensive about the prospect of replacing the highly esteemed Lighthouse Board with a single Commissioner. If so, they underestimated the worth of the first appointee, George R. Putnam, who served continuously until 1935. Putnam proved to be a superb administrator who genuinely loved his work. If his efficiency as Commissioner was impaired in any way, it was as a result of his wonderfully humane conscience which rebelled at inequities in the Lighthouse Service personnel system of that day. When Putnam took office, Lighthouse Service employees were not covered by federal retirement pension laws. Putnam immediately resolved that he would never turn a man or woman—however old or feeble—out of a job until he or she could draw a proper retirement pension. It was a dangerous game Putnam was playing, and he fully recognized the risks. Retaining employees beyond their productive years definitely contributed to inefficiency within the system. After nine shaky years, Congress finally relented and Lighthouse Service employes at last received the retirement perquisites which should have been theirs all along.

Putnam's 25-year administration was remarkable, both for its economies and its innovations. During its first 17 years, the number of aids to navigation in U.S. waters doubled. Yet, through an automation program which was years before its time, personnel numbers during the same period actually decreased by 200. Improved construction techniques within the period also allowed a net decrease of 9 lightships, the Service's most costly aids in terms of acquisition as well as maintenance. The radio beacon, introduced in 1921, soon became one of the Service's most important navigational aids.

In 1939, when President Franklin D. Roosevelt announced the transfer of the Bureau of Lighthouses to the Coast Guard, it came as a surprise to many in both organizations. Even during the 114 years in which the two Services had served together in the Treasury Department, there had been little contact between them. During the mid-1800's, in fact, the cutters had received orders *not* to assist in the supply of Lighthouse Service facilities except in emergencies. Viewed through the perspective of time the consolidation of the two Services seems completely logical. The central aim of each—preserving the safety of life and property at sea—was strongly reinforced by combining forces with the other. Transitional phases of the merger progressed so smoothly that most doubts about the wisdom of the move were quickly dispelled.

Equipped today, with a modern arsenal of navigational aids designed for both civil and military use, the Coast Guard has made U.S. waters the safest of any nation. Lighthouses, buoys, and fog signals are at least as important as they were in 1789. They are now complemented with navigational wonders such as the Service's worldwide system of Loran stations. Research continues in the effort to provide the public with even better services. One device, presently being evaluated, is a type of Radar beacon with many possible applications. It can be used to indicate the center line of a channel passing beneath a bridge, or to single out important buoys and landmarks for use as reference points. In many instances, colorful but costly old lightships have been replaced with more

economical offshore towers or gigantic automated buoys. A Harbor Advisory Radar System, which has already been satisfactorily tested in San Francisco, promises to provide improved marine traffic control in major ports and harbors.

The Department of Transportation, to which the Coast Guard was transferred in 1967, issued in the spring of 1970 a "National Plan for Navigation" in which the Coast Guard figures quite prominently. A major goal of the plan is the establishment of a highly accurate navigational system for the coastal/confluence zone. Two systems under consideration for this purpose are modifications of the Loran program presently operated by the Coast Guard. A third, *Omega*, is a system in which the Service is playing an active research and development role.

There are only a few personnel left in the Coast Guard who began their service with the old Lighthouse Service. Those remaining are proud to be Coast Guardsmen, and will vouch for the fact that their service is providing aids to navigation services in this country which are second to none.

The 157-foot coastal buoy tender *Red Birch* is representative of one of the Coast Guard's most important new classes of aids to navigation vessels. *Red Birch* was constructed at the Coast Guard Yard in Curtis Bay, Maryland. She is stationed in San Francisco.

Boston Light Station, A National Historical Landmark

On July 23, 1715, less than a year after George I was crowned King of England, his loyal subjects in the Province of the Massachusetts Bay passed an act calling for establishment of a lighthouse on Little Brewster Island at the entrance to Boston Harbor. Thus was born the vast system of navigational aids operated by the Coast Guard today. After more than 250 years of service, Boston Light is still an important part of that system.

The bill which authorized the light's construction was the first lighthouse act ever passed by a legislative body in the Western Hemisphere. Not for another 74 years was the U.S. Congress to pass a bill for similar purposes. In fact, when its first light was kindled on September 14, 1716, there were few lighthouses to be found anywhere in the world. Even England's historic Eddystone Light preceded the light at Boston by only 18 years.

In its early days the light was supported by a user tax so reasonable and logical that today's legislators might learn from its rationale. Vessels using the harbor were required to pay an impost of

On a rocky promontory, little changed since Revolutionary times, stands the famous Boston Lighthouse. The present light is the descendant of a primitive beacon erected early in the 18th century.

a penny for each ton of cargo transported, both entering and departing.

Young Benjamin Franklin scored his first success as a writer when the light's first keeper, George Worthylake, was drowned with his wife and daughter while attempting to return to the island during a storm. Franklin, only 13 at the time, commemorated the calamity with a dolorous ballad called, "Lighthouse Tragedy." The ballad was printed by Ben's brother and sold in the streets of Boston, where it found a ready market.

During its first 40 years of existence the structure was damaged by fire on several occasions, which is hardly surprising since its light was produced by an open flame burning in a wooden lantern. The lantern was finally reconstructed of metal after a particularly disastrous fire in 1751. A higher tonnage tax was enacted to defray repair costs.

As a point of contention during the Revolutionary War, the light was badly damaged by both sides. While occupied by the British, an American attacking force burned the lighthouse's wooden parts. The British attempted repairs, but

these were undone when another group of American raiders struck on July 31, 1775. When the British were finally driven out of Boston on June 13, 1776 they vindictively destroyed the light with a timed explosive charge. In 1783 the structure was restored and a new keeper was appointed.

In 1813 keeper Jonathan Bruce and his wife witnessed the famous battle between the American *Chesapeake* and the British *Shannon*. It was in this encounter that the mortally wounded Captain Lawrence uttered the immortal words, "Don't give up the ship."

The story of Boston Light is also the story of lighthouse technology. From the tallow candles which provided the structure's first source of light, there followed a continuous succession of improvements: the addition of a cannon which served as the nation's first fog signal; Argand lamps fueled by fish oil, sperm whale oil, lard, and, finally, kerosene; crude parabolic reflectors to concentrate the light's rays; a Fresnel lens in 1859 to concentrate the rays more efficiently; and in the late 1800's, a lamp which burned vaporized kero-

The lighthouse tender *Holly* at Point No Point Light, 1910.

sene. Not until 1948 was the light electrified. The Fresnel lens, with modifications, is still in use.

Keepers of the light have participated in a number of spectacular rescues over the years. Perhaps the most dramatic of these occurred on

To warn mariners of the deadly hazards posed by rocks and shoals in the area, an auxiliary light was built in 1890. It uses a white light to indicate the fairway, with red lights on either side indicating danger zones.

Since 1795, a light has been maintained by the U.S. Lighthouse Service and later, the U.S. Coast Guard at Montauk Point at the east end of Long Island, New York.

February 3, 1918 when the *USS Alacrity* was wrecked on the ice-covered ledges off the island. Keeper Charles H. Jennings and his men fought ice, rocks, and freezing surf in the station's dory during the four separate passages required to save the ship's personnel.

Today's light has 1.8 million candlepower and rises 102 feet above the water. It also has a diaphragm fog signal giving two blasts every sixty seconds during fog.

On May 13, 1964 Boston Light Station was designated a National Historic Landmark.

Lightships

Nantucket

Coast Guard service is inherently dangerous. Whether battling mountainous seas in a peacetime rescue mission or facing hostile fire in combat, almost any career Coast Guardsman, within the space of twenty years of service, will find himself in one or more operational situations where his life is in jeopardy. Curiously, the most dangerous duty in the Coast Guard is neither on board a rescue cutter nor a man of war. It is on board the Service's quaint little red lightships, which were never designed to do anything more than remain anchored in one spot, while serving as floating navigational aids for ships at sea.

Lightships are very much a part of American history. The first one established in the U.S. was off Craney Island in Chesapeake Bay. It was stationed there in 1820, nearly a century after the first British lightship, the *Nore*, was established at the mouth of the Thames. Since their inception in all parts of the world, lightships have represented concessions to technological limitations. Had the construction of conventional lighthouses in offshore waters been economically feasible in those early years, it is likely that we might never have constructed any of these picturesque oddities. And in fact, they have always been engineering anachronisms, in the process of being replaced by superior hardware capable of doing the same job for less money. In 1909, at the height of their popularity, U.S. lightships numbered 56. Successive engineering innovations such as screw-pile and caisson light structures in the 1860's, offshore towers in the 1960's, and the large navigational buoys which herald the progress of the 70's have all contributed to the lightships' declining numbers. Today, only a handful of the historic old ships remain in service, and most of them will soon be replaced by large navigational buoys (LNB's).

At least one lightship figures to be around for many years to come, however. She is *Nantucket*, manning a station with an incredible past and unpredictable future.

The first lightship stationed in Nantucket Sound bore the name *Davis South Shoal*. A tiny wooden craft, equipped with no means of locomotion other than a single staysail, she was towed to her place of anchorage in 1854. Anchored in 100 feet of often stormy water, she became at once what *Nantucket* still is today—the farthest offshore lightship in the world. But, she didn't remain offshore for long. Within less than six months, a raging New England blizzard snapped her anchor chain and tossed her unceremoniously up on the beach at Montauk Point, Long Island. Miraculously, her crew escaped to serve on other ships in other storms.

In 1856, the persistent U.S. Lighthouse Service sent out a new lightship to flash its warning from Nantucket Shoals. For the next thirty-odd years the new ship—now named *Nantucket*—weathered storms in a more sedate fashion. The chief hazard experienced by her crew during this period seems to have been her huge lantern's unfortunate propensity to occasionally topple from its clumsy rigging on the mast. A few lives were lost, and more than a few bones were broken as a result of these frequent accidents on board lightships of that era. Minor conflagrations usually accompanied the incidents, as burning whale oil spilled on wooden decks.

In 1892, bad luck struck the Nantucket Station with renewed vengeance. The year had hardly begun when a violent gale swept the powerless, 103-foot vessel from her mooring. For nine agonizing days she bobbed about helplessly in towering seas, before grounding at last off Gays Head near Martha's Vineyard. The worst was yet to come. Just three months later, on March 11, her anchor chain again parted in the midst of one of history's most extraordinary snowstorms. For days the blizzard continued unabated and all hope for the ship and her crew was abandoned. A few grizzled mariners who had successfully reached port through the storm swore they had seen some glimpse of the frail red craft, causing newspapers to speculate she had become another *Flying Dutch-*

man. Then, two weeks to the day after her disappearance, *Nantucket* was sighted rolling in the surf off "No Man's Land," an area as forbidding as the name indicates. Her crew members were half-starved and nearly dead from the miseries they had endured, but every man survived. The battered ship was taken in for repairs and never again manned Nantucket Station. Returned to service almost immediately, the spunky little cutter manned other light stations until finally decommissioned in 1930. She was 74 years old!

succeeded in taking *58* in tow after hours of arduous effort. It was to no avail. Perhaps the old ship simply yielded to an inevitable fate long decreed for the lightships of Nantucket. *No. 58's* crew abandoned her a few moments before she vanished forever beneath New England's dreaded graveyard of dead ships.

World War I brought new hazards for the lightships. One of *Nantucket's* southern sisters, *Diamond Shoals Lightship*, off the coast of North Carolina, was blown apart and sunk by a German

A U.S. Coast Guard HO4S-2G helicopter picks up ailing seaman by hydraulically hoisted basket out of a small boat from *Nantucket Shoals Lightship.*

After 1892, it was universally agreed that Nantucket Station was jinxed. The past 80 years have done nothing to dispel that belief. A relief light vessel, *No. 58*, broke her anchor chain during storms in both 1895 and 1896, drifting aimlessly for 65 miles on the latter occasion in spite of her "modern" steam propulsion plant. The same helpless ship developed a serious leak during a fierce gale in 1905. The tender *Azalea* fought her way through the heavy seas to offer assistance and

submarine. The gallant U-boat commander first warned the ship's personnel of his intentions and gave them ample time to make their escape before carrying out his plan.

For *Nantucket*, the war presented problems of another sort. A vicious, marauding sub, the infamous *U-53*, sank six merchant vessels, while operating in *Nantucket's* immediate vicinity. *U-53's* brazen commander had actually anchored in Newport, Rhode Island harbor, and gone ashore to

Top: Bush Bluff Lightship was stationed in Virginia's Elizabeth River during the early 1900's. Like most of her kind, she has long since been replaced by less expensive but superior technology. *Bottom:* This *Diamond Shoals Lightship* was sunk by a German submarine in World War I.

buy newspapers listing merchant vessel sailings, before proceeding with his ruthless mission. The U.S., at the time, was observing a state of "neutrality." At one time during the two-day action, *Nantucket* was a place of refuge for 115 survivors of *U-53's* depredations.

The war years spelled a different kind of disaster for one of *Nantucket's* neighbors, *Cross Rip Lightship*, in Vineyard Sound. During the abnormally severe winter of 1917, *Cross Rip* became frozen fast in threatening ice floes. Her skipper risked his life to walk across the perilous ice to seek help. His unconscionable superiors ordered him to return to his ship "and get back to duty." Two days later, clutching *Cross Rip* like a massive, frigid vise, the ice pack moved out to sea with its helpless prey. Ship and crew perished in the tumultuous Atlantic.

By 1934, the ship bearing the name *Nantucket* was distinguished by her advanced technology. Her steel hull displaced 630 tons. Her habitability standards were second to none. Her light could be seen for 14 miles. She was powered by a sophisticated diesel-electric propulsion system. Best of all, she was outfitted with the latest thing in electronics equipment—a radio beacon which would allow ships at sea to take lines of bearing or even home on her position if they so desired. Until merchant mariners learned how to properly use radio beacons, the new electronic devices posed a greater threat to the lightships than had all the storms in history.

Radio beacons were great! As long as a mariner's radio direction finder pointed to 000 degrees relative, he was steering directly for the lightship. Too many feckless mariners failed to consider that steering directly for an object over prolonged periods of time may cause one to collide with that object. On January 6, 1934, the United States Line's *Washington* came within inches of sending the new *Nantucket* to a watery grave. The liner scraped *Nantucket's* side, shearing off davits, a lifeboat, antennas, and other protruding appurtenances. For Captain George Braithwaite, *Nantucket's* 70-year-old skipper, the *Washington* collision was a little too close for comfort. Imagine the old seafarer's distress then, when five months later, the 50,000-ton liner *Olympic* came slicing through *Nantucket's* midsection at a speed of 16 knots! Captain Braithwaite and three of his men were saved. Seven others died in the tragedy. During the newspaper coverage of this sad disaster one enterprising statistician reported that if all the vessels lost in the Nantucket Shoals since recorded history were resurrected and floated bow to stern, they would stretch from Florida to Maine.

Nantucket is not the only lightship to have suffered the helpless humiliation of a collision. *Boston Lightship* was practically split in half by a collision in 1935. Her well-trained crew saved the ship by listing her over until water was no longer pouring in the fissure in her side. *Ambrose Lightship* was struck by other ships no less than four times within the 56 years of her existence. In 1960, a relief lightship on Ambrose Station was rammed and sunk by the freighter *Green Bay*. The lightship's eleven crewmen were rescued.

Modern-day storms have continued to hurl their wrath at poor little *Nantucket* and her lightship neighbors. Because of the United States' unfortunate experiences with U-boats during World War I, and because of *Nantucket's* exposed position, the station was temporarily placed on inactive status during World War II. The War quite possibly prevented the sinking of still another *Nantucket*. For, as *Nantucket* was tucked away safely in Portland harbor, her sister ship, *Vineyard Sound Lightship*, sank during the devastating September hurricane of 1944. Boatswain Edgar Sevigny and his crew of eleven were killed. The 1944 storm also sank two of the Coast Guard's 125-foot cutters, the *Bedloe* and *Jackson*.

Ten years later, *Nantucket* was back on station when Hurricanes "Carol" and "Edna" stormed through New England. "Edna", with her 110 mph winds and 70-foot seas was particularly hard on *Nantucket*, smashing her steel-plated flying bridge and pilothouse, destroying her rudder and steering gear, and generally demolishing every exposed object on the ship. The buoy tender *Hornbeam*, which would later win fame in her rescue of *Andrea Doria* survivors, got underway during "Edna's" height to rescue *Nantucket* and her crew.

Lightships are the most picturesque navigational aids operated by the Coast Guard. They are also the most expensive to build, maintain, and operate. The case against their continued service is an overwhelming one, the Coast Guard is well along with a program which will eventually place large navigational buoys at almost every site now occupied by a lightship. *Nantucket* is not yet earmarked for such replacement. If and when *Nantucket* is replaced by a buoy or other aid, however, Coast Guardsmen around the world can sleep easier with the knowledge that they will never have to serve on what history has proven to be the Coast Guard's most dangerous station.

Offshore Towers

Chesapeake Light Station

Generations of Coast Guard seagoing experience and much fine engineering went into the construction of this offshore structure, standing its lonely watch over the approaches to Chesapeake Bay. For the Coast Guard, the tower represented a revolutionary departure from its familiar lightships

The Chesapeake Offshore Light Structure stands in 38 feet of water about 14½ miles east of Cape Henry, Va. It is located about three miles from the site of the former *Chesapeake Lightship*.

which performed so faithfully in their century and a half of operation. In designing the towers, the Coast Guard sought to create a multi-purpose navigation aid, serving not only as a beacon for oceangoing ships, but also as a launching platform for helicopters and as a point of oceanographic research.

But like most modern technological advances, the tower did not come cheap. Its construction cost the Coast Guard about $2,000,000 when it was built in the early 1960's. Chances are that such a structure would be even more expensive in today's inflated economy.

Placed in operation in September, 1965, the Chesapeake tower has done all that has been

demanded of it and has managed to resist the relentless pounding of the sea and the often harsh weather of the Chesapeake area. The tower has been in every way worthy of the fine tradition established by the *Chesapeake Lightship* a picturesque and familiar navigational mark for nearly 35 years.

What are some of the advantages of the offshore tower? Only six men are required to operate it as contrasted with the 15 crewmen on a lightship. Ultimately it is expected that the Light Station will, through personnel and maintenance economies, pay for itself in its first 30 years of operation out of a total expected life of about 75 years. Life on a tower is far more pleasant than in a cramped and pitching lightship. To the anxious mariner, the tower provides a light visible up to sixteen miles away. Approaching aircraft can spot the light a hundred miles away. An advanced engineering prototype, the tower beacon is similar to an enormous photographic strobe light. It consists essentially of slender glass tubes filled with xenon gas, and is rated at 6 million candlepower for high intensity operation. Provisions have also been made for reduced illumination at 600,000 candlepower.

Screw-pile lights, such as this one at Thomas Point, Maryland, were early forerunners of today's offshore towers.

The xenon flash configuration has proved to be a highly effective innovation. Actual electric power required to produce the desired candlepower is far less than that of a conventional light.

From the bottom of its heavy steel pilings to its uppermost antenna, the tower is over 400 feet in height, the light proper being 131 feet above the average low water line. In addition to its powerful light, the tower also houses a fog signal with a ten-mile range and a radio beacon useable up to a rainwater catchment system on the roof. The roof, heavily reinforced with steel, also serves as a landing pad for helicopters on search and rescue missions and in the transfer of men and supplies.

Chesapeake Lightship sounds a blast of her whistle, bidding farewell to her offshore tower replacement.

distance of 70 miles. As a distinctive daymark for piloting, the station can be seen for a distance of nearly 15 miles during periods of good visibility.

Tanks beneath the tower's air-conditioned housing contain a four-month supply of fuel and water. The fuel is replenished periodically by Coast Guard cutters, but the water is provided by a

Life can be a bit lonely and monotonous on a tower, but this is softened somewhat by an excellently equipped and supplied galley and spacious living quarters, including television and other amenities. All things considered, the Coast Guard has succeeded in making the towers as much "a home away from home" as is possible.

Loran Stations

Kure Island

One of the most popular misconceptions about the Coast Guard is that the service's operations are confined to the coastal waters of the United States. Nothing could be further from the truth. Ocean Stations and military missions take Coast Guardsmen far from their home bases, and few federal agencies of any description can boast of a mission so global in concept as Loran.

All over the free world, at sites as varied as Germany, Thailand, Turkey and Iceland, Coast Guard Loran stations beam their signals for the navigational assistance of ships and planes. The names of many of these stations sound like something from a travel agent's sales pitch. Indeed, personnel fortunate enough to be assigned to one or more of the Service's choice locations, such as

A 625-foot Loran antenna towers above tiny Kure Atoll.

Spain or Japan, may regard Loran duty a year's vacation at government expense. For the vast majority of Coast Guard veterans, however, Loran is a word which conjures up dreadful visions of loneliness and privation hardly found outside a penal colony.

Until 1960, Kure Atoll's human inhabitants had always been unfortunate shipwrecked mariners who had fallen victim to its treacherous reef and

supply point. It is surrounded by an extremely hazardous reef which has been the ruin of an untold number of ships over the ages. Still another, a large seagoing tug, was lost during the station's construction. There was no fresh water supply and the island's solid coral structure is not about to yield any. The island is only 3/4 mile long and 1/2 mile wide, a challenge for any plane to land on, even after a runway had been cleared.

Not all Loran stations are as dull as Kure. In this photo, native girls perform a ceremonial dance at the dedication of a Coast Guard Loran station on the island of Yap, in the Carolines.

currents. Then the Coast Guard decided to build a Loran station there. By Loran construction standards the location was almost ideal. Kure was far enough away from civilization for its powerful electronic transmissions to radiate out into space without fear of creating commercial radio and TV interference. And it was properly aligned, in a geographical sense, with other proposed Loran sites at Johnston Island and Hawaii. These very features complicated construction, of course, but constructing a Loran station is seldom an easy task.

Kure was particularly difficult. It lies some 1,200 miles from Honolulu, the nearest major

Dynamite was used to blast a passage through the reef for the first construction barges. The barges carried heavy equipment which was immediately set to work clearing a runway so that the bulk of the station's electronics equipment could be air-freighted in by Coast Guard HC-130.

Perhaps the most perplexing problem facing the station's first crew was the endemic animal population: about 4,000 unusual birds, 300 rare Hawaiian Monk Seals, and incredibly, a quarter of a million rats! Like modern Robinson Crusoes the first Coast Guardsmen on Kure lived a very primitive existence. While permanent quarters were being constructed they slept in tents, bathed in a salt-water lagoon, and answered calls of nature behind the sand dunes. Each of these functions was complicated by the omnipresent rats. With typical Coast Guard ingenuity, the crew soon erected a

A Coast Guard seaman reads Loran charts at Con Son Loran Station, Vietnam. The charts tell whether the station's beacons are operating properly.

crude shower fashioned from two oil drums and an improbable assortment of piping. The sand dunes soon gave way to an old-fashioned outhouse, but not until dynamite was used to blast out a pit for it.

At last the rats became so intolerable that all-out war was declared. Armed with shovels, axe handles, and other available implements, the crew literally spent weeks in their extermination attempt. When

the rats' numbers had been thinned to the point that such direct methods were no longer effective, poison was finally shipped in with lasting and gratifying results.

After six months of tent dwelling the crew moved into modern and comfortable permanent quarters. Today's crew enjoys semi-private rooms and a wide array of recreational equipment, including a pool table, a boat for water skiing, and a fine stereophonic sound system. The station is also a skin diver's paradise, although sharks, barracuda, and moray eels abound within the reef.

There is plenty of work for the station crew now that the station's transmitters and timers are in operation. A 24-hour watch is required for the Loran equipment. Electronics technicians are the personnel backbone of a Loran station. On Kure, ET's stand watches or work as equipment repairmen on a rotating basis. Of course, when a major breakdown occurs, everyone pitches in. Loran stations take pride in their percentage of on-air time, and most can boast of averages well exceeding 95%.

During a one-year duty tour on a Loran station a man can develop many new interests: seashell collecting, bird-banding, amateur radio, writing, skindiving, or even self-analysis. None of these will ever replace wife, home, or family but a surprising number of Loran station personnel elect to extend their tours of duty. For the average man, though, a year away from girls, liquor, and the comforts of home is more than enough.

Loran—A Layman's Explanation

A man whose travels have been confined to land cannot begin to appreciate the problems which face the average seagoing navigator. For a land-locked motorist, traffic or confusing masses of road signs at a cloverleaf interchange are occasionally frustrating, but the most serious navigational problem he is likely to encounter is simply figuring out how to refold an awkward highway map.

The nautical navigator is much less fortunate. Coast Guard buoys and lighthouses mark the way in and out of ports, but once beyond sight of land, one sees nothing but miles and miles of nondescript ocean.

Until slightly more than 25 years ago a good chronometer and sextant were the best navigational tools available to the mariner. Under ideal conditions these instruments could deliver very precise navigational information, but the navigator was still faced with several intrinsic problems. For one thing, the amount of time necessary to take a series of celestial observations, to engage in the laborious computations necessary to solve them, and to plot the resultant information on a chart is excessive by any standard. Also aggravating is the relatively brief period of time available for celestial sights. Star sights can only be taken at twilight. Worst of all is the unpredictability of the weather. It is not uncommon to be at sea for several days on end without seeing the sun or any other celestial body. Obviously, celestial fixes are impossible under these circumstances.

During World War II, Coast Guard electronics engineers began developing theories which were to reach fruition in the vast Loran complex the service operates today; theories which were to overcome the navigator's dependence on lengthy mathematical solutions and whims of the weather. The theory is soundly based on one of the most immutable of all scientific phenomena—light and radio waves travel at a speed of 186,000 miles per second.

To initiate the Loran cycle a controlling station, designated as the "master," transmits a pulsed signal which is radiated in all directions. The signal proceeds along a straight line until it is received by a secondary unit called the "slave" station. Simultaneously, the signal travels to the position of any ship or aircraft in the area which may be equipped with a Loran receiver. At the receiver site, the signal is converted to a visual trace displayed on the face of an oscilloscope, a device which resembles a small TV screen in appearance. The slave station also receives the master's signal, waits a specified time (referred to as a coding delay), and then transmits a pulsed signal of its own. This signal is picked up by the receiving station, where it appears as a second trace on the oscilloscope. The Loran receiver is arranged in such a way that the master signal appears as the upper trace on the scope, while the slave signal appears below and slightly to the right of the master. Rotating a series of control knobs on the Loran receiver activates complex electronic counting circuits similar to those used in early binary computers. The controls are used to position the slave signal directly below the master, and then to superimpose the two signals. When this evolution has been performed by the receiver operator, he records a number from a direct-reading counter on the set. This number indicates how many millionths of a second (micro-seconds) transpire between the time a master signal reaches a receiver site and the slave signal triggered by that master signal arrives at the same point. With this information in hand, the receiver operator then consults an especially printed Loran chart of the general area he is in. The chart is over-printed with numerous hyperbolic lines, each of which represents a Loran time difference. The lines are labeled in micro-seconds. By matching his reading with the lines on the chart, the operator determines that his position is located somewhere along one of the lines. Since the lines usually extend for vast distances, however, a single line with no amplifying information is virtually valueless. By taking readings on two or more master-slave combinations, though, the operator can determine his position with great precision.

Navigational accuracy is only one of the advantages offered by Loran. Operation of the receivers is almost incredibly simple. Experienced operators seldom require more than two or three minutes to establish a position. The system is nearly independent of weather. Finally, Loran is usable at daytime ranges of up to 750 nautical miles and night-time ranges of almost double that figure. Another version of the system, called Loran "C," offers accuracy to within 1/4 mile, even at ranges in excess of 3,000 miles from the transmitting station. The "C" system was principally designed for use in defense and space programs, but the Coast Guard is attempting to develop inexpensive receivers which could be used by the general public.

Loran, as much as any other Coast Guard mission area, makes a vital contribution to the safety of life and property at sea.

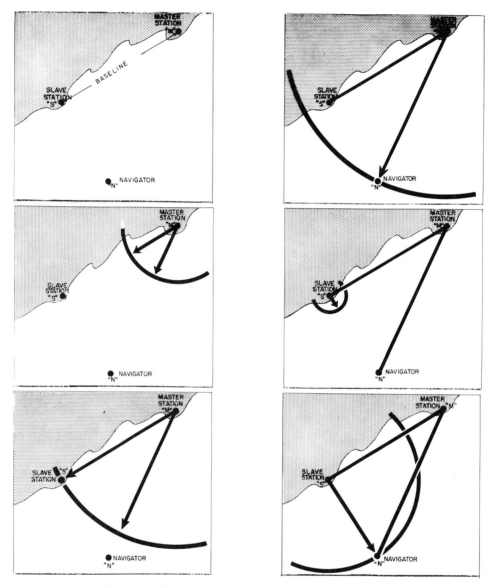

Sequence of operation of Loran transmitting stations.

Left (top to bottom): **Step I**—Navigator aboard ship at "N" is within range of stations "M" and "S" and is about to receive Loran signals. **Step II**—Loran transmission cycle is begun by "master" station. Pulse is radiated in all directions and travels toward both "slave" station and navigator. **Step III**—Pulse transmitted by "master" station arrives at "slave" but has not yet reached the navigator. *Right (top to bottom):* **Step IV**—Pulse from "master" station arrives at position of navigator. "Slave" station has already received "master" pulse and is waiting for proper amount of time to elapse before transmitting to assure correct synchronization with "master." **Step V**—After waiting for the proper amount of time to assure correct synchronization, the "slave" transmits its pulse. The navigator has already received the pulse from the "master" station. **Step VI**—"Slave" pulse arrives at navigator's position. Since navigator has already received the signal from the "master" station, Loran reading is taken by measuring the time elapsed between the arrival of the master and slave pulses. After both signals have travelled throughout their effective range, the cycle is repeated.

Cape Flattery Light Station

The founding of Boston Light Station in 1716 began a tradition of lighthouse keeping by entire families which has continued to the present day. To be sure, the tradition has faded considerably since the early days when virtually every station was tended by a keeper, his wife, and their children. The tradition was curtailed quite abruptly, in fact, when the Lighthouse Service merged with the Coast Guard in 1939. Nevertheless, the tradition still survives at a handful of scattered locations, one of the most interesting of which is Cape Flattery, Washington.

Tatoosh Island, the site of Cape Flattery Station, rises up dramatically and precipitately from the Pacific Ocean floor, only about three miles from the Washington mainland. The sheer stone sides of the rugged island jut upward nearly a

hundred feet before leveling into a relatively flat tableland forming an almost perfect circle, only three-tenths of a mile in diameter. For four Coast Guard families it is home.

A young bride's initial reaction to the prospect of life on Tatoosh is almost sure to be one of shocked surprise. Tossing in a boat at the base of the island's forbidding cliffs, it hardly seems possible that a person might ascend to the summit, let alone live there for a 15-month assignment. Docking a boat and climbing to the station would be almost impossible by conventional means, so the Coast Guard has installed a gigantic boom on the island for transferring personnel back and forth. The boom swings out from the edge of the cliffs and lowers a large box to a boat waiting below. As many as four people can be hoisted in

Cape Flattery Light Station, Tatoosh Island, Washington. Built in 1857.

the box at one time. The 84-foot ride can still be a perilous one under anything other than ideal weather conditions. Heavy winds can cause the box to swing wildly and the tiny 16-foot skiff below is pounded mercilessly by even a slight sea. In practice, no attempt is made to transfer personnel unless the wind and sea are calm. At times, this can mean that people desiring either to travel to the station or to leave it may have to wait for days or even weeks to accomplish their goals.

Arriving at the station on one of the infrequent days when such travel is possible will produce an incredulous reaction of an entirely different sort. The environment is peaceful, pleasant, and extraordinarily homelike. A profuse growth of rich, green lawn covers four acres of the station. The four-foot layer of topsoil which caps the base-rock of the island is also liberally planted with a variety of fresh vegetables, including potatoes, radishes, parsley, peas, and carrots. Quaint but beautifully maintained dwellings complete the domestic scene.

A Coast Guardsman is hoisted to the top of Tatoosh Island in this World War II photo. This method of ascending Tatoosh's rocky heights has not changed over the years.

During a 15-month residence at Cape Flattery there are unfortunately all too few of the kind of days which allow a person to enjoy the scene described above. According to personnel who have served at this station there are but two seasons: winter and August. Although air temperatures average about 45 degrees in the winter, the wind-produced chill factor can make life all but unbearable. Prevailing winter winds approach 50 to 60 knots and gusts of as much as 100 knots may be expected once or twice each year.

Time weighs heavily on the station personnel and their wives. Maintaining the station buildings and the three 75 KW diesel generators which power the light seldom taxes the abilities of the men. They rotate through a schedule of watches which allows for a 72-hour holiday after each six days of duty. Even if they are fortunate enough to have weather which allows them to leave the station, there is difficulty in escaping the isolation of their existence. They will have to travel 55 miles to the nearest town, Port Angeles, an industrial town of less than 15,000, or to the nearest large city, Seattle—130 miles away.

Luckily for the wives, a well-stocked commissary located at Makah Air Base puts grocery shopping within a short drive of Cape Flattery. Again, adverse sea conditions can confine them to the station for weeks at a time. Wives soon learn to manage their resources well enough to buy groceries for at least a month in advance.

Another fairly regular event at the station which requires special planning is childbearing. Although families assigned to the station list a number of hobbies such as tropical fish, sewing, gardening, and card games among their interests, a census taker might make a few conclusions of his own. A recent tabulation of station families revealed a two-year-old boy, a week-old boy, a four-month-old girl, and an expectant mother. Unpredictability of the weather will demand that the latter be evacuated from the island at least six weeks before her due date.

Cape Flattery is among the most important lighthouses in the United States. It marks the approach to the Strait of Juan de Fuca, which is the principal sea route to the port of Seattle. It seems likely that the light will undergo automation within the next few years, as the Coast Guard continues in its attempts to make living conditions and working conditions better, where possible, for service personnel.

When construction on the first Cape Flattery Light began in 1856, the first building raised was a blockhouse for protection against marauding Indians from British Columbia. A number of keepers have wryly commented over the years that the island should still be given back to the Indians. Perhaps they would not want it. Mariners entering and leaving the Strait appreciate the navigational assistance provided by Cape Flattery's light and radio beacon, so it seems probable that the U.S. Coast Guard will be beaming a light from Tatoosh's rocky heights for many years to come.

Top: The Coast Guard Cutter *Bittersweet* (WLB-389). *Bottom:* Coast Guard Base Ketchikan, where *Bittersweet* is berthed.

Buoy Tenders

Bittersweet, 180-foot Buoy Tender

On the buoy deck, crewmen exchanged tense glances of apprehension. For three frustrating days, they had been tossing about in the waters near Calder Rocks. The weather was miserable, but typical of Alaska in the fall. Nevertheless, the ship's captain had decided that this day's weather was as good as they might be likely to see for several weeks. With a bit of luck, he could at last dispose of the enormous buoy which had been cluttering his deck for more than a week.

The captain ordered another round of sextant bearings. His ship's effort would be wasted if the buoy should be stationed in the wrong spot. "Right on." The order was sounded, and the tender's superbly trained crew went into action.

The boom operator energized his equipment. Slowly, but with the graceful precision of a ballerina executing a pirouette, the 13 ton buoy "danced" lightly across the deck to the water's edge. A confident nod from the captain signaled his approval to lower the buoy into the cold sea below. Moving an object 38-feet high and 9 feet in diameter across the decks of a ship is never routine. The eight-foot seas and 25-knot winds then rocking the buoy tender made the operation downright dangerous. But, in a flawless display of coordinated seamanship, captain, crew, ship, and machinery combined forces to place the new Calder Rocks Buoy in the water with hardly a splash.

Things now moved at a furious pace. A last

Left: A buoy is "walked" across the deck. *Right:* A 4,000-pound buoy sinker is brought aboard ship.

round of sextant bearings. Still on station. The chain stopper was then released, allowing the 8,500-pound concrete sinker suspended over the cutter's side to plummet downward into the water.

A Coast Guardsman crewman repairs the flasher on a harbor entrance buoy.

The sinker's descent also dragged down the heavy 160-foot chain which connected it to the floating buoy. The chain was "faked down" on deck in orderly, oblong loops which permitted it to run freely without becoming fouled. Each loop was stopped off on deck with a knot of Manila line. Each knot snapped in sequence as the chain continued to pay out into the water. As the last loop disappeared over the ship's side, there was a terrible wrenching of metal against metal, sending a shudder throughout the vessel. The chain's motion had been abruptly stopped by a "pelican hook," the last thing connecting the buoy to the tender. A nod from the captain, and the third class boatswain's mate on deck struck the hook solidly with a sledgehammer, sending the last length of chain into the water and severing all connection between the tender and its buoy.

Considering the severity of the weather, it was a magnificent achievement, a victory of man over the sea. For the crew of the Coast Guard cutter *Bittersweet*, it was truly a bittersweet kind of victory, which more accurately could be

considered an admission of defeat. Just 11 months previously, the crew had attempted to do away with Calder Rocks Buoy forever. The "permanent" derrick-shaped aid to navigation they constructed with such care and labor on that optimistic occasion had now been pounded into oblivion by wind, tide, and derelict logs from a distant lumber camp. Thus, marking the treacherous reef with a buoy again was a sadly frustrating event for the tender's grizzled CO.

He and his predecessor had waited nearly three years for the precise combination of tide, daylight, and calm weather which might enable construction of a fixed structure. When the conditions finally did occur, *Bittersweet* was there and waiting. With no more than six hours in which to complete their task, there was not a moment to spare. The minute the rocks began to appear above the receding tide, the tender launched her workboat.

The workmen who began pouring the concrete foundation were frequently drenched by breakers during the first 45 minutes of their task. Then, the tide sank low enough for them to continue on a relatively dry surface. The concrete was mixed on *Bittersweet's* deck and transferred to the work site in the cutter's all-too-small boat. Getting the concrete from the rocking, unsteady boat to the reef was an awkward job at best. On several occasions, uncooperative waves caused the crew to lose nearly half its load of building materials into the surf.

By the time the waters began to rise again, the cutter's efficient crew had laid a remarkably solid concrete foundation supporting an eight-foot-square, four-foot-high structure with a warning light on top. The crew was exultant. They had done something that other crews and tenders had repeatedly tried and failed. When the tender's captain complimented the young damage control-man who had engineered the operation, the prescient lad ventured a guess that the structure might last a year if they were lucky. As previously mentioned, he was not far wrong in his prediction.

Coast Guard buoy tenders are named for flowers and shrubs. It seems incongruous for a hard-working, seagoing vessel to bear a name such as *Iris* or *Cowslip*. *Bittersweet* is named for a plant too. The metaphorical connotation of her name seems more appropriate, for this ship, which many consider to be one of the Coast Guard's finest duty stations, ran aground three times in as many years.

Running aground is an occupational hazard for buoy tenders, for they often are required to tend navigational aids in such tightly restricted waters that lightly touching bottom becomes almost routine. There was nothing routine, though, about *Bittersweet's* groundings.

In 1965, after an arduous session of working coastal lights and buoys, the tender's CO thought his crew deserved some special consideration. Almost every major trip made by the cutter brought her tantalizingly close to Baird Glacier, one of the most spectacular scenic attractions in a state famed for majestic scenery. Every enlisted man and officer on board was itching to see Baird Glacier. It was inside Thomas Bay, a body of water which charts showed to be easily navigable, and was no more than three or four miles off *Bittersweet's* scheduled route. The captain gave in to his crew's entreaties and headed up the Bay. The special sea detail was set and the CO listened confidently as his fathometer operator shouted out soundings: "35 fathoms—30 fathoms—23 fathoms." These soundings, within the space of less than ten seconds, were enough to send the captain running for the bridge. He made it up and backed full on his engines. Then, his vessel groaned and listed over several degrees, before righting itself in the uncharted alluvial sand extending out from the glacier. *Bittersweet's* bow was high and dry, yet her stern floated in 60 feet of crystal clear water. It took a reversal of tide to free her. The ship was undamaged, but her CO had endured an unforgettable experience which had nothing to do with the spectacular scenery he had seen. Already embarrassed, he was further chastened by a wry note from his District Commander, who suggested that sightseeing might better be left to commercial entrepreneurs.

The heights and depths found in Alaska make buoy tending more difficult there than in any other Coast Guard operating area. Tides range as much as 24 feet, and while some waters are thousands of feet deep and impossible to mark with buoys, others are so shallow that a captain hazards his ship each time he travels them. Wrangel Narrows is a famous Alaskan channel which is regularly traveled by *Bittersweet*. During average tide conditions a vessel can travel through the Narrows in an euphoric state. There appears to be water everywhere. At low tide, however, the channel is flanked by an eerie landscape of jagged and potentially destructive rocks. Dry Pass, another channel which has often been used by *Bittersweet*, is dredged only to a depth of 12 feet, a figure which exactly coincides with the tender's normal draft. Thus, without ideal tide conditions, travel through the pass is out of the question.

Equally problematical for the cutter is the fact that many of the lights for which she is responsible are located on sheer and lofty cliffs. Such a light is Cape Bartolome, where *Bittersweet's* personnel

A large navigational buoy (LNB) on station.

have to climb a rope up a 163-foot precipice while carrying batteries weighing as much as those used in automobiles.

Bittersweet's home port is Ketchikan, Alaska, a town of approximately 11,000, where the townspeople love the Coast Guard and the Coast Guardsmen love the town. The tender departs her berth every other Wednesday for a logistics run to the Coast Guard's air station on Annette Island. Each trip involves the transfer of 10 to 14 tons of supplies for the Coast Guard crew and their dependents. On any given supply trip, the ship may transport: an automobile and household effects belonging to a newly assigned man; aircraft repair parts; mail; and enormous quantities of groceries. *Bittersweet* is the air station's most direct and dependable life line, and as such, may be required to transport virtually anything. She also carries fuel

Top: The busy tender *Tern* is an experimental design. *Bottom:* The Coast Guard Cutter *White Holly* (WLM-543) is another Alaskan buoy tender.

and other supplies to five extremely isolated Alaskan lighthouses, whose crews consider the cutter's visits a major cause for celebration.

No matter what a cutter's routine mission may be, she inevitably will become involved in a number of search and rescue incidents. *Bittersweet*, which averages 12 such cases each year, is certainly no exception. Of all the rescues in which she has participated, perhaps none has given her crew a higher sense of achievement than one in 1966 when the ship rescued the crew of one of the Coast Guard's own helicopters that had crashed in a blinding winter snowstorm. The "helo" had been involved in a rescue mission of its own when it went down, all of which emphasizes the ever-present danger that typifies Coast Guard duty.

Somewhat less gratifying was the rescue case which caused the tender's second major grounding. It was June, 1967 and the cutter had been bucking heavy winds and seas all day as she searched for a disabled fishing trawler with a broken shaft. At last the tender located the object of its quest. Because the cutter still had several aids to tend, her captain decided to attempt repairing the faulty shaft, rather than tow the craft the long distance back into port. After considerable effort, the ship's small boat succeeded in transferring a repair crew to the trawler, but the latter was rolling so badly in the rough seas that welding the shaft was impossible. Consequently, it was removed and returned to *Bittersweet* to take advantage of the tender's machine shop. *Bittersweet* was also rolling badly so her CO decided to seek the protected waters of nearby Kritoi Basin. The crew was up practically all night, but the relative calm of the Basin enabled them to satisfactorily weld the trawler's shaft. As the tender attempted to depart the narrow Kritoi Basin, it drifted almost imperceptibly toward the beach. There was a sickening crunch. *Bittersweet* had done it again, and, again it was an uncharted shelf which was responsible for her predicament. She was damaged, but not critically. Pulling free immediately, she proceeded to complete her assistance to the waiting fishing vessel. This time the tender's CO, who had already attracted the attention of his superiors for the Thomas Bay fiasco, received a very dry and formal letter of reprimand from his District Commander. It speaks well of the officer who received this painful correspondence that he is still something of a legendary Coast Guard figure in Alaska because of his expert shiphandling and seamanship, despite his two unfortunate accidents. At any rate, he is philosophical about it all, and his letter of reprimand is displayed on the wall of his den for all to see. "It's a good reminder" he says, "of a couple of things I never want to do again."

Unfortunately, the next skipper of the *Bittersweet* didn't profit from the experience of his predecessor. While taking part in what should have been a routine search case, *Bittersweet* struck an incorrectly charted pinnacle. The chart said four fathoms (24 feet), but the tender's 12-foot draft struck solid rock. This time the jinxed cutter had really done a job of it. Seven holes were ripped in her hull, and water was pouring in from all directions. The cutter's well trained crew sprang into action, plugging the holes to remove the threat of a swamped engine room. The holes were too big and too many. *Bittersweet* was sinking!

The ship's executive officer kept his cool, and took the only available course of action. He had to save his beloved vessel. Steering a fine course for a strip of sandy beach, he headed her in, wary of the rocks that bordered his narrow target. The maneuver worked beautifully. The ship was nudged into soft sand from which she could easily be extracted. Most important, she might sink, but not very far. The water beneath her keel was only a few feet deep.

Word of the fiasco spread rapidly, and the townspeople turned out in force. Their Coast Guard friends were in trouble. Artisans with many skills converged on the ship's location to offer their services. One of the town's expert divers volunteered his abilities to temporarily repair the underwater damage. Others pitched in, and the following day, *Bittersweet*, without paying a cent for the work the townspeople had performed, was able to limp into Ketchikan under her own power. An extensive shipyard repair period would be required, but she was due for one of those anyway.

It has now been a while since the 180-foot tender suffered the humiliation of a grounding. In the course of tending the 136 buoys, lighted structures, and other navigational aids for which she is responsible, the *Bittersweet* constantly faces a calculated degree of danger. Her 16,900 square-mile operating area is one of the most difficult to be found anywhere.

Thus, the men who have responded, over the years, to the challenge of duty on board this fine old cutter can take pride in the knowledge that they have served on one of the best. Even those who shared in the cutter's darkest hours consider their service to have been more sweet than bitter. And when sailing's smooth for *Bittersweet*, how very sweet it is.

Top: Exhibits such as this one carry the Coast Guard's boating safety message to the public. *Bottom:* The need for a boating safety program is vividly illustrated in this 1968 photo.

Boating Safety

Within the past three decades, pleasure boating has become one of the fastest growing forms of recreational activity in America. At present, there are between 8 and 9 million small boats in the U.S., and that number is increasing at the fantastic rate of more than 5,000 each week. These figures may be compared with those from a census of July 1, 1940 which listed only 298,243 motorboats to which numbers had been assigned by the Department of Commerce (which had the responsibility for numbering boats until the functions of the Bureau of Marine Inspection and Navigation were transferred to the Coast Guard). Although the 1940 figures did not include sailboats without power, the astronomic increase is nonetheless awesome in its significance. By even the most conservative estimates, motorboating in this country has undergone more than a thousand per cent increase within the span of 30 years.

This incredible growth can be almost entirely attributed to two factors: an affluent society, and the emergence of boats as highly favored status symbols. Without any sort of license or a modicum of knowledge in the field, any man, woman, or child with sufficient funds can become the owner and operator of his own boat. Concentrate a few of these novices within an unregulated operating area and pandemonium is almost sure to erupt.

It is hardly surprising, then, that recent years have brought large scale expansion to the Coast Guard's safe boating program, with increasing emphasis on preventative measures. The logic of the preventative approach is underscored by statistics which indicate that an overwhelming majority of boating fatalities recorded in recent years could easily have been prevented.

In a strictly numerical sense, very few persons die as a result of boating accidents: only 1,450 in 1970. Tragically, those who do die are usually victims of their own foolish acts. Some people apparently find it impossible to take very seriously a sport as enjoyable as boating. Vessel capsizings have consistently accounted for more of the lives lost in boating accidents each year than any other

This harbor patrol boat of the Revenue Cutter Service helped carry out the Service's boating safety mission in the early 1900's.

type of casualty. Nearly all of these capsizings can be attributed to some fault of the operator in his handling of the vessel. Chief among these faults are improper loading or overloading of the boat; ignoring weather warnings and proceeding under unfavorable weather conditions; and operating in waters which exceed the limits of the craft and/or the operator's training or experience.

three times and nothing's ever happened to me yet."

Historically, the Coast Guard's boating safety mission dates back to an act of May 19, 1896. That act authorized the Secretary of the Treasury "to prescribe regulations to insure the safety of passengers on excursion steamers, yachts, and all other craft, whether as observers or participants,

A Coast Guard boating safety detachment (BOSDET), on the alert to prevent unsafe pleasure boating.

Blind euphoria and apathy seem to pervade almost all unpleasant boating statistics. In 1969, nearly 500 people who had lifesaving devices available—but were not wearing them—drowned in boating accidents. Exemplifying this type of boatman was a fellow encountered some years ago by a Coast Guard boat patrolling the mouth of North Carolina's treacherous Oregon Inlet. During periods of adverse or deteriorating weather, it is customary for the Coast Guard to warn boatmen that it is unsafe to cross the inlet's bar. As the hero of this anecdote was so cautioned, he indignantly demanded "By whose authority are you warning me?" "By no one's authority," the Coast Guardsman replied. "We simply want you to be aware of the danger you are facing." "Nonsense," the boatman insisted. "I've capsized out there

attendant upon amateur or professional regattas on navigable waters of the United States, and to detail revenue cutters to enforce such regulations." The modern Coast Guard is still very active in patrolling regattas and boat races. Such patrols, in fact, constitute one of the few controversial mission areas of the service. Occasionally, and particularly around the time of the America's Cup races, the Coast Guard receives letters from disgruntled taxpayers who feel that Coast Guard patrols of these events represent the interests of only the very wealthy, and should be abolished. Patrolling regattas may well remain controversial, but it is certain that races and regattas could not be conducted safely without some sort of supervision.

In 1908, federal activities in the safe boating field entered a lengthy phase which must have been frustrating for all concerned. The 1896 act was repealed in an action which effectively transferred identical enforcement responsibilities to the Department of Commerce and Labor. The transfer probably seemed logical enough to those aware of the newly created Bureau of Navigation within that department. Unfortunately, the logic was more apparent than real. Not a single agency or bureau within Commerce and Labor had any vessels at its disposal for attending to such matters. The new act did authorize the Secretary of Commerce and Labor to request the use of public vessels from any other department, but when such requests were made for the use of revenue cutters, they were flatly rejected. No provisions had been made for interdepartmental transfers of funds. The Treasury Department pressured Congress into correcting this oversight, but the resultant legislation still left matters in a relative quandary. Under the modified procedure Commerce and Labor could charter vessels of its own, or could reimburse other departments for the use of their vessels. Since an annual appropriation of only $15,000 was set aside for these alternatives, the program never amounted to much.

Meanwhile, the Motorboat Act of 1910 was passed, establishing solid precedents for many of the Coast Guard's modern responsibilities in boating safety. Once again, at the outset, enforcement powers were only vaguely defined. The Department of Commerce and Labor, which still had no floating units of its own, was assigned the leading role in enforcement. The Act of 1910 set requirements for numerous items of safety equipment, including navigational lights, whistles, fire extinguishers, and life preservers. The act had immediate and gratifying results. During the period from 1904 to 1910, motorboat casualties reached an alarming average annual growth rate of 45%. In the three years following passage of the act, the disaster rate dropped to 11%. These impressive results were realized despite the fact that neither the Revenue Cutter Service nor the Bureau of Navigation was adequately equipped to enforce the act.

Attempting a pragmatic approach, the Bureau of Navigation eventually procured two boats of its own to patrol the heavily travelled oyster beds of Chesapeake Bay. Revenue cutters, succeeded by Coast Guard cutters, continued to share much of the burden.

In 1918, a curious law was passed requiring each undocumented motorboat over 16 feet in length to be assigned a number, such number to be prominently displayed on the boat's bow. The somewhat tenuous rationale behind this act was improved enforcement of navigation laws through positive identification of a boat's owner. However unnecessary such an act may seem to a casual observer, similar provisions exist today, as restated by the Federal Boating Act of 1958.

On June 23, 1939, the Coast Guard's safe boating program recorded a major milestone with creation of what was then called the Coast Guard Reserve. The Reserve was defined as a voluntary, non-military organization of private boat owners, joined together:

"1. To promote safety of life at sea and upon navigable waters.

"2. To disseminate information relating to the laws, rules, and regulations concerning motorboats and yachts.

"3. To distribute information and knowledge concerning the operation and navigation of motorboats and yachts, and,

"4. To cooperate with the Coast Guard."

Renamed the Coast Guard Auxiliary on February 19, 1941, this remarkable organization has performed service of inestimable value during the short years of its existence. There are few, if any, contemporary parallels for the Auxiliary, whose unpaid members are banded together for the principal purpose of supporting a federal agency and its causes. There are no volunteer organizations helping the Post Office Department to deliver mail or the Customs Bureau to make border checks. The Auxiliary, however, works side by side with the Coast Guard in patrolling regattas, examining motorboats, educating the boating public, and assisting those in distress.

Because of the Auxiliary's demonstrated cost-effectiveness, the Coast Guard has launched a five-year plan designed to increase the volunteer group's size from its present membership of slightly more than 30,000 to 100,000. The impact of such growth will be considerable, for the Auxiliary's benefits extend far beyond its immediate membership. In 1971, the organization taught safe boating courses to more than 400,000 persons, examined more than 200,000 motorboats, screened safe boating films for more than 900,000 viewers, and participated in nearly 10,000 assistance cases.

Creation of the Auxiliary was quickly followed by passage of the Motorboat Act of 1940, a basic and very important updating of those safety standards established by the Act of 1910. The new law was primarily enacted to reflect and cope with vast technological changes which had taken place within the thirty-year span. A new classification system was established for motorboats, with specific safety equipment and navigational light requirements for each class. Carburetor flame arrestors were made mandatory for boats built after the date of the act. Special standards were also set for the ventilation of engine and fuel compartment bilges. Reckless or negligent operation became a punishable offense, and provisions were established for administering penalties. Accident reporting procedures were also stated in the law.

The 1940 law was reasonably adequate in those areas it covered, but it failed to come to grips with the problem of improperly operated boats carrying passengers for hire. Several grim disasters involving commercial craft pointed out these deficiencies, and in 1958, the act was amended. The new provisions required inspection and certification of all passenger vessels carrying more than six passengers. Operators of such vessels were required to be licensed by the Coast Guard. These measures dramatically improved the situation. Prior to enactment of the 1958 regulations, uninspected passenger vessels had a six year average death toll of 111. During the following six years, the average accidental death rate for both inspected and uninspected small passenger vessels dropped to six.

The Coast Guard's approach to boating safety has consistently been one of public education rather than punitive measures. The latter are used only in extreme cases or as a last resort. In carrying out its enlighted program, the service has organized Boating Safety Detachments throughout the country. These detachments usually consist of three or four specially trained and selected petty officers. They are equipped with a vehicle, boat, and trailer, allowing them great mobility in their operations. During the boating season, they travel to areas where pleasure boating is popular, boarding motorboats to insure conformance with existing safety regulations. Almost half of the boats boarded by the Coast Guard each year are found to be in violation of the laws. Where possible, the boarding teams also provide public instruction in motorboating safety.

Surging interest in boating has brought about a major restructuring of the Coast Guard's administrative organization. The boating safety mission acquired its general present form within the Coast Guard when it absorbed the former responsibilities of the Bureau of Marine Inspection and Navigation in the early forties. During that era, most boating safety duties were functions of the service's law enforcement subdivisions under the broad jurisdiction of Operations. During the mid-sixties, Recreational Boating Branches were set up as separate subdivisions under Operations Divisions at Coast Guard District Offices. After the Coast Guard's transfer into the safety-oriented Department of Transportation, Boating Safety was established as a separate Office at Coast Guard Headquarters in Washington. As an indication of the intense regard with which the Coast Guard views its growing mission in boating safety, the service named a Rear Admiral to head the new Office in 1967.

On August 10, 1971 President Richard M. Nixon signed the Federal Boat Safety Act of 1971, considered to be the most significant legislation in the long history of federal action in this field. The new Act repeals most of the Federal Boating Act of 1958, and amends the Motorboat Act of 1940. The new law shifts much of the responsibility for conformance with equipment regulations from boat operator to boat manufacturer. The Act also authorizes an annual 7-1/2 million dollar grant-in-aid program for the individual states to use in setting up safe boating programs of their own. The sweeping nature of the legislation has been designed to ensure maximum safety without detracting from the wholesome fun of recreational boating.

Icebreaking

On March 30, 1867, the United States completed negotiations with Russia for the purchase of 590,000 square miles of the obscure and chilly expanse of real estate known today as Alaska. Four months later, the Revenue Marine embarked upon a new mission: the exploration of that forbidding and little known region. Today, after more than a hundred years of experience in the Arctic and Antarctic, the Coast Guard's fleet of specially designed icebreakers continues to advance man's knowledge of the most inaccessible spots on this earth.

The revenue cutter *Lincoln*, which carried the first government inspection party into Alaska, completed her mission without benefit of special design features to facilitate her progress through ice. Accompanied by Professor George Davidson of the United States Coast Survey, Captain W. A. Howard of the *Lincoln* was directed to "make local surveys, investigate locations for lighthouses and coaling stations, determine suitable points for custom houses, search out probable haunts for smugglers, locate fishing banks, inquire into the physical characteristics and resources of coastal areas, and collect specimens for the Smithsonian Institution." The activities assigned to the Coast Guard's modern icebreakers are somewhat different but no less diverse.

Revenue cutters such as *Lincoln* and *Wayanda*

provided the earliest reports indicating the vast potential of Alaska's natural resources. A single haul of *Lincoln's* primitive seine yielded 2,500 salmon and herring. *Wayanda's* captain reported coal veins of incredible magnitude. The cutters also brought back word of the predaceous devastation of the area's valuable fur seals. When legislation was established for the seals' protection, cutters were given the difficult task of enforcing it.

Alaska's development brought still more cutters into the territory. In 1868, the cutter *Reliance* was assigned to duty in Sitka, which was her home port for the next several years. In 1880, the cutter *Corwin*, whose hull had been reinforced for ice travel, began the first of the Revenue Marine's regular cruises in the Arctic Ocean and Bering Sea. The many duties of *Corwin* and her sister ships *Thetis*, *Bear*, *Northland*, and *Storis*, included law enforcement, exploration, scientific research, and protection of a native population which had been cruelly exploited by the early white settlers. *Corwin*, in 1880-81, was involved in a dangerous but futile attempt to locate survivors of an Arctic exploration ship and two whaling vessels which had not been heard from for many months. Unfortunately, the fates of those *Corwin* was seeking had been sealed long before the 145-foot cutter began her mission. Nevertheless, the heroism and resourcefulness demonstrated by *Corwin's* crew

History-making icebreaker *Northwind*.

Top: Icebreaker *Southwind* when originally built for the Coast Guard. *Bottom:* Crewmembers of the USCGC *Snohomish* check the ship's progress as she breaks through foot-thick ice on the Penobscot River, Maine.

throughout the mission deserve recognition in history. In the absence of shipyard facilities in Unalaska, *Corwin's* hearty sailors careened their own ship on the beach and repaired its ice-resistant sheathing. In an action which presaged that of the famed *Bear's* overland expedition, two officers, a coxswain, and two natives were dispatched by dog sled to search the area of Cape Wankerem. After a month of travel through blinding snow and chilling rain, the courageous band reached their destination. There, with dismay, they learned that one of the whalers had disappeared without a trace, and the other's crew members were already dead from cold or starvation.

While continuing her search for *Jeanette*, the explorer ship, *Corwin* smashed her rudder in the ice pack. As the sea began to freeze around them,

and in the midst of a gale-driven snowstorm, the cutter's deck force managed to jury-rig a rudder which allowed *Corwin* to work clear. More ingenious carpentry allowed the vessel to fabricate and install a whole new rudder while still in the open sea. Later it was learned that *Jeanette* had been destroyed in solid pack ice, far beyond the reach of her potential rescuers. George W. Melville, later Rear Admiral, USN, was one of the few survivors. During a long, arduous trek to safety, through heavy snow and ice, the indomitable Melville carried, upon his back, a 175-pound fellow officer. Such were the deeds of early Arctic explorers.

In the immediate years that followed, cutters played an increasingly important role in Alaska and the Arctic. They delivered the U.S. mail, enforced

Using explosives to break free of the ice.

Top: America's largest icebreaker, the 310-foot U.S. Coast Guard icebreaker *Glacier*, is moored on Filchner's Ice Shelf for diving operations and a seal census hunt during the first organized oceanographic survey of the Weddell Sea in the Antarctic during 1968. *Bottom:* Winter patrol in the harbor area of her home port at South Portland, Me., grows a few ice whiskers on the hull of the 65-foot U.S. Coast Guard harbor tug *Shackle* (WYTL-65609).

a multitude of laws (including those which prohibited the sale of liquor to the natives), transported construction materials for government projects of every description, performed medical services, and generally made the area a far safer place for those who sailed and settled there.

Although cutters operated by the Coast Guard in the Bering Sea and Arctic Ocean were constructed to withstand occasional contact with ice, they could not be considered icebreakers in the truest sense. Even the diesel-electric powered *Northland*, which was built in 1927 as a replacement for the old *Bear*, had an extremely limited icebreaking capability. On the other hand, icebreaking was accomplished rather effectively in municipal ports, such as Baltimore, as early as 1837. Paddle-wheeled ferries were used for the purpose.

It was for domestic usage that the Coast Guard finally built—or modified—its first real icebreaker, the *Kickapoo*. The former seagoing tug was outfitted, shortly after the end of World War I, with one of the first bows ever designed to break ice by riding up over it. Her seagoing ability was so adversely affected by the bow modifications, that she was hardly an unqualified success. Though designed for general duty, five of the 165-foot cutters built in the early 1930's were modified to make them reasonably effective in sheet ice up to one foot in thickness.

Development of the oil barge during the 30's, coupled with a series of unusually severe winters in New England, caused President Franklin Roosevelt, on December 21, 1936, to issue an Executive Order directing the Coast Guard "to assist in keeping open to navigation by means of icebreaking operations . . . channels and harbors within the reasonable demands of commerce." Since no funds were appropriated for the construction of icebreakers, the Coast Guard attempted to carry out its new mission with existing cutters. Damage to screws and rudders was commonplace.

World War II provided the impetus necessary to establish the icebreaking mission as it exists in the Coast Guard today. Extension of the shipping season in the Great Lakes, which previously had been shrugged off as impractical, now became imperative to the national defense. Iron ore and other defense supplies had to reach their destinations without delay. As an interim measure, several Great Lakes ferries were chartered for icebreaking operations. The cutter *Mackinaw*, specifically designed to break ice in the Lakes, was not completed until 1945. Her peacetime

contributions to commerce have paid for her construction many times over. Today, a sizeable fleet of Coast Guard tugs and buoy tenders also operate in support of domestic icebreaking.

Another early wartime requirement was to keep harbors and channels open in sub-polar regions such as Greenland and Labrador. The cutter *Storis* was built for that purpose in 1942. Funds were also appropriated for construction of four polar icebreakers during the war years but three of the four were loaned to the Soviet Union immediately following their construction. The fourth became the Coast Guard's famous *Eastwind*.

Between 1946 and 1947 replacements were built for those icebreakers which had been transferred to the Russians. *Burton Island* and *Edisto* became ships of the U.S. Navy, while *Northwind* was added to the Coast Guard fleet. In 1950-51, when Russia returned the icebreakers she had borrowed, they became the Navy icebreakers *Atka* and *Staten Island*, and the Coast Guard cutter *Westwind*. *Westwind* has occasionally been employed in domestic icebreaking, although the majority of her activities have been in polar regions. In 1954, the Navy built still another icebreaker, the *Glacier*. While *Glacier* was patterned after the design of the "Wind Class" breakers, she was enlarged and improved over the earlier vessels. In 1964-65, all Navy icebreakers were transferred to the Coast Guard and that service was given sole responsibility in this highly specialized field.

To this day, Coast Guard cutters continue to make history in polar and sub-polar exploration. In 1957, the icebreaker *Storis*, accompanied by the icebreaking buoy tenders *Spar* and *Bramble*, became the first deep-draft U.S. vessels to transit the fabled Northwest Passage. When the supertanker *Manhattan* made her own epochal journey through the Passage in 1969-70, she was assisted by the cutters *Northwind* and *Staten Island*.

Northwind has many historic "firsts" to her credit. Between 1963-65, she became the first U.S. vessel to survey the East Siberian, Laptev, and Kava Seas. She claims the northernmost penetration of the Western Arctic ice pack ever made by a surface vessel: 79° 26. 5'N. Her transit of the Northwest Passage in July 1969 was the earliest ever made by a surface ship. Her return trip later that year marked the first roundtrip within a single season which had ever been made by a surface ship. In 1970, she became the first U.S. surface vessel to cross the Western Arctic Circle during winter.

The Coast Guard's polar icebreaking has not been confined to the Arctic. *Eastwind*, now decommissioned, participated in the first Opera-

Top: An artist's rendering of the icebreaker which Lockheed Corporation presently is building for the Service.
Bottom: The Coast Guard Cutter *Spar* (WLB-403).

tion Deep Freeze in 1955, and Coast Guard ice-breakers have visited regions of the Antarctic in numerous subsequent expeditions. On one such trip, in 1961, *Edisto* encountered 90-mph winds whose furious ice spray deposited ice six feet thick on her forecastle.

Today's Coast Guard missions near the poles relate to a number of national interests, including logistics support of military and scientific missions at remote outposts, maritime transportation research, and scientific research supporting economic development of Arctic Alaska and the Alaskan continental shelf. The service also foresees a growing potential need for search and rescue units in the Arctic as commercial activity increases.

To accomplish its current and future objectives in these far-ranging fields, the Service has begun construction of the first representative of a new and modern fleet. The Lockheed Shipbuilding and Construction Company of Seattle, Washington was awarded a $52,681,485 contract to build the new breaker. The 400-foot, 12,000-ton vessel is expected to be in operation by 1974. It will be the world's most powerful icebreaker.

Polar Icebreakers

Northwind

To have served on board one of the Coast Guard's polar icebreakers is to have tasted one of life's greatest adventures, and most probably to have shared in the making of history. Both the adventure and the history relate not so much to the danger of the undertaking as to the uniqueness of travelling frozen wastes which few, if any, men have ever travelled before. In the spirit and tradition of Peary, Amundsen, and Byrd, Coast Guardsmen return each year to the forbidding polar zones which represent man's last unconquered frontier on the surface of his planet. Even astronauts on the moon have hardly battled a more inhospitable environment.

The U.S. was relatively slow to recognize the need for a fleet of polar icebreakers. In contrast, Russia, with her 24,844 mile coastline, was building relatively sophisticated breakers by the end of the 19th century. As World War II approached, however, one man was visionary enough to anticipate the role such vessels might play in the strategic defense of the Western Hemisphere. He was Rear Admiral (later Admiral) Russell R. Waesche, Commandant of the Coast Guard. Waesche ordered E.H. Thiele, one of his lieutenants, to the Baltic states, where the young officer studied icebreaker design under some of the world's leading engineers in the field. After more than a year of intensive study, Thiele returned to the U.S. and developed plans for icebreaking vessels which would be superior to any then in existence. The war's outbreak provided impetus to forge ahead with the plans. It was decided to construct four polar icebreakers.

So imposing were the construction standards established by the Coast Guard for its new icebreakers that only one firm ventured to bid on the job. Even that firm, the Western Pipe and Steel Company of San Pedro, California, had many reservations about the task. The prospect of building all-welded, one and five-eighth's-inch steel hulls for the breakers posed such staggering problems, in fact, that Western nearly backed out of the job. The west coast shipbuilder was fully capable of the task before it, for the "Wind Class" breakers built by Western have exceeded their designers' expectations.

Before the first "Wind Class" icebreaker had even been launched, the U.S. received a request from the Soviet Union to borrow all four ships. At the time, Russia was one of America's staunchest Allies, so the U.S. eventually agreed to lend the Soviets the cutters *Northwind*, *Westwind*, and *Southwind*. The agreement was not finalized until 1945, however. By that time, the cutters *Southwind* and *Eastwind* had combined forces with two other Coast Guard cutters, *Northland* and *Storis*, to break up an insidious attempt by the Nazis to establish bases in Greenland. Together, the four cutters captured or destroyed two radio-weather stations and three German vessels. The cutters also took 60 German prisoners.

The cutter known today as *Northwind* might never have been built had it not been for the Russian transfer agreement. The first *Northwind*, launched in 1942, served with *Southwind* and *Westwind* as members of the Soviet fleet during the period from 1945 to 1950-51. The U.S. could not

Top: The Cutter *Burton Island* during her 1971 Antarctic expedition. *Bottom:* The ship's HH-52A reconnaissance helicopter returns to the U.S. Coast Guard icebreaker *Northwind* (WAGE-282) after searching for an open lead in the frosted crystal-paved Northwest Passage.

afford to be without icebreakers of its own, so almost immediately built three more of the 269-foot Wind Class breakers. They were *Burton Island*, *Edisto*, and a new *Northwind*. (When the first *Northwind* was returned to the U.S. in December, 1951, it was given the name, *Staten Island*. Thus, the cutter dealt with in the remainder of this article is the present, but second, ship named *Northwind*.)

also scheduled to accompany the group but her construction (for the Navy) had been delayed, and she would not be completed in time to make the first trip through the Ross Sea ice pack. Until *Burton Island's* arrival, *Northwind* would have to do the job of two. Specifically, she had to lead other ships of the task group through the treacherous polar ice so they could build a base on the ice shelf for Admiral Byrd.

Left: The Coast Guard Cutter *Northwind* in action. *Right:* The Coast Guard Cutter *Eastwind* is framed by a gigantic iceberg near Jakobshavn, Greenland, in this 1952 photo.

When the atomic bomb ended World War II sooner than almost anyone had expected, the newly commissioned *Northwind* became, during the first few months of demobilization, a problem ship. When peacetime priorities were reestablished, polar scientific missions were called for, and *Northwind* entered the pages of history.

Sailing from her home port of Seattle, Washington, the ship travelled south, then east through the Panama Canal, and north to Boston, Massachusetts. Staging out of Boston, she sailed to the Arctic for a brief summer expedition. Upon returning to the Massachusetts port, she took on a new commanding officer and a new assignment. She was to serve as the principal icebreaker for Rear Admiral Richard Byrd's epic Antarctic expedition of 1947, Operation High Jump. Another Wind Class breaker, *Burton Island*, was

On December 30, 1946, *Northwind* left other ships of Task Group 68 in the vicinity of Scott Island, just inside the Antarctic Circle. While the others waited, the cutter surveyed ice conditions ahead. Encountering few difficulties, she returned with a favorable report. *Northwind's* initial observations were misleading, and the 2 seaplane tenders, 2 oilers, 2 destroyers, 2 supply ships, aircraft carrier, submarine, and command ship following the plucky breaker soon found themselves battling ice conditions which many still consider to have been the toughest Ross Sea pack of all time.

One vessel after another became frozen fast in the ice. By the time *Northwind* could break through to free a ship that was stuck, two others might become entrapped. The group was facing ambient water temperatures of 28 degrees with the ice refreezing almost immediately after it had been broken. Thus, it was necessary for ships of the task group to maintain precariously close distances to one another. By the morning of January 3, 1947, the group faced mammoth ice floes towering as high as *Northwind's* pilothouse. Heavy winds thrust one huge mass of ice into *Yancey*, one of the supply ships, ripping completely through her 3/4-inch hull plating, and pouring tons of near-freezing water into her hold. *Yancey* was saved only by the monumental efforts of her crew. The perilous voyage was continued. It soon became obvious, that bringing along the submarine *Sennet* had been a serious mistake. The underwater craft was no match for the destructive ice, and would have to be led back to safety. Tightly snubbing the sub's bow into her stern towing notch, *Northwind* began a difficult return voyage to Scott Island.

One problem followed another. While *Northwind* continued her arduous task, a PBM plane from the carrier was reported lost in the vast polar expanse. Battling heavy ice and with *Sennet* still in tow, *Northwind* received an urgent message from the command ship *Mount Olympus*. *Yancey*, which had nearly been sunk by a berg, and *Merrick*, the other supply ship, were helplessly drifting down on bergs. They were in immediate danger. A swift decision had to be made. *Sennet* was left in the relative safety of a nearby ice lake, while *Northwind* returned to rescue the others. The supply ships' plight grew more desperate during the 24 hours it took the cutter to batter her way through one massive floe after another to reach their position. On January 7, 1947, shortly after midnight, *Northwind* successfully completed her first major rescue mission.

As these dramatic events were occurring, tragedy struck the expedition, underscoring the hardships and heartbreaks which must be endured by those who would explore the extreme latitudes. Rear Admiral Richard H. Cruzen, Commander of the High Jump Task Group, received word that his son had been killed in an accident. Both Cruzen's geographical position and his position of command presented him with no choice but to continue his mission.

Northwind was still faced with problems of her own. Because Antarctica is an enormous continental land mass, its temperatures run about 20 degrees colder, latitude for latitude, than those of the North Polar Basin. This was an exceptionally cold year, and heavy cold means heavy ice. Breaking ahead at a creditable 8 knots, *Northwind* suddenly sighted a series of threatening hummocks

in her path. The cutter couldn't possibly smash into the ice ridges at such an excessive rate of speed. To slow suddenly, was to risk collision from astern. To warn *Merrick*, charging up rapidly from astern, *Northwind* attempted to sound a whistle signal indicating that her forward motion was virtually at a standstill. The intense cold had frozen her whistle. Just as all seemed lost, the stubborn ice yielded, averting a collision by mere inches.

During the epic voyage, *Northwind's* commanding officer, Captain Charles W. Thomas, and Lt. James Cornish, one of the ship's pilots, made history's first helicopter flight south of the Antarctic Circle. The flight was one of many which would be made by *Northwind's* air crews as they searched for openings in the ice.

By now, the cutter had safely escorted the submarine *Sennet* out of the ice, but other ships of Task Group 68 continued to encounter grave difficulties. Both *Merrick* and *Mount Olympus* received severe ice damage, but were prevented from sinking by the outstanding performance of their damage control personnel.

The task group's destination was the Bay of Whales, a narrow identation in the Ross Ice Shelf. The Bay would provide the shelter necessary for off-loading the supplies needed for setting up Little America Number Four. There was cause for apprehension, however. When last visited, the Bay's solid ice walls had been converging on each other at a rate of four feet a day. Climatologists had predicted, in fact, that by 1947 the Bay would have ceased to exist! If the Bay was found to be completely ice-bound, the task group would be forced to battle its way 500 miles farther—to McMurdo Sound. The McMurdo alternative was to be avoided if at all possible for it was much too far from Byrd's intended base. Worst of all, the ships would be exposed to extreme peril there, because of constantly shifting pressure ridges.

The climatologists had not erred much in their predictions. *Northwind* and party arrived to discover that the Bay of Whales had narrowed to a mere 200 yards at its entrance. Those portions which were not solidly frozen were at least blanketed with thick bay ice. The Bay was functional as a seaport only to the extent that *Northwind* could break through it. After 63 hours of continuous pounding, the powerful breaker had cleared an area a mile wide and two miles long, having removed what Admiral Byrd later estimated to be 15 million tons of ice from the Bay of Whales. During the latter stages of this tremendous feat, *Northwind* was testing her strength against ice ten feet thick, as pressure ridges in the distance thrust upward to heights of 70 feet.

Clearing the Bay wasn't nearly the completion of *Northwind's* task, however. It was now necessary for her to return to Scott Island, where the carrier *Phillipine Sea* required her assistance as an escort through the ice. Furthermore, the carrier had cargo to be transferred—150 tons of it, including two small planes. The cargo was passed from the carrier to the cutter using a high line. The transfer took 32 hours, much of it during a howling gale.

Northwind's return to the Bay of Whales was even more difficult than her first trip. At times it was necessary to use high explosives to blast her way through the dense ice pack. She had hardly more than returned when the supply ships finished off-loading cargo, and announced their intentions of heading for warmer seas. The timing of polar missions is so critical that there is usually not a moment to spare in any phase of operations. An unplanned delay can result in a ship's becoming frozen fast in the ice, and damaged beyond repair. *Northwind* now became the vanguard of what was to be a necessarily hasty retreat. This time the task group was joined by the now-completed *Burton Island*.

At first, escorting the logistics fleet back to Scott Island promised to be an easy assignment for the two breakers. The ice was not compacted as badly as it had been during *Northwind's* earlier trips to and from the Bay of Whales. Then, a furious storm swept over the Ross Sea, creating a scene of violent turmoil, where massive bergs and floes became devastating, unavoidable instruments of destruction. A huge floe smashed into *Merrick*, tearing off her rudder and slashing two holes in her side. Once again, *Northwind* was confronted with a tow job through arduous ice conditions.

Getting *Merrick* out of the ice was the most demanding and dangerous task the cutter had faced thus far. On one occasion, *Northwind* was forced to back her engines at full speed in order to prevent *Merrick* from being struck by an iceberg which would have completed the supply ship's destruction. *Northwind's* maneuver essentially amounted to a collision between her and the supply ship, buckling frames and dishing in shell plating. The resultant damage, however, was far less than what the berg would have caused.

Once clear of the perils of the ice, the ships still faced a rugged voyage—nearly a thousand miles across latitudes which mariners refer to as the "screaming sixties" and "furious fifties" because of

the storms encountered there. The infamous latitudes lived up to their reputations. *Northwind* and company soon found themselves threatened by a full-blown hurricane with winds of ninety miles an hour. During the storm's peak, *Northwind's* towing hawser snapped, leaving *Merrick* helpless for a period of several hours.

The winds had only partially subsided when the dutiful *Northwind* again had her charge in tow. Following a nightmarish journey of two weeks, the ships reached their destination, Dunedin, New Zealand. For *Merrick*, Dunedin meant extensive shipyard repairs. For *Northwind*, though, the port was simply a place for a couple of days' rest and recreation before returning to the rigors of breaking ice on the Ross Shelf where Byrd needed an emergency landing field for his aircraft, and the *Northwind's* icebreaking ability was necessary for the job.

The 1947 expedition was, perhaps, more extensively chronicled than most of *Northwind's* subsequent voyages. But Operation High Jump was neither more nor less dramatic than any number of trips the cutter has undertaken subsequently. After the Byrd expedition, *Northwind* was assigned to Bering Sea Patrols for many years, during which she proved herself a worthy successor to the glorious traditions of the fabled *Bear*. To the Eskimos and Aleuts of Alaska, there were few more welcome sights during those years than the gleaming white cutter bringing civilized law, medical care, mail, supplies and 185 friendly crewmen eager to trade for native crafts. *Northwind* also played a dynamic role in enforcing sealing treaties in the Western Arctic.

One of *Northwind's* most exciting and tension-filled adventures occurred in 1965 when, at the request of the U.S. Department of State, she sailed for a transit of the so-called Northeast Passage, a hotly contested strait north of Siberia. Vil'kitskogo Strait, key to the passage, is supposedly less than 24 miles wide. Russia claims a 12 mile territorial limit, and insists that the strait is entirely within her territorial waters. The U.S. argues that they are international waters. *Northwind* approached the critical point in her voyage under constant harrassment by Soviet ships and planes. Nevertheless, the cutter carried out a wide-ranging and pioneering oceanographic program in waters never before visited by an American scientific expedition. Then, in a reversal of plans somewhat reminiscent of the Bay of Pigs disaster, the State Department apparently lost its nerve and refused permission for the cutter to travel across the top of Russia. It was a heartbreaking experience for *Northwind's* crew which had endured weeks of bitter and nerve-wracking frustration during their encounters with the Russians.

Like other cutters in the Coast Guard's icebreaking fleet, *Northwind* has begun to show her age. Twenty-five is a ripe old age for any ship, and is particularly old for one which has spent those years pitting her force against massive and occasionally unyielding ice packs. It is not surprising, then, that *Northwind* is no longer capable of performing her tasks quite as dependably as she once could. This was sadly true in 1969 as the old cutter joined forces with the Canadian icebreaker *John A. Macdonald* to assist the fabulous icebreaking supertanker *Manhattan* in her historic conquest of the Northwest Passage.

The trip was organized to test the feasibility of using the passage to exploit the extraordinarily rich petroleum fields on the Alaskan North Slope. To enable her to break ice, *Manhattan* was completely redesigned and rebuilt. When completed she was 1,005 feet long, longer than the Empire State Building is tall. Recognizing the Coast Guard's expertise in icebreaking, *Manhattan's* operators based the tanker's bow design on original studies which had been carried out by a Coast Guard officer. Coast Guard icebreaking experts conducted extensive operational briefings for the benefit of *Manhattan's* personnel. In addition, Coast Guard liaison officers were assigned to ride the icebreaking tanker for the duration of her voyage.

Unfortunately, *Manhattan's* heady victory was very nearly *Northwind's* most ignominious defeat.

After making history by transiting the Northwest Passage in July (earlier than it had ever before been travelled), the hardworking old cutter began suffering one mechanical failure after another. In time, the cutter could no longer keep up the pace being maintained by other members of the convoy. Lesser ships might have given up, but not the indomitable *Northwind*. Her crew was too proud and dedicated to be left behind. They worked feverishly—and well. Within a week, *Northwind* was running well enough to have caught up with *Manhattan*, and to continue with her to their Prudhoe Bay destination. For the tanker's return trip, *Northwind* was replaced by *Staten Island*, another of the Coast Guard's 269-foot icebreakers.

In the course of her own return trip to Seattle, *Northwind* again made history. She became the first ship to make a round trip through the Northwest Passage in a single season.

As the Coast Guard begins construction of its new, futuristic icebreaker fleet, it is obvious that *Northwind's* days are numbered. The number is substantial, though—approximately ten more years of polar operations. The Coast Guard has always gotten its money's worth out of ships.

What *Northwind's* last ten years will bring is anybody's guess, but it is certainly safe to predict that they will be eventful and productive ones. Already, the cutter's accomplishments have earned her an enduring place in the history of polar operations. There are polar operations specialists within the Coast Guard who would venture to say, that *Northwind's* most historic feats may still lie ahead of her.

Great Lakes Icebreaker

Mackinaw

The Coast Guard traditionally saves property each year valued at several times the Service's annual operating budget. In terms of service to the taxpayer, few cutters in the fleet can compare with the record compiled by the icebreaker *Mackinaw*, whose mission is facilitating commerce rather than search and rescue. *Mackinaw* does her job by breaking ice in the upper Great Lakes in early winter and spring, extending the shipping season by 45 days or more each year.

ten days after the Japanese attack on Pearl Harbor. Great Lakes shipping ports were logical loading points for a number of raw materials vital to the war effort, such as iron ore, coal, and limestone, so extending the shipping season assumed an importance it had never had before.

When finally commissioned in 1944, *Mackinaw* was rated as the most modern, powerful, and capable icebreaker in the world. She is still well equipped for the job she has to perform. Her hull

The Cutter *Mackinaw* on a summer cruise.

The magnitude of *Mackinaw's* contribution to the area's economy cannot be appreciated without some knowledge of the lakes. During the open navigation season approximately 480 million ton-miles of cargo are travelled by Great Lakes carriers each day. This figure multiplied by 45 additional days gives some idea of the value of *Mackinaw's* services. During one ten-day period in 1947, the 290-foot cutter is said to have more than paid for her $10 million original cost by escorting 84 ships in and out of heavy ice which was jamming Buffalo Harbor.

Mackinaw's construction was authorized as a result of increased demands for industrial materials. The authorization occurred, in fact, only

plating, from the keel to well above the water line, is made of steel 1-5/8" thick. The stout plating is heavily reinforced with deep and closely-spaced frames. Her stern propellers are each 14 feet in diameter and weigh 10.7 tons. She is powered by six 2,000 horsepower diesel engines. The cutter is also fitted with a bow propeller which plays a major role in icebreaking operations. The violent discharge created by this 7.2 ton screw can break up ice which is ahead of the vessel and can flush it away from piers, docks, and other vessels beset in the ice. As an additional propulsive force, the bow propeller issues a stream of water which reduces friction between ice and the ship's hull.

Like most icebreakers, *Mackinaw* is designed to

break ice by riding up over an ice shelf and letting the ship's weight do the work, rather than by ramming. The reasons, upon examination, are obvious. It is much simpler to apply the vertical force necessary to break through ice three or four feet thick than to apply the horizontal force necessary to break through a solid sheet of ice which may extend for many miles in a horizontal plane. The vertical force exerted by the specially shaped bow is enhanced by the bow propeller which draws water from under the ice, lessening the effort required to force the ice downward.

Mackinaw is prepared for almost any contingency and it sometimes happens that the thickness or consistency of the ice encountered may impede the ship's progress to a point where it is necessary to back and ram. Occasionally, the ship may become wedged so tightly in the ice that she is unable to back out, even with full power. When this happens, she turns to her efficient and advanced water transfer systems. Large water tanks are located on both sides of the ship, amidships. By pumping water rapidly back and forth from one side to another, through a system capable of trans-

ferring 160 tons in a minute and a half, can create a heeling motion which is usually enough to free her. Should this approach fail, however, there are further safeguards, in the form of a trimming system which pumps water from fore to aft. Using this system, the ship can transfer 120 tons of water in a little less than seven minutes.

When *Mackinaw* is called on for a rescue operation, she usually finds herself in ice as always. Here again she has special design features. Because a standard towing rig might allow a towed vessel to come crashing in from astern, *Mackinaw* is outfitted with a large constant tension towing winch. She also has a towing notch in her stern which allows the bow of the vessel being towed to be placed securely before the towing evolution is begun. Effectively, the two vessels become one, and the possibility for collision is greatly reduced.

During summers, *Mackinaw* spends much of her time on one or another standby status, where she may well be called out on conventional Coast Guard rescue missions. She also serves as a training vehicle for cadets of the Coast Guard Academy.

This is the berg believed to be the one which sank the *Titanic*.

International Ice Patrol

Human progress has usually resulted from some terrible disaster which has impelled us to take preventive action. This is the case with the International Ice Patrol operated by the Coast Guard since 1914. It took the sinking of the so-called "unsinkable" luxury liner *Titanic* in 1912, after colliding with an iceberg off Newfoundland's Grand Banks on her maiden voyage to stir the nations of the world to preventive action.

The much-travelled shipping lanes of the North Atlantic had been the setting of disasters long before the *Titanic*. In May, 1833, the *Lady of the Lake*, bound from England for Quebec, struck an iceberg with a loss of 215 lives. An American ship, the *William Browne*, suffered the same fate with the loss of seventy lives, while returning from England to Philadelphia in 1841. Between 1882 and 1890, fourteen ships were lost and about 40 seriously damaged by ice. Many more which departed port never to be heard from again were undoubtedly victims of the dreaded bergs. But, it required a disaster of the magnitude of the *Titanic* to shock the maritime world into positive cooperative action, resulting in the International Ice Patrol.

North Atlantic icebergs break away from Greenland's massive glaciers which extend over an area almost two and three quarters the size of Texas. Carried along by ocean currents, they drift inexorably southward toward the Grand Banks of Newfoundland. Relatively few of the bergs calved on Greenland's east coast ever reach the North Atlantic shipping lanes. Hampered and delayed by adverse currents and the earth's rotation, they usually are worn away by the sea before they have a chance to do any damage. Passage is quicker and easier for those thousands of bergs which originate each year on the west coast of the island. Not all of the bergs survive the eighteen hundred to three thousand mile trip to the Grand Banks, but the few which do make it pose a serious threat to shipping in the area.

Nothing has ever been found to stop the bergs, although many things have been tried. Explosives have proven impractical. Approximately 1,900 tons of TNT would be required to break up a single, average iceberg—and there are thousands of them! Nearly two and a half million gallons of gasoline would be required to melt one, and even then, the gasoline's combustion would have to be *complete*. Lamp black, to melt the bergs more

rapidly by absorption of the sun's rays, has also proven inadequate. Natural deterioration, in fact, is the only thing likely to reduce the threat of any given berg.

A monster which cannot be destroyed had better be avoided. The only sure way of avoiding these icy monstrosities is by keeping track of their whereabouts. Such has been the imminently practical approach of the International Ice Patrol since its founding in 1914. During the years since, except when prohibited by the exigencies of war, the Coast Guard has operated the patrol as one of the most patently successful of all its many missions. And, during the years when the Coast Guard has been on the job, not a single ship has been lost in major shipping lanes due to collision with an iceberg.

Carried out by the U.S. Coast Guard, the patrol is jointly funded by Belgium, Canada, Denmark, France, Germany, Great Britain, Greece, Italy, Japan, Liberia, the Netherlands, Norway, Panama, Spain, Sweden, Yugoslavia and the United States. The charge assessed for each nation is computed on the basis of the nation's shipping tonnage in the 33,000 square-mile patrol area.

In its earliest days, the ice patrol was exclusively a function of cutters. Increasingly over the years, aircraft, with their greater mobility, have come to dominate the operation. Visibility permitting, Coast Guard HC-130's search the patrol area three times weekly during the patrol season. Bergs are located, identified, and tracked. To facilitate identification in areas where confusion might otherwise result, some bergs are splattered with dye markers. Often flying at less than 500 feet, the ice reconnaissance aircraft routinely operate with only two of their four engines, to conserve fuel. In the frigid waters of the North Atlantic, almost any forced landing would prove fatal.

Twice each day during the season, which may run from February to July, the Service broadcasts the location, course, and rate of speed of bergs, floes and ice fields. Coast Guard Loran has greatly improved the accuracy of information provided. If poor visibility or inclement weather persists over an extended period of time, cutters again respond to needs of the patrol. Commercial vessels and planes are also requested to cooperate in furnishing the Coast Guard with information concerning ice conditions they have sighted.

Top: Coast Guard HC-130. Aircraft are mainstays of today's international ice patrol. *Bottom:* This 63-foot
cutter is one of a flea fleet of air-sea rescue boats in the icy dangerous North Atlantic.

There is always some difficulty in statistically documenting the effectiveness of any preventative program. The perfect record of the International Ice Patrol is impossible to fault. During that period of World War II in which the patrol was discontinued it is significant to note that a merchant vessel did sink after colliding with an iceberg, and several lives were lost.

The functions of the ice patrol are specifically designated by both international treaty and U.S. law. The patrol's geographical jurisdiction extends only to those ice-menaced regions of the North Atlantic through which pass the major trans-Atlantic shipping tracks. Many areas not covered by the patrol continue to be unsafe for mariners. The tragic sinking of the *SS Hans Hedtoft*, which struck an iceberg off the south coast of Greenland on the night of January 30, 1959, attests to the dangers which still exist.

For those lucky enough to travel the shipping lanes protected by the Coast Guard's International Ice Patrol, the Service's extraordinary 100% ice-track record has, for nearly sixty years, been a talisman which Saint Christopher, himself, might have blessed.

Law Enforcement

The Coast Guard, whose very creation stemmed from the necessity of enforcing our nation's early customs laws, faces the future with a whole new bag of law enforcement responsibilities. One hundred eighty-one years of history have produced vast changes, both in the laws the Coast Guard enforces and the equipment with which it enforces them. But, the Service is today, as it was then, the principal agency for enforcement of all federal laws upon the navigable waters of the United States, its possessions, and the high seas.

The need for a floating police as a part of the national fiscal organization was recognized by Congress in "An act to regulate the collection of duties imposed by law on the tonnage of ships or vessels, and on goods, wares and merchandise imported into the United States." Approved on July 31, 1789, the act was the first ever passed by the U.S. Congress. Section 5 of the act provided for a surveyor at each port, whose duties should include "the employment of the boats which may

be provided for securing the collection of the revenue," but no provision was made for the boats themselves. Without such boats, the act proved to be virtually unenforceable. Congress recognized this untenable condition by passing the Act of August 4, 1790, authorizing establishment of the cutter fleet which has grown into the modern Coast Guard.

The 1790 act charged the newly created Service only with enforcing collection of customs and tonnage duties, but other missions were soon added. When the introduction of slaves into the United States was prohibited in 1807, the revenue cutters were given primary enforcement responsibility. Quarantine and neutrality laws were other early additions to the growing list of laws to be enforced by the revenue fleet. The cutters were also used in suppressing piracy in the Gulf of Mexico during Jean Laffitte's supremacy there.

Some of the ecology issues which have so captured the public imagination today relate to

Because of Coast Guard law enforcement efforts these Alaskan Fur Seals are no longer in danger of extinction.
Photo: U.S. Department of the Interior

Top: The Boston trawler *Red Jacket* is being inspected by a boarding team of Coast Guardsmen and a U.S. Fish and Wildlife agent from the 210-foot U.S. Coast Guard Cutter *Vigilant. Bottom:* Small but sturdy, these 40-foot boats are designed primarily for law enforcement work and search and rescue under moderate sea conditions.

Coast Guard missions with long standing historical precedents. The 19th century had just begun when Americans started to think about the conservation of our natural resources. Poachers, operating on public lands of the U.S. soon threatened the young nation with a rapidly· diminishing supply of the timber stock needed for the construction of naval vessels. Landmark legislation, passed in 1822, prohibited the unauthorized cutting of timber on public lands in Florida. Coast Guard cutters were dispatched to see that despoliation ceased.

courage to advise a whaling captain that the catch he had just fought so long and hard for was a few inches too short to keep.

On inland waters and in the western rivers, the Coast Guard enforces navigational "rules of the road." These are regulations concerning lights, fog signals, speed, steering, and signaling for vessels in a comprehensive variety of operating situations.

The Outer Continental Shelf Lands Act of 1953 extends U.S. jurisdiction to the seabed of the shelf. It authorizes the Coast Guard to make and enforce

The Coast Guard is charged with enforcement of many of the nation's antipollution laws. Here the Service tests a floating barrier designed to keep oil pollution from spreading.

A host of other conservation activities followed; most are still in effect. Among the many fish and game species protected by laws presently enforced by the Coast Guard are halibut, sockeye salmon, tuna, whales, sponges, and fur seals. For a brief period, beginning in the mid-1930's, a Coast Guard officer was assigned to each large whaling vessel sailing under the U.S. flag. The officer's presence was to insure that the whalers were operating in accordance with the International Whaling Treaty. According to old-timers, it took a rare form of

regulations regarding lights, warning devices, safety equipment and other matters relating to safety of life and property on artificial islands and offshore structures. The large number of offshore oil discoveries made during the past two decades have made the Coast Guard's role in this area an increasingly important one.

The multitude of laws and regulations enforced by the Coast Guard encompasses areas of responsibility as diverse as: murder, kidnapping, robbery, the transport of narcotics, and numerous other criminal offenses; several laws relating to motorboat regulation and the safe conduct of marine parades and regattas; security regulations authorizing the control of the anchorage and movement of any vessel in United States waters; anchorage regulations established by the Army Corps of Engineers; the handling, storage, and use of all explosives or other dangerous articles or substances on both domestic and foreign commercial vessels; and illegal immigration attempts.

In any society, there may be a group of radical extremists who oppose law and order, and make life and order difficult for those officers charged with preserving them. It became the Coast Guard's miserable task during the 1920's and '30's to attempt enforcement of prohibition laws opposed—not by a lunatic fringe—but the public majority. Few missions have ever posed a greater challenge. The dedicated but unappreciated heroes, who waged war against dangerous criminals in the face of public hostility during those dark years, deserve more credit than history has ever accorded them.

Passage of the Water Quality Improvement Act of 1970 has thrust the Coast Guard into an area of law enforcement which seems certain to have a wider base of public support. The Service entered the anti-pollution field years ago under provisions of the Refuse Act of 1899 and the oil pollution acts which followed. Recent events have placed the Service in the vanguard of those agencies designated to cope with our nation's pressing pollution problems. Legislation has been advanced which would give the Coast Guard enforcement responsibilities in pollution incidents involving hazardous substances, such as mercury, pesticides, and explosives, in addition to oil. Under terms of other new legislation, the Coast Guard has been specified as the agency to which the public should report all pollution violations in navigable waters of the U.S.

Public concern over pollution of our seas indicates a probable continued expansion of Coast Guard law enforcement responsibilities in the years to come.

The Coast Guard Cutter *Reliance* (WMRC-615) as she appeared shortly after her commissioning. Today *Reliance* bears the Coast Guard's distinctive slash and seal on her bow.

Reliance, 210-foot class

During the Revolutionary War, smuggling by American colonists was almost considered an act of patriotism. With the establishment of the Union, it soon became apparent that smuggling would have to cease if the new government was going to survive. The federal budget was solidly based on anticipated revenues from customs duties. Alexander Hamilton, the United States' first

Coast Guard Commandant, Admiral E.J. Roland, presides at *Reliance's* christening ceremony on May 25, 1963 at Todd Shipyard, Houston, Texas.

Secretary of the Treasury, was quick to recognize the absolute necessity of rigidly enforcing the customs laws which had been passed. He requested, and Congress authorized, a fleet of 10 sailing cutters to ply the coast and secure the national revenue. Thus was born the Revenue Cutter Service which has grown into today's Coast Guard. Now, after nearly two centuries, the Service has added a multitude of other missions, but law enforcement remains an important responsibility of the Coast Guard. That responsibility in its modern form is exemplified by the swift and beautiful 210-foot class of cutters.

The commissioning of the cutter *Reliance* on June 20, 1964 was a major event in Coast Guard history. Almost twenty years had elapsed since the Service had built a major cutter of any kind. Other medium endurance cutters operated by the Service were 30-40 years old and the Coast Guard was approaching the threat of block obsolesence of its entire fleet of ships.

As the first representative of a radically new class of vessels, *Reliance* represented a two-million-dollar gamble. That gamble was based on the well calculated judgment of some of the best naval engineers in the country.

An HH-52A amphibious rescue helicopter comes in for a landing on the flight deck of the 210-foot Coast Guard Cutter *Reliance*.

It would be unrealistic to say that the gamble was an unqualified success. *Reliance's* design is a highly innovative one. She was the first ship of any consequence built in the U.S. to be equipped with a combined diesel engine and gas turbine engineering plant. She also has controllable-pitch propellers which can be shifted from full ahead to full astern within ten seconds. The controllable-pitch feature provides for automatic adjustment to obtain maximum thrust when towing, regardless of the size of the ship being towed. Extensive experimentation led to a combination of inward-turning propellers and spade rudders which give the cutter extraordinary maneuverability. The plant is operated by a sophisticated control system with a number of remote and automatic options. Because the ship is equipped with a flight deck for helicopter operations, the traditional vertical stack was abandoned as a design feature. Since a conventional stack would have obstructed a pilot's vision and created turbulence hazardous to the aircraft, the 210-foot cutters have internally installed exhaust pipes, water cooled, and extended from the engine room to the ships' sterns.

worthy of her name. Operating out of Corpus Christi, Texas, a city most of her crew members consider to be one of the Coast Guard's finest duty stations, the *Reliance* is involved in about 30 rescue cases each year. Because of the importance of the Texas Gulf Coast as a shrimping area, a majority of her cases deal with vessels of that type. For many years, until it was terminated in 1969, the Coast Guard maintained a continuous patrol in the Gulf of Campeche, protecting the interests of Gulf shrimpers. The rapid response made possible by the Service's new 210-foot cutters has now made it possible for them to provide virtually the same services while remaining on a standby status.

The 210-foot cutters have been constructed during a period when the nation has become

Reliance's sister ship, the *Vigorous*, is stationed at New London, Conn.

Considering the numerous engineering advances incorporated into *Reliance's* design, it is not surprising that she has endured a nominal share of mechanical failures. The problem of matching a 1,500 HP diesel running at 1,000 RPM with a gas turbine running at 22,300 RPM on the same shaft proved to be a far more difficult task than her designers had anticipated. This aspect of the design was altered after construction of the first five cutters, and subsequent members of the class have been equipped with standard diesel reduction gear plants, without the turbines. The lessons learned on *Reliance* showed the way to the very successful combined diesel and turbine installation on board the Coast Guard's 378-foot cutters.

The problems have been ironed out now, and *Reliance* has begun to demonstrate a reliability

increasingly conscious of conservation. A large part of the vessels' deployment schedules relates to enforcing regulations of the cod, haddock, halibut, salmon, and yellow-fin tuna fisheries. In 1969 *Reliance* sailed through the Panama Canal to conduct a tuna patrol off the coasts of Mexico and Central America. The patrol was in support of an international agreement between the U.S. and other nations of the Americas. The cutter also periodically patrols areas of the Gulf of Mexico in which off-shore oil rigs are located, to insure that the rigs are properly lighted and are not creating any pollution problems.

Reliance was awarded the Coast Guard Unit Commendation for her activities during the Cuban Exodus of 1965. During one two-month period the cutter rescued a total of 175 Cuban refugees.

Commercial Vessel Safety (CVS)

Of all the Coast Guard's many missions, it is probable that none is more complex or less understood than Commercial Vessel Safety. Like many programs of preventative action, CVS is seldom dramatic enough to be newsworthy in a society which would rather read about maritime disasters than precautions against their occurrence. Yet, the quiet accomplishments of the Coast Guard's very dynamic Commercial Vessel Safety Program have had inestimable impact in making the U.S. merchant marine the world's safest.

the recognized necessity of establishing more uniform regulations for navigation and shipping.

Most mission responsibilities established in those early acts still exist today in one form or another. It was not until some years afterward, though, that legislation was introduced in the interest of improved safety on board merchant vessels. Until the invention of Fulton's steamboat *Clermont* in 1807, it would appear that Americans were relatively apathetic about the dangers of water travel. Sinkings and groundings were common

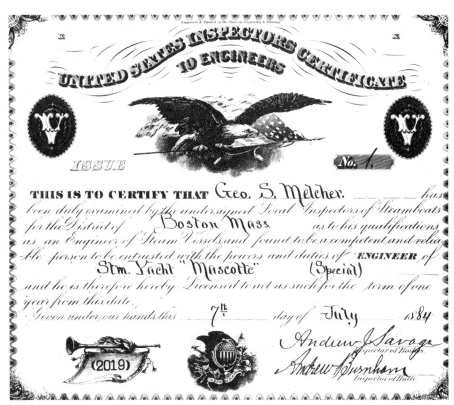

The original first issue of a United States Inspectors Certificate to Engineers was donated to the U.S. Coast Guard by Captain E.B. Ellis of Cooperstown, N.Y.

The historical origins of CVS as presently practiced by the Coast Guard, are far too detailed to be adequately covered in this text. Congress, in 1789, passed two acts which established tenuous precedents in the field of merchant marine regulation. One imposed a duty on the tonnage of vessels; the other provided for the registering and clearing of vessels, and regulation of the coastwise trade. It is significant, that one of the most pressing reasons for uniting the several states was

enough to have become accepted hazards. Steamboats were a novelty, and brought with them novel forms of danger—fire and explosion. In 1832, in fact, 14% of all steamboats in operation were destroyed by explosions. Obviously, something had ought to be done.

It was six years before Congress reacted to the problem, but the act finally passed was a good one. It provided for the periodic inspection of steam propelled vessels' hulls and boilers to determine their strength and durability. A requirement for certain safety devices such as lifeboats and fire-fighting equipment was also established. Engineering watches on board the steamers were to be stood by skilled and experienced personnel. In keeping with the times, the act was administered rather loosely. Inspectors were appointed by District Judges of the United States. Certificates of Compliance with the act were issued by Federal Port Agents. Without such a certificate it was illegal to carry passengers.

Administration of our national CVS Program improved considerably after 1852, when an act was passed creating the Steamboat Inspection Service. The new act provided for greater standardization of procedures through the appointment of a nine-man board of supervising inspectors. It also provided for the classification and licensing of engineers and pilots on board steam-driven vessels carrying passengers for hire. Despite these improvements, the program languished at less than maximum effectiveness for many years because it lacked a strong central administration.

Richard Henry Dana's famous *Two Years Before the Mast*, which was published in 1840, exposed to the public another type of problem facing our merchant marine: the scandalously inhumane treatment of its seamen and lower officers. Herman Melville's best works, written only about ten years later, added fresh new evidence to the system's indictment. Melville's *Typee* and *Omoo* also pointed out that disloyal and desertion-prone crewmen deserved, in many instances, the harsh treatment they received.

In 1872, Congress passed legislation providing for the appointment of "shipping commissioners" at important U.S. ports. These gentlemen numbered among their duties the arbitration of disputes and controversies between ships' masters and crewmen. The commissioners also provided liaison between mariners desiring employment and ship operators needing employees. Records kept on each individual indicated whether his performance of duty had been satisfactory. Twelve years later these missions, and others of a minor nature, were assigned to a newly created Bureau of Navigation, so-called because the laws involved had been traditionally known as navigation laws.

Until 1903, the two agencies operated separately under the Treasury Department. From then until

Coast Guard Marine Inspectors at work.

1932, they operated as separate agencies within the Department of Commerce and Labor. At that time they were merged in one of the many sweeping economy moves precipitated by the Depression. The new combination was at first called the Bureau of Navigation and Steamboat Inspection. In 1936, as an indication of changes in marine propulsion systems as well as the program's emphasis, the name was changed to Bureau of Marine Inspection and Navigation.

From the earliest days of their existence, these two organizations suffered from critical public relations problems. The fine preventative work done by the Steamboat Inspectors was never called to the public attention. In the case of a serious maritime disaster, the Inspection Service was invariably made a scapegoat. One unresponsive Congress after another would ignore the Inspection Service's requests for improved safety legislation—until one or more grim disasters made the need for such legislation obvious beyond doubt. Even then, a great deal of historical foot-dragging is in evidence. A boiler explosion on board the steamer *Sultana* near Memphis killed 1,450 persons in 1865, but it was 1871 before corrective legislation was passed. In 1904, the excursion steamer *General Slocum* caught fire in New York harbor, with the loss of 955 lives. On this occasion a purge of the Steamboat Inspection Service was ordered. In 1915 the *Eastland* sank in a disaster which claimed 855 lives. In 1934, after countless intervening disasters, the *SS Morro Castle* burned, killing more than 100. In 1936, Congress at last passed corrective legislation, precisely as it had been recommended by the Steamboat Inspection Service more than two decades previously.

A number of significant improvements were included in the 1936 act. Marine Casualty Boards were established, not only to assess fault where appropriate, but to analyze causes and rectify them. Most important of all was the establishment of a Technical Division with the responsibility for approving plans and specifications for construction of all machinery-propelled U.S. passenger vessels of over 100 gross tons.

As the Coast Guard's own responsibility in the general field of maritime safety became more clearly defined over the years, it became apparent that there might be advantages in consolidating all such Federal services within a single agency. In 1942, the Coast Guard was effectively chosen as that agency when all safety functions of the Bureau of Marine Inspection and Navigation were transferred to it "until further notice." In 1946, the transfer was made final.

As in other mergers leading to the Coast Guard's present composition, there was some apprehension on both sides. In this particular case, there may have been more just reason for concern. Until this time, all Coast Guard officers had been qualified for general duty, but merchant marine safety was a highly specialized discipline. Aside from a few awkward problems in the field of officer career patterns, the transition has been an unqualified success. A major part of that success can be credited to the talented personnel who first began their Coast Guard service as members of the old Bureau.

Today the Coast Guard has trained its own cadre of merchant marine safety specialists. Increasingly, they have been drawn from the ranks of Coast Guard Academy graduates, although many are former merchant marine officers and a few holdovers from the Bureau still remain on active duty. Former enlisted personnel with technical specialties have also effectively augmented the Coast Guard's MMS program.

Mission responsibilities have grown tremendously. From design to destruction, merchant ships come under Coast Guard supervision. Design plan and specification approval is still a major MMS job. Even the welders who construct a merchant vessel's hull must pass a Coast Guard examination. Once constructed, the Coast Guard determines what type and how many personnel will be required to man the vessel. The Service also examines and licenses the operating personnel. While operational, the vessel must be periodically inspected by the Coast Guard. If the vessel is involved in a casualty, the Coast Guard will investigate.

The Service's Safety Equipment Branch evaluates lifesaving equipment of every description, including lifeboats, first aid kits, emergency food and water rations, fire fighting devices and systems, and life preservers. The Branch also evaluates the fire resistant qualities of certain construction materials.

Horizons are constantly being expanded. Atomic power has resulted in entirely new inspection criteria. Pollution control has become a major concern, as MMS personnel seek improved construction standards which will minimize the possibility of pollution incidents caused by collisions and other avoidable contingencies which may occur within navigable waters of the U.S. Regulations have been established which relate to the transportation of hazardous cargoes which are toxic, strongly corrosive, or likely to react explosively in contact with other substances. In contrast with times past, the President has recently come to the Coast Guard's Office of Merchant Marine Safety seeking the Service's recommendations for pollution control legislation.

The Coast Guard's MMS program is international in scope. The Service has been a dynamic force in both the United Nations' Intergovernmental Maritime Consultative Organization (IMCO) and several international conferences on Safety of Life at Sea (SOLAS) for many years. Merchant marine details carrying on many of the old Bureau of Navigation's former functions operate in major world ports such as Rotterdam, Yokohama, and Manila.

Still suffering from a public relations problem (its outstanding contributions to maritime safety are unknown to many, even within the Coast Guard), the Coast Guard's Office of Merchant Marine Safety has emerged as one of the foremost entries in the Service's battle against catastrophes at sea.

Merchant Marine Inspection Offices

MIO New York

Commercial Vessel Safety (CVS) is one of the Coast Guard's biggest and most important jobs. As such, it occupies the efforts of approximately 15% of the Coast Guard's entire officer corps (nearly 600 out of slightly more than 4,000). And almost 15% of the Service's Marine Inspectors are assigned to duty at a single station, the Service's huge Marine Inspection Office in New York, N.Y.

From drawing board to scrapyard, U.S. merchant vessels come under Coast Guard regulation. To illustrate the pervasive responsibilities which MIO might exercise over a single merchant ship, the authors have chosen the convenient device of tracing the history of a fictional tanker, SS Flotsam.

The Flotsam was envisioned by her owner, the Enterprise Oil Company, as a rather routine addition to the company's already sizable tanker fleet. Physically, Flotsam would be almost identical to two other Enterprise tankers, SS Jetsam and SS Plankton. Flotsam would be the same length and have the same tank capacity as the other two vessels. In an effort to cut construction and operating costs, the oil company had made a few noteworthy modifications in Flotsam's design. The Enterprise Company hoped to utilize a new, inexpensive alloy in Flotsam's piping and boilers. Enterprise also hoped to install electrical wiring with insulation different than that employed in the previous two tankers. Finally, the company's new design incorporated a number of automated features into the ship's main propulsion plant, with the hope that these mechanical innovations might reduce the number of personnel necessary to operate the tanker.

Before Enterprise could begin work on Flotsam, the company had to win Coast Guard approval of the ship's design plans. In accordance with standard procedures, the plans were submitted to the Officer in Charge, Marine Inspection (OCMI), of the New York office. The OCMI (commanding officer) briefly reviewed the plans, attached his comments, and forwarded them to the Merchant Marine Technical Branch located in New York. Technical Branch offices are also located in New Orleans, Cleveland, and San Francisco. All come under the direct supervision of the MMT Branch at Coast Guard Headquarters in Washington, rather than under the supervision of the Coast Guard District in which they are located. Enterprise could have sent the plans directly to the N.Y. MMT branch, but thought the OCMI should have an opportunity to have a look at plans for a vessel which would be constructed within the New York MIO's geographical jurisdiction.

Coast Guard engineers studied the plans at great length, paying especially thorough attention to design factors which might detract from the ship's ability to perform its job safely. Particular emphasis was placed on evaluation of those systems which would be subjected to high temperatures and pressures. Electrical circuitry was analyzed at length. Personnel accomodations were studied to insure adequate ventilation, and other acceptable standards of habitability. The vessel's stability and water-tight integrity were given careful consideration. Materials to be used in the tanker's construction were checked to ensure they were on the list of such substances approved by the Coast Guard. Approval standards for materials are based on strength, durability, fire resistance, and other properties.

No other ship builder had ever attempted constructing its piping and boilers from the new alloy Enterprise proposed. Consequently, it was necessary for MMT to conduct and analyze tests of the alloy to ensure its adequacy for the planned application. The tests proved conclusively that constructing high pressure systems from the alloy would require piping and wall thicknesses almost double that shown in Enterprise's plans..

Other features of the design appeared

satisfactory, so the plans were returned to the Enterprise Company with an accompanying letter. The letter stated the plans were approved, subject to modification of the piping and boiler systems. Enterprise was left with the options either of using heavier applications of the new alloy or returning to acceptable conventional procedures. After weighing all considerations, the company decided to abandon the alloy idea and use the same materials it had used in previous tankers.

The Practical Shipyard of Paterson, New Jersey won the contract to build *Flotsam*. Practical was delighted to get the job, but faced immediate problems. As the shipyard already had what was virtually a full workload, it would be necessary to hire several new welders. Fortunately for Practical, an iron works nearby had just gone out of business, putting several welders out of work. Practical hired them all. Unfortunately, none had previously worked in a shipyard. Because welders working on some specific phases of ship construction must be certified by competent authority, OCMI N.Y. sent

out one of his inspectors to examine Practical's new men. Each welder was subjected to a stringent practical examination. Materials welded by the men were then taken to a laboratory where the welds were X-rayed for imperfections. Then, each weld was stressed to the breaking point. Welders who passed the examination were certified by the Coast Guard inspector, and were allowed to work on critical facets of *Flotsam's* construction.

Because Practical is one of the principal shipyards in the New York area, two officers from the N.Y. MIO are always assigned to the yard as Resident Inspectors. One of the inspectors is a hull expert; the other, a boiler expert. In reality, both are qualified in virtually all aspects of merchant vessel inspection. From the moment *Flotsam's* construction began, these two officers were on hand to ensure that the ship was built to required standards. Their efforts were directed not only toward ensuring that the vessel was built according to the approved plans, but according to approved construction practices as well. They inspected the

Marine Inspection Office, New York, N.Y.

materials used, as well as the *way* in which the materials were used. Other inspectors from the N.Y. MIO periodically visited the Practical yard to augment the Resident Inspectors' work.

As work on *Flotsam* progressed, representatives of Enterprise Oil Company and of the maritime unions met with the Coast Guard OCMI to determine an appropriate manning level for *Flotsam*. The automated systems Enterprise had incorporated into *Flotsam's* design had been used by several other shippers with conspicuous success. Consequently, both the Coast Guard and the unions agreed that *Flotsam* could be safely and satisfactorily operated by 25, rather than the 27 personnel normally required for tankers of *Flotsam's* size. Final decision in the matter rested with the Coast Guard, which approved the requested manning.

Flotsam's construction was now almost completed, and it was time for Enterprise to employ a crew for its new tanker. Enterprise practiced a merit system in the operation of its fleet, so most of *Flotsam's* crew would be composed of personnel the company felt had earned opportunities for promotion. Before they could be advanced, several of the men had to qualify for higher licenses than they presently held. Foster Driver, the First Mate on board *Jetsam*, had been offered command of *Flotsam* if he could pass the examination for his Master's license. A graduate of Marine Maritime Academy, Driver had very little difficulty in passing the rigid examination. The Coast Guard had put its seal of approval on the curriculum offered by the Marine Academy, so Driver was sailing familiar seas when he took the test.

Al K. Hall, an ordinary seaman who would be sailing on board *Flotsam*, visited the MIO to be examined for his Lifeboatman's Endorsement. As unlicensed merchant mariners acquire certain special skills, they can, after an appropriate exam, have their basic documents endorsed with a certification of those skills. Each merchant vessel is required to carry a certain number of qualified lifeboatmen on board, and personnel holding a Lifeboatman's Endorsement receive slightly more pay than they otherwise would.

Flotsam was now completed. The tanker's operating equipment had been tested, both at the dock and at sea, without turning up any disqualifying deficiencies. Then, the ship was given a final check by inspectors of the MIO staff. They found the vessel generally seaworthy. They did observe a number of minor problems which needed correcting. On the basis of the inspectors' report,

the OCMI issued *Flotsam* a Certificate of Inspection which would be valid for two years. Accompanying the Certificate was a list of deficiencies, all of which had to be corrected within 60 days. The Certificate also listed the number and qualifications of personnel legally required to operate the ship.

Civilian personnel of the MIO's Admeasurement Section computed and certified the tanker's cubic volume and issued a document authorizing her to engage in international trade. The MIO's Documentation Section recorded the tanker's title and mortgage, and assigned her both a name, *Flotsam*, and an official number. Documentation and Admeasurement functions are relatively recent Coast Guard responsibilities. They were acquired from the Customs Bureau in 1967, when the Coast Guard became a part of the Department of Transportation.

Only one thing further was required before *Flotsam* could sail: the tanker's personnel had to be signed on officially. This event is witnessed by the Coast Guard officer who serves as the MIO's Shipping Commissioner (SC). "Shipping," as used in his title, refers to a man's being hired to serve on board a ship. "Discharge" is the opposite of shipping. The SC witnesses both types of articles each time the documents are signed on board a ship.

Having completed these affairs, *Flotsam* embarked on her first sea voyage. Her first stop was Savannah, where she onloaded a cargo of petroleum solvent. While in Savannah, the tanker also corrected the faulty guardrails and fire extinguishers which had been her only uncorrected deficiencies when she left New York. Coast Guard inspectors from the Savannah MIO notified MIO N.Y. that the corrections had been made.

Approximately a year after her first sailing, *Flotsam* returned to New York, where she underwent what is known as a "mid-period inspection." These inspections are required between the 10th and 14th months after a vessel receives a Certificate of Inspection. Two inspectors spent a full day in carrying out *Flotsam's* mid-period check. They discovered a number of serious safety violations: cracked ribs on one of the tanker's lifeboats; several broken life rails on deck, and an insufficient number of life jackets on board. The inspectors also discovered one very serious violation. The ship's Chief Engineer had tied down the "overspeed trip" on his main turbo-generator. The trip is a safety device designed to prevent turbines from being operated beyond the speeds for which they are designed. The Engineer was severely chastised by the inspectors and ordered to untie the trip device so it could function properly. The Engineer sheepishly admitted that he knew he was taking a chance by disabling the safety trip, but said they were trying to get a bit of extra speed out of *Flotsam* and it was annoying to have the trip periodically cut out. Annoying or not, the trip was there for a purpose and if *Flotsam* wasn't fast enough, she should have been designed differently. *Flotsam's* captain was issued Coast Guard Form 835, citing the safety deficiencies and requiring that they be corrected before leaving for another port.

While *Flotsam* was in New York, she was also visited by the Senior Investigating Officer (SIO), another key member of the MIO staff. The SIO's visit was prompted by a complaint he had received from one of *Flotsam's* seamen. The seaman, Al K. Hall, accused Captain Driver of cruel and unjust treatment of the ship's unlicensed personnel. The results of the SIO's investigation, however, indicated that, in fact, Hall was a trouble-maker with a serious drinking problem. The SIO consequently served a charge of misconduct on Hall, requiring him to appear before the Coast Guard Hearing Examiner in New York. Because Hall's previous, rather lengthy service had been unblemished, and because Captain Driver personally intervened on the seaman's behalf the Hearing Examiner was lenient. Hall was placed on probation.

Normally, in order to renew her Certificate of Inspection, *Flotsam* would have required complete reinspection within another 12 months. Shortly before her 24th month of service, however, the tanker tragically and needlessly sank while enroute to Le Havre, France. *Flotsam's* Chief Engineer was known for his bull-headed stubbornness. Thus, the ship had hardly more than left the dock in New York when he once again wired down the overspeed trip. Captain Driver insisted on speed out of his ship, and the Chief Engineer was determined to provide it if at all possible. A short in the electrical circuit providing excitation to the main generator triggered the disaster. Under ordinary circumstances, the short wouldn't have amounted to much; the overspeed trip would have seen to that. With the trip disabled, and with a complete loss of load on the turbine, the turbo-generator began to race away wildly. The Engineer immediately recognized the problem and rushed toward the generator to untie the trip. In his panic, he dropped the wire cutters needed for

the job. And, as he bent over to pick them up, a jagged fragment of metal casing ripped completely through his abdomen. The generator had disintegrated from the tremendous centrifugal force of the overspeed.

The scene was now a holocaust. Shrapnel was flying everywhere. A two-foot hole was ripped through the engineroom hull, slightly below the water line. The tanker's Second Assistant Engineer was killed instantly when a metal fragment penetrated his neck as he was attempting to shut off the ship's main sea suction valve. Tons of cold seawater poured into the ship from condenser tubes which had been severed by other flying fragments.

Within twenty minutes, the ship disappeared forever beneath the sea. Three men, including *Flotsam's* Chief Engineer, were killed in the disaster. A Coast Guard cutter, diverted from Ocean Station Charlie, rescued the remainder of the crew.

A Formal Board of Investigation was convened. The Coast Guard Captain serving as the Third Coast Guard District Chief of Staff was named to head the Board. Four other Coast Guard officers, including two from Headquarters in Washington, rounded out the membership. Relevant testimony was sketchy at best, but at last, the Board succeeded in recreating essential details of the disaster.

Because the Chief Engineer, as the person most responsible for the disaster, was deceased, the Board made no recommendations concerning him. In the case of *Flotsam's* Master, however, the Board considered further action appropriate. Captain Driver had tacitly approved his engineer's hazardous practices, and had made no real effort to correct them. Thus, Driver appeared to have been negligent in the performance of his duties. He was served with charges requiring him to appear before a Hearing Examiner. The Examiner suspended Driver's Master's License for a period of six months, and in fact, the young officer was never again employed as master of a ship.

The *Flotsam* saga, as previously mentioned, is fictitious (although based on fact). Further, it has been perhaps excessively simplified. Maritime disasters, for example, rarely result from something as uncomplex as tying down an overspeed trip. Nevertheless, the foregoing account clearly indicates the sweeping responsibilities which Coast Guard MIO's have over the U.S. merchant marine.

It is worthy of note, that most MIO's have far fewer personnel than does New York. Of the 57

Merchant Marine Inspection units operated by the Coast Guard, many are located in places such as Wilmington, North Carolina, Lake Charles, Louisiana, and Ludington, Michigan. In areas such as these, two officers may be assigned the entire range of responsibilities managed by 68 at MIO New York.

It is also significant that the Coast Guard's Commercial Vessel Safety Program is so overwhelmingly effective, that situations involving the loss of a U.S. merchant ship are very rare indeed.

Using extremely conservative statistics, the Coast Guard estimates that CVS prevents 1,100 needless deaths each year, and saves $150 million in property.

The fundamentally undramatic nature of CVS has resulted in a large cadre of hardworking officers who wear very few medals on their chests. Whether working out of New York or Ludington, Merchant Marine Inspectors can be numbered among the real unsung heroes of Coast Guard service.

Having plunged into the icy North Atlantic from a Coast Guard combat cutter in shipwreck drill, Coast Guardsman Leonard Kadish clambers dripping back up the life net and over the side. A 1944 photo.

Military Readiness

Military readiness is a vital and pervasive part of the Coast Guard's duties. Nevertheless, the subject will not be treated as lengthily and definitively in this section of the book as have been some of the Service's other major missions. The reasons are obvious. Much of the Coast Guard's military role is classified. Further, the practical application of the Service's military preparedness has been repeatedly illustrated throughout this book's historical section.

It is noteworthy that the Coast Guard was originally conceived as a military service. Alexander Hamilton said that giving the officers military rank " . . . would attach them to their duty by a nicer sense of honor." In July, 1797, nearly a year before it legislated a navy into being, congress passed a bill authorizing augmentation of personnel and armament on board revenue cutters for purposes of national defense. After the navy was established, the Act of March 2, 1799 defined the Revenue Cutter Service's military role more specifically: "PROVIDED, the said revenue cutters shall, whenever the President of the United States shall so direct, cooperate with the Navy of the United States, during which time, they will be under the direction of the Secretary of the Navy, and the expenses thereof shall be defrayed by agents of the Navy Department."

In reality, the President had already anticipated the action of Congress by transferring, in October, 1798, the entire fleet of cutters to the Navy. They remained under Navy control for two years thereafter, during the quasi-war with France and the period of piracy suppression in the Caribbean.

In 1915, when the Revenue Cutter and Lighthouse Services combined to form the Coast Guard, the cutters had already won an enduring place in American military history. To ensure that there would be no misunderstanding, the act creating the new service states that " . . . the Coast Guard . . . shall operate under the Treasury Department in time of peace and operate as a part of the Navy, subject to the orders of the Secretary of the Navy, in time of war or when the President shall so direct . . . "

The historical section of this book is replete with instances of the Coast Guard's cooperating with or operating under the Navy. The invariable smoothness with which these transitions have taken place is not a product of chance.

Every Coast Guardsman is a military man and is trained as such from the moment he enters boot camp, the Academy, or OCS. Selected senior Coast Guard officers attend the most advanced military training programs in the U.S.: the Armed Forces

A fighting Coast Guardsman is given rigorous training under battle conditions. Plunging into the sea, rifle, helmet and all, he swims for shore, preparing himself for such an emergency in the far-flung sea fronts of the war.

Staff College; Naval War College; National War College; Industrial College of the Armed Forces; and others. Cutters are equipped with military armament and regularly conduct gunnery exercises. The Service's modern 378-foot cutters are outfitted with the latest developments in anti-submarine warfare ordnance.

The Coast Guard's major East Coast cutters participate in "Refresher Training" at Guantanamo Bay, Cuba, at intervals of 12 to 18 months. Each

161

grueling training session lasts from three to four weeks, during which 12-hour workdays are considered routine. Every facet of operational readiness is covered, but the military role is particularly emphasized. Similar training is conducted in Norfolk, Virginia, for the benefit of the Service's 210-foot cutters, as well as a few of its seagoing tugs and 180-foot buoy tenders.

In the Pacific, units utilize training facilities in San Diego or Pearl Harbor. All units, of whatever size, conduct regular training programs of their own.

It is no wonder then that the Coast Guard's motto "Semper Paratus" has the ring of truth to it. The service has spared nothing to ensure that it is always ready and ready in all ways.

Top: At a U.S. Coast Guard Training School during World War II, men are taught the difficult art of swimming ashore, weighted down with full battle equipment. *Bottom:* Coast Guard recruits at Cape May, N.J. Cadets and officer candidates receive instruction in major ordnance as well as small arms.

Taney, 327-foot class

Of the 101 U.S. fighting ships present during the Japanese attack on Pearl Harbor, only one remains in active service. She is the Coast Guard cutter *Taney,* a vessel which has performed distinguished service in three foreign wars, most recently in Vietnam.

Taney and her sister ships of the 327-foot class, whether because of their superior design or the historical time frame of their collective existence, have become classic representatives of the Coast Guard at war. Although smaller and slower than U.S. Navy ships doing similar jobs, the Coast Guard gunboats proved remarkably adept at anti-submarine warfare. *Campbell, Duane, Spencer,* and *Ingham* were all credited with U-boat sinkings in the Battle of the Atlantic. *Taney,* in addition to driving away a force of 5 enemy aircraft during the Pearl Harbor attack, dropped depth charges on a submarine the following day in an attack which was considered by most observers to have resulted in destroying the underwater craft. She also downed 5 Japanese aircraft during the Battle of Okinawa in 1945. Sadly, another member of the Class, the *Alexander Hamilton,* became one of the Coast Guard's first major casualties in World War II. An explosion from what was thought to be a torpedo ripped the vessel's mid-section asunder, killing the entire engineering crew and resulting in *Hamilton's* sinking while under tow into Reykjavik, Iceland.

When originally constructed in 1936, *Taney's* mission was that of a search and rescue cutter—the largest in the Pacific. From her first home port of Honolulu, Hawaii, she participated in numerous rescue missions and supported Department of Interior operations in the equatorial islands of Howland, Canton, Baker, Palmyra, Jarvis, Enderbury, and Tutuila. During the conflict with the Axis powers, she traveled the globe from Pearl Harbor to New York to North Africa, and back to Okinawa.

Following that great naval engagement, she returned to the U.S. mainland where much of her armament was removed and she again assumed a peacetime mission, manning ocean stations in the Pacific. The majority of her service during the years which have ensued has been spent on Ocean Stations Victor and November, where she provided

U.S. Coast Guard Cutter *Taney* answering a distress call near Ocean Beach, San Francisco, Cal., Feb. 9, 1960.

communications and meteorological support during the Korean War. In the fall of 1969 she was deployed to the South China Sea, patrolling the coast of the Republic of Vietnam and providing naval gunfire support.

For many years the 327's were the Coast Guard's "Capital Ships." Certainly, *Taney's* title, "Queen of the Pacific" is still a well-deserved one. The advent of the Service's 378-foot class has somewhat diminished Coast Guard pride in the older class of cutters, but in the minds of many old-time officers, never have finer ships been constructed than *Taney's* noble breed.

There are no plans for decommissioning them within the near future, despite their advanced years. The 2,400-ton displacement ships are powered by twin boilers, driving twin turbines, driving twin shafts. Their very respectable speed of 20 knots, combined with wonderful maneuvering characteristics, makes them fully capable of performing any task to which they are assigned.

Every one of the 143 men assigned to *Taney* attest that the old girl has a lot of life left in her yet. The prestigious place of the 327-foot cutters in Coast Guard history is well assured.

Top: Taney as she appeared during World War II. *Bottom: Taney* as she appears today.

Ocean Stations

If you were to ask a number of Coast Guardsmen to name the Service's toughest duty, you would probably receive as many answers as there are persons in the group. But most of them would agree that one type of duty—ocean stations—has hardly any redeeming qualities. One historian has described an ocean station as "44,000 square miles of bad weather." To Coast Guardsmen who have served ocean station vessels (OSV's), that description will probably seem an understatement.

As a mission of the Service, the stations had their origins during the nerve-wracking years of "neutrality" preceding World War II. After Hitler's invasion of Poland, in 1939, most merchant vessels felt too intimidated by the threat of German U-Boats to risk radio transmission at sea. An immediate and unfortunate result of this radio silence was the cessation of radio weather reports which merchant vessels had formerly provided the U.S. Weather Bureau on a voluntary basis. Although these reports had consisted of little more than on-scene surface conditions, they had been an invaluable aid to the Weather Bureau for its ocean predictions. To resolve this information crisis, the Bureau requested that the Coast Guard implement a program of "Weather Patrols." In February,

Crew members dig furiously to free the 311-foot U.S. Coast Guard Cutter *Castle Rock* of her 300-ton ice shroud caused by a severe winter storm in the North Atlantic.

A day on Ocean Station; 44,000 square miles of bad weather.

1940, two ocean stations were established between Bermuda and the Azores. Cutters of the 327-foot class were assigned to the new patrol duty

To increase the value and validity of the reports provided, the Service took upper atmospheric observations through the use of radiosonde balloons, while continuing to make surface observations. The radiosondes, which still play an important role in the Ocean Station Program, are ingenious, helium-filled balloons outfitted with tiny radio transmitters. By tracking the balloons on radar as they ascend into the upper atmosphere, and by monitoring the radiosonde's transmissions, National Weather Service meteorologists assigned to the cutters are able to determine upper-air wind speed and direction, in addition to temperature, and barometric pressure, at any given altitude.

Weather information provided to pilots making transatlantic flights was possibly even more important during the war than the reports relayed to shore-based weather facilities. As U.S. involvement in the war began in earnest, merchant vessels were being sunk at such an alarming rate that increasing quantities of vital cargo were transported across the Atlantic in aircraft. For the pilots engaged in this bold undertaking, the weather cutters represented a possible safe ditching site in the event of emergency, as well as a source of badly needed meteorological information. The relative success of air cargo operations soon necessitated the establishment of additional ocean stations. By 1944, the U.S. was operating 13 stations in the North Atlantic. America's European allies were operating an additional nine. At the war's end, there were a total of 24 ocean stations established in the Pacific theater.

During the confused period of readjustment following Japan's surrender, the U.S. ocean station program was drastically curtailed in both major oceans. At their lowest ebb, during 1946, only two stations remained in the Pacific and one in the Atlantic. Memories of the stations' benefits were etched too deeply in the minds of the world's pilots to allow complete abandonment of the program. As military pilots familiar with the program gravitated to employment in civil aviation, a worldwide wave of support for ocean stations began to swell. On September 17, 1946, representatives of the governments of the U.S., Canada, France, the United Kingdom, the Netherlands, Norway, Iceland, Ireland, Denmark, Sweden, and Belgium convened in London to consider development of an ocean station network suited for a world at peace.

Although consensus was strong that the program should be re-established, most of the participating nations were slow to honor the commitments agreed on at the London conference. Then, one of the most dramatic rescues in Coast Guard history underscored the potential of ocean stations so forcefully that no one could continue to question their value.

On October 14, 1947, the Coast Guard cutter *Bibb* was patrolling Ocean Station "Charlie," midway between Ireland and Newfoundland. A violent storm—not uncommon for the season and locale—was raging as a message of desperation was intercepted from *Bermuda Sky Queen*, an aircraft en route from Ireland to New York. The intense winds which were hurling massive waves over *Bibb's* bow and superstructure had impeded the *Sky Queen's* progress to the extent that the plane's fuel supply was exhausted. The only hope for survival of the 69 passengers on board the plane depended on the highly unlikely possibility of a successful ditching at sea.

Using her radio beacon, the *Sky Queen* homed on *Bibb*, the plane's only real hope of salvation. With the poised calm unique to those long accustomed to decisions where human lives may hang in the balance, the two captains laid their plans. While the *Sky Queen* circled overhead, *Bibb* readied her lifeboats and spread oil on the treacherous seas. When preparations had been completed, the *Sky Queen* made her perilous descent, plunging headlong into the crest of a 20-foot wave. Miraculously, the plane's hull remained intact.

As the plane appeared to be floating satisfactorily and in no immediate danger, the decision was made to await an expected moderation in the weather before attempting to launch the cutter's boats and rafts. By three o'clock in the afternoon the storm had showed no signs of subsiding while the plane was definitely beginning to leak. A chance had to be taken, and quickly. One of *Bibb's* rafts was dropped into the violent sea which was still capable of producing an occasional 35-foot wave. Four round trips, characterized by grave danger, resulted in the safe transfer of 44 persons to the ship. Then darkness fell, making further rescue attempts impossible. Though the storm raged unabated throughout the night, the *Sky Queen* was still afloat at daybreak the following morning, enabling the recommencement of rescue efforts. Four days later, as *Bibb* steamed into Boston harbor with the *Sky Queen's* 69 survivors on board, a broom was lashed to her masthead, signifying a "clean sweep." The program of worldwide ocean stations was off and running.

Today the Coast Guard operates six conventional ocean stations, one or two of which may be eliminated during 1972. All ocean stations are strategically located along major air and sea navigational routes. Other nations operate another six stations. Since 1969, the Coast Guard has also stationed the cutter *Gresham* on weather station "Hotel," north of Norfolk, Virginia, in a new operational concept. *Gresham* is classified as a weather ship rather than a full-service OSV. She is scheduled to operate away from her home port for approximately 210 days each year, which is commensurate with the schedules observed by high endurance cutters manning other Atlantic weather patrols. *Gresham's* operating time is compressed into an 8-month season from August through March. Liberal personnel leave policies actually make this type of schedule somewhat milder than that of conventional OSV's. The latter usually spend 21 days on station at one time. Travel time

to and from station can extend this period by as much as two weeks.

Despite recent developments such as the creation of weather station Hotel, and despite occasional rescue incidents as dramatic as the *Bermuda Sky Queen* case, the future of the Coast Guard's ocean station program has been questioned increasingly within recent years. No dollar value can be attached to a single human life, but as weather observation platforms, the cutters have become somewhat anachronistic since the advent of weather satellites and automated data buoys. It appears to some that weather cutters are simply not cost-effective. To a majority of those who have endured the misery, boredom, discomfort, and time away from their families brought by assignment to an ocean station vessel, abolition of the program would come as no great loss. National priorities will dictate the final decision.

Whatever the future holds, ocean stations have justly earned their place in history. Rough duty? Yes, but magnificent in the service they have provided humanity.

A Monomoy surfboat from the U.S. Coast Guard Cutter *Bibb* sets out to survey behavior of the ditched flying boat *Bermuda Sky Queen* and practice approaches when plane and cutter were determining safest way of removing plane's passengers and crew. October 14, 1947.

Chincoteague, 311-foot class

Changing operational requirements and economical considerations have made it necessary for the Coast Guard, at more than one juncture in history, to borrow ships from the U.S. Navy. In some instances, the vessels so acquired were motley castoffs, hardly fit for the tasks assigned. In the case of its now aging 311-foot class of cutters, the Service was fortunate enough to borrow naval vessels ideally suited for the job at hand. That job—ocean stations—and the 311-foot ship class were both a direct outgrowth of World War II.

The Norfolk, Virginia-based Coast Guard cutter *Chincoteague* was launched at Lake Washington Shipyard in Houghton, Washington. She was the ninth small seaplane tender of the 311-foot *Barnegat* Class built for the Navy. Like her sister ships, she was christened with the name of a bay.

Upon her commissioning in April of 1943, the sleek little warship departed almost immediately for duty with the Pacific Fleet. On July 6th, she arrived at Saboe Bay in the Santa Cruz Islands, where she was scheduled to serve as tender for Fleet Air Wing 1 during the New Guinea campaign. Eleven days later the young ship was nearly destroyed during a massive Japanese bomber attack on the bay. A direct hit in the after engine room killed one officer and eight enlisted men. Two near misses did extensive additional damage.

Many other ships were lost during the war after suffering damages far less serious than *Chincoteague's,* but this valiant little tender's history was just beginning. With extraordinary skill, *Chincoteague's* damage control team made emergency repairs which kept the ship afloat and allowed it to be towed away for overhaul. The composure, logic, and expertise demonstrated by *Chincoteague* during this incident have made it a classic in the history of damage control. The event is still being relived today as a part of the standard Navy Damage Control School curriculum.

By winter of 1944, *Chincoteague* was busily back in action. From then until war's end, she participated in a variety of campaigns which took her to the Solomons, the Marshalls (Kwajalein, Eniwetok), and Iwo Jima, where she again received severe battle damage. She ended the war in the Far East, serving as a base for seaplanes operating off the coast of China. She had earned six battle stars.

When decommissioned and placed in the reserve fleet on December 21, 1946, there was little reason to think that her most productive years of service might still lie ahead. In 1949 she and a number of her sister ships were recommissioned as Coast Guard cutters to fulfill the pressing needs of that Service's ocean station program. This program, which was originally founded at the outset of the war, was almost completely phased out after the armistice was signed. Then, just three months before *Chincoteague* was sent to the mothball fleet, the U.S., Canada, and several European nations entered into an agreement whereby the United States Coast Guard would undertake the manning of four North Atlantic weather stations. A dramatic rescue case in October of 1947, during which the cutter *Bibb* rescued 69 survivors of the aircraft *Bermuda Queen* when it was forced to ditch in the open seas, pointed out the need for accelerating entry into the ocean station program. A new fleet of ships was needed immediately but there was neither time nor money to build new ones. Enter *Chincoteague* and the other 311's.

On October 30th, 1956, while patrolling Ocean Station Delta, *Chincoteague* won an enduring place in Coast Guard history by rescuing the entire 35-man crew of the ill-fated German vessel *Helga Bolten.* The rescue was accomplished during heavy winds and 25-foot seas. For this action, the cutter received a bronze plaque from the Federal Republic of Germany.

Chincoteague also seems to have well remembered her lessons learned in combat. During the past decade, she has won a number of major awards for her excellence in anti-submarine warfare and gunnery exercises, as well as for general military readiness and over-all performance.

Presently, *Chincoteague* is one of more than 20 high endurance cutters assigned to Atlantic ocean station duties. Each year she makes five or six ocean station patrols, varying from 30 to 40 days in length. The abnormally large fuel capacity of the 311-foot cutters makes them particularly well suited for such duty. While on station, the cutters routinely transmit hourly weather observations to shore stations for further dissemination to the weather bureau. Several types of oceanographic observations are also made. In addition, the ship contacts overseas airline flights, furnishing them with communications services, and weather and navigational information. It is not uncommon to contact more than 2,000 such aircraft during a single patrol.

Four of *Chincoteague's* sister ships, the cutters *Yakutat, Bering Strait, Cook Inlet,* and *Castle Rock* were transferred to the Republic of Vietnam under the Coast Guard's unique turn-over program. The heroic *Chincoteague's* remaining days of service were growing short as this book approached its publication date. The Nixon Administration's economic policies insisted on major cost reductions during fiscal year 1972. The Coast Guard's proposed responses to the Administration's decree included the decommissioning of six high endurance cutters. *Chincoteague* is one of them.

It seems certain that the old girl's service will have ended by late 1972, but her memory will endure in the pages of Coast Guard and Navy history.

Top: The *Helga Bolten* wallows in heavy seas, 400 miles east-southeast of Cape Race, Newfoundland. *Bottom:* The 311-foot USCGC *Chincoteague.*

Oceanography

Early voyages of the revenue cutters *Lincoln*, *Wayanda*, and *Corwin* to Alaska and the Bering Sea were filled with significance for the future Coast Guard. The historical precedents established in those epic journeys to the Arctic north form the foundations of two of the Coast Guard's most important missions: icebreaking and oceanography. Thus, oceanography, thought of by many as one of the most modern of scientific disciplines, has figured importantly in Coast Guard operations for more than one hundred years.

Oceanography is a comprehensive study of the oceans in all their aspects. It combines physics, chemistry, geography, biology, ecology, meteorology, and geology as applied to man's search for knowledge of the sea. Not surprisingly, the oceanographic sciences interplay with virtually all Coast Guard missions.

The Service's first oceanographic efforts were made by the *Lincoln* in 1867 and they furthered U.S. knowledge of general geography in Alaska and the Bering Sea. Creation of the International Ice Patrol in 1914 brought the Coast Guard directly into the study of ocean currents, and launched a greatly expanded role for the Service in the oceanographic sciences. Within thirteen years, the Ice Patrol's observations made it possible to forecast, with considerable accuracy, the movements of icebergs in the area of Newfoundland's Grand Banks.

With the hope of learning more about the origins of these huge, icy threats to navigation, the 125-foot cutter *Marion* was dispatched on a major oceanographic cruise to Baffin Bay and Davis Strait in the summer of 1928. *Marion* was a tiny ship for such a large undertaking but she was outfitted, for the term of her mission, with some of the most advanced oceanographic apparatus of that day. Two deep-sea winches were installed, along with equipment which made it possible to take simultaneous water samples at several predetermined depths. Salinity and temperature measurements were also made. Installation of a new and promising invention, the fathometer,

Famous Revenue Cutters of the early Alaskan Patrols and Bering Sea Patrols at anchor at Sitka Harbor, 1895. They are (l. to r.) the Cutters *Wolcott*, *Rush*, *Grant* and *Corwin*.

Top: U.S. Revenue Cutter *Oliver Wolcott, Jr.* (1873-1897). *Bottom:* U.S. Revenue Cutter *Richard Rush* (1874-1913),one of the earliest of a long line of Coast Guard cutters that served on Alaskan patrols.

made it possible for *Marion* to determine the depth of waters in which she was operating. In subsequent years, *General Greene*, one of *Marion's* sister ships, made several similar voyages.

Gradually, as oceanography's importance became better recognized, increasing numbers of Coast Guard cutters were equipped with scientific apparatus and used as "ships of opportunity." Improvement of the Service's system of navigational aids lent greater validity to oceanographic observations made by vessels of whatever description. World War II, with its threat of Nazi submarines, expanded use of the bathythermograph, a device whose graphic depiction of temperature versus depth, provided insight into deceptive practices which might be employed by underwater craft.

The Ocean Station Program, established shortly before the war, continues to enrich man's progress in oceanography. While on station, and while travelling to and from their various destinations, the Service's ocean station vessels conduct a wide variety of oceanographic observations. The cutters have been particularly noteworthy in their cooperation with various other institutions and agencies connected with the oceanographic sciences. Plankton samples have been collected for Columbia University, the Scottish Marine Biological Association, American Museum of Natural History, the Smithsonian Institution and others. Water samples for specialized chemical studies have been collected for organizations as diverse as the Scripps Institute of Oceanography and the Atomic Energy Commission.

In 1948, the cutter *Evergreen*, a buoy tender of the 180-foot class, was outfitted as the Coast Guard's first cutter exclusively devoted to oceanography. She has performed splendidly over the years and has participated in numerous cooperative projects. Her collaboration on biological studies with the Florida Board of Conservation and the U.S. Bureau of Commercial Fisheries has been especially relevant to ecological interests.

In 1965, the Coast Guard Cutter *Rockaway*, a 311-foot former seaplane tender, was converted into the Service's second oceanographic vessel. She is equipped with chemical, biological, physical, and instrumentation laboratories. *Rockaway* has made extraordinary contributions to man's knowledge about the scientific basis for increasing the harvest of fisheries, as well as the effects of weather on food production from the sea. A third vessel, the former sea-going tug *Acushnet*, was converted for oceanographic purposes in 1968.

Today, icebreakers, automated buoys, lightships, and offshore towers participate in a variety of oceanographic programs, along with more than 40 of the Coast Guard's general duty cutters. An Oceanographic Unit has been established in Washington, D.C., adjacent to the National Oceanographic Data Center.

The oceanographic Cutter *Evergreen* as she appeared in 1963.

Facilities are only part of the story, however, for the Coast Guard has also trained its own skilled force of oceanographic personnel. For many years, selected Coast Guard officers have received postgraduate instruction in the oceanographic sciences. In 1968, the Service established a new "Marine Sciences Technician" rating for its enlisted oceanographers. Simultaneously, the Coast Guard set up its own "MST" school at Governors Island, New York.

The beginning of 1970 found the Coast Guard busier than ever before in this rapidly growing mission. As a part of the Service's dynamic anti-pollution program, research projects concentrated on determining what might happen to oil spilled in the Arctic environment, and on better defining the Arctic's present ecological status. Coast Guard participation in the "Tektite" projects of 1969 and 1970 was a major factor in man's first attempts to live for prolonged periods in underwater habitats. Cooperative projects in the Weddell Sea, the Caribbean, the eastern tropical Pacific, and other areas placed the Service in increasingly prominent roles in international oceanography. A special Search and Rescue Project, to study the effects of winds, waves, and currents on drifting life rafts and other objects was producing a priceless store house of information.

Then, in late 1970, a new National Oceanographic and Atmospheric Administration (NOAA) was legislated into existence. After extended controversy, during which a number of congressmen, lobbyists, and editorial writers advocated the Coast Guard's inclusion in the proposed new agency, NOAA was ultimately organized without the older seagoing Service. The move did strip the Coast Guard of its National Data Buoy Project.

Thus, as the seventies advance, the Coast Guard's future role in oceanography is somewhat indeterminate. At the executive level, speculation is that a growing NOAA will require growing Coast Guard support, and that the cutter *Lincoln's* heritage will extend to endless generations of Coast Guard units to increase man's domain over that 71% of his planet which consists of the oceans.

Constant probing for knowledge of the ocean currents (which greatly influence iceberg movements) is important to the Ice Patrol's predictions and tracking plots for iceberg seasons. The tests are being made on the Coast Guard's oceanographic ship *Evergreen.*

The Coast Guard Cutter *Marion* in front of the glacier at Port DeQuervain, Greenland.

Top: A five-liter sample of sea water (right) on board the U.S. Coast Guard Cutter *Casco* during *Equalant II* surveys. *Bottom:* Mark F. Miller, a student scientist from the University of Wisconsin, lowers a gravity meter by motor driven cable winch over the side of the U.S. Coast Guard icebreaker *Northwind* to the bottom of the Chukchi Sea.

Top: A new 31-foot fiberglass boat, designed specifically for reservists to use in port security work and training. *Bottom:* The Coast Guard Cutter *Courier*, formerly a Voice of America broadcast ship off the coast of Rhodes, Greece, and today, a floating port security school for reservists.

Port Safety and Security

Port Safety and Security, like the International Ice Patrol, joined the Coast Guard's mission roster in the wake of disaster. The disaster in this case was a catastrophic series of explosions which wreaked incredible havoc at Black Tom's Island, New Jersey, site of a World War I munitions facility. The Black Tom's explosion caused far fewer fatalities than *Titanic's* sinking, but the potential dangers posed by the blast's devastating force perhaps exceeded those of any ship or port disaster in history.

If the Black Tom's explosion had occurred just a few hours later, rather than at 2 a.m. in the morning, it would almost surely rank with the great holocausts of all time. A hundred barges, 85 loaded freight cars, 6 piers, and 13 brick warehouses were utterly destroyed. Ellis Island and the Statue of Liberty were pelted by a continuous barrage of three-inch shells. Property damage was estimated at $22 million. Fortunately, only seven persons were killed in the horrendous explosions that rained daggers of jagged glass from skyscrapers into the streets of Manhattan, and shattered windows in homes and offices all over Brooklyn, Hoboken, and Jersey City.

The date was July 31, 1916. America, in a state of somewhat uneasy neutrality, was enjoying the best of all possible economic worlds. As the richest and most powerful of the neutral nations, she was reaping huge profits from her exports to Germany as well as to that country's World War I adversaries. Public sentiment was with Britain and France. The Wall Street firm of J. P. Morgan and Company organized bond sales to the Allies resulting in a financial boon to them of $2.3 billion. In contrast, Wall Street loaned the less favored Germans only about $27 million during the same period.

A stoppage of American munitions shipments would have represented a substantial victory for the Germans. German and Austrian agents were ordered to carry out any surreptitious measures necessary to halt the lethal exports. In 1915, two German attaches in Washington and the Austro-Hungarian Ambassador were implicated in a scheme which would have used violence to disrupt the arms flow. Other enemy plots were also disclosed. Thus, when the Black Tom's facility was destroyed, there was considerable reason to suspect German involvement. No evidence to that effect was ever found, but many reputable historians persist in suspecting that the explosion was the work of German saboteurs.

John Stanley, hero of the *El Estero* incident, as he appeared in 1953 when a Coast Guard Captain.

The Black Tom's explosion, the sinking of *Lusitania* and numerous U.S. merchant vessels, and Germany's avowed policy of sinking any and all U.S. merchant ships, at last galvanized the Wilson Administration into a declaration of war which was ratified by both U.S. houses of Congress on April 6, 1917. On June 15, that year, Congress passed the Espionage Act, forming the basis for the Coast Guard's important mission of Port Safety and Security. The act authorized the President to require the Secretary of the Treasury to assume the virtual control of ports of the U.S., controlling the movements of vessels, establishing anchorages, and supervising the handling and storage of explosive cargoes. The Secretary immediately delegated responsibility for administering the act to the Coast Guard.

Coast Guard officers were designated as "Captains of the Port" in ten major areas. One of the most important provisions of the act related to the Coast Guard's supervision of explosives' loading. From December, 1917, until June 30, 1919, the Service oversaw the handling of hundreds of thousands of highly dangerous

Top: The scuttled munitions ship *El Estero. Bottom:* A Coast Guard 64-foot fireboat attempts to extinguish the blazing Monsanto Chemical Company plant during the Texas City disaster.

munitions without so much as a minor explosion. But, as the Espionage Act related exclusively to a state of war or national emergency, the Coast Guard's function in this area effectively ceased following the signing of the Armistice.

Then came World War II and the reawakening of the need for protecting our port facilities. President Roosevelt declared a state of national emergency in September, 1939, while the U.S. was again treading a precarious course of neutrality. The Coast Guard was ordered to provide reports of the movements of all foreign merchant vessels, public vessels, and aircraft within U.S. Ports. Almost immediately, similar requirements were imposed for domestic vessels, no matter what their cargoes or destinations. In late 1939, the Service was also assigned responsibility for sealing radios and checking armament of belligerent vessels arriving in American ports. On June 27, 1940, greatly expanded measures were authorized for the Coast Guard, pursuant to the Espionage Act of 1917.

During the next several months, Coast Guard Captains of the Port were given extraordinary powers, extending into many unprecedented areas of responsibility. An identification and fingerprinting system was established for U.S. longshoremen. Licensed exporters of explosives were required to report details of their activities to

A Coast Guard Chief Petty Officer points out a defective wire rope to the chief mate of a merchant vessel. Note kink and flat spot in runner.

A Coast Guard Port Security Officer supervises the safe loading of explosives. During the Vietnam conflict, the Service's Explosives Loading Detachments supervised the loading of more than five million tons of dangerous cargo without a single casualty.

Top: A three platform firefighter of World War II. *Bottom:* Coast Guard fire fighters play high pressure streams of water on a raging fire at the United Fruit Pier in Charleston, S.C. on October 6, 1944.

the Coast Guard. In October, 1940, the Dangerous Cargo Act was passed, giving the Service sweeping powers over the storage, loading, and shipping of practically all hazardous materials other than those transported on board vessels of the U.S. government or tankers. Captain of the Port offices were set up at key ports all over the country. The nation was gearing for battle.

The battles came and Coast Guardsmen around the world fought and died heroically. For the port security forces which remained at the home front, a different kind of war was waged, with results which may have been less dramatic, but were certainly no less significant. Thousands of volunteers from the Temporary Reserve, many of whom were too old or otherwise physically unqualified for combat duty, manned port security billets, performing a multitude of services. By now, a presidential order had placed the responsibility for port security in the hands of the Secretary of the Navy. The Coast Guard was operating under operational control of the Navy, and retained its traditional port security functions, while adding a number of new ones.

Small boats of all shapes and sizes patrolled the waters alongside port facilities, while specially trained Coast Guard security forces walked their beats ashore. Particular emphasis was placed on fire prevention, with Coast Guardsmen manning a large fleet of fire boats during latter stages of the war.

At the war's peak, port security personnel accounted for 22 per cent of the Coast Guard's total numbers. Temporary Reserves/Auxiliarists augmented the port security force by an additional 50,000. Many members of the Service's Womens' Reserve, the SPARs, also filled port security billets.

Under the watchful eyes of Coast Guard port safety personnel, there were no major port explosions or conflagrations during the war years, despite the enormous quantities of explosives and petroleum products shipped. There were, however, a number of near disasters.

On one occasion, a bomb fuse detonated in the arms of a stevedore loading ammunition into a magazine at a New York loading terminal. A pile of dunnage caught fire, threatening a large scale disaster. Although painfully injured in the groin by flying fuse fragments, Sandow Holdman, a Coast Guard seaman, quickly extinguished the blaze with a fire extinguisher and a ship's hose.

Another potential disaster was narrowly averted in the New York area on April 24, 1943, after a bilge fire started on board the Panamanian steamer *El Estero*, loaded with 1,500 tons of high explosives. When the alarm was sounded, Lieutenant Commander John T. Stanley, serving his first day on board *El Estero* as Coast Guard Munitions Officer, immediately assumed command. He and his men fought bravely but futilely in their efforts to extinguish the rapidly spreading flames, which were now engulfing much of the superstructure. In a final act of desperation, the ship was towed away from the harbor area toward the open sea, where she was at last scuttled near Robbins Reef Lighthouse. For his work in "preventing an explosion which might have done incalculable damage to other vessels and vital installations in the harbor", Stanley was awarded the Legion of Merit.

In the final analysis, the Coast Guard's accomplishments in the field of port security must be judged by those things *which did not happen*. Considering all the potential for disaster, the Service rated an A+ for its World War II performance.

Following the war, the Port Security program was again rapidly demobilized. People began to reappraise the situation, after the *Texas City* disaster of 1947 killed 561 persons, destroyed $67 million in property, and leveled an entire town. It was the Korean situation in 1950, accompanied by a wave of apprehension that the country was rife with communist subversives, which led to the Magnuson Act and the Coast Guard's present role in Port Safety and Security. Essentially an amendment to the old Espionage Act, the new bill authorized the President to invoke a strong port security program at any time he deemed the safety of U.S. ports to be in jeopardy. President Truman acted almost at once, ordering the Secretary of the Treasury to carry out the necessary safeguards.

Truman's executive order has never been rescinded, and Port Safety and Security remains a major Coast Guard mission. Thirteen Captain of the Port offices are vitally involved with port safety on a day-to-day basis. Most of the Service's Marine Inspection Units are also involved in the program to a considerable extent. Eleven thousand reservists assigned to the Coast Guard's 154 ORTUPS (port security) reserve training units stand ready to respond to any national call to arms.

USCG Reserve Training Center, Yorktown, Virginia, is the site of the Service's Officers' Candidate School as well as a number of special schools for reservists.

Reserve Training

Near the end of World War II, Coast Guard personnel strength reached its all-time high: more than 175,000 officers, enlisted men, and women. Approximately 78% of that total consisted of members of the Coast Guard Reserve, founded only shortly before the war began.

Few federal agencies have undergone more periods of radical augmentation and reduction in personnel strength than has the nation's oldest seagoing Service. Often, these periods were accompanied by acute disruptions in Coast Guard personnel practices. To those who endured these situations during the first 150 years of the Service's history, it must have occasionally seemed that conditions would never stabilize. National emergencies involving hasty expansion programs were invariably followed by slashing economy moves which threatened to put the Service out of business entirely. Invariably, a national emergency would place the Coast Guard in the position of frantically trying to train personnel to deal with the crisis at hand. Once normality was restored, the Service was faced with the equally sticky problem of figuring out what to do with personnel who were now in excess of Coast Guard needs. These awkward problems were further compounded each time a

merger with another agency, such as the Lighthouse Service, brought a whole new specialized personnel force into the Coast Guard.

World War I and the Prohibition Era created problems of extreme difficulty for the Service, although the latter resulted in a badly needed revitalization of operating facilities. The lessons learned in the field of effective personnel management during those critical years were not soon forgotten. The Coast Guard needed a trained reserve which could be mobilized in time of crisis.

The depression years, which upset many national priorities, prevented an immediate response to the problem. But, during the late 1930's, as war clouds began to darken European skies, both the Coast Guard and the Congress recognized that constructive action could be postponed no longer. A half-way measure, the Coast Guard Reserve and Auxiliary Act, was passed on June 23, 1939. It provided for a non-military, purely voluntary, unpaid reserve of civilian boat owners whose principal objective would be the advancement of safe boating. In light of the old Lifesaving Service's unsatisfactory experiences with unpaid volunteers, the creation of such an organization might seem a hopelessly naive

Coast Guard Reserve Boats during World War II.

anachronism, yet such cynicism would have been unwarranted in this particular case. Known since the Act of February 19, 1941 as the Coast Guard Auxiliary, the Coast Guard's first "reserve" continues today as a dynamic and vital force within the Service.

The Coast Guard selected Dorothy C. Stratton, former Dean of Women at Purdue University, to head the SPARS when they were founded. Captain Stratton is shown here with the Service's wartime Commandant (then Vice Admiral, later Admiral), Russell R. Waesche.

Although it has been modified many times since, the 1941 Act also established a military Coast Guard Reserve very similar to that operated by the Service today. Curiously, the act still provided for one classification of "Temporary Reserves," most of whom served part time and without pay. Many of these dedicated patriots were men whose age or physical condition prevented their serving in the regular establishment. For the most part, they were assigned to duties in the field of port security. Preserving the safety of our ports may have been somewhat less rigorous than combat duty, but it was nonetheless important to national security. Of 51,173 Temporary Reserves on the roles in June, 1944, more than 44,000 were part-time personnel, serving for a minimum of 12 hours a week and without pay. Their selfless volunteer efforts released more than 8,000 full-time Coast Guardsmen for other types of duty.

More relevant to today's reserve organization was the so-called "Regular Reserve" provided for in the 1941 Act. It was this arm of the Reserve around which was built the Coast Guard's expansion into all phases of wartime activity. In 1942, the Reserve and Auxiliary Act was amended, authorizing establishment of a Women's Reserve within the Coast Guard. Called the Spars (for Semper Paratus; Always Ready), the Women's Reserve grew within less than two years to a personnel strength of 8,371. The assignment of distaff reservists to shore-based administrative billets released still more Coast Guardsmen for combat. When the U.S. entered the war, the Coast Guard was operating only 267 cutters and boats more than 65 feet in length. During the hostilities this figure grew to 1,441 including 351 Navy ships and 288 Army craft which had been taken over by the Coast Guard. In addition, nearly 8,000 smaller craft were operated by Coast Guard personnel. Obviously, such growth would have been impossible without a viable reserve.

Reservists distinguished themselves in many capacities throughout the war. Many served as commanding officers of ships or in other positions of great responsibility. The wide range of expertise and experience which reservists brought into the wartime Coast Guard contributed inestimably to the Service's reputation as a formidable military force.

War's end brought a rapid demobilization of personnel, reducing the Coast Guard, by 1947, to only about one tenth of its peak wartime strength. The change was much too sweeping to be entirely free of problems. The transition was facilitated considerably, by the fact that most of those being demobilized were reservists.

Despite the demonstrated advantages of a strong Coast Guard Reserve, the program's postwar years have been fraught with difficulties. By 1949, the Reserve's size had been reduced to a mere 5,000, but the Korean conflict spurred a dramatic revival of the program with particular emphasis on the port security mission. Subsequently, numbers and programs have varied considerably, in flexible response to both the budget and needs of the Service.

A very important aspect of the Reserve program over past years has been the training of Officer Candidates to augment the junior officer corps. Reserve officers who graduate from the Coast Guard's Officers' Candidate School in Yorktown, Virginia must complete three years of active duty following their graduation. Without temporary personnel inputs such as these, the Service could not possibly maintain fluidity in its officer career patterns and advancements. Nearly half of the officers commissioned by the Coast Guard each year are reservists. Most leave the Service after their period of obligated duty, although ample career opportunities exist for those who wish to stay.

Requirements have fluctuated repeatedly over the years, but in general, a reservist with career aspirations can pursue any one of three routes. A method preferred by many is that of "Integration" into the regular establishment. Successful applicants in the integration program become regular officers with all the perquisites of that status. Another favored career opporutnity for reservists is that of becoming an RPA (Reserve Program Administrator). RPA's retain their status as reserves and can expect to spend significant portions of their careers in administration assignments at some level of the Reserve Program. They may expect to prove their versatility in operational assignments as well. An advantage of this career choice is that reservists are not affected by the dual compensation laws which prevent retired regular military officers from drawing full civil service pay in a second career. The third and most risky type of Reserve career opportunity is that of serving under contract for specified periods of time. Since there are no guarantees of contract renewal, most career-minded personnel avoid this as anything other than an interim arrangement.

Like the other military services, the Coast Guard operates several types of reserve training units throughout the land. Members of these units are required to attend periodic drill meetings for which they receive regular military pay. Some units meet for a few hours on one night of each week. Others meet for one full weekend each month. Members of these units are required to serve two weeks of active duty each year in addition to their drill meetings. In many instances, this duty may be performed on board a specially designated reserve training cutter, such as *Courier*, the Coast Guard's unique, floating port security school.

Coast Guard experience in World War II taught the Service that of all its many missions, none was likely to undergo a proportionally greater expansion during national emergencies than that of port security. Statistically, this was reflected in both prewar and post war port security programs involving less than 5% of the Service's active duty personnel, compared to a wartime effort which saw 22% of all Coast Guardsmen engaged in some form of port security work. This experience has been put to use effectively in organizing the Coast Guard Reserve Program. At present, approximately 70% of the Ready Reserve is committed to port security, 25% to vessel augmentation and activation, and 5% to miscellaneous activities such as Commercial Vessel Safety and electronics repair.

During 1970, the Coast Guard Reserve underwent one of the severest tests of its brief existence as the Nixon Administration proposed economy moves which would have eliminated the billets of all those reservists receiving drill pay. Congress balked at the proposal as stated, but compromised in an action which reduced the Reserve's size from an authorized 16,900 down to 10,000.

Experienced personnel management specialists within the Coast Guard shuddered at the thought of a future which might not include the Reserve. They recognized that the special skills and talents to be found within the Reserve personnel pool are invaluable management assets. This had been borne out repeatedly, and again very recently, when reservists with training in marine biology, law, public relations, economics, and other academic disciplines were voluntarily called to active duty as participants in a special study group developing anti-pollution proposals for the President. The Reserve Program made this talent available to the Coast Guard more quickly, and at far less cost than it could have been gotten in any other way.

In spite of the Nixon Administration's initiatives, it now appears that the Congress has granted the Coast Guard Reserve Program a reprieve. The Transportation Appropriations Sub-Committee reported out recommendations for fiscal year 1973 which would increase the Reserve's budget to nearly $28 million and its personnel strength to 15,000. To justify Congressional support, the Reserve is developing new peacetime missions to complement its traditional wartime contingency responsibilities. With the Service's increased activity in anti-pollution programs, it seems likely that new thrusts for the Reserve may also be aimed at environmental issues.

Politics is an unpredictable business, but if the lessons of history count for anything, then reserve training will be a major Coast Guard mission for many years to come.

Top: Little Kinakeet Life Saving Station on North Carolina's outer banks in a photo taken near the turn of the century. *Bottom:* A 1908 surfboat drill at Orleans Station near Cape Cod, Mass.

Search and Rescue (SAR)

To a broad segment of the public, Coast Guard means—search and rescue—and little more. Certainly, nothing else the Coast Guard does can compete with SAR when it comes to attention-grabbing news headlines. Viewed in its proper perspective, SAR is a mission of last resort. Ideally, if the Service's extensive efforts in Commercial Vessel and Boating Safety, Law Enforcement, Port Security and Aids to Navigation all prove effective, then Coast Guard SAR facilities will be necessary only for those few cases caused by the elements and acts of God. If recent statistics give a realistic indication of what the future holds, one might conclude that Coast Guard SAR units will be busy for many years to come. In 1971 the Service responded to more than 50,000 requests for assistance!

The Coast Guard entered the business of search and rescue by two converging paths based on the services provided by rescue cutters and shore-based lifesaving stations. By the time aviation units arrived on the historical scene, SAR as a major mission responsibility was already firmly established.

Lifesaving in this country was first conducted on a volunteer basis and at private expense. The first organization dedicated to lifesaving in America was the Massachusetts Humane Society. It was founded in 1785 upon the model of the Royal Humane Society of England, which dates from 1774. According to the quaintly-worded charter which the Massachusetts Society received in 1791, "The end and design of the institution is for the recovery of persons who meet with such accidents as to produce in them the appearance of death, and for promoting the cause of humanity by pursuing such means from time to time as shall have for their object the preservation of human life and the alleviation of its miseries." This broad policy included the relief of persons on distressed vessels.

To carry out its charter's goals, the Society built several small huts on exposed coastal points and equipped the huts with various articles of lifesaving equipment. The Society also offered monetary rewards to those who might make "signal exertions" to save lives. In 1807, it established at Cohasset a station equipped with the first lifeboat ever used in the United States.

The first federal funds expressly appropriated "for rendering assistance to the shipwrecked from the shore" were five thousand dollars for "furnishing lighthouses on the Atlantic coast with means of rendering assistance to shipwrecked mariners." Although approved in 1847 as an item in the following year's Lighthouse Service budget,

Major David A. Lyle, U.S. Army in an 1889 photo. Lyle was the inventor of the famous Lyle Gun which, for more than 60 years, was used to shoot rescue lines to distressed vessels. Photo: U.S. Army

there seems to have been some confusion about how best to utilize the money. Two years later it was finally turned over to the collector of customs at Boston to provide for the purchase of boat houses and appliances on Cape Cod for the use of the Massachusetts Humane Society.

By that time a series of disastrous wrecks off the New Jersey coast had focused new attention on the problem. Between 1848 and 1854, a total of $92,500 was appropriated for the placement of 137 lifeboats at stations on the Great Lakes and the Atlantic coast. Like the Massachusetts Humane Society stations, the new federal installations were little more than crude huts in which were housed food, blankets, fire building materials, clothing, boats, rockets, and carronades. A key to each boathouse was left in the custody of some responsible citizen who lived nearby. The volunteer caretaker was also provided with a set of printed instructions for use of the equipment.

From its own sad experience in the field, the Massachusetts Society could have told the federal government that such a system was not likely to be very effective. Vandals and thieves soon depleted or destroyed the supplies provided in almost every case. When Congress called the Treasury Department to task for this sorry state of affairs, the Secretary somewhat fatuously replied that "upon establishing the stations and furnishing them with apparatus, all care over them on the part of the government ceased."

Conditions did not improve appreciably until 1871, when Secretary of the Treasury George S. Boutwell reorganized the Revenue Marine Bureau, bringing lifeboat stations under the Bureau's supervision. At about the same time, Congress authorized the Secretary to employ full-time surfmen where necessary. Sumner I. Kimball, an outstanding administrator, was named to head the reorganized Bureau. In 1878 the United States Lifesaving Service was established, again separating the stations from the cutters, although both agencies continued to operate within the Treasury Department. Kimball's assignment as General Superintendent of the new organization heralded the beginning of a golden age of daring rescues and distinguished public service, an age in which such uncommon men as Joshua James would leave their marks in the annals of heroism. Kimball established his own place in history through dynamic administrative innovations such as the creation of a Board of Lifesaving Appliances to test and evaluate new rescue techniques and equipment.

The Coast Guard's direct predecessor service, the Revenue Marine, entered the rescue business a short time after the founding of the Massachusetts Humane Society, but long before the founding of the U.S. Lifesaving Service. History hasn't recorded the circumstances of the first Coast Guard SAR case, but it undoubtedly occurred in the early 1790's. Seagoing traditions have demanded for centuries that any ship in a position to assist must respond to the plight of another ship in distress. By 1831, the cutters' potential for rescue work had

been demonstrated often enough for Treasury Secretary Louis McLane to initiate a program of "winter cruising." The tiny sailing craft were assigned to cruising stations from which they were required to make contact with all vessels sighted within their operating areas. They were directed to provide any aid which might be necessary.

An act of Congress, passed in 1837, authorized the President "to cause any suitable number of public vessels, adapted to the purpose, to cruise upon the coast, in the severe portion of the season, when the public service will allow of it, and to afford such aid to distressed navigators as their circumstances and necessities may require; and such public vessels shall go to sea prepared fully to render such assistance." This law did not mention revenue cutters specifically, but performance of the duty was imposed, primarily, upon the Revenue Marine Service and immediately became one of its major activities.

In 1848, when the federal government made its first inept attempts at establishing lifesaving stations, officers of the Revenue Marine were appointed to inspect and administer the facilities. The new responsibility, at that point in time, was incongruous if not impossible. Virtually all of the Revenue Marine officers had seagoing assignments and no additional billets were authorized. The 1871 and 1878 reorganizations of the Treasury Department gave Revenue Marine officers similar responsibilities under more realistic mandates.

Thus, when the Lifesaving Service merged with the Revenue Cutter Service in 1915 to form the U.S. Coast Guard, the SAR tradition was one of many years' standing. Since that time the Service has registered nearly incredible successes in its search and rescue activities. In each of the past ten years, the Coast Guard has saved property valued at from four to seven times the Service's annual operating budget. Tens of thousands of lives have been saved within the same time frame, a statistic which is beyond monetary calculation. Hundreds of thousands of citizens have been assisted in lesser ways.

Any typical year of Coast Guard SAR activity could furnish an entire legion of adventure writers with sufficient material to last throughout their respective lifetimes. Yet, the Service's more idealistic planners look forward to the day when the Coast Guard's preventative safety programs will make SAR a relatively minor mission, or even a thing of the past.

A lifeboat used at Galveston, Texas around 1900.

By 1925, tractors such as the Fordson model pictured here had replaced horses in most areas.

Top: A Lyle gun in use in 1940. *Bottom:* By the mid-1940's, shoulder line-throwing guns like this one had replaced the dangerous and cumbersome Lyle guns for most types of rescues.

Top: Shore stations such as this one at Cleveland, Ohio, perform most of the Coast Guard's rescue missions. *Bottom:* At Honolulu in 1962, the 311-foot Cutter *Matagorda* and an HC-130B aircraft join forces in one of the Coast Guard's annual rescue seminars for airline personnel.

Top: Two crewmen of the Coast Guard Cutter *Castle Rock* based at Boston, Mass., brave the rough, cold North Atlantic in a rubber raft to rescue eight men from the 82-foot fishing vessel *Maureen & Michael* going down east of Newfoundland on February 23, 1967. *Bottom:* This 1968 photo of an actual crash clearly illustrates the importance of such rescue seminars for airline personnel.

Top: Coast Guardsmen from the Cutter *Rockaway* row to the rescue of the master and three crewmembers of the foundering American freighter *SS Smith Voyager. Bottom:* The Coast Guard Cutter *Coos Bay* maneuvers into position to rescue personnel of the foundering British merchant vessel, *Ambassador,* in 1964. In one of the most difficult rescues in modern Coast Guard history, *Coos Bay* succeeded in saving 11 of the 12 men remaining on board *Ambassador* at the time of the cutter's arrival on scene.

Gale winds churn the surf as Coast Guardsmen from Oregon Inlet, Cape Hatteras, and Chicamacomico, N.C. Stations bring a crewman from the grounded Honduran freighter *Omar Babun* safely ashore with a breeches buoy. This 1954 rescue was one of the last recorded instances of a rescue in which a Lyle gun and breeches buoy were employed.

The world's only Search and Rescue School is operated by the Coast Guard at its huge Governors Island, N.Y. complex.

14th Coast Guard District, Honolulu Rescue Coordination Center—Pacific coverage of U.S. Coast Guard rescue operations.

Hamilton, 378-foot class

Construction of the Coast Guard's first 210-foot cutter in 1964 marked the dawning of an exciting, modern shipbuilding age for the Service. The most important milestone of that age, however, occurred in 1967 with the commissioning of Hamilton, the Coast Guard's first high endurance cutter in over 20 years.

Hamilton's significance is reflected in the way she has been described. She has been called the Coast Guard's "ship of the future," and the "first jet-powered high endurance cutter." But whatever the description, Hamilton is clearly a superb ship whose advanced engineering and architectural characteristics point the way to the new and ultra-modern Coast Guard fleet of the future.

At 378 feet, these super cutters are the longest ships in the Coast Guard by a substantial margin of 39 feet. The highly specialized polar icebreakers and the cargo-carrying Kukui exceed the 378's in a few areas such as beam width, draft, displacement, and maximum range among Coast Guard cutters in general. Among search and rescue craft, however, the 378's have no peers. In fact, Hamilton's special search capability, speed, and high maneuverability are unmatched by any ship smaller than a cruiser!

The 378's have a top speed of 29 knots, almost 10 knots faster than the 327's which reigned for 30 years as queens of the Coast Guard fleet. Main propulsion plants in the 378's consist of the largest combined diesel and gas turbine systems ever installed in American vessels. Each of the twin shafts has its own propulsion unit consisting of diesel and gas-turbine engines. The diesels alone are capable of propelling these handsome ships at a respectable

20 knots. The gas turbines used in *Hamilton* and her sister ships are almost identical to the Pratt and Whitney turbojets which power Boeing 707 jetliners.

Predictably, the advanced engineering plant drives three superlative propellers. The stern props are 13 feet in diameter, the largest controllable

which careful maneuvering is required to avoid damage to expensive and delicate scientific equipment.

Hamilton's engineers can monitor the ship's functions from a soundproof, air-conditioned control booth. A profusion of indicating meters, gauges, lights, and other devices provide monitor-

New crewmembers report on board *Hamilton* during the cutter's 1967 trip to Norfolk, Va.

pitch propellers on any American vessels. The propellers' pitch can be increased, decreased, or reversed as circumstances warrant. Controllable pitch allows the ships to reverse their direction of travel without reversing or stopping shaft rotation. Perhaps the most futuristic feature of all, though, is the ships' 350 horsepower bow propulsion units. Retractable bow propellers, rotatable through 360 degrees, provide the 378's with near incredible ability to maneuver in restricted waters. Many a seasoned sailor has been baffled to see these sleek beauties turn what appears to be a poorly judged docking into a feat of fantastic seamanship. This feature is also a valuable aid in search and rescue, anti-submarine warfare, and oceanographic work in

ing of almost every detail of the propulsion and electrical systems. A closed-circuit television system with six TV monitors allows the commanding officer to see at a glance what is going on about the ship.

The 378's also have a formidable military potential which has already been used off the coast of Vietnam. Special emphasis has been placed on anti-submarine warfare, with torpedoes, an underwater fire control system, and a modern scanning Sonar installed for that purpose. A 5-inch/38 gun, 81-mm. mortars, .50 cal. machine guns, fire control system, and electronic countermeasure system round out each vessel's armament.

Search and rescue operations often require the

Top: Hamilton's sister ship, the *Mellon,* is based in Honolulu. *Bottom:* A crewman signals an *HH-52A* amphibious helicopter to safe alighting on the flight deck of the 378-foot U.S. Coast Guard Cutter *Hamilton.*

combined efforts of both air and sea craft. The 378's have an 80-foot flight deck which makes it possible for them to fuel helicopters at sea or even transport one if circumstances warrant.

The Boston-based *Hamilton* is the fifth cutter to be named for Alexander Hamilton, founder of the Revenue Marine which led to the establishment of today's Coast Guard. The great man might well take pride in the seagoing tradition which has produced the Service's 378-foot cutters.

Hamilton's ultra-modern bridge.

Pontchartrain, 255-foot class

Pontchartrain and her 255-foot sister ships are reminders of a classic form of inertia which has afflicted shipbuilders during twentieth century wars. More astute planners might have anticipated the need for these rugged old cutters considerably before the U.S. was plunged headlong into World War II. Instead, their construction was begun in reaction to the war's most threatening hours. The U.S. transferred ten 250-foot cutters (all bearing the names of American lakes) to the British in April, 1941. Now the American government badly needed additional ships in order to fight its own war. Ironically, by the time the first 255 was completed, the war had run its course.

Coast Guard legend would have you believe that the 255's were originally designed to be much larger ships but were reduced in size when the Congress failed to provide expected funding. The legend is impossible to document. It had its origins in the somewhat peculiar configuration of the 255-foot hulls. In order to walk from bow to stern below decks, it is necessary to negotiate a series of up-and-down ladders. According to those who propound the legend, this nuisance is a result of removing an entire center section from the cutters' original design.

As the last completed cutter of the new "Lake" class, *Pontchartrain* instantly became, in the years of postwar demobilization, an extraneous member of the Coast Guard fleet. Built at the Coast Guard Yard in Curtis Bay, Maryland in 1944, she was at first assigned to ocean station duty out of Boston.

The Coast Guard Cutter *Pontchartrain.*

Top: Pan American Clipper *10943* comes in for an emergency landing as the Cutter *Pontchartrain* stands by to assist.
Bottom: Impact!

As the Coast Guard's personnel strength was reduced from a wartime peak of 175,000 to a postwar low of only 18,500, the Service was forced to decommission many of its cutters and curtail many missions. In 1946, the 2,000-ton *Pontchartrain*, barely off the ways, was decommissioned.

Destiny had decreed a permanent place in Coast Guard history for *Pontchartrain*, and that destiny was not to be denied. In August, 1948, as the ocean station program began to hit its stride, the cutter was placed back in service. From a new home port in Long Beach, California, she has performed in outstanding fashion ever since.

remembered is one of history's most remarkable rescues. At the time of its happening, the ditching of Pan American Clipper 10943 and the subsequent rescue of the plane's 31 crew members and passengers by *Pontchartrain* so fired the public imagination that *Life* magazine featured the incident as its cover story. In retrospect, the rescue seems almost devoid of drama, but this is a deception created by the uncannily cool professionalism of the principal figures in the case.

At 3:22 on the morning of October 16, 1956, while patrolling Ocean Station November, *Pontchartrain* received an emergency call from the

Clipper 943 had taken off at about 9:30 p.m., October 15, 1956, from Honolulu on a routine trip to San Francisco with 24 passengers and 7 crew members. At 3:20 a.m., halfway across the Pacific past the point of no-return and 1,150 miles from her destination, the Clipper's No. 1 engine on the extreme port side began to run away. The pilot, Richard Ogg, was able to only partially control the propeller. Then the No. 4 engine, on the extreme starboard side, began to falter and then fail completely. There was nothing to do but to ditch the crippled plane. Here 943's tail breaks away as her wings disappear under a swell.

Ocean Station Sugar has now gone the way of the dinosaurs, but in the years of its existence, *Pontchartrain* pulled arduous three-month patrols in the often stormy waters of the Pacific. The average schedule for the plucky cutter on those lengthy itineraries carried her from Long Beach to Sugar (in midocean), from Sugar to Japan, Japan to Sugar, and Sugar back to Long Beach. When Sugar was discontinued in 1953, it seems certain that not a single tear was shed on board *Pontchartrain*.

The event for which *Pontchartrain* is best

Clipper stating that one of her engines was running away. The plane also requested continuous radio-beacon service, which the cutter promptly provided. *Pontchartrain's* radar showed the Clipper to be only 38 miles away.

Within less than ten minutes, the 943's situation had deteriorated to the point that she announced her intention to ditch alongside *Pontchartrain*. The Cutter immediately sounded her general alarm for ditch and rescue stations, setting off an evolution which *Pontchartrain*, like other ocean station vessels, had drilled for countless times. Evoking

Lifeboat carrying a rubber raft from the U.S. Coast Guard Cutter *Pontchartrain* speeds to the aid of the survivors of the broken and sinking Pan American Stratocruiser "Sovereign of the Skies." Twenty-four passengers and 7 crew members were out of the plane and safe aboard the *Pontchartrain* within 20 minutes after the plane was ditched and one minute before it sank, on October 16, 1956. The series of photos was taken by William Simpson, Commissaryman, second class, USCG, crewman of the *Pontchartrain*.

standard textbook procedures for ditching situations, the Cutter's CIC officer assumed his station as "Air Controller," advising the pilot of surface weather conditions, the proper course for ditching, and the procedures he should follow in carrying out his proposed plan of action. Throughout the ship, preparations were made for putting over small boats, rigging emergency lighting, and laying an illuminated sea lane for the aircraft.

After a brief period of indecision over whether to dump fuel and ditch at once or wait until daybreak, the pilot chose the latter course of action. *Pontchartrain* remained at the ready.

At 7:40 a.m. the sun was already beginning its climb into the morning sky as *Pontchartrain* began to lay a path of fire-fighting foam through the sea. The foam, which is closely related to many household detergents, would indicate the proper ditch heading for the Clipper, and would also have a flattening effect on the swells. The wind and seas were moderate, however, and posed no real threat, per se. The foam path had hardly more than been completed, and *Pontchartrain* had not quite assumed her proper station in relationship to that path, when 943 announced the beginning of her final run. Before the ship could adjust her position, the Clipper touched the sea surface, bounced off, and plunged into the face of the next wave, with twisting, violent impact. There is nothing routine about landing commercial aircraft on the open sea.

Pontchartrain surged forward toward the rapidly sinking hulk, whose forward section was smashed and whose severely damaged tail section served from the plane's main body within three minutes after impact. Within an instant, the well-briefed passengers began to appear on the plane's wings, and *Pontchartrain*'s small boats were launched to carry out rescue operations. Although the Clipper sank to the bottom within 20 minutes after impact, every soul on board was saved. Seldom in history has such a critical problem been resolved with greater calm or efficiency. It is that very efficiency which seems to detract from the drama of the incident. Nothing, however, can detract from the magnificent job performed by the personnel of *Pontchartrain* and the 943, or from the high place they will always hold in Coast Guard history.

During subsequent years, *Pontchartrain* has performed a variety of services, including special training cruises for reservists, and assignment to the Alaska Fisheries Patrol. She has also sailed to Honolulu on three occasions to participate in the annual SAR demonstration drills held for the benefit of commercial airlines. The majority of her service has been devoted to ocean station duty on stations Romeo (no longer in existence), November and Victor (tentatively scheduled for termination in 1972). But she had continued to distinguish herself in many other search and rescue cases as well.

At last, in 1969, the venerable *Pontchartrain* was called upon to perform the job she had been designed for 25 years before. Now her country was engaged in another kind of war, off the coast of Southeast Asia, but the 255-foot cutter was as ready as ever. In late 1970, after rendering highly meritorious service as a member of Coast Guard Squadron Three in Vietnam, *Pontchartrain*, again returned to her humanitarian role as an ocean station vessel. Her record in war had been no less honorable than her previous performance. The noble old ship, which had waited a quarter century to engage in its first battle, returned heaped with honors.

While in Vietnam, she was called upon, sometimes nightly, to provide naval gunfire support for friendly forces ashore. On occasion, within the space of 10 minutes, her hefty 5-inch gun poured as much as a ton of devastating explosives into enemy positions. Her accurate fire was credited with stopping at least two planned enemy attacks in the Mekong Delta. On another occasion, while providing support for the Army's American Division near Chu Lai, the cutter knocked out several Viet Cong bunkers, a bridge, and six other structures.

Like other members of her uniquely "Coast Guard" design, the famed *Pontchartrain* has proven her prowess time and again. Yet, despite the glorious past performances of these fine, reliable old cutters, it seems entirely possible that their best days may still lie ahead of them. *Pontchartrain*'s home port is expected to be shifted to the East Coast in 1972.

Top: The oceangoing tug *Yocona* is based in Astoria, Oregon. *Bottom:* The Seattle-based oceangoing tug *Modoc* is equipped for search and rescue, firefighting, and icebreaking.

Raritan, 110-foot Harbor Tug

The word "tug" is one of the least glamorous appellations in the entire lexicon of ship and boat categories. Whether glamorous or not, however, the Coast Guard's 14 medium-sized harbor tugs are worthy inheritors of the grand old cutter tradition. At least one member of the class, the *Raritan*, has earned a secure place in Coast Guard history.

On the 13th of June, 1943, *Raritan* was serving as a part of Task Unit 24.8.2, escorting convoy G.S. 24 from Narsarssuak, Greenland to Saint Johns, Newfoundland. The convoy, which had departed Greenland on June 10th, was also composed of the U.S. Army transport *Fairfax*, and the Coast Guard cutters *Tampa, Mojave, Algonquin, Storis,* and *Escanaba.*

It was a journey fraught with danger from the very beginning. Before departure of the entire convoy, *Storis* and *Algonquin* had been ordered to search for a submarine reported to be operating in Brede Fjord. The search was fruitless and the convoy departed on schedule. On June 12th, a number of icebergs and growlers were encountered which, combined with dense fog, made navigation both difficult and dangerous. It was under such conditions that the convoy was proceeding during the early morning hours of the 13th.

Suddenly at 5:10 a.m., observers on board the *Storis* spotted an enormous cloud of smoke and flames shooting upward from *Escanaba*. Within only three minutes *Escanaba* had disappeared beneath the surface of the waters. *Storis* and *Raritan* sped to the scene of disaster, arriving within ten minutes. Other ships in the convoy began evasive maneuvering as protection against attack by submarine.

Escanaba's destruction was uncannily rapid and complete. Despite the quick response made by *Raritan* and *Storis*, only small bits of wreckage remained afloat when the search units arrived on the scene. Then, after 40 minutes of searching, *Raritan* sighted and rescued two survivors. No others were ever located, although *Raritan* did

The 110-foot tug *Raritan* extinguished a fire on board a 40-foot cabin cruiser.

recover the body of one other man who was buried at sea the following day.

After the war, *Raritan* was transferred to Norfolk, Virginia, where she served as a multi-purpose unit under Norfolk's Captain of the Port. In October, 1962, she was reassigned to duty in the Ninth Coast Guard District, where she had served prior to World War II.

Raritan now performs a busy schedule of diverse missions under operational control of Coast Guard Group Two Rivers, Wisconsin. Her home port is Milwaukee.

The cutter's schedule varies significantly according to the season. During each summer she is assigned to patrol major yacht races in the Great Lakes, such as the annual Chicago to Mackinaw Island, Queen's Cup, and Port Huron to Mackinaw Island events. When increased summer boating activity combines with a squall, *Raritan* is as likely as any other Coast Guard cutter to find herself assigned to a rescue mission. Because of her near proximity to Group Two Rivers she is often spared the inconvenience of minor assistance cases. Other sub-units of the group can usually attend to these with greater dispatch, if nothing else. Like most of the Coast Guard's harbor tugs, *Raritan* is an effective floating fire department. In August, 1969,

a serious fire broke out on board a 40-foot cabin cruiser near where *Raritan* was patrolling a yacht race. *Raritan* extinguished and overhauled the fire within 25 minutes of the time she first learned of the situation. Her actions on that occasion received considerable attention and praise from the press.

As an actual tug, *Raritan* spends a great deal of time towing about and positioning a construction barge out of Toledo, Ohio, which is used to renovate Coast Guard docks and navigational aids.

From late December to early April each year, *Raritan* is a Great Lakes icebreaker, participating in "Operation Oil Can." The 110-foot cutter can hammer her way through as much as six feet of ice. Another seasonal responsibility is the removal of personnel from the Coast Guard's Minneapolis Shoals Lighthouse each year as winter approaches. The light is iced in and inaccessible for several weeks each year. When the cold subsides in early spring, *Raritan* also has the job of taking the men back to the light.

No doubt *Raritan* is an exceptional tug. On the basis of her accomplishments alone, the dictionary publishers should expand the definition of tugboat to read beyond "a small, powerful boat for towing or pushing ships and barges." *Raritan* is that and much, much more.

The Coast Guard Cutter *Cape Knox*—a seagoing command in every sense.

Command at Sea

Cape Knox, 95-foot class

Most young men who choose the sea as a career dream of the day when they can command their own ships. For those who have chosen the Coast Guard, that day is often not long in coming. Usually a young officer's first sea command is on a 95-footer.

The Service has long recognized the importance of highly developed senses of responsibility in its officers, and the surest way to develop responsibility in a man is to burden him with it. There are few responsibilities in the world more demanding than a sea-going command in the Coast Guard.

A ship of any size is a floating city. A crew of any size is a sort of family. A mission of any size is a job which must be done. Thus, a commanding officer can be compared to a mayor, a father, a boss. The CO must ensure that his floating community provides adequate housing, food, and utility services for its citizens. He must be sensitive to the dreams, ambitions, and frustrations of his family. He is also responsible for administering family discipline through a system of punishments and rewards. As a boss, he must fully understand the job which has to be done, coordinate and supervise the efforts of his subordinates, and be willing to share his successes with the certain realization that should he fail instead, the failure is uniquely his own. The peculiar nature of Coast Guard service extends these responsibilities still further, since many of the jobs undertaken involve risking crew members' lives, and other lives often hinge on the outcome of any given mission. Finally, the commanding officer must be able to independently make crucial decisions, without benefit of more mature council.

Each year the Coast Guard gives command responsibility to approximately 31 of its most promising officers serving in the rank of Lieutenant (junior grade). Most of these young men are graduates of the Coast Guard Academy with less than 24 months of Service experience. They are assigned as commanding officers on board the Service's 95-foot patrol craft. The cutters are small, but the job is still a big one.

The Coast Guard cutter *Cape Knox* is typical of the class. Until quite recently *Cape Knox* and other small cutters in the Miami area were busily engaged

Cape Knox's sister ship, *Cape Cross,* is based in Gloucester, Mass.

in patrolling the Florida Keys, acting as search and rescue units and maintaining a sharp lookout for Cuban refugees. In fact, *Cape Knox* was transferred to Miami from her original home port of Norfolk, Virginia because of the large numbers of refugees who were fleeing Cuba in the early sixties. The refugee problem has now somewhat subsided and the Keys Patrol has been discontinued, but *Cape Knox* is as busy as ever.

Cape Knox is the largest cutter assigned as a sub-unit of Coast Guard Group Miami, and Group Miami is probably the busiest search and rescue facility in the entire Coast Guard. Our affluent society has produced ever-increasing numbers of pleasure-boatmen, of whom many have selected Florida's fine fishing grounds as a base of operations. Because of this trend, *Cape Knox's* work load has increased from 21 rescue cases in 1969, to more than double that figure in 1971. Other units attached to Miami Group have logged similar increases.

Miami figures importantly in a number of the world's great yacht races, and these demand special attention from *Cape Knox* and her sister ships. Large numbers of boats, straining for every last knot of speed, almost inevitably result in a few rescue cases. The 128 sailing yachts competing in the 1969 Miami-to-Nassau Race encountered gale force winds and 20-foot seas. The several masts and rudders smashed during the storm made the Race a memorable one for the *Cape Knox's* crew.

When not specifically assigned to patrols *Cape Knox*, like most cutters with primary search and rescue missions, rotates through a schedule requiring her to maintain various degrees of stand-by readiness. A ship's status is referred to as either "Alfa," "Bravo," or "Charlie." Alfa means the vessel is actually under way. Charlie means the unit is in a maintenance status and can not ordinarily be called out. The bane of a Coast Guardsman's existence, however, is Bravo. This ominous word, followed by a number which indicates the number of hours within which a ship must be under way to assist, means a stand-by status is in effect. *Cape Knox* is assigned to a full measure of Bravo Six and Bravo Two. Every third

weekend the cutter also takes its turn in Bravo Zero status during peak boating hours. This means that her crew must be on board and ready to respond at a moment's notice when an emergency arises.

For *Cape Knox* and other small rescue units, Bravo means much more than just a state of readiness. It may mean being called out of bed in the middle of the night or the cancelling of long-planned social engagements. After extended periods of Bravo, the mere ringing of a telephone can be a shattering experience, an instant reaction of wondering whether the ship is being called out. A growing wind or unfavorable weather forecast can create a crisis. In contrast, no matter how much maintenance work may be scheduled, Charlie is sure to bring a sigh of relief.

Every moment of hard work, uncertainty, danger, and frustration faced by a commanding officer is offset by a hundred others which bring rare professional satisfaction. No artist in any field is likely to derive more pride from the results of his intensely personal artistic expression than will a man of the sea who has molded his ship and crew into a happy and efficient unit, bearing the imprint of his own personality.

Through its command training program on board 95-foot cutters, the Coast Guard affords its junior officers an opportunity to understand both the difficulties and rewards of command.

Point Warde, 82-foot Patrol Boat

A 130-foot Viet Cong junk was sunk in February, 1965 as it attempted to infiltrate the South Vietnamese coast through Vung Ro Bay. When investigated by Allied forces, the sunken hulk was found to contain enough supplies, including explosives, weapons, and ammunition, to outfit an entire battalion. The vessel was of North Vietnamese registry. Thus were U.S. and South Vietnamese planners made aware of a critical gap in their strategic defense.

A quick solution had to be found, but how? Coastal surveillance and interdiction was entirely unlike anything for which the U.S. Navy was prepared. Then somebody thought of the Coast Guard, which had, after all, fought in every American war after the Revolution. In April, the announcement was made that 19 of the Coast Guard's 82-foot patrol boats were to be armed and sent to Vietnam to prevent the smuggling of enemy arms, personnel, and supplies by coastal routes.

When the Department of Defense started looking for small boats and personnel with small-boat experience, it was inevitable that it would be attracted·to the 82-footers. They were large enough to mount additional armament, yet their relatively shallow (approximately 6½ foot) draft would allow them to get near the coast. Moreover, they had that built-in *sine qua non* for operating in the tropics, air-conditioning.

In May, approximately 10 additional tons of weight were added to the cutters through the addition of four .50 caliber machine guns and an 81 millimeter mortar forward, a food freezer, and other modifications. The beefed-up little cutters were then loaded on board merchant vessels and transported to the Phillipines for further staging to the combat zone. By July, they were indeed at war, and under way more than 70 percent of the time. In September, 1965, the cutter *Point Marone* sank the first enemy junk attempting to cross the coastal barricade. The battle was on. By the time the last member of the Coast Guard's 82-foot combat fleet had been turned over to the Government of South Vietnam in August, 1970, the Service had destroyed more than 3,000 enemy junks and killed almost 2,500 enemy personnel.

Coast Guard personnel deserve a full measure of credit for the outstanding service they rendered in Vietnam, but so do the spunky fighting ships on which they served. In truth, the peacetime performance of the 82-foot boats is as impressive as their service in time of war.

Point Warde, based in San Juan, Puerto Rico, is one of twenty-six 82-foot cutters which were authorized to replace those sent to Vietnam. Like most other members of her class, she is commanded by a Chief Petty Officer, although in Southeast Asia, the 82's were commanded by Lieutenants or Lieutenants (junior grade). Built in 1967 at the Martinac Shipyard in Tacoma, Washington, *Point Warde's* job, like that of all 82's operated by the Coast Guard today, is primarily one of saving lives. She is also extremely active in the areas of law enforcement and boating safety, and regularly conducts pleasure boat boarding operations in Mayaguez and Fajardo, P.R.

Puerto Rico's year-round good weather and the fact that the boat is air-conditioned, make duty on board *Point Warde* particularly attractive for Coast Guardsmen. The boat is normally berthed at the Coast Guard Base in the old port of San Juan, a city which was founded in 1521. Like all SAR cutters, *Point Warde* spends what often seems an unendurable amount of its schedule on Bravo Two or some other type of stand-by status. The boat's rescue accomplishments clearly underscore the importance of her being ready to respond at a moment's notice.

A typical year may see *Point Warde* involved in as many as 50 search and rescue incidents. Most of these are routine cases involving disabled fishing and pleasure boats ranging from 20 to 50 feet in length. Such cases usually occur relatively near *Point Warde's* base of operations.

Occasionally the boat is involved in cases which transcend the ordinary by almost any standard of measurement. In 1970, the boat was involved in at least three cases which will stand out in the crew's memory for many years to come. In the first of these, a shrimp boat grounded on a reef off the coast of the Dominican Republic. The boat sank, but its operators were rescued by another shrimp boat in the area. Then, that boat ran into serious troubles of its own. *Point Warde* ended up rescuing

both crews and towing the second boat to safety.

Point Warde also assisted in the rescue of 130 passengers off the hydrofoil *Sun Arrow*, after their pleasure cruise culminated on one of Puerto Rico's many treacherous reefs.

The Coast Guard Cutter *Point Warde*.

The 82-foot patrol boat made a major contribution to the success of a particularly difficult case in May, 1970. A distress call was intercepted from the merchant vessel *Charles Towne*. Communications were lost before the vessel's position could be determined. The Commander of the Coast Guard's Greater Antilles Section initiated a general communications check, using information gained from a hydrofoil which had moored astern of *Charles Towne* the previous day. The hydrofoil reported that the merchant vessel was a converted LCT carrying a load of cement bags from St. Thomas to St. Martin at a speed of 5 to 6 knots. The merchant vessel had departed St. Thomas at 5:20 p.m.

From the information obtained, the Coast Guard's Rescue Coordination Center in San Juan was able to develop a reasonably accurate estimated position for *Charles Towne*. Using that position as a point of departure, a search plan was established and two aircraft were deployed to carry it out. In practically no time, one of the aircraft located *Charles Towne*, capsized with six persons clinging to it. *Point Warde* was directed to the scene. Within an hour, the boat was on scene and had rescued the six survivors. Unfortunately, a seventh man had been trapped inside the vessel and divers were unable to recover his body. By any criterion the rescue was an outstanding success. At the outset, it was only known that a vessel was in distress. But where? The successful outcome was the result of careful application of standard procedures, good search planning, good search execution, and the efforts of a boat typical of a class which has served with conspicuous distinction in both peace and war.

Thanks to an incredibly successful training plan, 82-foot patrol boats formerly operated by the Coast Guard in South Vietnam are now operated by that nation's navy. In coastal waters of the U.S. and its possessions, it seems certain that *Point Warde* and other members of her versatile class will be saving lives for many years to come.

Self-Bailing, Self-Righting Motor Lifeboat, *44303*

After an arduous 3-hour training session in the heavy surf off the Umpqua River bar, the crew of CG44303 was understandably tired. They were satisfied, though, with the results of their training. Saving lives under conditions such as those routinely encountered at the mouth of the Umpqua requires exceptional skills which can only be obtained through hard practice. It was time to call it a day. The boat coxswain, who was also Officer in Charge of the Coast Guard's Umpqua River Station, set his course for the station and prepared to cross the treacherous bar for the last time that day.

For nearly an hour the surf breaking over the bar had been building, fanned on by the brisk, penetrating October sea breeze. The coxswain was unperturbed for these were the conditions he had wanted his inexperienced crew to see for themselves. They were now directly over the bar, the most precarious point of their return passage. Suddenly, he had the awful feeling that a situation had developed over which he had no control. A huge breaker of 20 feet or more was cascading over his stern, causing his boat's head to swing violently to one side. His instant master-seaman's reaction, to control his heading by backing down on his

Umpqua River Station. *CG-44303* has operated out of here as well as Cape Disappointment Station.

engines, was answered by still another sign of trouble—the frenzied sound of propellers spinning through air rather than water. There was no help for it now. The boat had already begun capsizing.

The brutal immensity of the breaker pounded mercilessly over the small boat. Within a split second the boat had rolled over 90 degrees and was on its side. "Hang on!," shouted the coxswain. For a moment, the throbbing mass of the boat strained to hold its position. Then it continued the agonizingly slow process of turning completely over. Aside from his own strong survival instinct, the coxswain had but a single other thought—the safety of his men. "Dear God, let's hope they learned what I was trying to teach them," he prayed intensely. Thankfully, they had.

From the first instant that they realized the boat was rolling, each man who wasn't strapped into position assumed the safety stance he had been taught. With knees bent for cushioning effect, they pushed upward with every last ounce of strength, wedging themselves solidly between the safety grab rails and the deck. No amount of practice or mental preparation could completely condition them for what followed. In an instant they were deluged by tons of thundering water. By now they were upside down, engulfed in the shockingly cold water.

For the men undergoing this traumatic experience for the first time, there was a maddening compulsion to do all the things they had been told not to do. There had been no time for a good breath of air before the deluge, so their submersion seemed an eternity. Fortunately, each resisted the temptation to let go of the grab rails and swim for the surface. The admonitions of the Master Chief Boatswain's Mate who was serving as coxswain had been firmly implanted in the mind of every man present. "Hang on long enough and we'll roll back on over. Let go and you've got two big screws back there spinning around, just waiting to cut you into pieces."

One man was lucky. A large air bubble had been captured beneath the boat when it rolled. It swept over his head, giving him a chance for a surprise breath of air. For the others, it seemed their lungs would burst before the boat could ever right itself again. But right it did, just as it was designed to do.

Safely on the other side of the bar, and hardly worse for the experience, CG44303 continued on to her moorings. Her superbly balanced diesel engines had never missed a lick.

For two of the men on board, October 12, 1969, was a day which would never be forgotten. As for the 44-foot boat which had been especially designed for·such service, and her skipper, the Chief Petty Officer, an uncommon man who had pioneered in the use of such boats, it was simply another of five such experiences.

Necessity, indeed, is the mother of invention, and the peculiar bottom features of the Pacific coast off Washington and Oregon inspired the development of what is surely one of the most impressive pieces of boating hardware to be found in the world. A deep, deep ocean, stretching in a wide, unbroken expanse from Japan to North America creates unusual opportunities for build-up of massive swells. It is the rapid shallowing at river bars along the coast which accounts for the really heavy surf in the area. A nominal increase in sea conditions outside the bar may be increased tenfold in the area of breaking surf.

Skilled boatmen in these areas treat the bars with humble respect. There are ever increasing numbers of not-so-skilled boatmen who are attracted to the coast each year. And no wonder! Salmon and albacore tuna abound there in quantities sufficient to lure even the most timid landlubber out to sea. Approximately 800 pleasure boats regularly tie up in Winchester Bay, near the Umpqua Station, and future dredging will make room for 1,500 more. Countless others are brought down on trailers each summer and launched into the bay and river.

For the station personnel, it all adds up to a monumental work load. More than 350 assistance cases were logged during an average year. Since arrival of the first 44-footer in 1964, it is estimated that station personnel have rescued more than 500 people who might otherwise have lost their lives. Other stations in Washington and Oregon can claim similar statistics.

CG-44303 crashes through the surf *(continued on facing page)*.

Automated Merchant Vessel Report System (AMVER)

Modern rescue at sea is a complex operation, involving close cooperation between land, air and sea units. Promptness of response to a call for help is essential to carrying out a successful rescue. One of the most effective instrumentalities for achieving this is the Coast Guard's Automated Merchant Vessel Report System (AMVER), initiated in 1958 in New York City. Since then it has steadily refined this electronic communications network until today it extends to all the world's oceans.

Heart of the AMVER system is a Coast Guard-manned communications center on Governors Island, New York. Service personnel there receive and transmit messages to and from all parts of the globe. Data contained in the messages is linked with a high-speed electronic computer at Coast Guard Headquarters in Washington, D.C. AMVER is easily the most revolutionary advance in search and rescue within the past half-century.

Participating voluntarily in the program are ships of most of the world's maritime nations. In accordance with the centuries-old tradition of the sea, each vessel stands ready to provide whatever assistance it can to another distressed ship or person. Through AMVER, the Coast Guard maintains a tracking system, keeping continuous check on the locations of merchant ships both in the Atlantic and Pacific Oceans. Thousands of vessels are taking part in the program, and the number is rising each year.

Vessels participating in the program send sailing messages to the Coast Guard's AMVER Center in New York. Data included in the reports consist of time and place of departure, routing, speed, and time and place of destination. The reports also indicate any special radar or communications capabilities which might be valuable in search and rescue situations, and whether the vessel carries a doctor on board.

If an emergency occurs at sea in a known location, AMVER's computer can be consulted to determine what potential rescue units are in the distressed vessel's vicinity. The computer prints a listing of these units, indicating each one's predicted position, course, speed, destination, and special search and rescue capabilities. Vessels shown on the list, which is called a "Surface Picture," can then be contacted and requested to assist the unit in distress.

Coast Guardsmen punch computer cards with information on passages of merchant vessels at sea. The cards are fed to an electronic computer's memory bank from which they can be recalled for use if a distress occurs.

The computer is programmed to provide three basic types of Surface Pictures: the "Radius," which is a listing of vessels within a given number of miles of a specified position; the "Hi-Lo," providing lists of vessels within a rectangular area defined by specified parallels of latitude and meridians of longitude; and the "Trackline," a listing of vessels within a given number of miles on either side of a trackline extending between two specific positions. The Surface Pictures requested may be further condensed to include only doctor-carrying vessels, only eastbound or westbound vessels, or just eastbound or westbound vessels with doctors.

During 1969, 5,650 vessels representing more than 60 countries participated in the AMVER program. A total of 96,537 passages were plotted and 1,476 emergency surface pictures were provided. Of the various distress cases, 76 involved aircraft, 180 involved vessels in distress, 433 were emergency medical cases, 28 involved persons who had fallen overboard, and 759 were related to other causes.

Countless lives have been saved by AMVER since the computerized program's inception in 1958. The program's success presents a shining example of the benefits to be derived from international cooperation, unfettered by politics, and directed only toward the general good of mankind.

Top: The VC-11A, Grumman Gulfstream II, is one of the Coast Guard's two VIP planes. *Bottom:* The Elizabeth City Complex: U.S. Coast Guard Air Station; U.S. Coast Guard Air Base; U.S. Coast Guard Aircraft Repair and Supply Center.

Coast Guard Aviation

The Elizabeth City, North Carolina complex: U.S. Coast Guard Air Station. U.S. Coast Guard Air Base; U.S. Coast Guard Aircraft Repair and Supply Center.

The first hint of trouble was sounded a little after three in the morning, November 12, 1968. *Napeaque*, a 150-foot fishing trawler, reported that she was foundering and in danger of capsizing six miles southeast of the Hatteras Inlet Sea Buoy. The trawler's situation was serious, but not yet desperate. For the harried duty officer at the Coast Guard's Rescue Coordination Center in Portsmouth, Virginia, it had already been quite a night. Six other rescue cases were in progress, and he was faced with the difficult task of coordinating all of them. Most of the District's available SAR units were already committed to other cases.

The seas grew heavier, though, and it became increasingly apparent that *Napeaque's* crewmen were in real danger. At 5:30 a.m., the trawler jettisoned two 40-foot boats, complete with purse seines and equipment, with the hope that lightening the craft might make her more stable in the steadily building seas. The effort was futile. Twenty-five-foot swells came crashing over her pilothouse, shattering her windows and dumping hundreds of gallons of water into her interior. Fifteen minutes later, one of Elizabeth City Air Station's off-duty helicopter pilots was awakened at home by the all too familiar ring of his telephone. Whether pilots or ship operators, Coast Guardsmen soon become accustomed to middle-of-the-night telephone calls.

Helicopter No. 1425 is pictured here rescuing survivors off the foundering trawler *Napeaque*.

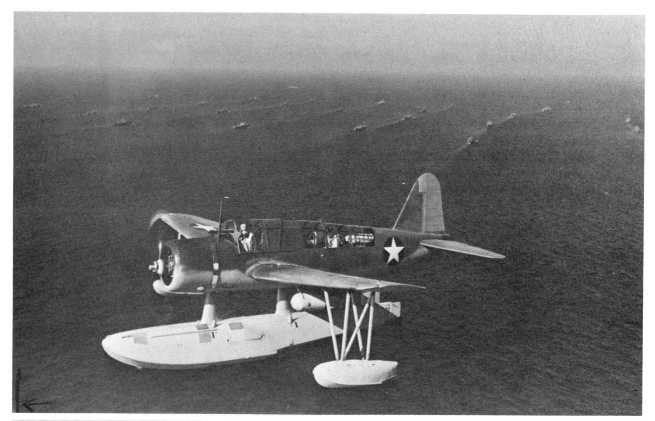

Top: A Coast Guard pilot scouts ahead of his convoy on World War II anti-submarine patrol. *Bottom:* Coast Guard cutters, such as the 327-foot *Campbell*, won reputations as submarine killers during convoy escort operations in World War II. The *Campbell* was built in 1936 at Philadelphia, Pa.

The pilot reached the station within minutes. There had been some problem in getting through to his regularly assigned crewman. The critical nature of *Napeaque's* plight required the earliest possible response, so the pilot elected to depart without his regular man, taking, instead, another petty officer who had volunteered for the assignment.

By now, *Napeaque's* communications equipment had been destroyed. The distressed vessel had been located by one of Elizabeth City's HU-16E fixed-wing aircraft, which now orbited over *Napeaque's* position. Flying one of the station's HH-52A helicopters, the rescue pilot soon arrived on scene. But what a scene it was! Enormous waves violently rolled and pitched the helpless trawler about, flinging spray so high in the air that it often obscured the pilot's vision. The tremendous force of the sea caused the trawler's 40-foot mast and radio antenna to gyrate wildly. The pilot maneuvered in as closely as he dared, and attempted to communicate with the trawler by displaying a message he had inscribed in large letters on a blackboard. The crew was practically hysterical and the pilot's attempts to communicate were unsuccessful. One thing was obvious: *Napeaque's* crew wanted off—and quickly. With remarkable courage and skill, the pilot brought his craft into a position which would allow him to

drop his rescue basket to the trawler's deck. Timing was critical. At each moment the

A Sikorsky turbine-powered helicopter rescues survivor of Hurricane Betsy in September 1965.

The HC-130B *Hercules* in flight over the Pacific Ocean.

threatening mast-antenna combination might come smashing into the helicopter. Insane with fear, two of the trawler's crewmen leaped into the basket—standing up. As the rescuers attempted to shout instructions, the trawler lunged forward erratically, casting the basket clear of its decks.

crazed crewmen might begin piling on in such numbers that their weight would bring the copter crashing down on deck. A similar accident had occurred in 1965 during Hurricane Betsy, as a Coast Guard helicopter attempted to rescue several flood-stranded persons from a rooftop.

Top: This Curtiss Flying Boat was one of the earliest aircraft used by the Coast Guard for search and rescue. *Bottom:* A Douglas Dolphin used by the Coast Guard during the 1930's and early 1940's.

With two men clinging desperately to the basket, the Coast Guardsmen were now committed to a hoist, but without benefit of prearranged signals or coordination. The petty officer at last succeeded in making the men understand they would have to sit down. Then, despite the turbulent, storm-driven winds, he executed a perfect hoist.

During each successive hoist, the Coast Guardsmen were faced with the constant danger that their basket and line might become entangled in the tossing trawler's rigging. They were also threatened by the possibility that the vessel's

The savage and unpredictable sea made the *Napeaque* rescues much more difficult than the rooftop rescues had been. The lashing motion of the mast and antenna allowed the pilot no more than 5 seconds to put his basket on deck, load survivors, and retract. The understandable eagerness of *Napeaque's* crew should have facilitated the operation, but there was too much disagreement between hoists about which man or men would have an opportunity to be next. On one occasion, three men simultaneoulsy jumped into the basket. Their combined weight would have been dangerously near the limits of the hoist's capability, so the pilot was forced to dump the basket back on the deck.

After three hours against all but insuperable odds, the crew of Coast Guard helicopter Number 1425 had successfully rescued nine of *Napeaque's* 13 crewmen. Two Marine Corps helicopters, which had been called on to assist by the Coast Guard Rescue Coordination Center, rescued the other four.

Such daring rescues are very much a part of Coast Guard aviation, and each year aviation seems to assume greater importance in the Coast Guard's overall organization and missions. The hub of Coast guard aviation is the Service's vast Elizabeth City complex, consisting of an air station, an air base, and an aircraft repair and supply base. The station is primarily concerned with search and rescue, the supply center's name is self-descriptive, and the air base operates and maintains the facilities used by both the other two.

Other Coast Guard air stations, notably Miami and Saint Petersburg, have busier search and rescue schedules than Elizabeth City. "E" City can claim, among other distinctions, to be the station out of which operate the aircraft flown by the Coast Guard's famous International Ice Patrol. The HC-130 planes used for the Ice Patrol are among the best capital investments ever made by the Service. They can fly to the site of a search at speeds of 350 knots or more. Once on scene, they can descend to search altitude, cut two engines, and search for seven to ten hours at a speed of 125 to 150 knots. It should be emphasized that high speed is not desirable for search operations, and that the HC-130's characteristics provide optimum flexibility. The 130's also have large plexiglass windows on the sides, permitting wide-range scanning during searches.

The HC-130's are remarkable cargo and passenger carriers. For transporting VIP's, they can be outfitted with a beautifully appointed "pod" which accommodates as many as 15 passengers in absolute luxury. With this configuration, there is still sufficient space in the rear of the aircraft to carry a full-sized automobile and other cargo. The planes can provide spartan, but adequate, accommodations for as many as 66 passengers with cargo space to spare. Every two years, each of the Coast Guard's helicopters is brought to the Elizabeth City Aircraft Repair and Supply Base for major overhaul. In the case of the service's HH-52A helicopters, most have their rotors disassembled and are loaded into HC-130's for transportation to the repair site. HC-130's are extensively utilized for logistics support of the Coast Guard's remote Loran stations. Paradoxically, these enormous powerhouses require considerably less space for takeoff and landing than do many smaller aircraft. Further, the 130's can take off and land on unprepared sod and sand fields if necessary.

One of Elizabeth City's HC-130's is frequently equipped with a pod somewhat different than the luxury model described in the foregoing. The aircraft is then designated as EC-130E, denoting the fact that it is simply loaded with electronics equipment. Several times each year the aircraft flies to points all over the world, monitoring signals from the Coast Guard's widely scattered Loran stations. Loran, which is the greatest boon to the navigator since the development of the compass, is only as good as it is accurate. The Coast Guard leaves nothing to chance. Loran charts are based on mathematical predictions of the speed at which radio waves travel. Crewmen of the electronics aircraft fly to spots which have been surveyed and established as landmarks. At each location they monitor Loran signals to ensure that the actual readings compare with the mathematical predictions. If any discrepancy exists, the Loran transmitting station is directed to correct its error by adjusting the delay time of the signal. This duty might prove very tedious to the air crews, were it not for the fact that Loran calibration flights routinely take them to famed travel spots such as Keflavik, Copenhagen, Oslo, Tokyo, Taipei, and Hong Kong. Occasionally the electronics plane carries along a van which is also equipped with Loran monitoring equipment. Thus, while the plane makes airborne observations, the van can operate independently on land. Whimsically called the "pizza wagon" by those who operate it, the van has, on at least one occasion, created something of an international furor. Innocent as the motive may be, imagine the difficulty of trying to take a van filled with mysterious electronics equipment across an international border.

Filling out "E" City's aircraft inventory are three HU-16E medium range fixed-wing aircraft. These are the well-known Grumman "Albatross" amphibians which formerly bore the military designation UF-2G. Most of these planes are now approaching their twentieth year of service. They have proven so dependable that the Coast Guard is hard-pressed to find a replacement for them. More than one experienced Coast Guard aviator has been quoted as saying "the only way you can replace an HU-16 is with another HU-16." Because of this, there is currently some talk of resurrecting a few HU-16E's from an aircraft "boneyard" in Arizona. The planes would be employed in pollution surveillance flights.

Although the HU-16's are nominally referred to as amphibians, it takes a very daring aviator to land one on anything other than protected waters. History has recorded a few instances where aviators have made water landings with fixed-wing amphibians and saved a few lives in the process.

of being swamped. To make matters worse, the boat was surrounded by sharks which the youth had repeatedly attempted to drive away by pummeling them with his oar. The sharks' tenacity seemed predicated on the sure knowledge that it was only a matter of time before the heavy waves would serve their dinner for them.

Nightfall was only 90 minutes away. The nearest surface rescue craft was 86 miles away in Palm Beach. Von Paulsen realized that if the boy were

00-1 Viking Flying Boat. Six of this model were in the U.S. Coast Guard service between 1931 and 1939.

Such a case occurred in 1932, shortly after the establishment of the Coast Guard's Miami Air Station. A young man in a small skiff had been blown offshore by squall winds in the vicinity of Cape Canaveral. Lieutenant Commander C.C. von Paulsen, one of the Coast Guard's most celebrated aviation heroes, was ordered to begin searching for the boy. Piloting *Arcturus*, a flying lifeboat whose place in Coast Guard history is as secure as that of its pilot, von Paulsen conquered rugged headwinds and poor visibility in locating the missing skiff. The situation was critical. The weather had deteriorated to the point that the skiff was in immediate danger

not rescued immediately he might never be located again. Before attempting a landing, it was necessary to dump all surplus gasoline. In doing so, something went wrong and much of the gas was blown into the plane's interior. To reduce the possibility of fire, the plane crew sprayed "Pyrene" on the gasoline. The result was a noxious miasma which threw the crew into fits of violent retching.

Fire was still a distinct possibility, but von Paulsen set his craft down in the heavy seas alongside the skiff and rescued the boy. The flimsy plywood plane was only a little more seaworthy than the skiff it had come to rescue, and the left wingtip float-struts collapsed. Radioman Third Class Thomas McKenzie volunteered to enter the shark-infested waters to clear away the wreckage. After 15 minutes of immersion in the stormy January sea, the young petty officer, assisted by the force of the sea itself, tore away the dangling wing tip.

Takeoff in a ten-foot sea could never be simple, but with a wing tip missing, it was all but impossible. With flawless airmanship, von Paulsen gracefully soared into the sky. The plane's damage began to spread. The remaining plywood on the left wing began peeling off like a discarded banana

skin. Helplessly, *Arcturus* began losing altitude until she was once again a prisoner of the storm-torn waters. With the calm for which he was famous, von Paulsen ordered that a sea anchor be put out. The anchor soon parted, but under von Paulsen's sure guidance, *Arcturus* continued her travel toward the shoreline. At last, nearly six hours after the time when she first entered the water, the flying lifeboat beached herself near a mangrove swamp, as neatly as if she had been a surfboat. Both her wings had virtually disintegrated. For their outstanding heroism, von Paulsen, McKenzie, and three other *Arcturus*

U.S. Coast Guard Fokker PJ-1, shown here at former Coast Guard Air Station in Cape May, N.J. Upper photo was taken in May 1935; lower photo in October 1935.

crewmen received the Treasury Department's Gold Lifesaving Medal, the highest peacetime medal bestowed by the U.S. Government. *Arcturus* was rebuilt and went on to win her greatest fame in Florida's severe hurricanes of 1934.

C.C. von Paulsen as a Captain during World War II.

Arcturus and von Paulsen had a considerably more difficult task to perform than the amphibious helicopters which Elizabeth City and other Coast Air Stations operate today. "E" City operates only the medium range HH-52's but the Aircraft Repair and Supply Center overhauls both HH-52's and the Service's long-range models, the HH-3F's.

The Elizabeth City complex began inauspiciously in August 1941. Only three officers and 52 enlisted men were assigned to the station at that time. Today, the complex employs nearly 500 military personnel and more than 300 civilians. Located at the site of the old Hollowell Plantation, on the shore of the Pasquotank River, the "E" City site has been an ideal one for the Coast Guard. The protected waters of the river are ideal for amphibious operations and the broad expanse of land has provided plenty of room for expanded runways. Because Elizabeth City is a relatively out-of-the-way spot, there are no problems with air control when it comes time to launch a major search or rescue. The central nature of the "E" City site has also proved convenient, as has the near proximity to Cape Hatteras, where many of history's greatest maritime disasters have occurred.

Aviation has grown tremendously since the Elizabeth City complex was begun. At one time, aviation was an insecure career field in the Coast Guard. An aviator, in the middle of his career, might find himself grounded and reassigned to a ship or other non-aviation unit. An indication of the changing times is that the two most recent Coast Guard Commandants, Admiral Willard J. Smith and Admiral Chester R. Bender are aviators. Other examples of the current trend are the new training facilities for helicopter pilots in Mobile, Alabama, and for technically qualified petty officers in Elizabeth City. Formerly, the Coast Guard sent its aviation personnel to Navy training commands.

In 1970 the Elizabeth City complex celebrated its 30th anniversary of service. On that occasion the Coast Guard received many congratulatory messages, including the following one from Admiral Ephraim P. Holmes, Commander in Chief of the Navy's Atlantic Fleet:

"On 15 August 1940, the Coast Guard Air Station, Elizabeth City, North Carolina, was established to provide important airborne search and rescue coverage for the Virginia and North Carolina coasts. From this early beginning, the Air Station, together with the establishment of the adjacent Coast Guard Air Base in 1964, has grown to become the center of Coast Guard aviation.

"The Air Station's outstanding accomplishments in search and rescue, from the original three assigned aircraft to today's fleet of modern fixed-wing and rotary aircraft, have brought national recognition. Equally important was the valiant service performed by Coast Guard personnel and aircraft from the Air Station in combating the submarine menace off our coasts during World War II.

"During these thirty years, the Coast Guard has flown alongside CINCLANTFLT aviators in peace and war. The records contain many cases of much appreciated assistance to the Navy by your Station and aircraft. On this 30th anniversary of the Coast Guard Air Station, Elizabeth City, North Carolina, we of the Atlantic Fleet send warmest best wishes for continued success."

Aircraft

The HH-3F Helicopter

The HH-3F helicopter is the most sophisticated aircraft to join the Coast Guard's air fleet. Fully amphibious, with a search radius of more than 300 miles, its dual engines and expanded fuel capacity give it a search and rescue (SAR) range far beyond that of other helicopters currently in service.

The most outstanding feature of the HH-3F is its airborne navigational computer. This marks the first time that this avionics system has been adapted to peacetime uses. Coast Guard pilots flying search and rescue and other missions now have at their command an advanced navigational system for humanitarian uses. Automatic flight control is achieved through a central navigation computer into which information is fed from six navigational sources. From data put into the computer, a pilot can develop a present aircraft position which is shown both in numerical form on a display unit and in graphic form on a chart. Any standard navigation chart may be used with the display. With the present position known, many other important navigational problems can be worked out by the computer. They include range and distance to preselected positions or destinations, the distance off a selected track and time to destination.

Behind the HH-3F lies more than a quarter of a century of Coast Guard experimentation with helicopters. From the very beginning of helicopter use in the 1940's, Coast Guard flyers were aware of the potential of the "whirlybird." Their dream of a vehicle—a flying lifeboat—which could hover over a target, land easily on rough water or terrain, pick up survivors of a disaster, and return to safety, was given fresh impetus by successful flights of early

helicopters. To turn that dream into reality, the Service set up a helicopter training base at Floyd Bennett Field in New York, in November, 1943. Coast Guard pilots instructed both British and U.S. Navy pilots. One year after the base was established 150 specialists were graduated. In 1944, Coast Guard Commander Frank Erickson flew the first helicopter mercy mission, carrying badly needed plasma from New York to victims of a ship explosion at Sandy Hook, New Jersey.

The computer revolution of the 1960's and the growing usefulness of the helicopter spurred Coast Guard electronics engineers to study the feasibility of adapting computer techniques to an area in which it would be especially effective—air navigation. The present system in the HH-3F is the fruition of their efforts.

Over the years the Coast Guard has logged many thousands of miles of helicopter flight, often under the most hazardous conditions. Its helicopters have landed on the rooftops of buildings in flooded areas to rescue stranded persons, have flown needed medicine to persons ill at sea, and they are presently carrying out reconnaissance in the Coast Guard's operations in the Arctic and Antarctic. Through experimentation, engineers have increased helicopter lifting and towing capabilities. More than half of the Coast Guard's air fleet consists of helicopters, reflecting their growing importance in the Service.

It has been a busy quarter of a century for the Coast Guard's helicopters. Unquestionably, the helicopter is one of the Coast Guard's most effective weapons in its humane war against the hazards of the sea.

Top: The HH-3F performs a basket rescue demonstration. *Bottom:* An HH-3F twin-turbine helicopter gives crewmen at Coast Guard Station, Barnegat Inlet, N.J., a lift with the heavy aids to navigation daymark they are assembling for an offshore site. Later the new versatile helicopter lifted the whole assembly to a rockpile in the water where it was anchored to an erected foundation.

The U.S. Coast Guard Academy

On the banks of the Thames River which flows past New London, Connecticut, stands the Coast Guard Academy. With its Georgian-style brick buildings rising from meticulously kept lawns, it is one of the most attractive educational establishments in the country.

Most of the Coast Guard's career officers are trained at the Academy where for four arduous years they carry out a combined program of work and study intended to fit them for their future careers in one of the most varied and dynamic services in the world. The young men studying here will have much to live up to. They will be following in the footsteps of men who have served their country with distinction in peace and war. Those capable of meeting the stiff competition will

An aerial view of the U.S. Coast Guard Academy, New London, Connecticut. The administration building, Hamilton Hall, is shown in the center. The Cutter *Eagle*, training vessel for cadets, is moored at the dock (background).

emerge at the end of their four years with the degree of Bachelor of Science and a commission as ensign in the regular Coast Guard.

The process by which an applicant may qualify for admission is highly selective. The only way is via a nationwide competitive examination given in December of each year. There are no Congressional appointments. Those who reach the Academy have done so on the basis of their high school or preparatory school records and their ability to meet the high physical, mental and moral standards. Examiners reviewing test papers have no way of knowing an applicant's race, creed, or color, nor do they care. After an applicant has met

the written standards, he is in line for an interview. But the heavier part of his total score is based on his score in the written examination, and on his school record. In view of the urgent need for high-caliber human material, the Coast Guard cannot afford to overlook any promising young man.

It must be understood, however, that there is a significant difference between the Academy and a civilian college or university. Those who come to it are presumably motivated by the desire for a military career with all that it entails. It is not only a question of mental alertness but of capability to adjust to the disciplines of military life. Discipline

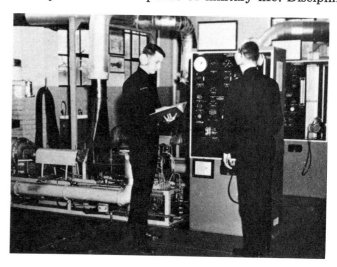

Classes in session at the Academy.

is at the core of the system in which they will spend their adult lives. Therefore, they must learn the military way of doing things. They must be capable of performing competently under the stresses which will undoubtedly face them in the Service. It is at the Academy that they have a chance to find out whether they are suited to this kind of regimen.

In addition to outstanding scholastic ability, prospective cadets must also possess a measure of athletic prowess, as well as an interest in extracurricular activities. The ideal sought for is a well-rounded personality. Scholastic excellence is not in itself a guarantee of successful performance as an officer. Yet it is nevertheless important since those entering the Academy are usually in the top quarter of their high school class.

Because the Coast Guard is a Service which

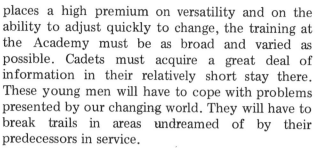

places a high premium on versatility and on the ability to adjust quickly to change, the training at the Academy must be as broad and varied as possible. Cadets must acquire a great deal of information in their relatively short stay there. These young men will have to cope with problems presented by our changing world. They will have to break trails in areas undreamed of by their predecessors in service.

Recognizing that in the new scale of educational values, sea duty, however traditional, is only one phase of an officer's career, the Academy is placing greater stress on modern managerial techniques, psychology, and other fields related to administration. Some Academy graduates will have the responsibility of representing their country on international maritime groups in which they will meet men of other countries, often with

Roland Field House (top l. & r. and bottom r.) and Billard Hall provide cadets with some of the finest athletic facilities in New England.

viewpoints very different from their own. They will have to think in global rather than in parochial terms. The narrower concept of education which served well enough in an earlier day will not suffice now. That is why the administrators of the Academy, over the last several years, have embarked on a program designed to widen the choice of studies available to cadets.

is probable that its functions will undergo further change. Traditions and precedents of the past will be less controlling than they have been before.

In line with the new thinking, Academy administrators have made some significant curriculum changes. Beginning with his third year, a cadet may choose to pursue a course of education much more closely akin to that of a conventional

U.S. Coast Guard cadets line up for gun drill with caisson and gun in tow at historic Fort Trumbull, New London, Conn., in 1916. The Fort was the site of the Coast Guard Academy from 1910 to 1932, after which the Academy was relocated permanently at its present site on the Thames River in New London.

In the past, the Academy tended to be an engineering and science-oriented school. This approach is gradually giving way to the realization that the modern Service needs capable administrators as well as operational types. Although the seagoing tradition continues to be important, those responsible for shaping the Academy curriculum know very well that, for every man at sea, a substantial body of personnel will have to stay ashore. As the Coast Guard becomes increasingly involved in the Department of Transportation, its new organizational home, it

college or university. Among the options open are history, French or Spanish, political science, and psychology. Under the Department of Humanities, a cadet may take courses in colonial American history, modern Russian history, and studies in Asian and Latin-American culture. That is a far cry from the old days when an officer's training was primarily in the operational, seagoing skills.

Reflecting man's reawakened intellectual curiosity in all aspects of his physical environment, the Academy has included a course of study in the marine sciences. The expanding scope of the Coast

Guard's work in oceanography and its allied fields makes it imperative that greater numbers of young men trained in this sector be available to the Service. Today, it is possible, therefore, for a cadet to obtain the degree of Bachelor of Science in Oceanography.

How is the new approach working out? Apparently, very well. Currently, only from 50 to 60 percent of the total cadet enrollment is taking the engineering curriculum. Also, the change in

faculty. The atmosphere is far less casual than that of a conventional campus. Everyone here realizes that what is being done at the Academy will determine the quality of the future Service. It is a solemn responsibility and everyone accepts it as such. There is universal agreement that in today's world a knowledge of the humanities is essential to the training of a successful officer. What has been going on at the Academy is nothing less than a revolution.

The Revenue Cutter *Salmon P. Chase* served as a cadet schoolship at New Bedford, Mass. from 1878 to 1899, when she was laid up because of pressure from the Navy Department. In 1894, *Chase* was recommissioned and in 1900, she was transferred to Arundel Cove, Maryland, site of the Academy until 1910. *Chase* was decommissioned in 1907.

teaching has been from a primarily specific to a conceptual approach. The theory behind this is that applications of principles may change, but principles themselves seldom do.

Emphasis is on turning out a whole man rather than a specialist. After all, it is impossible to turn out specialists in the four years of training allotted to the Academy. For this reason, the Coast Guard is sending out many of its more talented young graduates to leading colleges and universities throughout the nation. There they may take advanced training in their chosen field.

One of the most impressive aspects of life at the Academy is the degree of sincerity and devotion brought to their work both by students and

As one looks at the beautiful campus of the Academy, it is difficult to realize that it was not always so sumptuously housed. The first Academy was the revenue cutter *Dobbin*, in the historic old whaling town of New Bedford, Massachusetts. It had been authorized by Congress only a short time before it began functioning in the winter of 1876. The first small class of cadets studied a very narrow curriculum, aimed almost exclusively at turning out competent ships' officers. Training was strictly operational and there were no frills. Later, another cutter, *Chase*, was added as a schoolship. The arrangement worked well enough until the expansion of the Coast Guard's duties rendered the original educational concept inadequate. Consequently, in 1910, the Academy moved to Fort Trumbull on the outskirts of New London. Here the curriculum was significantly broadened. But by 1929, the Academy was no longer adequate to meet the Service's officer requirements. At this point, ground was purchased for the site of the present Academy. Its construction was completed in 1932 when the Coast Guard moved in. In the years since then it has continued to grow.

What is life like at the Academy? In general, it is quite rigorous. One of the most difficult things a young man must learn to do, is to put aside his easygoing civilian ways for the more stringent demands of military life. As soon as a cadet has been enrolled and assigned to a platoon, he is ready to begin his work. As the routine takes hold, he will find that his time has been fully budgeted. He will be up at 6:10 a.m. and will stay on the go until 11 p.m. With occasional variations, this will be the pattern of his life for the next four years. Not everyone can take it, and there are many casualties, usually in the first two years.

Yet life at the Academy is not unrelieved drudgery. There are many opportunities for non-academic pursuits, including all kinds of clubs catering to each cadet's interest. Sailboating on the Thames rates a high priority on the list of outdoor activities. On Saturday and Sunday afternoons in spring and summer, the Thames is dotted with sailing craft, often with a young lady aboard as the crew. Athletic facilities are excellent and Roland Field House is one of the best in the country.

Key to success at the Academy is motivation. A young man must want to be a cadet strongly enough to adjust to a far less permissive environment than that to which he has been accustomed. Without this strong inner drive, he probably will not survive. For those who come through the demanding routine, the rewards make it all worthwhile.

Sails open to the wind, the *Eagle* is one of the most beautiful ships in the world. She embodies the romantic traditions of the days of sail.

Eagle, The Extraordinary Classroom

With the construction of the 210-foot and 378-foot classes of cutters during the past decade, the Coast Guard has emerged as a builder of some of the world's most beautiful ships. Ironically, the most spectacular cutter in the Coast Guard fleet was not only not built by the Coast Guard, but was not even built in the U.S.

Almost anyone who has ever seen her will agree that the Coast Guard cutter *Eagle* is probably the most picturesque vessel flying the U.S. flag. When built in Hamburg, Germany in 1936, the three-masted sailing barque was christened as *Horst Wessel.* She was named for an early leader of the Nazi Party, who also gave his name to the official party anthem. She was originally intended as a training vessel for the German Navy, but the exigencies of war soon brought about her conversion to a cargo carrier.

At the war's end, the 1,816-gross-ton barque was awarded to the U.S. as a part of war reparations. In January, 1946, ten Coast Guard officers boarded her in Bremerhaven to take possession and change her name to *Eagle.*

In the years which have followed, *Eagle* has provided the first practical seagoing experience for cadets at the U.S. Coast Guard Academy at New London, Connecticut. That experience is piled on in heavy doses. On the first morning under way, each new cadet is required to make a full tour of the rigging. Going "over the top" for the first time can be a terrifying experience for the uninitiated, but in the course of a cruise, cadets go up so regularly, furling and unfurling canvas, that they become old hands at it in no time at all. A whole new vocabulary is learned while young men, who may have never previously been out of sight of land, master the intricacies of *Eagle's* stays, sails, yards, and masts. *Eagle* has also provided countless cadets with their first cases of seasickness, although under sail she rides as well as almost anything afloat.

Eagle's 21,350.8 feet of sail area can carry her along at speeds approaching 17 knots. A 728-horsepower diesel engine is available for maneuvering or when becalmed. From stern to bowsprit she measures 295 feet. Her foremast and mainmast stand slightly more than 150 feet above the water line.

Laying aloft, U.S. Coast Guard Academy Cadets on a summer practice cruise scramble up the ropes to the main shrouds of the training bark *Eagle.*

First year cadets at the Academy are called "fourth classmen." They are the ones who perform most of the menial tasks on board *Eagle.* They stand watches as helmsmen, lookouts, messengers, members of the ready boat crew, and quartermasters. They also do "day work" as mess cooks and compartment cleaners. In the execution of these tasks, they are supervised by second classmen who function as Officers of the Deck, Navigators, Bos'ns of the Watch, Combat Information Center Watchstanders, Engineers of the Watch, and Masters at Arms.

The real lessons to be learned on board this extraordinary floating classroom extend far beyond marlinespike seamanship and the esoteric art of cruising before the mast. *Eagle* provides almost unparalleled opportunities to learn teamwork and leadership. Changing the cutter's tack is an all-hands evolution. Every man has a highly specialized job and must know how and when to do it. Those in positions of leadership must coordinate each sequence of events down to the finest detail. Knowledge, skill, and that raw strength which seafarers call "Norwegian steam" are all called into play.

Sailing *Eagle* is a vastly more complicated feat than operating one of the Coast Guard's more modern cutters. A bewildering maze of halyards and other rigging must be mastered by those who would sail her. A man must learn that the act of hauling a certain halyard hoists a certain sail, and that each sail has a certain effect on the ship's travel.

Fifteen officers and 45 enlisted men supplement the 200 cadets who sail *Eagle* on her 4 two-week cruises each summer. The officers act as instructors and step in to correct the cadet watchstanders if an error is made. In former years *Eagle* has visited many of the world's great ports: Le Havre, London, San Juan, Bergen, Havana, Lisbon, and a great many others. Today the *Eagle* cruises independently, making ports between Portland, Maine, and Norfolk, Virginia. She is acclaimed for her great beauty wherever she goes.

Beautiful or not, this splendid anachronism has received her share of curses and vituperation. What else might we expect from a cadet who has suffered one crick after another from sleeping in her hammocks, nearly frozen on board her in the North Atlantic, sweltered in the calm of the Caribbean, spent hour after hour polishing her more than one hundred belaying pins, and been awakened in the middle of the night and called upon to furl or set her sails?

With the objectivity which comes with time, that same cadet can be trusted to look back on his sailing days on board *Eagle* as one of life's supreme experiences. Long may she sail!

Kukui, One of a Kind

Of all the ships in the Coast Guard, none is more unique than *Kukui,* the floating life line to Pacific Loran stations.

Kwajalein, Truk, Guam, Taiwan, Okinawa, Iwo Jima, Marcus Island, and six or eight stops in the Philippines. These back-breaking deployments keep

Kukui underway.

Taken solely as a piece of sea-going machinery, *Kukui* is as ordinary as they come. She is identical in design to dozens of "AK's" operated by the U.S. Navy and the Maritime Administration since the early 40's. Her design is also identical to the Coast Guard's reserve training cutter *Courier.* Under Coast Guard operation, *Kukui* has no peers. Each year, the 339-foot cargo carrier sails the wide Pacific, taking badly needed supplies to remote Coast Guard Loran stations. The aging cutter also carries a crew of skilled specialists capable of repairing, or even building the important stations.

Kukui is the only ship in the Coast Guard that includes a civil engineer as a regular part of its personnel complement. The cutter also carries a physician.

A typical deployment may take *Kukui* from her home base in Honolulu to Johnston Atoll,

Kukui away from Honolulu an average of nine months each year. Even when in her home port, the ship is fighting time as she loads cargo for the next deployment.

There is almost no limit to the types of work the cutter may be called on to perform. On a recent stop at a single station, Naulo Point, she was required to excavate, fill, grade, and compact both ends of the station runway; extend the sewer outfall system, replace the station's septic tank; install a fuel oil filter for the water heater; completely overhaul the station's antenna guys and lamps; and rebuild a large wooden bridge. Those who are in a position to know agree that there isn't a harder working ship in the entire Coast Guard.

The variety of cargo carried on by *Kukui* also staggers the imagination. On any given deployment, she may be taking spare electronics parts for the station's Loran and communications equipment, a new stereophonic record player for a station's recreational use, a new range for a station's galley, and a new jeep for a station's transportation use, are only a few examples. When fully loaded, in fact, the cutter can carry up to 3,800 tons of cargo, an amount equivalent to more than the entire dead weight of one of the Coast Guard's 378-foot cutters! The vessel's cruising range is also exceptional—20,000 miles; almost completely around the world without refueling.

Although search and rescue is not one of *Kukui's* major missions, the cutter has performed many missions of mercy over the years. In 1969, after a devastating summer typhoon, *Kukui* transported 350 tons of emergency food, medical supplies, and building materials from Manila to Batanes Island in the Northern Philippines. Routinely, the ship carries books and clothing donated by the Chinese Catholic Society of Honolulu to missions in the Trust Territory and the Philippines. There are few more welcome sights in the Western Pacific than *Kukui* and the two LCM's she carries. Frequently, as time permits, the ship's force assists the native population with local construction projects. In the past, she has helped to bulldoze a basketball court, dig a garbage dump, clear drainage canals, build and repair schools and hospitals, and perform many other jobs.

Because of *Kukui's* age and recent budget cuts, the future is presently somewhat uncertain for the Coast Guard's only cargo carrier. If she is to continue in operation, extensive overhaul of her deck machinery and living spaces will have to be made.

Whatever the future may hold, the hard-working Coast Guardsmen who have manned *Kukui* for the last 27 years can look back with justifiable pride on the fine service they have rendered to Loran stations of the Western Pacific.

Supply Depots

USCG Supply Depot, New Orleans

The Eighth Coast Guard District, with headquarters in New Orleans, Louisiana, has gained a well deserved measure of renown for its proven ability to respond rapidly and effectively to the demands of heavy SAR loads, frequently aggravated by natural disasters such as the devastating hurricanes which struck the area in 1961, 1965, 1967, and 1969. Naturally, a major part of the credit for this ability lies with the District's splendid array of boats, cutters, and aircraft and the finely trained crews which man them. An equal measure of credit rightfully belongs to the Coast Guard Supply Depot in New Orleans. Nearly lost in anonymity, all but forgotten when words of praise are handed out, the Supply Depot provides a vital and dynamic service to the field, without which

even the best operational units could not long survive.

With a seemingly endless inventory, ranging from items as mundane as paint and brushes to computer-age electronics components, the Supply Depot exists only to service the field.

Prior to World War II, each of the military services had its own peculiar system of supply. Integration of various operating forces soon made it clear that some degree of uniformity was highly desirable. Nevertheless, the services labored frustratedly through the war, spending countless hours cross-referencing through supply catalogues of the other branches. After the war, a standardized Federal Stock Number system was instituted, bringing about badly needed reform. Advantages

USCG Supply Depot, New Orleans, Louisiana.

realized by the elimination of duplication through consolidation were almost counterbalanced by complexities of the new system. For a unit without supply specialists attached, filling out MILSTRIPS (Military Standard Requisitioning and Issue Procedures) became a dreaded nightmare. Each item ordered had to be requested individually on a coded document which could be filled out by the nonspecialist only by numerous references to various manuals and catalogues. It was at this point that the New Orleans Supply Depot innovated one of the many improved procedures which have come to characterize this progressive unit.

By carefully analyzing the Depot inventory and identifying all high demand items, a special consolidated requisition was prepared. All of the coded details which formerly had to be looked up were printed right on the sheet so that it was only necessary for the unit to indicate the quantity desired of each item. Submission dates for the Conreqs, as they are called, are staggered to balance the depot's work load. Obscure and little-used items must still be ordered by conventional MILSTRIP, but the savings in man-hours has been tremendous.

The New Orleans Supply Depot holds one particularly unique distinction: it is the only supply point for Cummins diesel parts in the entire Coast Guard. To the uninitiated this may seem to be an inconsequential fact, but there are probably more Cummins diesels powering Coast Guard boats and cutters than any other type of engine. The centralization of these parts has taken place somewhat recently—between June and December 1969. Maintenance of the approximately 200 Cummins engines in use throughout the Coast Guard had become quite problematical over a period of years. No individual district could afford to stock adequate spare parts for its units, and lead time for orders from either the Cummins factory or wholesale distributors was often as long as six months, which was not at all satisfactory. Stocking all Cummins parts in New Orleans has produced two major benefits—nearly all parts can now be bought directly from the factory at a very

significant savings, and lead time for most orders has been reduced to about two days.

For nearly twenty years the New Orleans Depot has also offered the units it supplies complete door-to-door service. Because a number of Eighth District units, such as Freeport, Florida, Dauphin Island, Alabama, and Port Isabel, Texas, are not serviced by commercial freight carriers, the depot operates its own logistics trucks. Aside from the convenience offered by this system, the Coast Guard realizes a net savings of approximately $36,000 each year by providing its own transportation services.

People automatically associate the Coast Guard with search and rescue, so it is not entirely surprising that the Supply Depot has, despite its unspectacular mission, been actively involved in several SAR missions. On one occasion a collision between a ship and a gasoline barge threatened grave danger to the New Orleans waterfront facilities. The depot was the only unit in the area with large quantities of fire-fighting foam on hand, and was requested to stand by to assist. Within less than an hour, and in spite of the fact that the incident occurred on a Sunday, a depot truck was on hand with a full load of foam. During the several hurricanes which have struck the Gulf Coast in recent years, the depot has been manned 24 hours a day to process emergency requisitions. In a fairly recent incident, involving the forced landing in a swamp by a Coast Guard helicopter, the depot responded in the grand Coast Guard tradition by furnishing a large amount of plywood to build a ramp for recovering the aircraft.

Located for many years at the site of the old New Orleans Mint, the depot moved in 1958 to its present location at the U.S. Naval Support Activity on the east bank of the Mississippi River. The "can-do" spirit of the two chief warrant officers, ten enlisted men, and 22 civilians who man the New Orleans Supply Depot are living proof that every Coast Guard unit plays its own important role in making the Service the effective agency which it is today.

Miscellaneous Training and Support Facilities

Top: Approximately 4,000 recruits are trained annually at the Service's Training Center in Cape May, New Jersey. *Bottom:* The Coast Guard Training and Supply Center, Alameda, California, trains recruits enlisted west of the Rockies and is the main supply service for Western Area Coast Guard units.

Top: A different kind of Coast Guard cutter. This ferry transports passengers to and from Governors Island and Manhattan. *Bottom:* U.S. Coast Guard Base, Governors Island, New York, is the Service's single largest installation. It encompasses five tenant commands: Eastern Area Headquarters; Third District Headquarters; Base New York, Captain of the Port of New York, and U.S. Coast Guard Training Center, Governors Island. A number of the Service's important cutters are also berthed here.

Top: **This important radio station in Miami is one of 12 such stations operated by the Service.** *Bottom:* **The Coast Guard Yard in Curtis Bay, Maryland. Most major East Coast cutters undergo shipyard availabilities here. The Yard also has constructed a large number of the Service's boats and cutters.**

III
COAST GUARD PROFILES

Alexander Hamilton, Founding Father

Like a meteor, Alexander Hamilton flashed across the American sky, leaving behind him a legacy that still endures. In his 49 years of life, from 1755 to 1804, he guided the young Republic along paths which were to determine its destiny.

The man who at 34 was to become the first Secretary of the Treasury, was in every respect remarkable. Slim, elegant in manner and dress, gifted with a rapier-like intellect, he resembled an 18th century French marquis rather than an American statesman. Fiercely ambitious, he burned with a cold intellectual passion. Even in an age of giants, Hamilton was conspicuous.

Hamilton's origins made him vulnerable to his political enemies. He had been born on the West Indies island of Nevis on January 11, 1755, out of the union of a Scots trader, James Hamilton, and Rachel Fawcett Lavien, daughter of a French Huguenot and wife of John Michael Lavien, a Danish or German merchant who had settled on the island of St. Croix in the Danish West Indies. Hamilton's father was a descendant of Scottish nobility, being the fourth son of Alexander Hamilton, Laird of Cambuskeith, Ayrshire, Scotland. Rachel Lavien had been living with James Hamilton since 1752, although she was not divorced by Lavien until 1758. Thus the taint of illegitimacy attached to Hamilton's birth, a fact which was to cause him acute embarrassment all his life and probably had enormous impact in shaping his personality.*

In 1765, James Hamilton abandoned his family in St. Croix, and the 11-year old Alexander became a clerk in the counting house of Nicholas Cruger and David Beekman, New York merchants who had recently established themselves at St. Croix. By the time Hamilton was 16, his ability and intelligence had so impressed his employers that they promoted him from bookkeeper to manager. In that same year, some friends who admired his brilliance sent him to the American mainland to further his education.

The 1770's were tempestuous years in the American colonies and the very air at King's College (later Columbia University) was charged with the gathering revolt against Great Britain. Hamilton's passionate nature was caught up in the cause and he gave himself to it without reservation.

At the age of 19, he authored several powerful revolutionary pamphlets, attacking British policy in the New World. The pamphlets were so brilliantly written that at first they were attributed to John Jay and John Adams, two of the greatest intellectuals produced by this country. The pamphlets attracted the attention of some of the leading men of the time and Hamilton's career was under way.

No man contributed more to the strength and security of his country than the brilliant Alexander Hamilton, first Secretary of the Treasury under President George Washington, and founder of the U.S. Coast Guard.

For the remainder of his life, one achievement was to follow another with astonishing consistency. In February 1777, General Washington invited him to serve on his staff as aide-de-camp with the rank of lieutenant colonel, a considerable achievement for a young man of 22! Hamilton served with great distinction, making friends to whom he would be attached until his death. During lulls in the military campaigns, notably in the winter, he continued his interrupted education, reading deeply in the classics, especially in the literature of economics and public finance. The reading left its imprint upon his later style and fiscal attitudes.

*Some historical sources disagree on Hamilton's birthdate and his mother's last name.

Hamilton's public career was furthered by his marriage in December 1780 to Elizabeth Schuyler, daughter of General Philip Schuyler, the head of one of New York's most distinguished families. Hamilton's star was definitely in the ascendant, and was to remain so until it was so tragically cut short by a duelist's bullet in 1804.

Alexander Hamilton.

A Treasury Department engraving.

Admitted to the New York bar in 1782, Hamilton was shortly thereafter elected to the Continental Congress where the Republic's future shape would be forged. Already in his many writings, Hamilton had indicated that he was a strong Federalist, being convinced that the nation's first constitution, the Articles of Confederation, was a source of weakness and disunion. Behind Hamilton's passionate espousal of a dominant central government lay an unconscious distrust of the judgment of the common man. He was essentially an aristocrat, believing that the destiny of the nation should be confided only to those with the education and intellect to determine it. This tendency would in later years lead him to make some unwise statements, including his reference to the people as a "great beast."

What Hamilton had in mind politically was something akin to a constitutional monarchy with a president elected for life with the power to appoint state governors. The president would be selected by a double set of electors and would have an absolute veto over the legislature. It was a system closely analogous to the British model which Hamilton greatly admired. At one time he said, ". . . the British Government is the best in the world, and I doubt much whether anything short of it will do in America." These were strange words

for a man who had spent several years helping to throw off the yoke of just such a government! But Hamilton was a paradoxical man, and not at all easy to understand.

Undoubtedly, the event which most influenced Hamilton's life was his meeting with George Washington. Washington, with his flair for spotting talent, took immediately to the young officer. Despite the 23-year difference in their ages, the two men worked well together. The general so much admired Hamilton's brilliant mind and courtly manners that he placed him at the head of the headquarters' table, sitting himself at one side. This nettled many senior officers who thought themselves more deserving of the honor.

Hamilton soon made himself indispensable to the older man. His natural tact and courtesy tended to offset Washington's occasional brusqueness and abrasiveness. Hamilton also had a graceful way with correspondence and eventually wrote many of the letters for Washington's signature. However, this arrangement did not satisfy Hamilton, who like most young men, hungered for military glory. It was in deference to this desire that Washington, during the final battle at Yorktown, permitted Hamilton to storm a British redoubt, thus winning military fame.

In learning and intellect, Hamilton was Washington's superior. No one knew better than he that he lacked the stability and assurance that were Washington's by birthright. He was, after all, a gifted immigrant who had to make his way in the world with whatever talents he possessed. As he himself put it later, he needed the "aegis" or sponsorship of someone with the stability and social status of Washington. The result of this relationship was an alliance, inuring greatly to the benefit of the young Republic.

As he rose to power, Hamilton made some powerful enemies, one of them being John Adams who once referred to him as "the bastard brat of a Scots peddler." That gives some idea of the virulence of the politics of that era. Nevertheless, Hamilton and his adherents at the Constitutional Convention did manage to push through a Constitution which was a compromise between Hamiltonian absolutism and the loosely-bound system of the Articles of Confederation.

When Washington launched the new federal government in April, 1789, he called on Hamilton to serve as his Secretary of the Treasury. His instructions to Hamilton were that the latter draw up a plan for the "adequate support of the public credit." The task facing the 34-year old secretary was staggering. The Nation was almost bankrupt. With his strong sense of honor, Hamilton was determined that the Nation pay all its debts with full interest, including those of the States. Altogether, the sum of the obligations came to more than 74 million dollars, an immense sum for a country with a population of less than four million people.

Nor was that all. During the years before the Revolution, smuggling had been developed to a high art to evade unjust British levies. It was so profitable, that it was continued even after the Revolution had been won. Millions of desperately needed dollars were being diverted from the federal treasury. The amount of revenue lost could make the difference between solvency and bankruptcy. Unless it could be recovered for national use, the world's newest experiment in democracy could go down to failure. It was an emergency of the highest order and a solution had to be found quickly.

It was in this grave crisis that Hamilton conceived the idea of a revenue fleet whose mission would be to suppress smuggling. In correspondence in 1789 with Customs Collector Colonel Sharp Delaney of Philadelphia, Pennsylvania, he had suggested the formation of such a fleet on the Schuylkill River on an experimental basis. Approximately one year later, on a hot August 4, 1790, the First Congress authorized the construction of "ten boats for the collection of revenue." Hamilton's dream had come true.

Hamilton asked that the vessels be allocated as follows: two for the coasts of Massachusetts and New Hampshire; one for Long Island Sound; one for New York; one for the Bay of Delaware; two for the Chesapeake; one for North Carolina; one for South Carolina; and one for Georgia. That small revenue fleet was one of Hamilton's most brilliant accomplishments in a lifetime filled with achievement. It was to serve as the nucleus of what was to develop into today's Coast Guard. Not only did it help to keep the young nation afloat fiscally, but it also proudly asserted its sovereignty at sea against some of the world's mightiest sea powers. The modern U. S. Coast Guard is a monument to a very great American.

For as long as he lived, Hamilton was steadfast in advancing his dream of a strong and secure central government. Seen in this perspective, the Revenue Fleet represented another step along this road. Other steps included establishment of a national bank based on implied constitutional powers, passage of protective laws, bolstering the country's infant industries, and use of over-whelming force to put down a rebellion by farmers of western Pennsylvania against an excise tax on distilled liquors. This episode came to be known as the "Whiskey Rebellion."

Hamilton envisoned a government of superior persons who would be above party, influenced perhaps by the Dialogues of Plato. Instead, he became the leader of the Federalist Party, favoring a strongly centralized government. President Washington, sympathetic to Hamilton's views, joined himself with his Secretary of the Treasury as a leader of the Party. A good deal of the attraction which the two men felt for each other sprang from their similarity of temperament. Both were pronouncedly aristocratic in attitude, regarding service to country as a patrician obligation.

Hamilton's views brought him sharply into conflict with another giant of American history, Thomas Jefferson, whose brilliance and versatility surpassed even Hamilton's. While Hamilton leaned toward closer ties with England, Jefferson tended toward stronger alliance with revolutionary France. Hamilton especially detested the egalitarian principles of the French revolution and feared their importation to the United States. The feud between the two men grew so bitter that for two years, from 1791 to 1793, they tried to drive each other from the government.

Hamilton's opposition to the reelection of John Adams in 1800 made him another powerful enemy. Adams was not the kind of man to forgive so deep an injury. The result of Hamilton's efforts was to split the Federalist Party so that Jefferson and Aaron Burr, an intensely ambitious man, both received the same number of electoral votes. Putting aside his long-standing enmity to Jefferson, Hamilton urged the former's election. The controversy ended Hamilton's public career and insured the burning hatred for Burr.

It now seemed as if fortune had turned her back on her favorite. Arising to plague Hamilton was an affair he had had several years earlier with an attractive adventuress, Mrs. Maria Reynolds. It appears that her husband, a confidence man, had sent certain blackmailing letters to Hamilton. These fell into the hands of a political enemy and were published. Hamilton admitted the affair but denied any corrupt dealings with Reynolds. His defense was successful, but the entire incident was a deep humiliation to a man of his proud spirit.

In 1804, after a hard-fought and bitterly partisan campaign for the governorship of New York, Aaron Burr was defeated. Burr attributed this setback to his enemy, Hamilton. In June 1804,

Burr demanded satisfaction of Hamilton for having said that he (Hamilton) held a "despicable opinion" of Burr. The two antagonists met a dawn of June 11 on the heights of Weehawken, New Jersey, where Hamilton's eldest son, Philip, had died in a duel three years before. Burr was a crack shot, and his bullet found its mark. Hamilton fell mortally wounded. Before lapsing into unconsciousness, he said, "This is a mortal wound, doctor." He was never to regain consciousness. One of the great lights of the Republic had been extinguished forever.

Louis McLane—a Treasury Department engraving.

Louis McLane, Builder of a Service

Few men have had a more distinguished career in the service of their country, than Louis McLane, Secretary of the Treasury under President Jackson. Born in 1786 in Delaware, this remarkable man, in the course of his 71 years of life was to serve as U.S. Congressman, diplomat, cabinet officer and business executive. By the time he died in 1857, he had left a lasting memorial of service to the young Republic.

McLane's career and that of the growing Revenue Cutter Service coincided in 1831 when he was recalled from his post of U.S. Minister to England to serve as Secretary of the Treasury at a very critical time. For a long time a bitter dispute had been going on between the southern states over the tariff laws enforced by the officers of the Customs Bureau. Duties, they argued, should be levied solely for the original purpose stated by Alexander Hamilton—to produce revenue.

The southern philosophy ran directly contrary to that of President James Monroe and others who believed that the Congress should enact laws that would protect "those articles which we are prepared to manufacture or which are more immediately connected with the defense and independence of the country." In other words, they espoused the doctrine of the protective tariff about which controversy has raged until the present.

Protectionism had wide appeal for a young, weak nation struggling to build its economy. The protective-tariff block had achieved a major victory in 1824 when rates rose drastically. Then in 1828, they had pushed them even higher. As might be expected, the exporting nations did not take to these actions kindly. All the elements of a trade war were present. The effect could have been devastating to the United States.

Recognizing the danger, Congress in 1832 lowered the tariff rates slightly. Nevertheless, protectionism appeared to have gained the day.

It was during the troubled early 1830's that the country embarked on a great debate which would ultimately shake it to its foundations. Out of the tariff dispute rose for the first time the issue of States' Rights. This idea, pursued further, carried within it the doctrine of state sovereignty and secession. To put it another way, the tariff debate brought into sharp focus the question which had been troubling Americans ever since the days of Hamilton: Did the preservation of a strong federal union take precedence over all other considerations? Less than 30 years later, this issue would no longer be debated in Congress but with shot and shell on the bloody battlefields of the Civil War.

Jackson's position was emphatically clear. "Old Hickory," whatever his faults may have been, never left anyone in doubt as to where he stood on an issue. In a speech made at that time, he gave the toast, "Our Federal Union; it must be preserved." It was a battle cry to be repeated many times in the tumultuous years ahead.

Soon after Jackson's reelection in November 1832, the South Carolina legislature called a convention. After five days of fevered debate, they announced the Ordinance of Nullification, declaring the Tariff Acts of 1828 and 1832 null and void in South Carolina's ports.

But even before the nullification vote, Secretary McLane had sent instructions to the Customs Collector at Charleston to resist any measures adopted by the South Carolina convention. Said the Secretary: "You will consider yourself authorized to employ the Revenue Cutter which may be within your district. You will cause a sufficient number of officers . . . to be placed on board and in charge of any vessel arriving from a foreign port or place . . . and direct them to anchor her in some safe place within the harbor. And it will be your duty against any forcible attempt, to defend and retain custody of said vessel by the aid of the Officers of the Customs . . . until the requisitions of the law shall be fully complied with."

Simultaneously, the revenue cutters *Gallatin*, *Alert*, *Jackson*, *Dexter*, and *McLane* were ordered to get under way for Charleston, pausing only at Norfolk, Virginia, for arms, ammunition and provisions. Treason was to be met with force. And above everything else, the federal revenue and sovereignty was to be protected. It was the ugliest crisis to confront the nation since its establishment 56 years earlier.

Evidently McLane's positive nature resembled the President's. Some of McLane's directness and authority may have stemmed from his long service in the U.S. Navy which he had entered as a boy of 12 under the celebrated Commodore Stephen Decatur! It had been an early apprenticeship in service to our country.

The situation reached the stand-off stage, with neither side willing to make any concessions. Vessels arriving from foreign ports were boarded by an Officer of the Customs, piloted up to Sullivan's Island and ordered to drop their hooks under the guns of Fort Moultrie. There they discharged their cargoes, to be held until duties were paid.

After four months of violent argument, the peacemaker, Henry Clay, stepped in and averted an outright rebellion against federal authority. The result of his efforts was the Compromise Tariff Act of 1833; but it was only a palliative and not an answer.

The new legislation provided for a gradual lowering of the duties over a period of years. The South Carolina legislature called another convention to revoke the Ordinance of Nullification, and the country went back to normal, for the time being.

McLane had shown himself to be a strong administrator, but that was by no means the extent of his contribution. Not long after taking over as Secretary of the Treasury, it occurred to him that the vessels of the revenue fleet could render an invaluable service to coastal merchant shipping. He issued an order, laying the foundation for one of the primary duties of the U.S. Coast Guard: "rendering assistance to vessels in distress and saving life and property at sea." Today, the Coast Guard's maritime safety program goes far beyond that early instruction and extends to preventive safety measures as well. The seed of this magnificent program was sown long ago by Louis McLane and his short, simple instruction to the Collector of Customs at Wilmington, Delaware, ordering on December 16, 1831, the preparation of the *Gallatin* for sea duty without delay.

"In the present inclement season," McLane wrote, "it is thought proper to combine with ordinary duties of the cutters that of assisting vessels found on the coast in distress and of ministering to the wants of their crews." Very shrewdly, McLane reasoned that the cutters would thus be utilized to their maximum extent. The revenue cutter fleet was turning out to be one of the best values the taxpayer ever received for his money. This concern for using appropriations to the best national advantage is still one of the driving forces of the Service.

The *Gallatin* was to cruise between Cape May, New Jersey, and Hog Island, Virginia, keeping as close as possible to the mainland without endangering herself. She was not to return to Wilmington until forced to do so by bad weather or need for supplies. She was to speak to all vessels approaching the coast and give them any aid they might need. Similar orders were issued to the *Wolcott, Dexter, Hamilton, Morris, Portsmouth* and *Swiftsure*. McLane's humane order of 1831 was one of the most lasting contributions ever made to the Service. It gave new scope and meaning to the work of a small fleet whose original purpose had been law enforcement and little more.

McLane turned his attention to solving some intractable problems of administration and personnel management within the Service. One of the most troubling aspects of the situation was that each Collector of Customs, although under the nominal control of the Treasury Secretary, was in fact, a little potentate. Washington exercised scarcely any control over the various districts. An officer's progress depended largely on his relationship with the Collector of his district. This meant that those who cultivated the friendship of the Collector in a given locality could expect preferential treatment in promotions and other perquisites of office. Politics was king in that heyday of "Jacksonian democracy," and there was open acceptance of the cynical maxim: "To the victors belong the spoils."

As an able administrator, McLane could see that the current system spawned many evils, the greatest of which was the retention of incompetent personnel whose primary talent lay in toadying to their superiors. It was time, he believed, to bring the Service together as a national entity, replacing the many little fiefdoms which had sprung up over the years. Personnel procurement, promotions, pay, and regulations had to be established on a Service-wide basis. The loosely-tied, uncoordinated administrative system had to be replaced by a strong, coordinated one.

McLane was not the first man to criticize the inequity of Revenue Cutter Service administration. Many senior officers had already called attention to that. Considering the grossly partisan nature of the times it was a courageous thing to do. The fact that these men persevered and made distinguished records attests more to their innate decency and ability than to the vicious political spoils system prevailing.

Soon after taking office, McLane initiated an investigation of service personnel procedures. But he was too practical a man to engage in a quixotic tilt at political windmills. After all, he was a member of the official Jackson cabinet and could not afford to make a public issue of reform. He decided that a middle road would be the best to pursue, retaining some elements of patronage but also deferring to some kind of merit system. Thus, in 1832, he promulgated the following policy:

"With a view to greater efficiency in the Cutter Service in the future, vacancies will be filled by promotion from among the officers in the Service, when that shall be found preferable to other appointments, having regards to fitness as well as seniority."

It was not exactly a Declaration of Independence, but at least it was a step down the road to uniform Service administration. The wording of the announcement was deliberately ambiguous, allowing some freedom of interpretation. Yet its meaning was clear: outright political "cronyism" was not to be the sole determinant of advancement.

McLane discovered that, because of slow promotion and lack of ships in the Navy between 1825 and 1832, a number of Navy officers had been commissioned in the Revenue Marine. Many were unhappy with the arrangement, and their despondency was reflected in their lackluster performance of duty. McLane, therefore, formulated a new policy—the two Services were to be separated. Commissions held in the Revenue Service by naval officers were revoked on April 30, 1832. The result of this action was to eliminate from the Revenue Service all officers whose primary interest did not lie in that sector. It was a big step toward enhancing the pride and special professional status of the officers of the revenue fleet.

The early 1830's ushered in a new period of expansion for the Service. Cutters enforced customs and navigation laws; anti-wrecking, piracy, plundering, and slave-trade acts; quarantine regulations; neutrality laws; and one of the first federal conservation laws, the Timber Reserve Act. This statute prohibited export of the Florida live-oak lumber needed to build strong hulls for U.S. warships. Cutters also assisted vessels in distress, and their captains served as inspectors of lighthouses and buoys whenever such work did not interfere with their legal duties. The character of the Service by the 1830's closely approached that of the modern Coast Guard. It was a law enforcement agency with the additional functions of preventing loss of life, property and liberty, and of supporting the Navy in time of war.

Andrew Jackson's America was in a ferment of expansion and development. The advent of the steamboat was part of that bustling era. Steam power as employed in the 1830's was hazardous and unpredictable. The danger was so great that Congress entered the field and in 1838 enacted the first navigation law for the "better securing of the lives . . . on board vessels propelled in whole or in part by steam." The act established a precedent for federal regulation of private enterprise of a national character in the interest of marine safety. The legislation set up the machinery for a steamboat inspection program and was the prototype for a series of laws aimed at the same general objective. From it dates the Coast Guard's concern with the preventive aspects of marine safety.

Although the burden of enforcing the law was given to a separate Steamboat Inspection agency, much of the responsibility spilled over to the Revenue Service. The reason for setting up a separate agency was that the Revenue Service in those early days did not have a sufficient shore establishment to meet the requirements of the statute. Many years later the situation changed, and ultimately, the full responsibility for merchant marine safety accrued to the Coast Guard.

Despite the enormous advances toward greater efficiency of the Service made by McLane, his tenure of office was quite short. He left the post of Secretary of the Treasury in 1833 to become Jackson's Secretary of State. This amounted to a "kick upstairs" to give the President the opportunity for carrying out the destruction of the Bank of the United States—a move to which McLane was fundamentally opposed. McLane served in his new office for a little over a year, resigning when overruled on a matter of policy.

But his amazing career was not over. In 1834, after leaving government service, he became president of the Morris Canal and Banking Company of New York. Three years later, he began a successful ten-year period as president of the Baltimore and Ohio Railroad Company. While holding this position, he was selected in 1845 by President James K. Polk to go to Paris to negotiate a settlement of a dispute between England and the United States over the boundary of the Oregon Territory. The end came in Baltimore on October 7, 1857, just a few years before the Civil War. In the 71 years of his life, McLane had served his country well.

John C. Spencer.

A Treasury Department engraving.

The Legacy of John Canfield Spencer

A contemporary and rather unsympathetic observer described him as "tall and slender, with eyes fierce and quick rolling, and a face bearing the line of thought and an unpleasant character of sternness." Obviously, the Honorable John C. Spencer, Secretary of War and later Secretary of the Treasury under President John Tyler, did not possess the easy amiability of some public men of his time. What he did have was one of the most brilliant and incisive minds of his day, and a genius for administration which enured to the benefit of the still young Revenue Service.

Born into a wealthy and patrician family in upper New York State, Spencer did not fit in the "log cabin" tradition of early America. Instead, he enjoyed the advantages of an excellent education at Williamstown, Massachusetts, and at Union College, New York, from which he graduated with high honors in 1806. The excellent political connections of his father, Ambrose Spencer, as well as the young man's own ability, soon brought him to the notice of the leading political figures of New York.

Like most of the public men of that time, Spencer chose the law as a career, for which his analytical mind was eminently fitted. His political ascent was rapid, and by 1817, he was elected to Congress, serving on a House Committee which reported unfavorably on the affairs of the Bank of the United States so vehemently hated by Andrew Jackson.

By 1841 he had achieved sufficient national reputation to be selected by President John Tyler as Secretary of War. Two years later he succeeded Walter Forward as Secretary of the Treasury. It was in this capacity that he first came into contact with the tangled affairs of the Revenue Service.

Times were difficult both for the country and for the Service. The Panic of 1837 had wrought havoc with the country's financial structure. Government credit was at an all-time low, and in Congress, economy was the order of the day. In 1843, a group of Congressmen had recommended the elimination of the revenue fleet on the somewhat capricious ground that its revenue collections between 1830 and 1840 had declined from $22 million to $13.5 million, and that the Collectors of Customs had sometimes used the

cutters for their own pleasure or interest. Conveniently, the report overlooked the lowering of tariffs during that time, the serious economic depression, and the many other duties carried out by the cutters such as winter cruising, fighting of the Seminole War, and other tasks.

In response to the urgent need for economy, the previous Secretary of the Treasury, Walter Forward, had instituted a series of economy measures. In a Circular Letter to the Service, he ordered that the cutters extend their revenue patrols for longer periods to increase government receipts from the newly established higher tariffs, and that furnishings on the cutters be held to a level of austerity.

When Spencer entered upon his duties as Treasury Secretary in 1843, he found that its morale was flagging. The officers and men felt quite justly aggrieved at being made the political whipping boys by the administration in power. Nevertheless, the Service had survived the attack on its existence. Spencer was determined to build its stature so that it might never again be subjected to another such humiliation.

Spencer's first move was to set up a stronger and more efficient central authority in Washington. In his Report to Congress on January 10, 1844, he announced that he had established a Revenue Marine Bureau at Washington, D.C., and had placed it under the charge of a cutter captain, who could be spared from sea duty. His choice was Captain Alexander V. Fraser, one of the most outstanding administrators in Coast Guard history. The choice of Fraser could not have come at a better time to help mend the sagging fortunes of the Service.

Being a canny Scotsman, Fraser was cautious in his approach to his new job. His acceptance was conditioned on an increase in salary and a suitable allowance for living quarters and a servant.

When these matters had been ironed out, Spencer sent Fraser a formal letter, detailing the responsibilities of the new position. Spencer wrote:
"Sir:
"It has occurred to me that the interests of the Government and the advantage of all concerned would be much promoted by placing this branch of the public business in charge of an officer familiar with its details and qualified by practical

knowledge to judge of the wants and necessities of the Service. Confiding in your intelligence and disposition faithfully to serve the public in the premises, I have, therefore detailed you for duty in the Department and now assign you under the supervision of the Secretary of the Treasury, the charge of the business referred to. Generally your duties will consist in the supervision of all matters appertaining to the Revenue Service requiring the interposition of the Department. Your duties are comprehended under the following heads, viz:

"1st. The charge and investigation of all estimates for the Revenue Service and the administrative examination of all accounts for disbursements made by Collectors for the Revenue Vessels previous to their being sent to the Auditor for settlement.

"2nd. The construction and equipment of new vessels and the repair or other disposition of the old ones.

"3rd. The charge of all applications for appointments in the Service, the transmission of commissions, the assignment of officers to their stations, disposition of the vessels, force to be employed in them, and the arrangement for their cruising.

"4th. The care, preservation, and superintendence of all public property placed on board the Cutters and deposited on shore.

"5th. The investigation of all charges for neglect of duty or other misconduct and the preparation under the direction of the head of the Department of all letters touching these details.

"Suitable accommodations will be provided for you in the Department and a subordinate officer to be selected by yourself will be detailed to assist you in case it should become necessary."

As usual, Spencer left no detail unclarified. He was not a man to do things by halves. This meticulousness was one of his great strengths, and yet it could on occasion prove to be a weakness.

Under Spencer, second and third lieutenants no longer performed whatever duties came to hand. Under the new regulations, the second lieutenant found himself the navigating officer charged with the care of the navigating instruments and the flags and signals. Cables, standing and running gear were also within his control. In addition, he was responsible for the cutter's hold and had to draw a plan for the logbook, showing how he stowed ballast, water and provisions.

The keeping of the log was the responsibility of the third lieutenant who helped to prepare himself for promotion by supervising generally the boats, spars, sails, rigging and general stores.

In the case of enlisted men, all unnecessary brightwork was abolished, eliminating a major cause of discontent. New duties included small-arms drill and exercise at the guns twice a week, instead of once, with an occasional night exercise.

On top of these changes, the Secretary instituted a new military smartness by ordering strict observance of naval honors and etiquette. The effect of the latter order was tonic throughout the Service. It gave all members of the Service a new feeling of pride in their organization and enabled Spencer to report: "The officers and men feel that the service has been elevated, and a corresponding zeal in the discharge of their duty has been strikingly exhibited." In his short tenure as Secretary of the Treasury, Spencer had put the Revenue Service on a very firm footing. His achievements were to pay large dividends in the increased efficiency of the Service in the years to come.

After leaving the post of Treasury Secretary, Spencer left the federal government to take up a distinguished career at the bar. Yet his life was not without tragedy. One of his sons, Philip, who had been serving as acting midshipman under Captain Alexander Slidell Mackenzie of the brig, *Somers*, was executed for attempted mutiny on the brig. The elder Spencer was Secretary of War at the time, but made no attempt to intervene on his son's behalf. It is no wonder that Spencer's face bore "the line of thought and an unpleasant character of sternness."

Joshua James, Greatest Lifesaver of Them All

The annals of the Coast Guard are filled with heroic exploits. Each year new names are added to the list of honor as the Coast Guard assumes an ever-increasing rescue burden. Yet, among the hundreds of heroes produced by the Service, one man towers above all. He was Joshua James, perhaps the greatest lifesaver of all time. So impressive are his feats of heroism that the exploits of fictional heroes seem pale by comparison.

Whether acquired or hereditary, heroism was a James family trait. Joshua's mother saved one of his older brothers from the bottom of a 40-foot well in a descent so perilous that none of the men present would dare to attempt it. His father was a prosperous ship owner and a volunteer member of the Massachusetts Humane Society (a voluntary organization similar to the U.S. Lifesaving Service, which merged with the Revenue Cutter Service in 1915 to form the Coast Guard).

Joshua's dedication to lifesaving may have sprung from a tragedy which befell the family when he was only a boy of ten. His mother and a baby sister drowned when a schooner belonging to the same brother the mother had saved from the well, sank in the North Atlantic.

From earliest boyhood he followed the sea, participating in his first rescue mission at 15 as a member of a Humane Society boat crew. At 25 he began his own shipping business, having already established a formidable reputation as a pilot and navigator. During the 37 years in which he was self-employed, he compiled a record of lives saved unequaled in the seafaring tradition. Although most of the archives of the Massachusetts Humane Society were destroyed by a fire in 1872, existing newspaper clippings and biographical accounts indicate that Joshua was credited with saving more than a hundred lives as a volunteer lifesaver.

It seems natural that when he married, Joshua chose a girl who had saved a companion from drowning only two years before. It is hardly surprising that Osceola, their one son who reached maturity, finally became a lifesaver whose fame almost equaled that of his father. Joshua's brothers and their sons also made notable contributions to the James family tradition of lifesaving.

In 1886, when Joshua was 60, the Massachusetts Humane Society honored the grand old man with a large silver medal commemorating his 45 years of brave and faithful service. Remarkably, his most outstanding accomplishments still lay ahead of him.

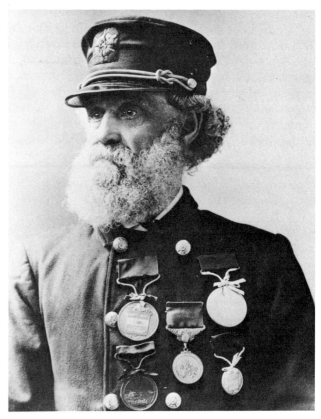

Joshua James.

On November 25 and 26, 1888, one of the most devastating winter storms ever recorded swept the coast of New England. Through blinding snow, Joshua and his fellow volunteers climbed to the top of Telegraph Hill to survey the situation. The distant seascape was cluttered with schooners fighting for their very survival. Joshua's crews were alerted and a beach patrol was scheduled to begin at two in the afternoon. It had no more than begun when the three-masted *Cox And Green* beached on the outer bar. Using the primitive line-throwing guns of the day, Joshua and his men succeeded in safely evacuating the nine-man crew by breeches buoy. Just as they were completing the first rescue, another three-master, the *Gertrude Abbott*, grounded a few hundred yards up the beach. The

Gertrude Abbott was beyond range of the line-throwing gun so Joshua asked for volunteers to attempt a rescue by surfboat. Night had fallen now, but the men launched their boat through the freezing, raging surf. Bailing frantically as they rowed, they at last reached the distressed vessel and picked up the eight crewmen on board. On the return trip to shore the surfboat crashed into jagged rocks, almost overturning. Another massive wave from astern demolished the boat on a second rock formation, but all made it safely ashore. The patrol was resumed.

A new boat was brought to the beach in time for a third rescue in which seven men were saved from the schooner *Bertha F. Walker.* While that incident was still in progress, a messenger on horseback arrived with news of a fourth wreck, the *H. C. Higginson,* with five men in the rigging. A boat crew from another station had failed in its attempts to save the *Higginson* survivors. Although

they had been battling the elements continuously for over 24 hours, Joshua and his men headed for the *Higginson.* After struggling desperately for 45 minutes, they were swept back ashore without having reached their destination. Undaunted, the rescuers patched two large holes which had been staved in the boat and resumed their quest. After several more hours of backbreaking effort the five men were saved and the Humane Society boat crew took a badly needed rest. For their efforts in these rescues Joshua and his boat crews all received either gold or silver Lifesaving Medals from the Treasury Department. Joshua and his son Osceola were both awarded the gold medals.

The following year the U.S. Government established a Lifesaving Station near Joshua's home town of Hull, Massachusetts. For the first and only time in the history of the Lifesaving Service the maximum age limit of 46 was waived in order to appoint Joshua as the station's keeper. Seven of

An early Massachusetts Humane Society Life Boat Station.

the brave men who had accompanied him on previous rescues were employed to round out the station crew. Despite his advanced age, the ever-vigorous Joshua participated in rescues which saved 540 lives during the remaining 13 years of his life. When he was 72 he engaged in six successful rescues within 48 hours during a storm even worse than that of 1888.

On March 17, 1902, another severe storm swept New England. During its course every man save one of the Monomoy Point Lifesaving Station boat crew was killed in a rescue attempt. News of the tragedy profoundly affected the 75-year-old Joshua, who conjectured they might have survived had they been better trained. To better protect his own crew against the possibility of such an occurrence, he took them out in the boat for a training drill two days afterward. With gale winds and seas still running high, Joshua, himself, manned the sweep oar. Satisfied, after an hour of exhausting drills in the heavy surf, Captain James ordered the boat back to the shore. As it beached, he jumped out with the graceful energy of a much

younger man and glanced back toward the sea. "The tide is ebbing," he remarked; then fell dead on the beach.

Very appropriately, his coffin was one of the surfboats in which he had performed 60 years of public service as the greatest lifesaver of them all.

The burial place of Joshua James.

The funeral cortege of Joshua James proceeds to the grave site in a horse-drawn lifeboat. James also was buried in a lifeboat.

Reindeer being hoisted aboard *Bear*, August 28, 1898, at a Siberian port for transportation to Alaska. During a ten-year period, beginning in 1891, more than a thousand deer were transported by the Revenue Cutter Service. These animals were used to introduce domesticated reindeer herds into Alaska, insuring freedom from starvation for great numbers of Alaskan natives.

Mike Healy, Black Hero of the North

It was Independence Day, July 4, 1855, when the East Indiaman, *Jumna*, moved out of Boston Harbor, Massachusetts, to begin her long voyage to Calcutta, India. On board was a 15-year-old cabin boy, Michael A. Healy, making his first sea journey in a lifetime of sailing that would take him from the warm latitudes of the Mediterranean and Indian Ocean to bleak northern seas where his name would become legendary.

But that was far in the future. At the moment, Healy was a slightly frightened, homesick lad, wondering what the years held in store for him. The *Jumna* was a beautiful clipper ship in the golden age of sailing ships. She and her sister vessels were carrying the U.S. flag to all the harbors of the world and opening new markets to Yankee ingenuity.

It was an exciting time, and the clipper fleet represented the vanguard of American progress. But as the Boston docks receded in the distance, young Healy's thoughts turned to his family—his brothers and sisters and the plantation at Macon, Georgia, where he had been born. He was a handsome youngster, of average height with regular, sensitive features and the light coffee-colored skin associated with the Mediterranean area. An air of reserve made him seem older than his years.

Why was Michael on the *Jumna*? The decision to sail on her had not been his. It had been made despairingly by his older brother, the Reverend James Augustine who had assumed responsibility as head of the family on the death of the father, Michael Morris Healy. James was an ordained priest of the Roman Catholic Church on the way to a brilliant career. Right now, the problem of what to do about his unruly younger brother was uppermost in his mind. Repeatedly, the boy had run away from schools selected for the strictness of their regimen, but none of them had any effect on him. The scholastic routine was not for him. Unlike the other members of his family who had shown exceptional aptitude as students, Healy hungered for a life of adventure. There was a headstrong, rebellious streak in the boy that could not be curbed. The Reverend James Augustine reasoned that perhaps a stint of service at sea might instill that discipline which the schools had not been able to do.

Accordingly, the older brother secured a berth as cabin boy on the *Jumna* for his wild younger brother. It was an agonizingly difficult decision for James Augustine, amounting to a confession of defeat. He knew the hardships of a sailor's life in the mid-19th century. Sailors at that time did not rate very high on the social scale, and it was quite possible that the young Michael would be exposed to many temptations. It was a calculated gamble.

Captain Michael A. Healy of the U.S. Revenue Cutter Service. Known as "Hell-roar'n Mike," he skippered *Bear* longer than any other officer. A colorful, resourceful individual, he helped to introduce domesticated reindeer culture into Alaska.

The unusual air of reserve surrounding young Michael could be attributed in part to his origin. He was one of ten children born to Michael Morris Healy, an Irish immigrant to Georgia early in the 19th century, and Mary Eliza, a comely, mulatto slave girl working as a domestic on the neighboring plantation of Sam Griswold. The elder Healy had come to Georgia by way of Halifax where he had served briefly with the British during the War of

1812. Tiring of boring garrison duty, he had headed south to Georgia where rich Indian lands were being opened to settlement. A cousin had already arrived there before him.

It was a time of great opportunity. Rich farmland could be purchased cheaply from the government. In a few years of hard work and shrewd dealing, the elder Healy was well on the way to becoming a prosperous plantation owner. He built a fine house near Macon with a well-stocked library. The time had now come, he felt, to take a wife and raise a family. His eye fell on Mary Eliza, and she became his wife. In the rural Georgia of those times this was a risky undertaking. Local customs tolerated a black mistress but not a wife. Recognizing the dangers to which his family would be exposed, Healy made arrangements for their education in the north.

The family fathered by Michael Morris was destined to become one of the most distinguished in the country. His eldest son, James Augustine, became the first black Roman Catholic bishop in North America at Portland, Maine. Another son, Patrick Francis, served as president of Georgetown University in Washington, D.C. Three sisters took Holy Orders and another brother served at the Vatican in Rome. Surrounded by all this scholastic brilliance, it is no wonder that for a long time young Mike thought of himself as the stray sheep of an illustrious family. Even after his northern exploits had made him famous, he was haunted by feelings of inadequacy. Years later, in 1865, when applying for an officer's commission in the Revenue Cutter Service, he asked the Examining Board "to look leniently upon" his faults.

For a decade Healy remained in the maritime service, a part of that time on a "fruiter" sailing to Mediterranean ports. Those ten years between 1855 and 1865 turned the young cabin boy into a seasoned, competent sailor. The wildness of his younger years seemed to have been curbed in the harsh school of the sea. In 1865 he applied for and received a commission in the Service.

Within a few years after entering the Revenue Cutter Service, First Lieutenant Michael A. Healy, on the cutter Rush, was patrolling Alaska's Pacific Coast. The United States had only recently acquired the sprawling territory and hardly anything was known of its vast natural riches. In 1868, Healy made his first trip north, but by 1881, "Cap'n Mike" was known from Attu to the Farallones as a brilliant seaman. By 1895, at the close of his Pacific cruise, he had become one of the best known figures in the north. In a feature article, the New York Sun rhapsodized: "Captain Healy is a good deal more distinguished person in the waters of the far Northwest than any president of the United States or any potentate of Europe has yet become. He stands for law and order in many thousand square miles of land and water, and if you should ask in the Arctic Sea, 'Who is the greatest man in America?' the instant answer would be, 'Why, Mike Healy.' When an innocent citizen of the Atlantic coast once asked on the Pacific who Mike Healy was, the answer came, 'Why, he's the United States. He holds in these parts a power of attorney for the whole country.' "

These glowing words were enough to turn any man's head, but they were substantially true. In all that wilderness of ice and water, Mike Healy's small cutter represented the only civilizing influence in the new frontier. Yet in 1881, he was only on the threshold of fame, with his major exploits still before him. His most remarkable period of service was to be as skipper of the cutter Bear, considered by many as the greatest polar ship of all time. In her nearly 90 years of sailing, she was like a shuttle on the loom of history, moving from the Arctic to the Antarctic and pioneering in the development of America's last frontier.

Like the Bear, Healy's reputation was made in northern waters. In 1886, when Healy took command of her, she assumed the police duties of the Corwin which Healy had commanded before coming to the Bear. The Bear was extremely well suited to a northern career. She had been built as a sealer by the famous firm of Alexander Stephen and Son at Dundee, Scotland. The company had specialized in building tough ships for the northern trade, but the Bear was the sturdiest they had ever built. She had massive beams, heavy oak frames, reinforced bow, and Australian iron-bark sheathing to enable her to work safely in the ice.

The Bear was substantially larger than the Corwin and therefore far better able to transport from Alaska a motley group of castaways, federal agents, destitutes, missionaries, madmen, scientists, and prisoners who had taxed the Corwin's limited capacities on her homeward trip to San Francisco. She was 200 feet long, 32 feet broad, with a depth of 18 feet, 2 inches, and displacing about 703 tons—a small ship by modern standards. She was a barkentine with auxiliary steam power, and her speed was eight knots by sail and nine by steam. The figures in themselves are not too impressive. But what they do not tell is the extraordinary durability of this famous ship. In her long saga of service she would take the worse that the far north had to give and still keep going.

At the time Healy assumed command of the *Bear*, the migration to the Northwest was in full swing. Not only were whalers voyaging into the North Pacific for their quarry, but hordes of miners and fortune hunters had begun their trek to the mineral wealth of the northwest and Alaska.

way to impress the poachers was to make up in ruthlessness what he lacked in facilities. His first blow came in 1887 when the Bering Sea Fleet captured 12 Canadian schooners. Each captured vessel was sent south to Sitka under a prize crew. In spite of much bluster on the part of the sealers and the British government, Healy stood firm.

By 1892, the *Bear*, *Rush* and *Corwin* of the Bering Sea Patrol had made so many seizures that

Bear drying sails in St. Lawrence Bay.

To Kotzebue and Nome they came, seeking to become rich in one bold stroke. Most were doomed to failure, returning broken in health and with none of the precious yellow dust they had been seeking. Behind the fortune hunters came traders and suppliers, as well as federal agencies to help provide governmental controls, education, and other civilizing influences.

The job facing Healy was enough to dishearten most men. One of his first orders was to "seize any vessel found sealing in the Bering Sea." The order was simple enough, but it was a gigantic task. Healy's means for carrying it out were pitifully inadequate. Against hordes of tough seal poachers, the United States had sent the three small cutters of the first Bering Sea Patrol, later renamed the Alaska Patrol. In 1886, the sealing depredations had reached their height. Knowledge that the government was planning to crack down on the practice stimulated the hunters to a last prodigious effort.

Healy was shrewd enough to know that the only

tension developed between the United States and Britain. The British contended that the seizures were illegal since they had been made for the most part outside the three-mile limit. They argued also that the seals, as wild animals, were lawful prey to anyone. The United States countered that the Bering Sea was under its jurisdiction, and then went on to emphasize that the further butchery of seals would not be tolerated.

Just when it seemed that the affair had reached the shooting point, both sides agreed to turn the matter over to an international arbitration tribunal. The British agreed not to oppose any seizures while the case was being considered.

Meanwhile, the slaughter of the seals continued with undiminished fury. The hunters paid no attention to the legal proceedings and made devastating inroads on the seal population.

Eventually, the tribunal decided against the United States, holding that the Bering Sea was an open sea, and therefore available to the ships of all nations. To Healy and the hard-working men of his command, the decision was a bitter blow. But they continued to guard the seal herds and to convoy them on their annual migration.

The dreadful butchery did not end before 1911 when a treaty was signed by the four nations principally involved: Great Britain, Russia, Japan, and the United States. The treaty prohibited all seal hunting in the North Pacific and the Bering Sea. Only the natives were allowed to hunt seals for their own use with their primitive equipment. Instead of putting the seal rookeries of the Pribilofs under a private company, the U. S. undertook their guardianship. A system of fur-seal conservation was begun, permitting only a limited number to be killed each year. The senseless massacre of the seal herds was over. The original treaty ended in 1941, but was renewed in 1957 and once again in 1963.

Today, the seal herd is estimated at about 1,750,000, or about eight and one-half times the number in 1911. The foundation for this great achievement in marine resource conservation was laid by Mike Healy and his patrol.

In the 1890's the term "genocide" had not yet come into use. But it was evident to Healy that Alaska's native population was steadily declining. The coming of "civilization" to Alaska had had a devastating impact on the Eskimos' primitive culture. The unrestrained killing of seals, walruses, salmon and other sea creatures was depriving the natives of their primary source of food. The damage was compounded by prohibiting the Eskimos from using repeating rifles for hunting, putting them at a crucial disadvantage with white hunters who used the modern firearms.

Another of the white man's blessings imported into the Alaskan Territory was alcohol. Soldiers of the first U.S. Army units to occupy the Territory had introduced the natives to "firewater." The craving for it became so intense with many of the Eskimos that they learned the art of distilling it. The raw spirits were called "hoochenoe" which was later shortened to "hootch." Healy was zealous in enforcing the ban on sale of alcohol to the natives. But with the very limited facilities at his command it was a difficult matter. Within a short time after the arrival of the American vanguard, the once proud, self-respecting native tribes had been reduced in many instances to beggary and starvation. It was a sardonic commentary on the "benefits" conferred by a so-called superior civilization.

The compassionate side of Healy was deeply touched by the misery and suffering of the natives.

An incident during his annual spring visit to King Island in 1890 turned Healy into an activist. As the *Bear* approached the island, the men on board could see that the shore was crowded with strangely quiet people. Craft put out for the *Bear* and Eskimos climbed aboard. They were gaunt and starved and could hardly stand. They could scarcely beg for food. Yet this was a proud people ordinarily scorning charity. The chief told Healy that more than 200 of his tribe had died during the winter. Only 100 men and women were still alive on King Island. The walrus on which they normally depended for food had not appeared during the previous fall. Harsh winter storms had barred passage to the mainland. The survivors had been reduced to eating dogs and seaweed.

Before leaving for Point Barrow, Healy ordered that supplies be ferried ashore. Crewmen of the *Bear* built platforms, according to Eskimo custom, for burial of the dead. The pitiful remainder was slowly nursed back to health. But the experience kindled in Healy a fierce determination to prevent another such tragedy.

Together with Dr. Sheldon Jackson, a missionary and eloquent speaker, who had also witnessed the King Island tragedy, Healy embarked on a plan to import reindeer from the Siberian Chukchi, a people very much like the Eskimos. Healy reasoned that if the Chukchi could manage to exist healthy and well fed with their reindeer herds, the same could hold true for the Eskimos. He and Dr. Jackson agreed that the importation of reindeer could be a solution for the problem. But that was easier said than done. For one thing, the Chukchi were reluctant to give up their reindeer, being superstitious about selling live animals. And there was the matter of transporting the reindeer across the Bering Sea to Alaska. Even if all this were accomplished, there would still remain the knotty problem of converting the Eskimos from a hunting to a pastoral life. Last but by no means least, was the difficulty of persuading the Washington bureaucracy of the need to make funds available for this project.

Only two idealists such as Healy and Jackson could undertake so arduous a mission. But somehow these dedicated men brought it off. During the next decade revenue cutters brought about 1,100 reindeer to Alaska. Dr. Jackson's Bureau of Education took charge of the deer on landing and distributed them among government and mission schools where the natives were trained in reindeer culture. Each graduate received the nucleus of a herd from which to breed additional deer. It was one of the most successful and significant social experiments in history. It aspired at nothing less than to change the way of life of an entire people within a short time span. Ordinarily such change comes about slowly and tortuously. By 1940, Alaska's domesticated reindeer herds had risen to about 500,000, providing both food and clothing for the native population. Yet, somehow, this humane endeavor received little recognition in a world generally given over to the more sensational aspects of progress. The work conducted by Healy and Jackson was one of the most constructive measures ever carried out by the United States in Alaska. Compared to the cost of most social change, the amount of money involved was nominal. But it saved a people from extinction.

Sometimes Healy's cabin served as a floating court of justice. One of his most unusual cases took place in the spring of 1893. It involved a murder by Eskimo boys. The victim was H. R. Thornton, a missionary and schoolmaster at Teller. From the evidence it appears that Thornton, a stern, self-righteous man, had threatened to whip three boys, including a chief's son, for some minor infraction. Such physical punishment was the very worst kind for a proud people who dreaded physical humiliation above all things. It was an affront to their dignity which could not be tolerated. Rather than submit to the whipping, the boys decided to kill Thornton. They went to his house, and when he answered their knock, they shot him through the chest.

The gunshot brought the villagers to the scene. In their shock at the killing, they immediately stoned two of the boys to death. Then they dug a grave for the chief's son. Before lying down in the grave, he announced he was thirsty and the entire village escorted him home for his last drink. Then he was led back to the grave and his personal treasures were laid beside him to take into eternity. His nearest of kin, an uncle, pointed a rifle at the boy's head and killed him. The sentence of execution had been carried out.

When Healy heard the facts, he was puzzled about what course of action to pursue. It would be obviously difficult to explain advanced Anglo-Saxon concepts of justice to a primitive people who had followed their own traditions. Unquestionably, the boys had deserved some punishment, but scarcely death. Healy made it clear that he strongly disapproved of the executions. However, he recognized and praised the elementary sense of justice underlying the actions. But he warned that, in the future, punishment would be dispensed only after a proper trial in a court of law. The Eskimos had had their first contact with the white man's legal procedures. Surprisingly, in a shorter time than anyone would have thought possible they succeeded in understanding the new procedures.

The years were rolling on, and by the 1890's the long and hard duty in the north was beginning to take its toll of Healy. The once smooth and boyish face now had deep lines in it. It bore the determined look of a man who demanded strict obedience from his subordinates. Brother Augustine, who had worried so much about his wayward younger brother, could put his mind at rest. Mike was carving out a brilliant career.

But a cloud hung over the years of achievement. The hard duty, the isolation of command, and possibly a gnawing awareness of his origin had their effect on Healy. Word was going around that he was drinking more than was good for him. This was not very unusual among professional sailing men. Most of Healy's colleagues enjoyed a convivial drink or two. But now also, as Healy grew older, there developed a widening gap between him and his junior officers. A new century, the 20th, was just over the horizon. The ways of an earlier, heartier era were gradually giving way to a new mode of life.

The first hint of trouble came in 1889, after Healy had completed more than 20 years of service in Alaskan waters. The man about whom the newspapers had written so glowingly some years previously was brought before a court of inquiry on charges of drunkenness and abuse of subordinates. At this distance in time, it is difficult to determine what really happened. Healy was then about 50, and it appears improbable that a man at this phase of his life would jeopardize his entire career by unwise action.

The charges themselves were not major. Healy had reproved several sailors of the whaler, *Estella*, for slipshod performance of duty and their insubordinate attitude toward their superior. They were rough, foul-mouthed men, contemptuous of authority and typical of many whalers of the time. Healy warned the men to mend their ways. When they persisted in ignoring his warning, he had them taken to the *Bear*, put in irons and "triced."

The latter punishment consisted of handcuffing a man with his arms behind him and lifting him by the manacles so that his feet barely touched the ground. Admittedly, it was a cruel penalty. But even by the statements of the men themselves, it lasted no more than 15 minutes. Aside from hurt feelings and some bruises, there were no serious injuries. Healy felt that he had to instill some respect for authority in these mutinous crewmen and there were few alternatives open to him. Whalemen, generally, hated the Revenue Cutter Service which had put an end to indiscriminate killing of whales. Unfortunately, some news of the unpleasant affair drifted back to the United States and some local groups on the west coast whipped up much indignation.

Throughout this humiliating ordeal, the enlisted men of the *Bear* remained steadfastly loyal to their skipper. In the November 16, 1889 issue of the *San Francisco Examiner* appeared an article under the banner, THEY STAND BY HEALY.

"A Tribute to the Captain of the Revenue Cutter by the Forward Hands.

"The crew of the United States Revenue Cutter *Bear* remain steadfast to their commander, no matter what may be the feeling between Captain Healy and his officers. The men say with one accord that a better master never issued an order. Some of the crew have felt the result of the captain's discipline, but from all accounts they like him the better for it."

In reading the detailed testimony of the hearings, it becomes apparent that some of the junior officers of the *Bear* bore a deep personal resentment against their commander. Although they seemed more interested in paying off old scores than in justice, Healy was found innocent of all charges.

Fortune seemed to have turned her back on Healy. In 1895, another lacerating incident occurred in which Healy had to undergo a similar ordeal. Once again, the pattern was that of younger officers eager for command turning against an older officer whose ways they regarded as outmoded. This episode was even uglier and more bitter than the earlier affair, and Healy did not escape unscathed. After 30 years of distinguished service, he was in the humiliating position of having to defend himself against minor charges. In spite of an able defense, Healy was found guilty of "some" charges, his name was dropped to the bottom of the Captain's List, and he was placed on an "awaiting orders" status in San Francisco.

The trauma of the judgment would have broken a lesser man, but it is a mark of Healy's hardihood that he survived the ordeal without breaking. Eventually, in 1902, he regained his position on the Captain's Seniority List and was given command of the *Thetis*. Yet there is no question that he had been deeply hurt by the inquiry. On September 22, 1903, at the age of 64, Healy retired from active service. Less than one year later, in August 1904, he died in San Francisco. Some think that he died from a broken heart; that is as good a guess as any. In any event, it was a shabby reward for one of the most exemplary officers ever to wear the uniform of the Revenue Cutter Service. Nevertheless, by the time he died, his place was secure in history. His greatness has been confirmed by time.

Perhaps *Bear*, too, died of a broken heart. At the age of almost 90, following an incomparable career of Navy and Coast Guard Service, the immortal *Bear* sank in a storm as she was being towed to Philadelphia to become a floating restaurant. This photo was taken March 19, 1963, a few hours before she sank.

David H. Jarvis, Leader of the Overland Expedition

Few rescue missions in history have attracted more public attention than the famous overland expedition of 1897-98. Few heroes in history have accomplished greater feats of daring than Lieutenant David H. Jarvis who led that humane mission.

Winter cold struck the north coast of Alaska unusually early in 1897, trapping an entire fleet of whaling ships in heavy ice near Point Barrow. The eight ships affected by the freeze had carried only enough provisions to last until their planned return to San Francisco in December. By early November the whalers and their 265 crewmen were stuck solidly in ice which no ship would possibly be able to penetrate until July or August of the following year. Without provisions they were doomed.

President William McKinley ordered that a relief expedition be organized. The immortal revenue cutter *Bear*, commanded by Captain Francis Tuttle, was chosen for the job. Because of the extremely hazardous nature of the task, Captain Tuttle refused to take anything other than a volunteer force. Every officer and crew member on board offered to go.

The plan was for *Bear* to land a rescue party as far north as possible. Because of the extreme conditions encountered, the gallant ship was unable to approach Alaska's northern limits and was forced to put the rescue party ashore almost 2,000 miles from the position of the desperate whalers. Lieutenant David Jarvis was chosen to lead the expedition. He was ably assisted by Second Lieutenant E. P. Bertholf (later a Commandant of the U.S. Coast Guard), and the ship's surgeon, Dr. S. J. Call.

The party landed at the tiny Eskimo village of Tununak on December 15, 1897. There they met Alexis Kalenin, a half-breed trader who agreed to guide them to St. Michael, 250 Miles to the north. The *Bear* turned back and wintered at Unalaska Island.

The trip to St. Michael required 13 arduous days. In order to pick up a fresh dog team, it was decided to split up the party and Lt. Bertholf proceeded on independently. In St. Michael, Jarvis and Call were able to get two new dog teams from the commander of the local U. S. Army post. The elements proved to be much less cooperative. Each step of the way had to be fought through subzero temperatures.

Heroes of the Overland Expedition. (L. to r.) 2nd Lieut. E.P. Bertholf (later a Coast Guard Commandant), Surgeon S.J. Call, and Lieut. David H. Jarvis.

Upon reaching Point Rodney, they succeeded in obtaining a herd of 138 reindeer from Charlie Artisarlook, an Eskimo. Artisarlook also agreed to go along with the herd to care for it. The deer were turned over to Lieutenant Jarvis on the basis of nothing more than a handshake and a promise of reimbursement. They were to serve as food for the icebound whalers.

Wearing the primitive but remarkably efficient clothing of the Eskimos, Jarvis and Call continued their journey. The weather was so intensely cold that even the reindeer and Eskimos were miserable.

After extreme hardships they reached Cape Prince of Wales, where a U.S. Government reindeer station was located. The Reverend William Lopp, keeper of the station, also agreed to turn his deer over to the rescue party and to personally accompany the group. They were still 700 miles from their destination.

Captain Francis Tuttle who commanded *Bear* at the time of the Overland Expedition.

Never before in history had such a group attempted crossing the rugged mountains and frozen tundra in the middle of winter. There were no paths to follow—only driving winds and snow. At times the temperature dropped as low as 70 degrees below zero.

In order to reach Point Barrow, it was necessary to cross either the frozen waters of Kotzebue Sound or take a longer route which would have added almost another two weeks to the journey. No time could be spared. They would have to try the Sound, although ledges of jagged ice jutted up to heights of 40 feet, making the passage so perilous as to be nearly impossible. A few deer succumbed to the hardships of the frantic pace,

but the rescuers fought onward toward Point Barrow. One deer was killed when the herd came under attack from starving wolves.

Jarvis and Dr. Call rendezvoused with Lt. Bertholf on the other side of Kotzebue. Bertholf, too, had faced many hardships and had not been nearly so fortunate as the others in his choice of traveling companions. On more than one occasion he had been abandoned by Eskimos and dogs. It was decided that he would stop over at Point Hope to set up an intermediate way station for the whalers in the event food shortages forced Jarvis to send any of the men down from Point Barrow.

Proceeding ahead of the herd, Jarvis and Call at last reached their destination on March 29, 1898. The reindeer arrived a day later. The stranded, starving whalemen were incredulous. Most had already reconciled themselves to gradual death from cold and hunger.

David H. Jarvis. This is thought to be a portrait taken during his honeymoon at Newport, R.I. in 1896.

There was still much to be done. Many of the men were already near death from scurvy and other diseases. Others had reverted to violent and almost animalistic behavior. Some of the ships had been completely destroyed by the pressure of ice. The situation was further aggravated by the fact that some ships were separated from the others by as much as a hundred miles.

Jarvis soon demonstrated that his organizational

Top: The whaler *Rosario* crushed in ice at Point Barrow. *Rosario's* surviving crewmen were crazed and dying of hunger when rescued by David Jarvis. *Bottom:* A group of the whalers rescued by Jarvis, Call, and Bertholf.

skill equaled his courage. Systematic medical treatment was begun. Housing was built. Food was intelligently distributed and rationed. Daily cleanliness inspections were instituted. Recreational and work programs were begun to raise the whalemen's spirits.

A previously unpublished photograph of Lt. David Jarvis made during his tour of duty in Alaska. His colorful uniform is obviously not of Service issue. The photo was made available by his daughter, Miss Anna T. Jarvis of New York City, who was born while her famous father was leading the successful Overland Expedition.

It was July 28 before the *Bear* was able to reach Point Barrow, and even then the ice pack had hardly receded. Jarvis saw to it that the whalers whose ships were still seaworthy were well provisioned. Then, with 97 men whose ships had been destroyed, the rescued and their rescuers boarded *Bear* for the long voyage home.

In volunteering for the expedition, Jarvis had had to make a difficult personal decision. His wife was expecting their first child within the next few months. His natural inclination was to stay with her until the child was born. But the plight of the whalers was desperate and there could be no delay. Soon he would be in a vast and frozen wilderness, defying the bitter winter of northern Alaska. There was always the chance that he might not return but his strong sense of duty won out in the end.

According to Jarvis' daughter, Miss Anna T. Jarvis of New York City, her father was a quiet, almost taciturn man who shied away from personal publicity. The enormous amount of publicity that followed the completion of the expedition and made him one of the most celebrated men of his time was embarrassing to him. His attitude toward his work in the rescue of the whalers was completely professional. He was that rare kind of man who placed the honor of his country and his Service above personal advantage.

In 1905, following his advancement to Captain and a three-year appointment as a Collector of Customs for Alaska, Jarvis resigned from the Revenue Cutter Service to accept an important executive position with the Northwest Fisheries Company. When this company was taken over by a vast syndicate operated by the Morgan and Guggenheim families of New York, Jarvis was appointed treasurer of the entire organization. His manifest ability and broad knowledge of almost every aspect of Alaskan industry made him particularly well suited for such a position.

In 1911, to the complete surprise of his family and associates, Jarvis tragically and inexplicably ended his life. He was 48 years old, with a wife and three children. A brilliant career lay before him, making his death all the more tragic. But his heroism had earned him an enduring place in the annals of human achievement.

Admiral Russell R. Waesche, Wartime Leader

Sunday, December 7, 1941, was a bright, moderately cold day in Washington, D.C. Despite the crisis atmosphere pervading the capital, life went on very much as usual. On this morning, small groups of tourists were gathered in front of the White House, taking pictures. Across the street in Lafayette Park, Andrew Jackson sat proudly astride his charger, rallying troops in some bygone battle.

The *Washington Post* carried ominous headlines of reported concentrations of Japanese troops and naval forces in Indochina and the Gulf of Siam. Orders had just gone out to the U.S. Coast Guard to seize all Finnish ships in U.S. harbors, and

armed Coast Guardsmen were boarding the vessels and taking them into custody.

Yet the country had not entirely abandoned its hopes for keeping out of war. President Franklin D. Roosevelt had made a personal appeal to Emperor Hirohito of Japan for peace. At this very moment, Japanese envoys were at the State Department ostensibly to consider these peace overtures. As the world was to learn shortly thereafter, the decision to make war on the United States had already been made. Before the day was over, the country would be stunned by the vicious Japanese attack on Pearl Harbor, putting an end to U.S. neutrality. From now on it would be a fight

Arundel Cove, Md., site of the Coast Guard's first training school for officers. Cadet R.R. Waesche is third from right, top row.

269

to the finish as the nation mobilized its resources for the enormous effort that lay ahead.

On the seventh floor of the Coast Guard Headquarters building on 13th and E Streets, the tempo of activity was at fever pitch. For months, both military and civilian aides had worked to prepare the Service for its wartime role.

R.R. Waesche as a young cadet.

Focal point of the activity was a lean, trimly-built man whose quick movements belied his 55 years. He was Rear Admiral Russell R. Waesche, a veteran of 39 years' service and in his second term as Commandant of the Coast Guard. A tireless worker, he was known as a hard-driving leader who spared neither himself nor his subordinates. With the fall of western Europe to the Nazis, Waesche had thrown all of his energy into building the military readiness capability of his Service. He knew that, sooner or later, the European holocaust was bound to engulf the United States.

By the time the United States declared war on Germany, Italy, and Japan, on December 8, 1941, the Coast Guard was well along in its military preparedness program. Service strength had risen from 17,000 to 30,000 men. Eventually it was to reach a peak of more than 175,000. Long before the country was formally at war, Coast Guard units had been active during the period of neutrality, operating the Greenland Patrol, escorting convoys, and performing many other war-related tasks. A part of the Service had already been transferred to the Navy. Under Admiral Waesche's direction, the Coast Guard was to play a prominent part in helping to win victory for the Free World.

In this critical time, no man was better fitted by training or temperament to lead his Service than Admiral Waesche. His leadership had been abundantly proved in nearly four decades of outstanding service. It had been a remarkable career, beginning early in the century, in 1903, when young Russell entered the U.S. Revenue Cutter Service Training School at Arundel Cove, near Baltimore. During a tumultuous year as a freshman at Purdue University, the lively, athletic 17-year-old took part in student high jinks with enthusiasm. Hoping to curb the young man's exuberance a little, his older brother urged him to take the entrance examinations for the Revenue Cutter Service school. Waesche passed the examinations and in 1904, he embarked on the two-year course to prepare himself for the Service.

Waesche was a popular and successful student at the training school. He did well in his studies and also showed great athletic promise. Besides playing second base on the varsity baseball team, he was a formidable tennis player. Many years later, when he was already in his forties, he played tennis with his son Russell R. Jr. (later to become an admiral himself) and defeated him by his superior court strategy.

At the training school, Waesche's agility was made to order for climbing the rigging of the large sailing ship used for summer cruises. In 1906, he graduated number three in a class of seven. He was at the threshold of a new career.

The early 1900's were exciting times for a young man just beginning to make his way in the world. The country was still growing. In the great Pacific Northwest new fortunes were being made by enterprising men. The hardier and more adventurous spirits of the time had answered the call of adventure and had come, a few years before, to the Klondike and its fabulous gold fields. It was America's last frontier. Tough, brawling men from everywhere were filling up the jerry-built towns and packing the shabby, hastily constructed saloons whose proprietors were growing rich exchanging rotgut whiskey for gold dust.

But before young Waesche reached the Alaskan

wilds, a fascinating journey lay ahead of him. His first orders put him aboard the revenue cutter *Tahoma*, which was about to make a trip around the world "to show the flag." He was to serve as second lieutenant on the *Tahoma*. The cutter was to depart Hampton Roads, Virginia, on April 3, 1909, and make a west-to-east circumnavigation of the globe. The ports of call were as exotic as any young man could wish: the Azores; Alexandretta, in the Gulf of Iskanderum; Port Said; the Suez Canal; Aden; Colombo, Ceylon; Singapore; and then northeastward in the China Sea, returning to the United States in midsummer, 1909. It was a magnificent prelude to a naval career.

1910 found Waesche on the revenue cutter *Perry*, on seal patrol in the Bering Sea. The patrol had begun shortly after the United States purchased Alaska from Imperial Russia, and one of its most pressing duties was to halt the dreadful slaughter of the valuable North Pacific fur seal which, by 1910, had been hunted nearly to extinction. These were poorly charted waters, and in June of 1910, while proceeding through a heavy fog at a slow speed near the seal rookeries of the Pribilof Islands, the cutter ran aground on an uncharted rock and could not be pulled off. Luckily, the sea was calm enough to permit the crew to remove whatever stores and equipment could be carried. Eventually, they were picked up by another ship, but the *Perry* remained aground, a total loss. Although Lieutenant Waesche was the navigation officer, he was not charged with responsibility for the loss. These were, after all, treacherous and uncharted waters. But it was a sobering experience for the young officer. It made him realize more deeply than ever the grave responsibilities of his calling.

In spite of this misfortune, Waesche tremendously enjoyed his tour of duty in the Bering Sea. In a long letter filled with youthful enthusiasm, he wrote to his future mother-in-law, Mrs. Luke, On September 23, 1910:

"My dear Mama:

"We have made our last cruise in Bering Sea and on October 1st we leave here for Valdez. On our last cruise we went out to Attu, my second trip out there this summer. We left here about the 12th and got back day before yesterday. On our way out we stopped at Bogoslof and everything was changed: there had been a eruption since the *Perry* was there in June. We went ashore and repeated everything we did in June, made sketches, took temperatures, gathered specimens, took photo-

graphs, etc. Captain Quinan divided the work up among the officers, that is among seven of us. I had the photographic end and took about fifteen pictures, all of which turned out very good. Bagger and I were the only ones that explored the new land and it certainly was an interesting sight. At first we thought we could not get across the lagoon but we groped our way through the steam and followed a cliff along which finally brought us to the top. Then we went down the other side and walked around to the center of activity. Over an area of two hundred square yards the water was boiling out of the beach, and in the center of this area were two small geysers, the water being thrown about six feet in the air ... The ground was very treacherous—several times we stepped on apparently solid ground and sunk in mud over our ankles, nearly cooking our feet before we could pull them out ... You remember I told you of all the Murres that were on the island in June— millions of them. Well there were none on our second visit but the island was strewn with their skeletons. The sea lions, however, were just as numerous ...

"On our way back, we came by Bogoslof again and I never expect to see a more wonderful or beautiful sight. The volcano was in violent eruption. We arrived at the island about seven o'clock in the morning and at three o'clock when we were forty miles from there I saw a brilliant display of forked lightning right ahead which of course was the direction of Bogoslof. The moon was full and it was a very clear night. I was on watch and it certainly was an unusual sight to see this full moon and this display of lightning at the same time.

" ... We stopped again at Atka for a day to see the new schoolhouse which is not quite completed. The U.S. is building it and it is a fine little building for that native village ... "

Originally, plans called for putting Lieutenant Waesche on the island of Bogoslof to take pictures for a week. At the last minute, however, the plan was scrapped—a very lucky development for the lieutenant since the section of the island to be charted disappeared in a volcanic eruption.

In 1960, when the Admiral's son, Russell R. Jr., commanded the *Northwind* in Alaskan waters, the Native Care program took him to every one of the places noted in the letter to Mrs. Luke. The frame schoolhouse on Atka Island was still there, but it was an old schoolhouse now.

In 1911, when Waesche was 25 years old, he met

and married an attractive young woman, Dorothy R. Luke, of Seattle, Washington. Four children were born of the marriage, the first of them, Russell, Jr., being born in 1913. For the next several years, he was stationed on ships operating out of the west coast. At the end of this period, he was given command of the Coast Guard cutter, *Snohomish*, as a senior lieutenant. A few years before, in 1915, the Revenue Cutter Service had merged with the U.S. Lifesaving Service to form the U.S. Coast Guard.

Waesche handled his new command with great success, notably in search and rescue. In May 1921, *Snohomish* rescued all hands from a Japanese ship which was foundering some hundreds of miles west of the entrance to the Straits of Juan de Fuca. In appreciation for this feat, the Japanese officers and crew presented a sterling silver tray inscribed to Lieutenant Commander R. R. Waesche. In 1967 this tray was presented to the Commandant and Mrs. W. J. Smith as an historical memento to remain in the Commandant's quarters. What made the rescue so noteworthy was that it was effected by securing a heavy hawser between the mast of the *Snohomish* and the mast of the Japanese ship and running a breeches buoy between the vessels in a heavy sea. This was one of the few successful breeches buoy rescues ever carried out under such hazardous conditions.

By 1924, the Coast Guard was fully committed to the "Rum War" of the Prohibition Era. It was a very arduous assignment for a small Service whose vessels were often outrun by the faster and more powerful craft of the rum smugglers. Waesche's assignment at that time was as commanding officer of the destroyer *Beale* on rum patrol. Since this meant moving to the east, he left his wife and four children behind. Later, in 1926, the marriage was dissolved. The two older children, Russell, Jr. and Harry Lee, went east to be with their father. In the summer, they spent their vacations on board the destroyer or at the family homestead in Thurmont, Maryland. Perhaps it was at this time that the second Admiral Russell R. Waesche acquired his taste for the sea.

Rum patrol duty was hard. To put down rum-running, the Patrols employed 25 World War I Navy destroyers that had been transferred to the Coast Guard. They were between 270 and 300 feet long, had a narrow beam of only 27 to 32 feet, and could make the very impressive speed of 30 knots. Since they were not built as pleasure yachts, in a rough sea, their pitching and tossing often made the boys seasick. The youngsters had things very

much their own way while in port, occasionally raising a bit of Cain. At one time they turned the hose on the crew of the destroyer *Tucker* commanded by Lieutenant Commander Waesche. The lieutenant commander was in his cabin when the incident took place. Hearing the commotion outside, he hastily came out to see his two young sons playing the hose on several members of the crew. Taking in the situation at a glance, he quickly reached the boys and gave them two resounding open-handed slaps across the face. For quite a while things were quiet on the ship.

With the ending of the destroyer duty, Waesche went to Coast Guard Headquarters at Washington, D.C., where he held a series of administrative posts. Between 1930 and 1936, he held nearly every position in the small Coast Guard administrative staff. He was Chief of Budget, Chief of Communications, Chief of Operations, along with several other posts. In that period he was promoted to Commander. As an administrator he displayed the same talents which had distinguished him on shipboard. The then Commandant, Rear Admiral Harry Hamlet, selected Commander Waesche to be his Administrative Assistant and Senior Aide. Admiral Hamlet was nearing the end of his term and the Treasury Department had decided not to appoint him for a second term. The search began for someone capable of filling that demanding assignment. Waesche's outstanding record had already won him considerable recognition. Some of his friends in high places made secret overtures to the Commander, urging that he enter the competition. They offered behind-the-scenes support which was bluntly refused by Waesche. It was something which ran counter to his nature. Whatever he achieved would have to be done openly without secret maneuverings of any kind.

The Secretary of the Treasury, Henry Morgenthau, Jr., discussed the problem with his confidants, and after deliberation, decided to recommend to the President that Commander Waesche be jumped over all the Captains in the Service and promoted to Rear Admiral, to become the Commandant in 1936. It was an unprecedented decision and a great tribute to Commander Waesche. To young Russell R. Waesche, Jr., who was about to receive his diploma and commission in the Coast Guard Academy class of 1936, the first inkling of the honor to be bestowed on his father came when he received a cryptic letter in May of that year, saying that he (Commander Waesche) would be able to come to the Academy only for a few hours on June 8 for the graduation ceremonies. After that, he would have to leave immediately for Washington. The Commander's decision did credit to his sensitivity. Knowing that Admiral Hamlet was to be the principal speaker, and realizing also that many of the guests present were already aware of his appointment, he chose not to detract from Admiral Hamlet's appearance at the graduation by his presence.

Quite naturally, Waesche's extraordinary good fortune was bound to be resented by the senior officers who had been passed over. But Waesche's total lack of vanity and his dedication to work soon won them over. In a short time, he had the wholehearted support of everyone.

Meanwhile, Waesche had remarried. His wife was the former Mrs. Agnes Rizutto Cronin, widow of a New London doctor. They had one son, William A. Waesche. Since no official quarters were provided, the couple lived in a Washington apartment to which the two eldest sons, Russell, Jr. and Harry Lee, were visitors.

Shortly after Waesche became Commandant in 1936, he approached the Department of Commerce with the suggestion that its Lighthouse Service be amalgamated with the Coast Guard. He also recommended through the Treasury Department that the Commerce Department's Bureau of Marine Inspection and Navigation be transferred to his Service. His reasoning was that, in addition to the responsibility for rescue at sea, the Coast Guard should also have the responsibility for taking preventive safety action. This included making sure that ships were built well and safely and manned by qualified and competent crews. Included within the same safety spectrum was the responsibility for maintaining and operating an efficient aids to navigation network. Waesche was partially successful in this. He was able to persuade the federal government of the desirability of amalgamating the Lighthouse Service with the Coast Guard. This was accomplished in 1939. But in the case of the Bureau of Marine Inspection and Navigation, he ran into some determined opposition. It was not until the U.S. involvement in World War II that President Roosevelt approved the latter transfer. All of these transactions were carried out in a completely aboveboard manner with ample opportunity for all to participate.

As the United States moved into high gear during the war, Waesche found himself working literally around the clock. Only a man in superb physical condition could have withstood the rigors of the work. Fortunately, he was blessed with the ability to take cat naps, something he shared with the great wartime leader, Sir Winston Churchill. At any moment, when he felt his energy was failing, he would lie down for 15 or 20 minutes to rest. Then he would return to his work with a freshness and a vigor which amazed his younger subordinates.

Admiral R.R. Waesche,
wartime Commandant of the Coast Guard.

In August 1943, with the war at its peak, Waesche made a 30,000-mile flying trip to the fighting front in the South Pacific to observe at first hand the operation of Coast Guard forces. He visited Admiral Nimitz and Vice Admiral Ghormley in Honolulu and then flew westward to Palmyra Island, Canton Island, Fiji Islands, Noumea, then Brisbane, Australia and several other stations there. New Zealand, Esperitu Santo, Guadalcanal, Honolulu, and San Francisco followed before his return to Washington after a journey of 36 days and 30,000 miles with the purpose of finding out at first hand the kind of support needed by Service units.

Then came the climactic day of June 6, 1944, the famous "D"-day, when the United States and her Free World allies threw a mighty punch at the weakening Axis Powers. Within a few weeks after the first beachheads were established, Vice Admiral Waesche went overseas on the Coast Guard transport *Wakefield* debarking in England to visit and inspect Coast Guard units in southern England. He also visited a number of Service units and personnel on the northern coast and harbor areas of France. His eldest son, then Lieutenant Commander R. R. Waesche, Jr., was in command of a destroyer escort, the *USS Camp, De 251*, on convoy duty between New York and Londonderry, Ireland. Father's and son's paths probably crossed at this point, but the son seldom saw his father except on his rare trips to Washington between convoy assignments.

In March 1945, Congress enacted legislation elevating the Commandant of the Coast Guard and of the Marine Corps to four-star rank. This made Admiral Waesche not only the first three-star, but also the first four-star admiral in Coast Guard history. The young lieutenant of 1909 had come a long way indeed since that first cruise.

Just when he had reached the pinnacle of a brilliant career and was preparing for the reward of a well-deserved retirement, a new enemy struck.

Against this new foe there was no defense. The Admiral's associates noted that he seemed weaker each day as he continued to carry out his duties as Commandant. When it became evident that he could no longer support the burden of his position, he applied for retirement as of January 1, 1946. In response to a request from Fleet Admiral Ernest J. King, USN, he recommended that Rear Admiral J. F. Farley be named as his successor. Waesche was then in his third four-year term as Commandant.

The name of the enemy draining Admiral Waesche's life was cancer of the stomach. It had been discovered during an exploratory operation in 1945. The finding was relayed only to top officials in the government. On October 17, 1946, his heart gave out, and his long voyage was over. But he had left behind him a contribution to the Service he loved which will not be forgotten.

Perhaps the best tribute to Admiral Waesche was paid by his son, retired Rear Admiral Russell R. Waesche, who said: "He was a leader by example, exemplifying in honor, sincerity, integrity and loyalty every fine leadership precept. The devotion of his immediate circle of associates, staff members and subordinates was always evident."

Waesche being sworn in for his last term as Commandant.

The Burning Sea

To most observers, the North Atlantic looked much as it had always looked on a midsummer day. But John Allen Midgett, keeper of a Coast Guard lifeboat station on the Outer Banks of North Carolina, was no ordinary observer. He was one of a famous family who had been bred to his calling. For generations, the Midgetts had provided the Coast Guard with some of its finest lifesavers. Today, as Midgett surveyed the blue and inscrutable expanse of ocean, he was filled with foreboding. Eighteen years of experience had given him an instinct for the ocean's moods. He was aware of its caprice and of its capability for shifting from sunlight to storm with alarming rapidity. He had seen the victims of its fury, and more than once had helped bury them.

There were other reasons for Midgett's disquiet. This was the wartime summer of 1918, and the United States was fully committed to the cause of its European allies against the German enemy. Only six days before, on August 5, a bold German U-boat had sunk a Dutch ship, the *Diamond Shoals* lightship, and had forced two steamers ashore with shellfire. To the north of the Coast Guard station at Nag's Head, North Carolina, a steamer had been torpedoed. Always, there was the possibility that the shark-like hull of a marauding U-boat would come into view. It kept the men's nerves taut.

Then at 4:30 p.m. on August 11, the dreaded eventuality happened. Midgett heard his lookout scream: "A big geyser of water has just shot up from the stern of a tanker proceeding up the coast. She bears east by south, distance of seven miles." The words were followed by the roar of an explosion.

Immediately, Midgett raced to the top of the tower where he could see that the stricken tanker had changed course and was headed for land. Flames were shooting out of her stern. In minutes she would become a blazing torch. And of all the disasters to befall a seaman, none was more terrible than a fire at sea. It turned decks into giant griddles from which crazed men often jumped into the sea, usually to their death.

Ordering his crew to prepare to launch a lifeboat, Midgett also rushed a call through to the Navy base at Norfolk, Va. He was told that destroyers and a squadron of planes had been

dispatched to the scene. While this was going on, the tanker was hit by another torpedo, putting her completely out of control, and blazing from stem to stern.

John Allen Midgett, some years after the *Mirlo* rescue.

A 30-knot nor'easter had sprung up, creating mountainous waves hitting the beach like pile drivers. It took all of Midgett's and his crew's expertise to launch the boat in that foaming cauldron of sea. Meanwhile, precious time was slipping by. Thirty minutes had elapsed since that first frantic message had been received—time enough for the raging fire to wreak terrible damage. British seamen were floundering in the maddened ocean; their endurance was limited.

Five miles from shore, Midgett's lifeboat met a boat from the torpedoed tanker, *Mirlo*, carrying Captain W.W. Williams, her commander, and 16 other burned and blackened survivors. In a voice trembling with emotion, Williams told that the tanker had been bound from New Orleans to Norfolk with a cargo of gasoline and refined oil. As such she was a prime target for enemy submarines.

flame, about one hundred yards apart. Like a giant bellows, the wind was fanning the flames to ever-increasing intensity. Midgett decided that he

The motor surfboat in which Midgett performed his extraordinary rescue of the *Mirlo* survivors. Photo: Cape Hatteras National Seashore.

Williams also revealed that two other lifeboats filled with *Mirlo* crewmen lay behind a wall of fire blazing all around the tanker. Sheets of flame 500 feet high sealed off the men in the lifeboats from their rescuers. If they managed to survive the fire, it was still possible that the U-boat would shell the men with Teutonic thoroughness. One of the men in Williams' boat reported that he had seen the conning tower of the U-boat as they had pulled away from the vessel. That explained Williams' haste in getting away from the vessel. There was no point in giving the Germans another target. It also meant that the rescuers would have to contend not only with this inferno, but also with possible enemy action.

Instructing Captain Williams to continue toward the station and to anchor outside the breakers, Midgett made his decision. He and his men were going to penetrate that flaming barrier and bring the men to safety. How would they do it? He wasn't sure, but he knew he had no alternative, whatever the outcome. If he failed to return, that was part of the risk of his profession.

The *Mirlo* had broken up into great islands of

would wait for the wind to make an opening in the solid mass of fire and then enter. If that curtain of fire closed behind them, they would be finished.

It had begun to grow dark and the flames lit up the area with a lurid glow. The flickering of shadows distorted everything and turned men's faces into tortured masks. When a shift in the wind gave Midgett the opening he had been seeking, he drove his boat in through the flames. The screams of the trapped seamen had an almost inhuman quality that made him shudder.

The heat given off by the burning fragments of the tanker was so great that it seared the lifesavers. At any moment, a blazing piece of the vessel could strike them and set them afire. The acrid smell of burning paint mixed with fumes of burning oil and gas made many of the rescuers sick. Some of them vomited in the boat, but the rescue continued.

Briefly the haze lifted, and Midgett could see six men clinging to a capsized lifeboat. The exhausted men were trying to protect themselves from the fire and the churning sea. They were the only survivors of the first boat launched by the *Mirlo*; it had capsized on hitting the water. The men had

The American Cross of Honor

INCORPORATED BY ACT OF CONGRESS, 1906

THE PRESIDENT OF THE UNITED STATES, HONORARY PRESIDENT

For Heroic Conduct

OF

AN EXTRAORDINARY NATURE, FAR ABOVE THE CALL OF DUTY

The Grand Cross

OF THIS ORDER

Is Hereby Awarded To

JOHN A. MIDGETT

WHOSE HEROIC CONDUCT IS BRIEFLY DESCRIBED AS FOLLOWS

FOR COMMANDING A BOAT CREW WHICH SAVED 42 LIVES, AT GREAT RISK TO THEIR OWN, INVOLVING UNUSUAL AND EXTRAORDINARY HEROISM OF THE MAXIMUM DEGREE, AS REQUIRED TO WARRANT SELECTION AS RECIPIENTS OF SIX OF NOT TO EXCEED TWELVE GRAND CROSSES AWARDED IN 1930.

On August 16th, 1918, in a heavy northeastern storm, the British S.S. "Mirlo" carrying oil and gasoline, was torpedoed by a German submarine off the coast of North Carolina. The ship was immediately enveloped in a mass of flames and the burning oil spread upon the waters. Under command of John A. Midgett, members of Coast Guard Station No. 179 launched their power surf boat. The boat was tossed back upon the beach and the crew washed away from the oars time after time. Undaunted they returned to their task. After succeeding in getting their boat through the surf they were compelled to steer into a blazing inferno and were in serious danger of being burned to death if not drowned. They picked up a number of the crew of the Mirlo and towed four of the ship's boats to shore. Being unable to take the ship's boats through the surf they anchored the same beyond the breakers and then made four trips in their surf boat bringing the entire 42 survivors safely ashore.

The extraordinary degree of heroism attested by this award cannot be adequately described in this citation. Not to exceed twelve Grand Crosses are awarded in any calendar year for the twelve most heroic acts brought to the attention of the order, and performed any time or any place in saving or attempting to save human life.

In testimony whereof, By order of the Board of Governors, this certificate is awarded and the seal of the order affixed this *fifteenth* day of *July* 1930

Secretary

Midgett's citation for The Grand Cross, one of many honors recognizing his heroism in the *Mirlo* case.

been showered with flaming oil and gasoline as the tanker was torn apart by explosions. One by one, they had surrendered to exhaustion, leaving only these six. The hair had been burned off their blackened scalps.

After taking the men on board, Midgett continued to search the area for additional survivors. He concluded that if the other boat were still upright, it would be downwind. But the strain was beginning to tell on him and his crew. It had been hours since they had first undertaken the rescue—hours filled with extreme labor and danger. Then somehow, in a black haze, he could make out the third boat from the *Mirlo.* Submerged to its gunwales, it carried 19 men who had been able to paddle away barely in time to escape the flames.

Above the crackling of the flames and the shouts of the men, Midgett could hear the welcome drone of an approaching Navy bomber, one of six dispatched from Norfolk. The U-boat would never attempt a shelling now; the odds had turned against it.

Covered by the Navy plane, the lifeboat crew took the survivors' boat in tow and headed for home, nine miles away. In the face of the most fearful odds, they had succeeded in carrying out one of the most hazardous rescues in the long history of the sea.

From his grateful countrymen, Midgett received a Victory Medal and a Congressional Lifesaving Medal. The latter also went to each member of the crew. King George V of England had a special medal struck for Midgett and each of his crew and the British Board of Trade gave Midgett a silver loving cup.

Midgett went on to serve in the Coast Guard for another 20 years—for a total of 38 years of service. He participated in 40 major rescues and in hundreds of smaller ones. The man who had defied death so many times at sea died in an automobile accident, two days before Christmas, 1937. He and his brave kinsmen lie buried in the family plot at Manteo, North Carolina, on windswept Cape Hatteras.

Death on an Icecap

Had anyone called Lt. John A. Pritchard a hero, he would have been embarrassed. A naturally modest man, Pritchard did not conceive of himself in heroic terms. What he did pride himself upon was his professionalism as an aviator. He had decided upon a flying career shortly after his graduation from the Coast Guard Academy in New London, Conn. He had entered upon his duties with the same quiet dedication he had shown in his other tasks.

Greenland icecap was especially dangerous. Treacherous crevasses and openings in the ice could appear at any time.

Only a few weeks previously, Pritchard had directed a party to rescue the Canadian airmen who had been stranded on the Greenland icecap. As Pritchard and his men picked their way through the icy wasteland, the *Northland* fired flares and star shells to guide the Canadians to the cutter's anchorage. The cutter also transmitted a Morse

Radioman First Class Benjamin A. Bottoms.

Lt. John A. Pritchard.

By November 1942, he had successfully flown the North Atlantic air lanes for nine months. In that time, he had operated a small Grumman amphibian from the Coast Guard cutter *Northland* on coastal patrol and over convoys making their way with supplies to war-torn Europe via the northern route. Far more dangerous than the Germans were Greenland's gales, icy rains, heavy fogs, and unexpected storms. Landing on the

Code message: "Move back from the edge of the glacier and bear south to meet a landing party." To the weary Canadians who had already undergone 14 days of privation, those simple words brought the greatest joy they had ever known. The icecap would not be their grave after all.

Five days after the rescue of the Canadians, the *Northland* received word that contact had been established with an American Flying Fortress

Lieutenant John A. Pritchard, Jr. stands alert as his plane is readied aboard the CG Cutter *Northland*. His heavy clothing stood him in good stead, when, after landing his aircraft, he was forced to trudge four miles over the icy terrain to reach the Army fliers, all of whom were suffering intensely from cold and hunger.

which had been lost for two weeks in the Greenland interior. The Coast Guard was asked to attempt the rescue. The *Northland* smashed her way through the ice as far as possible toward the reported scene of disaster. The situation was made even more desperate by knowledge that the men were short of supplies and suffering from the intense November cold and from injuries.

Pritchard requested permission to fly to the rescue, proposing to land his amphibian on the snow and ice with pontoons which would serve as runners. But it was a very risky business and his skipper, Cdr. Francis G. Pollard, had some serious reservations about the undertaking. Pollard was fully aware of the difficulty of making a successful landing on the icecap and he did not want to lose one of the best men in his command. Pritchard finally convinced the commander of his ability to land on the ice with his wheels retracted, pick up the Army men, and get into the air again.

The cutter's crew put the plane over the side, and Pritchard and his radioman, Benjamin A. Bottoms, taxied for the takeoff. The tough little amphibian sped into the wind, leaving a white wake in the dark blue water as she lifted and headed inland.

After half an hour's flight over the icecap, the downed plane was sighted. Radioman Bottoms sent a message to the Army fliers that they were going

Pritchard and Bottoms flew their historic rescue mission and met their tragic deaths in a Grumman J2F plane like the one pictured here.

to put down. Quickly, a reply came back from the ground: "Don't try it. You'll never make it."

But Pritchard already had his eye on a long, snow-covered downslope. He put the plane into a glide and made a perfect landing. Climbing out, he directed Bottoms to stand by and keep the engine turning over and maintain radio contact with the cutter. Then he started out on foot to reach the fliers over four wearying miles across the snow.

What Pritchard found was even worse than he had anticipated. Three men had survived the crash. One had a broken arm, two were suffering from gangrene, and all three were badly weakened by hunger and the terrible cold. The strongest gave Pritchard a hand in carrying the other two back to the Grumman and putting them aboard. Since the plane could carry only two passengers, the third man, Corporal A. L. Hayworth, stayed behind with the understanding that Pritchard would return and pick him up the following day.

Now began the most dangerous part of an already hazardous mission. Pritchard would have to get his aircraft back into the air, using the downward slope as an airstrip. With her nose pointed downhill and Pritchard gunning the engine, the Grumman shot forward, striking her belly on the hummocks of snow and ice, bounding a little higher with each blow, until she suddenly soared upward in full flight. It was a masterful exhibition of flying skill under the most difficult conditions.

By the time Pritchard reached the *Northland* it had grown dark and a heavy snowstorm all but blotted out visibility. The cutter's crew could hear the drone of the plane's motors but could not see it. Anxiously, they aimed the powerful ship's searchlight in the direction of the sound, managing miraculously to spot Pritchard. Following the narrow beam of the light in the all-embracing darkness, Pritchard made a successful landing on the rough water. Both he and his radioman had achieved an outstanding rescue.

Lieutenant Pritchard and Radioman Benjamin A. Bottoms remove one of the two rescued Army fliers from the cockpit of his J2F plane on returning to the Cutter *Northland*. Another Coast Guardsman stands ready to assist. The Army men, members of a B-17 crew, were rescued 15 days after their bomber was forced down.

But Pritchard could not relax. On that bleak icecap, a third man remained, who was counting on him for rescue. His duty was clear; he had to return. The weather had worsened and a blinding snowstorm had set in. Despite repeated warnings from the *Northland* not to make the landing, Pritchard continued on his way. Once again he made a flawless landing on the ice and picked up the remaining survivor. But his luck had run out. Somewhere along the return route, he lost his way, and the brave rescue attempt was not successful.

Reconnaissance flights later discovered the wreckage of the plane but no signs of life could be seen in the vicinity. For their gallantry, both Pritchard and Bottoms received posthumous Distinguished Flying Crosses.

Coast Guardsmen carry out their wartime duties from the Arctic waters to the African shores and to the beaches on the Solomons. Like the painting of 'Washington Crossing the Delaware' is this photo of the Coast Guard rescuing R.A.F. fliers, who were forced down on the Greenland Ice Cap.

The Gift of Douglas Munro

He was only 22 when he was struck down by an enemy bullet on a steaming Guadalcanal beachhead on Sunday, September 27, 1942. At that age most ordinary young men are preparing for a career, considering marriage, or simply enjoying the good years of youth. But Douglas Munro, Coast Guard Signalman, First Class, was no ordinary young man, and these were no ordinary times.

By 1942, the greatest war in human history had already been raging for three years. The ancient continent of Europe, the scene of so many bloody encounters between nations, was echoing to the march of Hitler's legions, as they ruthlessly smashed one frontier after another in their quest to establish a German hegemony, first in Europe, and then over the entire world. It was a mad dream born out of an insensate thirst for power. But the superbly trained German armies, aided by their allies, had been winning with frightening ease. So far, it had been largely a European affair, with the United States serving as the self-styled "arsenal of democracy." But when the Nazi steamroller crushed France and stood at the edge of the English Channel, it was clear to everyone that U. S. participation could not be long delayed.

Then came the slashing Japanese attack on Pearl Harbor on December 7, 1941, and the war was no longer exclusively European. The warlords of Japan had flung down the gauntlet to the hated United States. It would be winner take all, with no quarter given. The quiet beaches of the Pacific, celebrated by writers and poets as veritable Edens, suddenly were stained by the blood of wounded men.

So pervasive was the impact of the Pearl Harbor attack that no section of the nation would henceforth be immune from the war's horrors. Not even the peaceful little town of Cle Elum, Washington, where young Douglas Munro had grown up and been educated.

Those who remember Douglas recall that he was a quiet, slender young man, with a tendency to self-effacement. Yet there was also in him a deep spiritual strength which had yet to be discovered. Tragically, it took a terrible war to bring it to the surface.

When Munro enlisted in the Coast Guard in 1939 at the age of 20, he had completed one year at the Central Washington College of Education. As so often happens in life, he developed, quite by chance, an enduring friendship with another enlistee, Raymond Evans, whom he had met at the Port Angeles, Washington, recruiting station. For the next three years these two young men were inseparable. A Japanese machine gun bullet on the remote Pacific beach would eventually shatter this friendship.

Douglas A. Munro.

By September 27, 1942, the two friends had attained the rank of first class petty officers. The arduous "island-hopping" campaign to break the Japanese hold on the Pacific had begun, and it promised to be more difficult than any other campaign undertaken by the United States. In the years prior to Pearl Harbor, the Japanese had strongly fortified all strategic islands in the South Pacific. That meant that U. S. forces would have to carry out the most difficult of maneuvers—the attack of a heavily fortified enemy point from the sea. Japanese guns would literally be "pointing down their throats." But the decision had been made to roll back the Japanese forces.

Now the United States began the long, hard task of uprooting the Japanese forces from their fortress at Guadalcanal. It was months before this was accomplished and many a brave man left his blood on the white beaches.

This painting of Munro hangs in Munro Hall, the enlisted barracks at the Coast Guard Academy in New London, Conn.

Both Munro and Evans had been selected for a Guadalcanal landing craft assignment by Lieutenant Commander Dwight H. Dexter. This was not the first dangerous assignment given to Munro. Previously, he had risked his life to save the two-man crew of a U. S. Navy dive bomber forced down off Savo Island. Now, he volunteered to evacuate an expedition caught at a point raked by murderous Japanese gunfire and was placed in charge of ten landing boats to ferry a Marine battalion to a small, sandy area about four miles away. At 1 p.m. in the blazing heat of noon, the boats lowered their landing ramps as the tough, battle-ready Marines scrambled from the boats, across a narrow stretch of sand, to the cover of the dense jungle.

Everything had gone well. The Marines had made it safely to shore, and the craft had miraculously escaped damage. The mission had been accomplished. The problem now was to get off the island and back home.

It had been a particularly fierce encounter, and the Marines had run into savage, raking shellfire. As they worked their way back to the beach under galling enemy fire, Lieutenant Commander Dexter was waiting at the water's edge, signaling for the boats to approach. The situation was made even more precarious by the artillery fire of U.S. forces.

Cupping his hands, Dexter called out, "Will you two lead these boats to take them off?"

Munro's unhesitating reply was, "Hell, yes." Evans recalled later, "The three of us had done duty together for a long time, and I'm sure the commander knew the answer before he asked."

Munro and Evans gathered ten additional volunteer craft and moved across the bay to rescue the beleaguered Marines. Munro ordered his flotilla to stay off shore, while he drove his own boat to the beach to figure out the best course of action. He sighted the Marines and headed directly for them. Immediately, a hellish cacophony of Japanese machine-gun fire broke out, raking Munro's craft. He came safely through to the shore and coolly began making arrangements for the evacuation. True, the odds were not in his favor. The beach was hard but so narrow that only three boats could land at any one time.

Thirty Marines clambered into Munro's boat as he turned back to the waiting flotilla; they were transferred to another boat. Back into the hell of Guadalcanal, Munro led a small group of boats, to take troops off the beach. Japanese fire had risen to such intensity that the air was alive with the whine of bullets. Munro and his party were sitting ducks for enemy gunners.

Munro made his decision. He placed his boat in a position to serve not only as a shield against Japanese fire but to divert the enemy's attention from the main effort of evacuation. The enemy was so close that one could hear excited commands being barked out by Japanese commanders.

Over the exposed stretch of beach, wounded Marines were dragged and carried to the landing craft. One Marine captain told Evans he was certain that no Marines were left on shore.

As the craft retreated to safety, Munro noted that one of the boats had grounded on the coral. Its occupants were frantically attempting to free it from its deadly position. Munro ordered that his boat go alongside the stranded craft. A line was passed to start towing operations. The men attached the line and succeeded in pulling the boat into deeper water.

At that very moment, Evans recalls, "The Japs managed to get a gun set up on the beach and cut loose with it. As I swung to answer it, I heard Doug doing likewise. I emptied a full pan of ammo and

as being the whole of life, that would be true. But there is a flaming life of the spirit which long survives our frail mortality. Some call it the soul. In his brief 22 years of life Douglas Munro had made the greatest gift to his country that any man can give—his life. And he had given it willingly to preserve the lives of his comrades.

Named for the World War II hero, the Coast Guard Cutter *Munro* (WHEC-724) is side-launched at Avondale Shipyards, New Orleans, La.

screamed for another, but we were out of range by the time I reloaded. It's strange that I didn't notice something queer then, but I didn't notice that Doug wasn't visible until one of the fellows motioned for me to come forward. What I saw when I jumped over the intervening armor plate caused me to swear and drop quickly to my knees on the deck. It was Doug, and as I tried to ascertain how badly he was hurt, he opened his eyes and spoke, so softly I had to bend down to catch the words.

"Did we get them all off?" and seeing my affirmative nod, he smiled with the smile I knew and liked so well, and then he was gone."

Gone? Perhaps if one thinks of the mortal frame

The full evacuation of the nearly 500 Marines was carried out in about half an hour despite extreme enemy harassment. For his unselfish courage, Munro was awarded our country's highest honor, the Congressional Medal of Honor.

There have been other battles since then, and many other young men have died bravely. Sometimes in the turmoil of the world it is easy to concur in the despairing lines written by the English poet, Matthew Arnold, more than a century ago:

"And we are here as on a darkling plain,
Swept with confused alarms of struggle
    and flight

Where ignorant armies clash by night."

Yet it is not entirely so. Sometimes the darkness is lit up by an act of compassion and self-sacrifice so great that it lifts us above ourselves and closer to the God in whose image we are made. This high and tragic destiny was reserved for Douglas Munro. He is in a select company.

Douglas A. Munro Hall.

Grand Haven, Michigan, Coast Guard City, U.S.A.

Many cities and towns of the United States have formed mutual admiration societies with the Coast Guard. It is safe to say that Grand Haven, Michigan, a town of only 15,000, qualifies as the most uniquely "Coast Guard" of any city of any size in America.

There are other municipalities in the U.S. which **can** boast of a greater number of Coast Guard units **than** Grand Haven, although the friendly town on Lake Michigan's relatively unpolluted shore has a lighthouse, a rescue station, and a 180-foot buoy tender, the *Woodbine.*

Historically, the Coast Guard's presence in the area can be traced to the establishment of a U.S. Lifesaving Station there in 1870. Grand Haven's strong association with the Service began in a later era—1932, when the cutter *Escanaba* was first assigned to the town now known as Coast Guard City. It was a love affair from the beginning. *Escanaba* earned a place in the hearts of the townspeople by breaking ice in the Grand River, and by her many rescue feats. Grand Haven became known as one of the Coast Guard's finest duty stations through its open hospitality. The love affair grew, until in 1938, Grand Haven launched the first and only Coast Guard Festival. Highlights of the first festival included boat races, breeches buoy demonstrations, and other public displays of

Grand Haven's beloved *Escanaba* breaking ice in the Straits of Mackinac during the relatively carefree days prior to World War II (c. 1935).

the Coast Guard's expertise. The idea was simple, but sensational, and within two years the festival was attracting visitors from all over the state. Today, they come from all over America and Canada.

Following the outbreak of World War II, *Escanaba* was assigned to duty with the "Greenland Patrol." Grand Haven continued to observe the anniversary of the Coast Guard's founding, but no longer in such festive style. In truth, these

from the freezing waters. This incident marked one of the first uses of rubber "wet suits" in rescue operations.

On June 13, 1943, while escorting a convoy from Narsarssuak, Greenland, to St. Johns, Newfoundland, the 165-foot *Escanaba* was blown up, apparently by an enemy submarine. She sank within three minutes. Only two survivors were picked up, and they could offer no clue to what had transpired.

Escanaba goes to war.

occasions more closely resembled solemn patriotic services. *Escanaba* served with great distinction, and was involved in rescuing survivors of one of the war's greatest disasters, the sinking of the transport ship *Dorchester*, with 904 men on board. The *Dorchester* sinking, later commemorated on a U.S. postage stamp, is remembered for the four chaplains on board who gained immortality by giving their life jackets to others and going down with the ship.

Escanaba rescued 133 survivors of the disaster

Grand Haven was grief-stricken. Then, fighting back from its initial shock, Coast Guard City immersed itself in one of the war's most patriotic campaigns. In practically no time, the citizens of Grand Haven organized and succeeded in raising funds with a War Bond drive that more than equaled the cost of *Escanaba's* replacement. This was one of the most extraordinary civic achievements of the entire war.

It was only fitting that following the war, the city that had effectively purchased a cutter for the

Coast Guard, should be furnished with a replacement for the beloved *Escanaba*. *Woodbine*, a 180-foot buoy tender built in 1942, was transferred to Coast Guard City in 1947. The people of Grand Haven were grateful and the Coast Guard Festival was renewed with greater vigor and flair.

A major festival attraction was added in 1963, when a 10-year effort culminated in completion of the world's largest musical fountain. Funded by Grand Haven and its surrounding communities, the fountain defies description by mere words. Even color photographs fail to capture the dazzling extravaganza which awaits those who travel to Grand Haven to personally view its splendor.

The most spectacular feature of the musical fountain is its ability to present an unlimited

The sole survivors of the *Escanaba* tragedy: Boatswain's Mate 2nd Class Melvin Baldwin (l., now deceased) and Seaman First Class Raymond O'Malley.

Raymond O'Malley lays a wreath at the *Escanaba* Memorial during Grand Haven's annual Coast Guard Festival.

variety of programs. Ingenious electrical devices regulate the flow of water in endless formations. They also operate switches, changing the color of the lighting to match the moods of the music and flowing water. The variety of illumination and water displays is virtually endless and the effects are dazzling.

1963 also marked the beginning of what has now become a Grand Haven tradition, as the five officers and 50 crewmen of the cutter *Woodbine* were made honorary citizens of the city. The ship was also presented with the first City of Grand Haven flag. These unprecedented honors represent some of the reasons why many Coast Guardsmen have come to think of Coast Guard City as a real home away from home. They have shown their appreciation over the years by behaving in exemplary fashion during their shore leaves in the pretty resort town.

Arrangements for each year's festival begin as much as a year in advance. The clockwork precision with which the various events are carried out clearly reflects the careful planning and dedicated work which make it all possible.

Many highlights of the annual show are events especially organized to honor and entertain local and visiting Coast Guardsmen. Parties, receptions, marksmanship and athletic competitions, and retired officers' reunion, make for a full schedule. Each year, as permitted by operational commitments, the famous icebreaker *Mackinaw* visits the area, where she and *Woodbine* hold open-house celebrations. *Mackinaw* usually brings along a contingent of cadets from the Coast Guard Academy. They are treated to a cotillion dance and other activities. Visiting Coast Guard dignitaries from Ninth District Headquarters in Cleveland, Ohio, and from Coast Guard Headquarters in Washington, D.C., round out the guest list.

The Coast Guard Festival's most exciting moments are open to everyone and crowds which have been estimated at nearly three hundred thousand attend the most popular events. The annual Festival of Bands and the Street Parade are wonderfully refreshing glimpses of Americana. The fireworks display and the air show are among the best to be found anywhere. The latter has brought the U.S. Air Force Thunderbirds, Navy Blue Angels, and the Army Golden Knights to Grand Haven so many times that they, too, have come to hold Coast Guard City as a very special place. A memorable feature of the 1969 air show was the unveiling of an AF-100 aircraft, mounted on a pylon and dedicated to those Thunderbirds who have died on active duty. Since 1962, the festival has presented several performances of a water thrill show which compares favorably with Florida's famed Cypress Gardens.

Contrasting poignantly with the festival's gala activities is a quiet but colorful ceremony held each year to commemorate *Escanaba's* tragic fate, and to honor all officers and enlisted men of the Coast Guard who have given their lives in service to their country. Grand Haven remembers. Grand Haven cares. And the Coast Guard holds in high esteem its special Coast Guard City.

Bibliography

Bibliography

Adamson, Hans Christian, *Keepers of the Lights*, Greenberg: Publisher, New York, 1955.

Baarslag, Karl, *Coast Guard to the Rescue*, Farrar and Rinehart, Inc., New York, Toronto, 1936.

Bailey, Thomas A., *The American Pageant*, D.C. Heath and Company, Boston, 1966.

Beard, Charles A. and Mary, *Basic History of the United States*, The New Home Library, New York, 1944.

Bell, Kensil, *Always Ready*, Dodd, Mead & Company, New York, 1943.

Bloomfield, Howard V. L., *The Compact History of the United States Coast Guard*, Hawthorn Books, Inc., New York, 1966.

Capron, Captain Walter C. (USCG Ret.), *U.S. Coast Guard*, Franklin Watts, Inc., New York, 1965.

Evans, Stephen Hadley, *The United States Coast Guard, 1790-1915*, The United States Naval Institute, Annapolis, Md., 1949.

Flexner, James Thomas, *George Washington and the New Nation, 1783-93*, Little, Brown and Company, Boston and Toronto, 1970.

Hogan, Captain W.C., USCG. (Revised by Dickenson and Behrens), *The Coast Guardsman's Manual.*

Lorant, Stefan, *The Glorious Burden*, Harper & Row, New York, 1968.

Janes Fighting Ships, 1968-69 Edition, McGraw-Hill, New York and London, 1970.

Morison, Samuel Eliot, *The Battle of the Atlantic*, Vol. I, Little, Brown and Company, 1964.

Morris, Richard B., *Alexander Hamilton and the Founding of the Nation*, The Dial Press, New York, 1957.

Official Transcript of Testimony Taken at the Investigation into the Conduct of Captain M. A. Healy, of the Revenue Cutter Bear. Two documents dated March, 1890, and February, 1896 were studied intensively at the National Archives, Washington, D.C.

Petrow, Richard, *Across the Top of Russia*, David McKay Company, Inc., New York, 1967.

Powell, Hickman, *What the Citizen Should Know About the Coast Guard*, W. W. Norton and Company, Inc., New York, 1941.

Putnam, George R., *Lighthouses and Lightships of the United States*, Houghton Mifflin Company, Boston and New York, 1933.

Rapaport, Stella M., *The* Bear — *Ship of Many Lives*, Dodd, Mead and Company, New York, 1962.

Report of the Cruise of the U.S. Revenue Cutter Bear *and the Overland Expedition for the Relief of the Whalers in the Arctic Ocean from November 27, 1897 to September 13, 1898*. Washington, D.C., Government Printing Office, 1899.

Shannon, Terry, *Ride the Ice Down!*, Golden Gate Junior Books, San Carlos, California.

_____ and Payzant, C., *Sentinels of Our Shores*, Golden Gate Junior Books, San Carlos, California, 1969.

Short, Lloyd M. (Institute for Government Research) *The Bureau of Navigation — Its History, Activities, and Organization.*

Smith, Darrell H. and Powell, Fred W. (Institute for Government Research), *The Coast Guard— Its History, Activities, and Organization*, The Brookings Institution, Washington, D.C., 1929.

Smith, Captain, H.D.S., USRCS, *Early History of the United States Revenue Marine Service 1789-1849*, Press of R.L. Polk Printing Company, 1932.

Swanberg, W.A., *Citizen Hearst*, Charles Scribner's Sons, New York, 1961.

The Coast Guard at War, Greenland Patrol. A historical monograph prepared by the Historical Section, Headquarters, U.S. Coast Guard, Washington, D.C., 1946.

Thomas, Captain Charles W., USCG, *Ice Is Where You Find It.* The Bobbs-Merrill Company, Inc., Indianapolis-New York, 1951.

Weiss, George (The Institute for Government Research) *The Lighthouse Service, Its History, Activities and Organization*, The Johns Hopkins Press, Baltimore, Md., 1926.

Willoughby, Malcolm F., *The U.S. Coast Guard in World War II*, United States Naval Institute, Annapolis, Md., 1957.

_____ , *The Rum War at Sea*, Government Printing Office, Washington, D.C., 1964.

Index

ACV. *See* Air Cushion Vehicles
ADAPTS. *See* Air Deliverable Anti-
    Pollution Transfer System
AK's, 235
AMVER. *See* Automated Merchant
    Vessel Report System
Acacia, 66
Act of 1799, 3, 4
Active, 9
Acushnet, 54, 173
Adams, John, 4
Admeasurement Section, 158
Admiral Cervera, 36
Admiral Montojo, 36
Agassiz, 24
Aid to seafarers, 10
Aids-to-navigation, 39, 97-126, 187,
    226
Air cargo, 167
"Air Controller," 203
Air Cushion Vehicles (ACV), 92
Air Deliverable Anti-Pollution Transfer
    System, 89, 90
Aircraft, 65, 82, 93, 145-6, 167, 191,
    209, 217-27
    See also Helicopter
Alabama, 10
Alabama (State), 19, 21
Alameda, Calif., 239
Alaska Fisheries Patrol, 203
Alaskan Fur Seals, 147, 261-2
Alaskan Patrol, 28, 41, 78, 79, 171-2
Alaskan Territory, 28, 131, 141, 171,
    258
    continental shelf, 137
    King Island, 262
    North Slope, 142
Alcatraz Island, Calif., 101
Alderman, 54
Alert, 13, 249
Alexander Stephen and Son, 31
Alexander Hamilton, 62, 63, 163
Algonquin, 42, 44, 63, 205
Amagansett, L.I., 71
Ambassador, 193
Ambrose Lightship, 109
American Merchant Marine, 2, 13
American merchant ships, 3, 4
Amer. Museum of Natural History, 173
Amphibious. *See* Helicopter
An Thoi, 82
Anderson, W.S., 48
Anderson, Major, 20
Andrea Doria, 109
Androscoggin, 78
Annapolis, Md., 24
Annette Island, 123
Antarctic, 131, 134, 138-9, 225

Antietam, 24
Antigua, B.W.I., 66
Anti-pollution, 150, 173, 185
Antisubmarine units, 44, 161, 218
Anzio, 70
Arage, 21
Archduke Francis Ferdinand, 43
Archer, 24
Arctic Ocean, 31, 131, 135, 225
Arcturus, 222-4
Argand lamps, 104
Arkansas (State), 92
Armed forces of the U.S., 3, 4, 60, 90
    Staff College, 161
Army Corps of Engineers, 150
Army Golden Knights, 290
Artisarlook, Charlie, 265
Arundel Cove, Md., 231, 269
Ashuelott, 22
Astoria, Oregon, 204
Atka, 135
Atlantic Air Sweepstakes, 47
Atlantic City, N.J., 53
Atlantic Fleet, 44
Atlantic flight, 46
Atomic Energy Commission, 173
Austro-Hungarian Empire, 43-4
Automated Merchant Vessel Reporting
    System, 76, 215-7
Aviation, 45-8, 65, 93, 187
    See also U.S.C.G. Air Station
Aviators, 224
Avionic system, 55, 225
Avondale Shipyards, 285
Axis powers, 60, 65, 68, 274
Azalea (tender), 107
Azores, 46, 63, 167

BOSDET, 128, 131
Ba Dong, S. Vietnam, 84
Bachelor of Science. *See* Ocean-
    graphy
Baffin Bay, 31, 171
Bagley, Worth, 37
Bahamas, 66
Baird Glacier, 123
Baldwin, Melvin, 289
Baltimore, 24, 135
Barnegat Class, 169
Barnegat Inlet, N.J., 226
Barnegat, N.J., 16
Barricades, 22
Basket rescue. *See* Rescue basket
Bathythermograph, 173
Battle of Okinawa, 163
Battle of the Atlantic, 65-6, 73, 163
Bay of Whales, 40, 141

Bear, 31, 60, 131, 133, 135, 141,
    259-61, 263-4
Beauregard, Gen. P.G.T., 101
Bedloe, 109
Belgium, 60, 145, 167
Bender, Adm, Chester R., 224
Bennett, James Gordon, Jr., 24
Bering Sea Patrol, 28, 31, 38, 135,
    141, 171, 262
Bering Strait, 86, 170
Bermuda, 63, 167
Bermuda Sky Queen, 167-9
Bernadou, Lt., 37
Bertha F. Walker, 256
Bertholf, Ellsworth P., 41, 265-7
Bibb, 15, 21, 31, 167-8
Bicker, Capt., 13, 15
Billard, R. Adm. F.C., 53
Billard Hall, 229
Binns, Jack, 39
Bismarck (Ger. battleship), 60
Bittersweet, 120, 123, 125
Black Tom's Island, N.J., 45, 177
Blockade, 21
Blockading fleet, 36
Blunt's Coast Pilot, 100
Board of Lifesaving Appliances, 188
Boating safety, 126-30
Boilers
    square-shaped, 16
Boston, Mass., 104, 167, 187, 192, 199
Boston, 35
Boston Harbor, Mass., 103
Boston Light Station, 103-5, 109, 117
Boston trawler, 48
Bottoms, Benjamin A., 63, 279-82
Boutwell, George S., 27, 188
Boutwell, 33
Bowdoin, 60
Braithwaite, Capt. George, 109
Bramble, 78, 135
Brede Fjord, Greenland, 205
Brest, France, 44
Bristol Channel, 44
British, 8, 54, 57, 60, 62, 65, 104
    pilots 225
British Board of Trade, 45
British Navy, 5, 9, 10
British Prime Minister, 59
British vessel, 39, 40, 44-5
Brooklyn, N.Y., 177
Brooks, Capt., 6
Brown, John, 19
Bruce, Jonathan, 104
Brucker Survival Capsule, 155
Brushwood, Capt. John G., 19
Buchanan, James, 17
Buffalo, N.Y., 55, 61

Buoy boats, 74
Buoy flasher, 122
Buoy sinker, 121
Buoy tenders, 121-5, 135, 162, 173, 289
Buoy tending, 97-8
Buoys
    automated data, 168, 173-4
    breeches, 194
    marking system, 100
    structure, 101
Bureau of Lighthouses, 101
Bureau of Marine Inspection and Navigation, 130, 156
Bureau of Navigation, 129, 154
Bureau of Navigation and Steamboat Inspection, 156
Burton Island, 135, 138-9
Bush Bluff Lightship, 108
Buskoe, 61
Butler, B.F., 24
Bwiza (Poland), 68
Byrd, R. Adm. Richard, 137, 139-41

CINCLANTFLT, 224
CQD, 39
CVS. *See* Commercial Vessel Safety
C. Price & Morgan, 13
Cabin cruiser, 205
Cadets, 233
Calder Rocks, Alaska, 121-2
Caldwell, Lt., 19
Caleb Cushing, 24
California (State), 17
Call, Dr. S.J., 265
Campbell, 67-8, 163, 218
Canada, 145, 167
Canadians rescued, 279-80
Cape Bartolome, 123
Cape Canaveral, Fla., 222
Cape Cod, Mass., 15, 54, 186-7
Cape Cross, 207
Cape Flattery Light Station, 117-20
Cape Florida Light, 57
Cape Hatteras Light, 100
Cape Hatteras, N.C., 65-6, 194, 224, 278
Cape Henry, Va., 30, 97
Cape Horn, S.A., 17
Cape Knox, 207-8
Cape Lookout, N.C., 66
Cape May, N.J., 65, 162, 223, 239, 250
Cape Race, Newfoundland, 170
Cape Wankerem, 133
Captain-commandant, 15, 16
"Captain of the Port," 178-80, 206, 240
Cardenas, Cuba, 32, 36
Cargo carrier, 223, 235-6
Caribbean, 32-3, 78, 161, 173
Cary Island, 31
Casco (tug), 24, 175
Castle Rock, 86, 165, 170, 192
Cat Lo, 83

Cavite Arsenal, P.I., 36
Cayuga, 62, 65
Central America, 152
Certificate of Compliance, 154
Certificate of Inspection, 158-9
Chamberlain, Neville, 59
Champlain, 62, 65
Chance Vought, 55
Chandeleur Island, G. of Mexico, 25
Charles Towne, 209
Charleston, S.C., 10, 13, 100, 180
Charleston Harbor, 20
Chase, Salmon P., 21, 23-5
Chelan, 62, 65
Chesapeake, 104
Chesapeake Bay, 9, 21, 23-5, 66, 99, 106, 110, 129
Chesapeake Lightship, 110-1
Chesapeake Offshore Light Structure, 110-1
Chicamacomico, N.C., 45, 194
Chief of Revenue Marine Bureau, 16
China, 13, 80
China Trade, 33, 35
Chincoteague, 169-70
Chinese Catholic Society, 236
Chronometer, 13
Chu Lai, 203
Chukchi Sea, 175
Churchill, Sir Winston, 45, 60
Circular letter, 21
Civil War, 18-25, 27, 33
Civilian Conservation Corps, 57
Clarence (Conf. raider), 24
Cle Elum, Washington, 283
"Clean sweep," 168
Clermont, 153
Cleveland, Ohio, 14, 191, 290
Clipper ships, 13
Co Chien River, 84
Coast Guard. *See* U.S. Coast Guard
Coast Survey, 16
Coastal Surveillance Forces, 83
Coasts, 15, 224
Coffin, E.A., 48
Cohasset, 187
Colfax, 33
Collector of Customs, 268
Colleges, Military, 161
Collier, J., 17
Columbia River, 93
Columbia University, 173
Comanche, 60, 63
Combat artist, 7
Command at Sea, 207-14
Commander of Union Forces, 23
Commercial Vessel Safety Program, 75, 93, 152-60, 185, 187
Commissioner of Revenue, 99
Commissions, 2, 251
Committee on Naval Affairs, 15
Commodore Perry, 21
Communications Center, N.Y., 76
Communists, 80-1
Computer Information, 215, 225

Con Son Loran Station, Vietnam, 114
Confederacy's Stars and Bars, 19
Confederates, 20-2
Congress, 2, 3, 5, 10, 15, 20, 27-8, 31, 34, 40, 44-5, 53, 55, 60, 75, 97, 99, 100, 103, 129, 147, 153, 161, 177, 183, 185, 188, 231, 274
Congressional Lifesaving Medal, 45, 278
Congressional Medal, 48, 285
Conservation, 149
    enforcement, 152
Controllable-pitch, 151-2
Convoy, 205, 218
Cook Inlet, 86, 170
Coolidge, Calvin, 51
Coos Bay, 193
Cornish, James, 140
Corpus Christi, Tex., 152
Corwin, 21, 131, 133, 171, 260
"Cotton fleet," 22
Courier, 176, 185, 235
Cowslip (Br. sloop), 122
Cox and Green, 255
Craney Island, Chesapeake Bay, 106
Crawford, 19, 21
Crerie, Capt. John, 6
Crew stations, 59, 211
Crisfield, Md., 74
Crocus, 98
Cronin, Mrs. Agnes Rizutto, 273
Cross Rip Lightship, 109
Cruising stations, 188
Cruzen, R. Adm. Richard H., 140
Cryolite, 60-1
Cuba, 33
    exiles, 33, 152
    refugees, 76-7, 207
Cuban Patrol, 76
Cullen, John C., 71-2
Cummins diesel parts, 238
Curtis Bay, Md., 102, 199, 241
Curtiss Flying Boat, 220
Customs Bureau, 158
Customs Collectors, 11, 21
Customs laws, 2, 151
Customs Officers, 16, 27
Cutter fleet, 22, 31, 65
Cutters, 66-7, 71, 81, 187, 241
    armed, 161
    cost, 2
    iron ships, 15
    Lake Class, 65
    "Secretary Class," 65
    service pay, 2, 10
    Squadron One, 81
    Squadron Three, 83
    steam, 15
Cutters
    See also: *Acacia, Acushnet, Active, Agassiz, Alabama, Alert, Alexander Hamilton, Algonquin, Androscoggin, Antietam, Atka, Bear, Bedloe, Bering Strait, Bibb,*

Cutters (*cont.*)

Bittersweet, Boston, Boutwell, Bowdoin, Bramble, Burton Island, Caleb Cushing, Campbell, Cape Cross, Cape Knox, Casco, Castle Rock, Cayuga, Champlain, Chelan, Chincoteague, Colfax, Comanche, Cook Inlet, Coos Bay, Corwin, Courier, Crawford, Dallas, Dexter, Dianthus, Diligence, Dobbin, Duane, Eagle, Eastwind, Edisto, Escanaba, Evergreen, Ewing, Faunce, Forward (Walter), Gallatin, Galveston, General Greene, Glacier, Grant, Gresham, Guthrie, Hamilton, Harriet Lane, Hercules, Hudson, Icarus, Ingham, Iris, Itasca, Jackson, Jeanette, Jefferson, Jeremiah S. Black, Kickapoo, Lawrence, Legare, Lewis Cass, Lincoln, Louisiana, McClelland, McCulloch, Mackinaw, McLane, Madison, Manning, Marion, Massachusetts, Matagorda, Mellon, Mendota, Merrick, Miami, Midgett, Mojave, Morrill, Morris, Mount Olympus, Munro, Nashville, Nemeha, North Star, Northland, Northwind, Oliver Wolcott, Jr., Olympia, Onondaga, Ossippee, Owasco, Penrose, Phillip Allen, Pickering, Point Chico, Point Comfort, Point Garnet, Point Grey, Point League, Point Marone, Point Partridge, Point Slocum, Point Warde, Polk, Pontchartrain, Portsmouth, Raritan, Redwing, Reliance, Rockaway, Rush, Saranac, Sebago, Seminole, Seneca, Shackle, Shawnee, Sherman, Shoshone, Smith, Snohomish, Southwind, Spar, Spencer, Staten Island, Storis, Surveyor, Swiftsure, Tahoe, Tahoma, Tampa, Taney, Tern, Thetis, Tiger, Van Buren, Vigilant, Walker, Washington, Wayanda, Westwind, White Holly, Windom, Windsor, Winona, Wolcott, Woodbine, Woodbury, Yakutat, Yancey

Da Nang, 82
Dade, Francis, 10
Dallas, 9, 15, 36
Dana, Richard Henry, 154
Dangerous Cargo Act, 60, 181
Daniels, J.T., 48
Dart 6
Dauphin Island, Ala., 238
Davidson, George, 131
Davis South Shoal (lightship), 106
Davis Strait, 171
Dean of Women, 184
Denmark, 60, 62, 167

Department of Transportation. *See* U.S. Transportation Dept.
Depression, The, 56-7, 79, 183
Dewey, Adm. George C., 35-6, 43, 101
Dexter, Dwight H., 284
Dexter, 36, 249
Diamond (Cartel Brig), 6
Diamond Shoals Lightship, 107-8, 275
Dianthus, 68
Dien Bien Phu, 80
Diesel system, 195
Diligence, 78
Direction finder, 67
Dix, John A., 19
Dobbin, 28, 231
Documentation Section, 158
Donohue, Robert, 48
Dope, 53
Dorchester, 63, 288
Douglas A. Munro Hall, 286
Douglas Dolphin, 220
Downes (destroyer), 51
Dred Scott, 19
Driver, Foster, 158-9
Drury's Bluff, Va., 22
Dry Pass, 123
Duane, 61, 163
Dundee, Scotland, 31
Dunedin, New Zealand, 141
Duong-Dong, S. Vietnam, 82
Dye markers, 145

E.A. Stevens. See Naugatuck
Eagle 4, 6, 8, 227, 232-5
    Horst Wessel, 233
    world ports, 234
East India trade, 13
East Siberian Sea, 135
Eastern Area Headquarters, 240
Eastwind, 135, 139
    Operation Deep Freeze, 137
Eaton, P.B., 48
Ecology, 147, 173
Economic depression, 5
Eddystone Light, England, 103
Edisto, 77, 135, 137, 139
Eighth District Units, 238
El Estero, 177-8, 181
Electronics, 73, 76, 93, 109, 113, 236
    aircraft, 221
    computer, 215
    engineers, 76, 225
    repairs, 185
Elizabeth City Complex, 216-7, 219, 224
Elizabeth River, Va., 108
Ellis, John F., 155
Ellis Island, N.Y., 177
Embargo Act, 5
Emergency at sea, 215
Emergency training, 161
England, 5, 13, 22-3, 44, 70-1, 145
Ensign and pennant, 5
Enterprise Oil Co., 156-8
Equalant II, 175

Equatorial Islands, 163
Erickson, Frank, 225
Escanaba, 63, 205, 287-90
    Memorial, 289
Eskimos, 31, 61, 141, 262
Espionage Act, 45, 60, 177, 179-81
Estella (whaler), 263
Evans, Raymond, 283
Evergreen, 41, 155, 173-4
Ewing, 15
Explosives, 145, 150, 178-81

Fascism, 59
Fairfax (U.S. transport), 205
Fajardo, P.R., 209
Farley, R. Adm. J.F., 274
Fathometer, 171
Faunce, Captain, 20
Faunce, 55
Federal Boat Safety Act, 130
Federal credit, 2
Federal Port Agents, 154
Federal Republic of Germany, 169
Federal revenue protection, 23
Federal sovereignty. *See* National Sovereignty
Federal Stock Number system, 237
Federal Treasury. *See* National Treasury
Federal Union, 19
Fengar, Alvin A., 23
Fernessia, 39
Fessenden, 22
Fiberglass boat, 176
"Fifth Auditor," 99
Filchner's Ice Shelf, 134
Fireboat, 178
First amphibious landing, 10
First ship radio, 38
Fish and game, 149
Flea Fleet, 146
Fleet Air Wing I, 169
Floating police, 147
Florida (State), 10, 19, 21, 149
    Forts, 10
    Governor, 10
    Keys, 10, 66, 207
    Seminole Indians, 10, 19
    Straits, 32, 53, 76
Florida, 39
Florida Board of Conservation, 173
Flotilla, 20, 22, 24, 70, 76, 284
Floyd Bennett Field, 225
Flying Dutchman, 107
Flying Fortress, 63
Flying Lifeboat, 45, 222-4
Foam, 203, 238
Fog signal, 105
Fokker, 223
Forest City, 24
Formal Board of Investigation, 159
Fort Brook, Fla., 10
Fort Clark, 20
Fort Hatteras, N.C., 20

Fort King, Fla., 10
Fort Lauderdale, Fla., 54
Fort Moultrie, S.C., 10, 250
Fort Sumter, S.C., 19-21
Fort Trumbull, Conn., 230, 232
Forward, 14, 24, 32, 33
Foss, Capt. Alex, 45
Fox, Rev. George L., 63
France, 44, 60, 80, 167, 177
    physicist, 97
Franco, Colonel Francisco, 59
Franklin, Benjamin, 104
Franklin, Sir John, 31
Fraser, Alexander V., 11-18, 27, 253
Freebooters, 10
Freeport, Fla., 238
French, 2-5
    brig, 7
    privateers, 3
    raiders, 4-5
Fresnel, Augustin, 97, 101
Fresnel prismatic lens, 97, 101, 104-5
Freud, 19
Fulton, Robert, 153
"Furious fifties," 141

Gallatin, 249-50
Galveston, Tex., 20, 189
Galveston, 36
Gas turbine, 195
Gay's Head Martha's Vineyard, Mass., 106
Gedney's Channel, N.Y., 98
General Greene, 60, 172
Georgia (State), 21
Germany, 43, 57, 59-60, 65, 177
    ships, 62, 137
    station, Loran, 112
    submarine, 65-8, 107-8
Gertrude Abbott, 255-6
Gibraltar, 38, 44
Gillis, R.F. 48
Glacier (icebreaker), 134-5
Glenn Curtiss organization, 45, 47
Gloucester, Mass., 207
Gold Lifesaving Medal, 224
Gold Rush, 17
Goode, Rabbi Alexander D., 63
Governor General of the Philippines, 34
Governor's Island, N.Y., 173, 194, 215, 240
Grand Cross, The, 277
Grand Haven, Mich., 63
    Coast Guard City, U.S.A., 287-90
Grand River, Mich., 287
Grant, 38, 171
Great Britain, 5, 65, 177
Great Lakes, 78, 98, 135, 187
    ferries, 135
    icebreaker, 143-4, 206
    Pilotage Staff, 90
Greece, 145
Greely, Adolphus Washington, 31
Green Bay (freighter), 109

Greenland, 58, 60, 61, 63, 78, 135, 137, 146, 174
    Ivigtut, 60
    Patrol, 60, 62-3, 270, 288
Greenland glaciers, 40, 145
Greenland Ice Cap, 63, 179, 282
Gresham, 39, 40, 168
Griffin, C., 48
Group Miami, 207-8
Grumman Albatross, 73, 221
Grumman Gulfstream II, 216
Guadalcanal, 70, 284
Guantanamo Bay, Cuba, 161
Gulf of Campeche, 152
Gulf of Mexico 32-3, 66, 147, 152
Gulf shrimpers, 152
Guns, 190, 194
Guthrie, 36

HAR. *See* Harbor Advisory Radar System
H.C. Higginson, 256
Hall, Al K., 158-9
Hall, Norman B., 45, 47
Hamburg, Germany, 233
Hamilton, Alexander 1-2, 40, 65, 97, 151, 161, 198
    Founding Father, 245-8
Hamilton, 33, 36, 195-8, 250
Hamilton, Hall, 227
Hampton Roads, Va., 16, 19, 36
Harbor Advisory Radar System, 93, 102
Harbor cutter, 49
Harbor tug, 205-6
Harper's Ferry, W.Va., 19
Harriet Lane, 17, 20-1
Hatteras, N.C., 25
Hatteras Inlet Sea Buoy, 217
Havana, Cuba, 10, 34
Hawaii, 113
Hayes, George, 15
Healy, Michael A., 31
    black hero, 259-64
Hearst, William Randolph, 34
Helga Bolten, 169-70
Helicopter 55, 75, 90, 107, 125, 138, 217, 219-21, 225-7, 238
    amphibious, 75, 151, 197
    "Jolly Green Giant," 90
    "Pelican," 91
Henrietta (yacht), 24
Henry, Joseph, 101
Hercules, 24, 219
"Hi Lo," 215
Himmaleh, 13
Hirshfield, V. Adm. James A., 67-8
Hitler, Adolf, 59, 65, 165
Ho Chi Minh, 80
Hoboken, N.J., 21, 177
Hog Island, Va., 250
Hohenzollerns, 43
Holdman, Sandow, 181
Holland, 60, 167
Hollingshead, Platt & Company of Phila., Pa., 13

Hollowell Plantation, 224
Holmes, Adm. Ephraim P., 224
Honolulu, Hawaii, 163, 191, 197, 201, 203, 235, 236
Honolulu Rescue Coordination Center, 195
Hood (Br. warship), 109
Hornbeam (b. tender), 109
Horsepower, 196
Horst Wessel. See Eagle
Hospital Point Light, Mass., 96
Houghton, Wash., 169
House of Representatives, 15
Houston, Texas, 151
Hover 01, 92
Hover 02, 92
Howard, Capt. W.A., 13, 16, 130
Howell Cobb, 21
Hudson, 32, 36-7, 45
Hull, Mass., 256
Hurricanes, 237
    Betsy, 219-20
    Carol, 109
    Edna, 109
Hyde, Capt. Amasa L., 24
Hydrofoil, 209

Iberian Peninsula, 59
Icarus, 66
Ice floes, 140
Ice Patrol. *See* International Ice Patrol
Ice ships, 31
Icebergs, 40, 141, 144, 171
    dye markers, 145
    spotting, 145, 174
Icebreakers, 55, 77-8, 135, 137-42, 171, 173, 195
    Edisto, 77
Icebreaking, 131-46, 171
Iceland, 62, 167
    Loran Station, 112
I'm Alone (Can.), 54
Indo-China, 79
Industrial College of the Armed Forces, 161
Industrial revolution, 33
Ingham, 163
Integration program, 185
Intergovermental Maritime Consultative Organization, 76
International cooperation, 216
International Ice Patrol, 40, 79, 145-6, 171, 174, 221
International safety, 76
International Whaling Treaty, 149
Ireland, 167
Iris, 122
Iron steamers, 15
Ironsides. See Naugatuck
Italy, 57, 60, 62, 145
Itasca, 62, 65
Iwo Jima, 169

J.P. Morgan and Co., 177
Jackson, Andrew, 10, 13, 19, 251, 269
Jackson, Dr. Sheldon, 31, 262

Jackson, 24, 109, 249
Jacob Jones (destroyer), 66
Jakobshavn, Greenland, 139
James, Joshua, 188
    burial, 257
    greatest lifesaver, 255-7
James River, Va., 22
Jamestown, Va., 33
Japan, 13, 59, 70, 73, 145, 169, 201, 269, 283
    hegemony, 59
    Loran station, 113
    Pearl Harbor, 61, 63, 65
    surrender, 167
Jarvis, Anna T., 268
Jarvis, David H., 265-8
Jeanette, 133
Jefferson, Thomas, 1, 5, 97
Jefferson, 6
Jennings, Charles H., 105
Jeremiah S. Black, 24
Jersey City, N.J., 177
Jester, Maurice D., 66
Jewett, Jehediah, 24
John A. Macdonald (Can.), 142
Johnson, Andrew, 28
Johnston Island, 113
"Jolly Green Giant." *See* Helicopter

Kadish, Leonard, 160
Kalenin, Alexis, 265
Kankakee, 22
Kava Sea, 135
Kearny (destroyer), 62
Kennedy, John F., 79
Ketchikan, Alaska, 123, 125
Ketchikan Base, 120
Kewanee, 22
Key West, Fla., 25, 33, 36, 66, 76, 78
    Naval Base, 36, 78
Kickapoo, 135
Kill Devil Hill Lifeboat Station, N.C., 45, 48
Kimball, Sumner I., 27, 188
King, Ernest J., 274
Kitty Hawk, N.C., 45, 48
Korea, 79
Korean War, 163, 184
Kotzebue Sound, Alaska, 266
Kritoi Basin, 125
Kukui, 195, 235-6
Kure Island, 112-3

LNB. *See* Navigational aids
Labrador, 135
Lady Franklin Bay Expedition, 31
Lady Le Merchant, 23
Lady of the Lake, 145
Laffitte, Alexander, 10
Laffitte, Jean, 9, 10, 147
Lake Charles, La., 160
Lake Class cutters, 62
Lake Washington Shipyard, 169
Lamby, Victor, 54
Lamp black, 145

Lamp fuels, 104
Laptev Sea, 135
Law enforcement, 147-52, 187
Lawrence, Capt. James, 104
Lawrence, 16-7
Lee, Adm. S.P., 23
Lee, Robert E., 19
Legare, 16
Legion of Merit, 181
L'Egypte Conquise, 5
Lewis Cass, 19
Liberia, 145
Life Magazine, 201
Lifeboat Stations, 28, 188
Lifeboats, 155, 187, 189
Lifeboatman's Endorsement, 158
Lifesaving Service 27-8, 40-1, 183, 188
Lifesaving Stations, 28, 30, 187-8, 256
Light stations, 62
Lighthouse, 97-100
    keepers, 104-5, 117
Lighthouse Board, 101
Lighthouse Establishment, 25
Lighthouse Service, 2, 16, 57, 98, 101, 106, 117, 187
    Commissioner, 101
    pension laws, 101
Lighthouse tender, 98
"Lighthouse Tragedy," 104
Lightship, 16, 100, 106-9, 173
Lincoln, Abraham, 18-21, 23
Lincoln, 28-30, 78, 131, 171, 174
Linwood, 50
Little America Number Four, 140
Little Brewster Island, Mass., 103
Little Kinakeet Life Saving Station, 186
Livingston, Robert, 1
Lockheed Corp., 136-7
Lodge, Henry Cabot, 33
London, England, 40, 167
Long Beach, Calif., 69, 201
Long Island, N.Y., 6, 15, 62
Long Range Aid to Navigation. *See* Loran
Lopez, Gen. Narciso, 33
Lopp, Rev. William, 266
Loran, 39, 57, 75-6, 86, 102, 115-6, 145, 236
    Loran "C," 91, 116
    operation, 115-6
Loran Stations, 112-4, 221
    calibration flights, 221
Louisiana (State), 21
Louisiana, 10
Ludington, Mich., 160
Luke, Dorothy A., 272
Lunar observations, 13
Lusitania, 177
Lyle gun, 190, 194

MILSTRIPS, 238
MIO. *See* Marine Inspection Office
MMT. *See* Merchant Marine Technical
McClelland, 19

McCluskey, Leroy, 61
McCulloch, 16, 34-5, 37
Machias, 36
Mackenzie, Alexander Slidell, 254
Mackinaw, 135, 143-4, 290
    commissioned, 143
    water transfer system, 144
McKinley, William, 33-4, 37, 265
McLane, Louis, 188, 248
    Builder of a Service, 249-51
    career, 251
McLane, 15, 16, 33, 36, 249
McMurdo Sound, 140
Madison, 6
Magnuson Act, 181
Magruder, General, 20
Mahan, Alfred Thayer, 33
Mahoning, 22
Maine (U.S. battleship), 34
Major. *See* Sarany and Major
Malayan Archipelago, 13
Malew, W.R., 48
Man-O'-War Anchorage, Hong Kong, 34
Manhattan (supertanker icebreaker), 78, 135, 142
Manifest destiny, 33
Manila Bay, P.I., 34-6, 43, 79
Manning, 38, 44
Manzanito, 29
Marconi, Guglielmo, 39, 40
Marine Conservation, 90
Marine Inspection Office, 156-60
    Officer in Charge (OCMI), 156
Marine Maritime Academy, 158
Marine safety, 73, 75-6, 86, 90, 93
Marine sciences, 30, 41, 90
    M.S. Technician (MST), 173
Mariners Museum, 42-3
Marion, 171-4
Maritime Administration, 235
Marshall Islands, 169
    Eniwetok, 169
    Kwajalein, 169
Martinac Shipyard, 209
Mary Langdon, 56
Maryland (State), 74
Massachusetts (State), 33
    Senator, 33
Massachusetts, 3
Massachusetts Bay, 103
Massachusetts Humane Society 187-8, 255
    Life Boat Station, 256
Master, 2, 3, 13
"Master and Mate," 3, 13
Matagorda, 191
Matanzas Bay, Cuba, 36
Mathematical formulae, 15
Mathematical, Nautical, and Commercial School, N.Y., 13
Maureen & Michael, 192
Mayaguez, P.R., 209
Mead, Lt., 37
Meade, Gen. George Gordon, 101

Medals, 45, 48, 68, 71, 169, 181, 224, 256, 278, 285
Mediterranean, 34
Meduskey, J., 48
Mehitabel (brig), 7
Mekong Delta, 203
Melka, L.M., 48
Mellon, 197
Melville, R. Adm. George W., 133
Melville, Herman, 154
Mendota, 62, 65
Merchant Marine Technical Branch (MMT), 156
Merchant shipping, 5
Merchant vessels, 215
Merit system, 11, 13, 27
Merrick, 140-1
Mexican War of 1845, 14-5, 17, 19
Mexico, 152
Meyers, J., 48
Miami, Fla., 207-8, 222
    radio station, 241
    Nassau race, 208
Miami, 23
Midgett, John Allen, 45
    burning sea, 275-6
Midgett, 90
Military ranks, 3
Military Readiness, 161-3
Miller, Mark F., 175
Minefields, 36
Minneapolis Shoals Lighthouse, 206
Minnesota (State), 49
Mirlo (Br. tanker), 45, 275-8
Mirs Bay, China, 34
Missile crisis, 78
Mississippi (State), 21
Mississippi River, 101
Missouri River, 101
Mistinguette, 50
Mobile, Ala., 19, 224
Mobile Point Light, 99
Modoc (tug), 60, 204
Mojave, 63, 205
Monitor, 22
Monomoy Point Lifesaving Station, 257
Monroe, James, 33
Monroe Doctrine, 33
Monsanto Chemical Co., 178
Montauk Point,L.I., N.Y., 106
Montauk Point Light, N.Y., 99
Morgenthau, Henry, 55
Morrill, 33, 36
Morris, 250
Morrison, Capt. James J., 19
Mosquito fleet, 36
Motor Lifeboat, 210-5
Motor surfboat, 75, 93, 276
Motorboat Act, 129, 130
Motorboat regulations, 129-30
Mount Olympus, 140
Munitions, 177-82
Munro, Douglas, 283-6
Munro, 285
Munro Hall, 284

Musical fountain, 289
Mussolini, Benito, 59

NOAA. *See* National Oceanographic Atmospheric Administration
Nancy (brig), 7
Nanok (trawler), 63
Nanshan, 35
Nantucket, 106-9
Nantucket Sound, 106
Napeaque (trawler), 217-21
Narcissus (man-of-war), 6
Narsarssuak, Greenland, 205, 288
Nashville, 20
Nassif Building, 88
National Archives, 46, 97
National defense, 161
National Historic Landmark, 105
National Navigation Plan, 76
National Oceanographic Atmospheric Administration (NOAA), 91, 92, 174
National Oceanographic Data Center, 173
"National Plan for Navigation," 102
National Socialists (Nazi), 59, 60
National Sovereignty, 5, 19
National Treasury, 1, 2, 4, 5
National War College, 161
Natsek (trawler), 63
Naugatuck, 21, 22
    (*Ironsides* or *E. A. Stevens*)
Naulo Point, 235
Naval affairs, 15
Naval Base, 36
Naval engines, 151
Naval force, 34
Naval Patrol Force, 23
Naval victory, 36
Naval War College, 161
Navigation & Nautical Astronomy, 13
Navigational aids, 76, 91, 96, 173, 225
    LNB, 91, 103-26
    regulations, 153
Navy, 2, 5, 40, 81
    N. Cross, 68
    cutters assigned, 21, 28, 31, 40
    flagship, 20
    fleet units, 78
    gun boats, 36
    See also U.S. Navy
Navy Atlantic Fleet, 224
Navy Aviation School, 47-8
Navy Blue Angels, 290
Navy Damage Control School, 169
Nemeha, 24
Netherlands, 145
Neutrality laws, 147
New Beford, Mass., 231
New England, 62, 100
New Guinea Campaign, 169
New Hampshire (State), 3
New Haven, Conn., 6
New Jersey (State), 15 28, 45

New London, Conn., 152, 227, 229-30, 232-3, 284
New Orleans, La., 10, 19, 237, 285
New Orleans Mint, 238
New Orleans Supply Depot, 238
New York (State), 6, 13, 15, 22, 24, 33, 34, 163, 215, 225
New York Herald, 24
New York Sun 260
New York Times, 53
Newburyport, Mass., 3
Newcomb, Frank H., 36, 37
Newfoundland, 46, 63, 192
Newfoundland's Grand Banks, 145, 171
Newport, R.I., 107
Newport News, Va., 42
Newspapers, 34, 36, 53, 260
Nietzsche, 59
Nixon, Richard M., 131, 170, 185
No. 58, 107
Nones, Capt. Henry B., 14, 17
Nore (Br. lightship), 106
Norfolk, Va., 23, 38, 81, 162, 168, 169, 196, 206-7, 234
Norfolk Navy Yard, 21
Normandy, 70
North Africa, 70, 163
North Atlantic Blockading Squadron, 23
North Carolina (State), 20, 21, 100, 107, 186
North Pacific fur seal, 79
North Polar Basin, 140
North Star, 60
North Vietnam, 80, 82
Northeast Passage, 141-2
Northeastern Atlantic coast, 78
Northland, 58, 60-1, 63, 131, 135, 137, 279-82
Northwest Fisheries Company, 268
Northwest Passage, 78, 135, 138
Northwind (icebreaker), 75, 131, 135, 137-42, 175, 271
    "Firsts," 135
    name change, 139
Norway, 60, 145, 167

ORTUPS, 60, 181
Ocean Stations, 163, 165-70
    Charlie, 167
    Delta, 169
    Hotel, 168
    November, 163, 201, 203
    Romeo, 203
    Sugar, 201
    Victor, 163, 203
Ocean Station Vessels, 41, 163, 165-70
Ocean Station Vessel Program, 79, 173, 201
Oceanographic ship, 41
Oceanographic Unit, 173
Oceanography, 60, 63, 78, 141, 169, 171-6, 231
    Bachelor of Science, 231
    survey, 134
Officers' Candidate School, 182, 184
Offshore oil, 149

Offshore towers, 110-1, 173
Ogg, Richard, 201
Ohio River, 101
Oil
    barge, 135
    rigs, 152
    spills, 90-1
Okinawa, 163
Oklahoma (State), 92
"Old Hickory." *See* Jackson, Andrew
Oliver Wolcott, Jr., 172
Olympia (flagship), 36
Olympic (liner), 109
O'Malley, Raymond, 289
Omar Babun (Honduras), 194
Onondaga, 42
Operation Deep Freeze, 78, 137
Operation High Jump, 139, 140
    task group, 140
Operation Market Time, 81, 83-4, 86
Operation Oil Can, 206
Ordnance training, 162
Oregon (State), 93, 210-13
Oregon Inlet, N.C., 128, 194
Oregon and California Territories, 16
Orleans Station, 186
Osceola, 10
Ossippee, 44
Ott, George, 48
Ottinger, Capt. Douglas, 28
Outer Continental Shelf Lands Act, 1, 149
Overland Expedition, 265-66, 268
Overstreet, Dr., 17
Owasco, 84

Pacific fleet, 169
Pacific fur seal, 31
Pacific lighthouse, 101
Paddle-wheels, 15
    ferries, 135
Pan American Clipper, 200-3
Panama, 145
    steamer, 18
Panama Canal, 152
Paraguay, 20
Parker, S.V., 48
Parrot gun, 22
Pasquotank River, N.C., 224
Patoka (river tender), 92
Patriot, 6
Paterson, N.J., 157
Patrol Boat, 205-10
Pawtuxet, 22
Pearl Harbor, 61, 63, 65, 143, 162, 163, 269, 283
"Pelican." *See* Helicopters
"Pelican hook," 122
Penobscot River, Maine, 132
Penrose, 36
Pensacola, Fla., 47-8
Pernambuco, Brazil, 20
Petroleum fields, 142
Philadelphia, Pa., 2, 145, 218, 264
Phillip Allen, 24

Philippines, 34, 36, 208, 235, 236
    Cavite Arsenal, 36
    Sangley Point, 36
Philippine Sea (carrier), 141
Phu Quoc, 82
Pickering, 4, 5
"Piggy-back" gun, 85
Piracy and slavery, 9, 147, 161
Pirate fleet, 10
Pitch, 196
Pitkin, Dr. York Nones, 14
Pizza wagon, 221
Pleasanton, Stephen, 99, 100
Pleasure boating, 127, 207, 209, 211
Plymouth, England, 46
Point Barrow, Alaska, 78, 266-8
Point Chico, 92
Point Comfort, 82
Point Garnet (patrol craft), 81, 83
Point Grey (patrol craft), 81, 83
Point Highland, 74
Point League, 84
Point Marone, 208
Point Partridge, 85
Point Rodney, Alaska, 265
Point Slocum, 85
Point Warde, 208-10
Poland, 68, 165
Polar icebreakers, 137-42, 195
Poling, Rev. Clark V., 63
Polk, 16
Pollard, Francis G., 280
Pollution flights, 222
Pontchartrain, 62, 65, 199-203
Port Angeles, Wash., 42, 283
Port De Quervain, Greenland, 174
Port Isabel, Tex., 238
Port Royal, S.C., 25
Port safety and security, 177-82
Port Security, 45, 60, 176, 185, 187
    Officer, 179
Porter, Adm. David, 10, 20
Porter, Capt. Winslow, 16
Portholes, 39, 41
Portland, Maine, 24, 134, 234
Portsmouth, Va., 217
Portsmouth, 250
Potomac River, 23
Power engineering, 15
Powers, J.F., 48
Practical Shipyard, 157
Pratt and Whitney, 196
Presidents of U.S.
    See Adams, John; Buchanan, James; Coolidge, Calvin; Jackson, Andrew; Jefferson, Thomas; Johnson, Andrew; Kennedy, John F.; Lincoln, Abraham; McKinley, William; Monroe, James; Nixon, Richard M.; Roosevelt, Franklin D.; Roosevelt, Theodore; Taft, William H.; Truman, Harry S; Washington, George

President's Proclamation, 21

Pribilof Islands, 31
    seal rookeries, 262
Princeton University, 43
Prinz Eugen (Ger. battleship), 60
Pritchard, John A., 279-81
Pritchard, John K., 63
Privateer, 5
Prohibition, 49-58, 183
Prohibition Amendment, 47
    laws, 150
Propulsion, 15, 144, 152, 195, 196
    side-wheel, 15
    underwater, 15
Protectionist measures, 2
Provincetown, Mass., 39
Prudhoe Bay, Alaska, 78, 142
Public lands, 149
Pulitzer, Joseph, 34
Purdue University, 184
Pusey and Jones Co., 32
Putnam, George R., 101
"Pyrene," 222

Quarantine laws, 147
"Queen of the Pacific," 163
Qui Nhon, 82

Radio
    beacons, 62, 101-2, 109, 119, 167
    silence, 165
    station, 241
Radiosonde balloons, 167
"Radius," 215
Raritan, 60, 63, 205-6
Rats, 113-4
Read, Charles W., 24
Reade, A.C., 47
Ready Reserve, 185
Rear Range, 99
Red Birch (buoy tender), 102
Red Jacket, 148
Red Wing, 56
"Refresher Training," 161
Refuse Act of 1899, 150
"Regular Reserve," 184
Reindeer, 258, 262, 266
Reliance, 131, 150-3
Republic, 39
Rescue basket, 219-21, 226
    fleet, 31
    unit, 207-16
Research, 90
Reserve Program Administrator, 185
Reserve Training Center, 182
Resident Inspectors, 157
Reuben James, 62
Revenue Act, 2
Revenue Captains, 21
Revenue Cutter, 3, 7, 14, 24, 25, 78, 128
Revenue Cutter Service, 2, 5, 8, 14, 15, 17, 19, 21, 25, 27, 28, 31, 33, 37, 40-1, 127, 129, 151, 161, 250, 264
    law enforcement, 251

Revenue fleet, 2, 9, 40, 72, 147
Revenue Marine, 2, 6, 9, 10, 11, 13
    Bureau, 11, 15, 16, 27, 188
Revenue Service, 5, 13, 15-18, 21, 254
Reykjavik, Iceland, 163
Rhodes, Greece, 176
Rio de Janeiro, Brazil, 17
Rio Grande, 21
Richmond, Va., 22
Rivers
    See Cho Chien, Columbia, Eliza-
    beth, Grand, James, Mississippi,
    Missouri, Ohio, Pasquotank, Pe-
    nobscot, Potomac, Rio Grande,
    Schuylkill, Tabasco, Thames,
    Umpqua, York
Robbins Reef Lighthouse, 181
Rockaway, N.Y., 46
Rockaway, 173, 193
Roland, Adm. E.J., 79, 151
Roland Field House, 229, 232
Roosevelt, Franklin D., 59, 60, 62, 65,
    70, 101, 135, 179, 269
Roosevelt, Theodore, 33, 34, 43
Roper (destroyer), 66
Rosario (whaler), 267
Ross Sea, 139, 141
    ice shelf, 140-1
Royal Humane Society of England, 187
Rubber raft, 192, 202
Rudolph, Capt. T.C., 33
"Rules of the Road," 149
Rum Fleet, 49-58
Rumrunners, 49
Rush, 90, 100, 171-2, 260
Russia, 43, 59, 78, 80, 131, 135, 137,
    141, 142

SAR. See Search and Rescue
SIO. See Senior Investigating Officer
SOS, 39
SPAR. See Service Women's Reserve
Saboe Bay, Santa Cruz Islands, 169
Sabotage, 45
Saigon, 83, 86
St. Johns, Newfoundland, 205, 288
St. Louis, 34
St. Martin, V.I., 209
St. Michael, Alaska, 265
St. Thomas, V.I., 209
Salary, 2, 10
Sallisaw, Okla., 92
Salmon P. Chase, 231
Sampson, Adm. William Thomas, 36
San Antonio, Tex., 55
San Diego, Cal., 55, 162
San Francisco, Cal., 17, 28, 34, 49, 78,
    92-3, 102, 163, 201
    Collector of Customs, 17
San Francisco Examiner, 36
San Juan, P.R., 209
San Pedro, Cal., 137
Sanderlin, Sydney, 54
Sandy Hook, N.J., 91, 225
Sangley Point, P.I., 36

Sanibel Island, 36
Santa Paula (liner), 155
Santiago, 38
Saranac, 62, 65
Sarany and Major, 14
Satellites, 168
Satterlee, Charles, 44
Savannah, Ga., 9, 22, 33
"School of Instruction," 28
Schooners, 6, 50, 52
    Wade, 6
    French, 50
Schuylkill River, 3
Science of ecology, 79
Scott, Lt., 37
Scott Island, 139-41
Scottish Marine Biological Assoc., 173
"Screaming sixties," 141
Screw-pile lights, 110
Scripps Institute of Oceanography, 173
Sea weather, 16
Seal trade, 31, 79
    census, 134
    herds, 262-3
Seaplanes, 47, 55
Seaplane tender, 169, 173
Search and Rescue, 76, 93, 125, 137,
    148, 163, 187-204, 207, 209,
    217, 237
Search and Rescue Project, 173
Search and Rescue School, 194
Search and seizure, 5
Seattle, Wash., 119, 137, 142, 204
Sebago, 62, 65
"Secretary" cutters, 65
Secretary of State, 28
Secretary of the Navy, 4, 20, 31, 181
Secretary of the Treasury, 1, 2, 10, 13,
    15, 19, 21, 25, 27, 32, 55, 97,
    99, 100, 127, 151, 178, 188,
    250, 253
Secretary of War, 23, 254
Security regulations, 150
Seminole, 43
Seminole Indians, 10, 19, 57
"Semper Paratus," 25, 41, 72, 162
    marching song, 37
    SPARS, 72, 184
Seneca, 39, 44-5, 47
Senior Investigating Officer, 159
Sennet (submarine), 140
Service Women's Reserve, 181, 184
Sevigny, Edgar, 109
Seward, William H., 28
"Seward's Folly," 28
"Seward's Ice Box," 28
Sewell's Point, 22
Shackle, 134
Shamrock (brig), 6
Shannon (Br.), 104
Shawnee, 58
Sherman, 90
Ship Master. See Master
Shipping Advisor, 86

"Shipping Commissioners," 154, 158
"Ships of Opportunity," 173
Shipwreck drill, 160
Shoemaker, Charles F., 19
Shore stations, 191
Shoshone, 62, 65
Shubrick, Adm. W.B., 101
Siberia, 141
Sicily, 70
Side-wheel, 15, 20, 24
Sikorsky helicopter, 219
Silvatrice, 54
Simpson, William, 202
Singapore, 34
Sitka, Alaska, 28, 171
Small arms training, 162
Smith, Edward H., 60-2
Smith, Adm. Willard J., 224
Smith, 36
Smithsonian Institution, 22, 30, 101,
    131, 173
Smugglers, 2, 3, 27, 50, 51, 53, 151
Snohomish, 42, 132, 272
Solomon Islands, 169
South Carolina (State), 10, 13, 19, 21,
    250
Southwind, 132, 137
"Sovereign of the Skies," 202
Spade rudder, 152
Spain, 57, 59
    Civil War, 59
    Loran station, 113
Spanish
    Admiral Montojo, 36
    Gov. General, 34
    Republic, 59
    Rule, 33
Spanish-American War, 32
Spanish fleet, 36
Spar, 78, 135, 136
Specified contract time, 185
Spencer, John C., 10, 11, 15, 16, 18,
    252
    legacy, 253-4
Spencer, 15-6, 64, 67-8, 163
Squadron One, 81-3
Squadron Three, 83-4
Stand-by status, 208
Stanley, John, 177, 181
Stanton, Edwin M., 23
Stars and Bars, 20
Staten Island, N.Y., 99
Staten Island (icebreaker), 78, 135
States' Rights, 19
Statue of Liberty, 177
Steam cutter, 15, 18, 20
Steam-propelled, 15, 107
Steamboat Inspection Service, 154,
    251
Steamers, 22, 24
    armed, 15
    iron, 15
    Manzanita, 29
    Nashville, 20

Steamship, 13, 39, 153
SS Flotsam (fictional), 156-9
SS Hans Hedtoft, 146
SS Jetsam, 156
SS Plankton, 156
SS Smith Voyager, 193
SS Steel Admiral, 81
"Stevens Battery," 22
Stoddert, Benjamin, 4
Stone, Elmer F., 45-8
Storeships (supply), 35
    Nanshan, 35
    Zafiro, 35
Storis, 63, 78, 131, 135, 137, 205
Strait of Juan de Fuca, 119
Straits of Mackinac, 287
Stratton, Dorothy C., 72, 184
Stringham, S.H., 19
Subic Bay, P.I., 34
    El Fraile Rock, 34-5
    Squadron Three, 83
Submarine. *See* U-boat
Subsistence, 2, 10
Suez Canal, 34
Sugden, C.E., 48
Sun-Arrow, 209
Supertanker, 78
Supply Depot. *See* U.S.C.G. Supply
    Depot
Supply ships, 140
Supreme Court, 19
"Surface Pictures," 215
Surfboat, 168, 186
    Monomoy, 168, 257
Surfmen, 28
Survey vessels, 21
Surveyor, 6
Susan, 6
Sweden, 145, 167
Swiftsure, 250
Szumiel, Alphonse, 61

TV monitors, 196
Tabasco River, Mexico, 14
Tacoma, Wash., 209
Tacony, 24
Taft, William Howard, 40, 43
Tahoe, 62, 65
Tahoma, 271
Tampa, 44, 63, 205
Taney, 33, 163-4
Tariff
    "nullified," 10, 13
    revenue, 2
    sugar, 13
Task Force, 205
Tatoosh Island, Wash., 117-9
Tax dollars, 2
"Tektite" project, 173
Temporary reserve, 181, 184
Tern (buoy tender), 124
Terry (destroyer), 50
Texas (State), 21
Texas City disaster, 178, 181
Texas Gulf Coast, 152

Thailand, 82-3
    Loran Station, 112
Thames River, Conn., 227, 230, 232
Theater of Operation, 70
Thetis, 31
Thiele, E.H., 137
Third District Headquarters, 240
Thomas Bay, 123
Thomas, Capt. Charles W., 140
Thomas Point, Md., 110
Thompson, John W., 57
Thompson, Gen. Wiley, 10
Three platform firefighter, 180
Thrun, C.T., 48
Tiger, 24
Timber, 149
Timber Reserve Act, 251
Titanic, 40, 144, 145
Todd Shipyard, 151
Toledo, Ohio, 206
Towing rig, 140, 144
Tracking system, 215
"Trackline," 215
Trade agreement, 20
Training vessel, 227, 231-4
Trans-Atlantic flight, 48
Transportation, 89
Transportation Appropriation Sub-
    Committee, 185
Travis, Capt. William, 6
Trawler, 125, 217-21
Treasury Fleet, 2, 40
Truman, Harry S., 181
Trust Territory missions, 236
"Trusts," 43
Tugs, 135, 162
Tununak, Alaska, 265
Turbojets, 196
Turkey, 112
    Loran Station, 112
Tuttle, Capt. Francis, 265-6
Twin-turbine, 226
Two Years Before The Mast, 154
Typee and Omoo, 154

U-Boat, 64, 66-8, 72, 107, 109, 163,
    165, 205, 275
U-53, (Ger.), 107-9
Umpqua River, Ore., 210
Unalaska Island, 265
Underwater propulsion, 15
Union fleet, 20, 21
UNIROYAL, Inc., 89
United Fruit Pier, 180
United Kingdom, 167
U.S. Air Force, 90
    Thunderbirds, 290
U.S. Armed Services, 45, 73
U.S. Army Signal Corps., 31
U.S. Border Patrol, 55
U.S. Bureau of Commercial Fisheries,
    173
U.S. Coast Guard,
    Air base, 55, 216-7, 224

U.S. Coast Guard *(cont.)*
    armed forces, 3
    aviation, 45
    beach, patrol, 70-1
Depot, 96
    explosive loading, 87
    headquarters, 76, 85, 215, 290
    marching song, 37
    patrol boats, 68, 74, 83
    rescue fleet, 70
    Reserve, 77, 129, 183, 185
U.S.C.G. Academy, 28, 144, 207,
    227-32
    applicants, 228
    classes, 228-31
    educational options, 230
U.S.C.G. Aircraft Repair & Supply
    Center, 216-7, 221, 224
U.S.C.G. Auxiliary, 71, 76, 129, 183,
    184
    Women's, 72
U.S.C.G. Festival, 287-8
    air show, 290
U.S.C.G. Greater Antilles Section, 209
U.S.C.G. Marine Inspector, 154-6
U.S.C.G. Squadron Three, 203
U.S.C.G. Rescue Coordination Center,
    209, 217
U.S.C.G. Supply Depot, 237-8
U.S.C.G. Training and Supply Center,
    239
U.S.C.G. Umpqua River Station, 210-4
U.S.C.G. Unit Commendation, 152
United States Commerce, 33
U.S. Consul, 23, 60
U.S. Dept. of Commerce, 57, 91, 129,
    156
    Bureau of Marine Inspection, 72
U.S. Dept. of Defense, 76, 208
U.S. Dept. of State, 141
U.S. Dept. of the Interior, 28, 147,
    163
U.S. economy, 43
U.S. Fish and Wildlife, 148
U.S. Inspectors Certificate, 153
U.S. Interior Dept. *See* U.S. Dept of
    the Interior
U.S. Lifesaving Service, 189
U.S. Lighthouse Service. *See* Light-
    house Service
U.S. Lines, 109
U.S. Marine Corps, 221, 284
U.S. Merchant Marine, 75, 153, 177
U.S. Naval strategist, 33
U.S. Navy, 2-5, 31, 33, 44, 62, 161,
    169, 235
    Dept. 28, 161, 230
    pilots, 225
    Military Sea Transportation Service,
    86
U.S. Post Office Dept., 28
U.S. Presidents. *See* Presidents of U.S.
U.S. Revenue Cutter, 4, 5, 14, 22
U.S. Revenue Marine, 23
USS Alacrity, 105

USS Endurance, 90
USS Guadalupe, 84
U.S. Transportation Dept., 75, 88, 89,
    90, 102, 230
    Federal Aviation Administration, 76
U.S. Treasury Dept., 4, 11, 31, 75, 89,
    129, 154, 161, 224
U.S. Weather Bureau, 165
University of Wisconsin, 175
User tax, 103-5

Van Boskerck, Capt. Francis S., 37
Van Buren, 16
Versailles Treaty, 59
Vessels (British)
    Dart, 6
    Diamond (cartel brig), 6
    Dispatch (brig), 8
    Narcissus (man-of-war), 6
    Patriot, 6
    Shamrock (brig), 6
    sloop, 6, 8
Victoria, B.C., 29
Victory, 5
Victory Medal, 45, 278
Viele, Egbert, 23
Viet Cong, 203, 208
Vietnam, 81-8, 90, 163, 170, 203,
    208-9
Vigilant, 6, 148
Vigorous, 152
Viking Flying Boat, 222
Vil'kitskogo Strait, 141
Vineyard Sound, Mass., 109
Virginia (State), 21-3, 108
Virginia Capes, 24
Vixen, 21
Volstead, Andrew J., 49
Volstead Act, 49
Von Paulsen, C.C., 222-4
Vung Ro Bay, Vietnam, 82, 208

Wade, 6
Waesche, R. Adm. Russell R., 62, 65,
    137, 184

Waesche *(cont.)*
    administrative posts, 272-3
    wartime leader, 269-74
Walke, H., 14
Walker, 16
"Walrussia," 28
War of 1812, 5-9
War of Independence, 3
Warrington (Br. destroyer), 45
Washington, George, 1-3, 97
Washington, Father John P., 63
Washington, D.C., 15, 16, 18, 53, 76,
    88, 100, 173, 215, 290
Washington, (State), 117, 211
Washington, 10, 109
Washington Post, 269
Water Quality Improvement Act, 90, 150
Water samples, 171, 173
Water transfer system, 144
Wayanda, 22, 131, 171
"Weather Patrols," 165
Weather ship, 168
Weather stations, 61
Webster, Robert K., 54
Weddell Sea, 134, 173
Welles, Gideon, 20
Wellington (Br. collier), 44, 45
West Indies, 10
West Point, N.Y., 19
West Virginia, 19
Western Arctic Circle, 135
Western Area Coast Guard, 239
Western Pipe and Steel Co., 137
Westwind, 135, 137
Wet suits, 288
Whaling vessel, 149
White Holly (buoy tender), 124
White Star liner, 39
Whittaker Corp., 155
Wicks, John, 48
Wilhelm, Kaiser, 43
William Browne, 145
William J. Duane, 21
Williams, Capt. John Foster, 3

Williams, Capt. W.W., 275
Wilmington, Del., 32
Wilmington, N.C., 160
Wilmington, 36, 37
Wilson, Woodrow, 43, 44, 177
Winchester Bay, Ore., 211
"Wind Class," 137, 139
Windom, 33
Windsor, 33
Winona, 36
Winslow (torpedo boat), 32, 36-7, 45
Wireless telegraph, 38-40
Wolcott, 171, 250
Wolf Trap Light, 99
Wood, Hunter, 7
Woodbine, 287, 289-90
Woodbury, 13
Woodbury, 16
"World power," 33, 34
World War I, 38, 40, 43-8, 79, 107-9,
    135, 177, 183
    Archduke Francis Ferdinand, 43
    Austro-Hungarian Empire, 43
    Hohenzollerns, 43
    Kaiser Wilhelm, 43
World War II, 57, 59-64, 79, 109, 118,
    135, 137, 139, 146, 162-5, 173,
    179-81, 183, 185, 218, 224, 237,
    270, 285, 287, 288
Worthylake, George, 104
Wrangel Narrows, Alaska, 123
Wright, Orville, 48
Wright, Wilbur, 48

Yakutat, 86, 170
Yancey, 140
Yap Island, Carolines, 113
Yeaton, Hopley, 3
Yocona (tug), 204
York River, Va., 6
Yorktown, Va., 182, 184
Young, Ora, 48
Yugoslavia, 145

Zafiro, 35